UNDERSTANDING INTERNATIONAL ARBITRATION

Tony Cole and Pietro Ortolani

LONDON AND NEW YORK

First published 2020
by Routledge
2 Park Square, Milton Park, Abingdon, Oxon OX14 4RN

and by Routledge
52 Vanderbilt Avenue, New York, NY 10017

Routledge is an imprint of the Taylor & Francis Group, an informa business

© 2020 Tony Cole and Pietro Ortolani

The right of Tony Cole and Pietro Ortolani to be identified as authors of this work has been asserted by them in accordance with sections 77 and 78 of the Copyright, Designs and Patents Act 1988.

All rights reserved. No part of this book may be reprinted or reproduced or utilised in any form or by any electronic, mechanical, or other means, now known or hereafter invented, including photocopying and recording, or in any information storage or retrieval system, without permission in writing from the publishers.

Trademark notice: Product or corporate names may be trademarks or registered trademarks, and are used only for identification and explanation without intent to infringe.

British Library Cataloguing-in-Publication Data
A catalogue record for this book is available from the British Library

Library of Congress Cataloging-in-Publication Data
A catalog record has been requested for this book

ISBN: 978-1-138-80603-0 (hbk)
ISBN: 978-1-138-80604-7 (pbk)
ISBN: 978-1-315-75186-3 (ebk)

Typeset in Times New Roman
by Apex CoVantage, LLC

UNDERSTANDING INTERNATIONAL ARBITRATION

Understanding International Arbitration introduces students to the primary concepts necessary for an understanding of arbitration, making use of illustrative case examples and references to legal practice throughout.

This text offers a comprehensive overview of the subject for those new to arbitration. Making use of a unique two-part structure in each chapter, *Understanding International Arbitration* provides a clear and simple statement of rules, followed by detailed discussion of the ideas underlying those rules, illustrated with relevant comparative law and case examples.

Designed with students of arbitration in mind, this text provides both a clear introduction to the subject and a comprehensive course text that will support students in their preparation for exams and practical assessments.

Tony Cole is an arbitrator at JAMS and 33 Bedford Row, and is Reader in Arbitration and Investment Law at Leicester Law School.

Pietro Ortolani is an Assistant Professor of International Arbitration and Transnational Dispute Resolution at Radboud University.

CONTENTS

Table of cases		vi
Introduction		xii
1	**What is arbitration?**	1
2	**The laws and rules applicable to arbitration**	26
3	**The agreement to arbitrate**	51
4	**The arbitral tribunal**	97
5	**Arbitral proceedings**	128
6	**The arbitral award**	171
7	**Challenging and enforcing arbitral awards**	201
	Index	246

TABLE OF CASES

International Courts and Tribunals

Arbitral Awards

Dow Chemical France, The Dow Chemical Company and others v ISOVER Saint Gobain, Interim Award, ICC Case No. 4131, 23 September 1982

FR German buyer v Thai seller, Award, WVHB Case No. 23/1982, 12 March 1984, in Albert Jan van den Berg (ed.), *ICCA Yearbook Commercial Arbitration*, XVI (ICCA 1991) 11

ICC Case No. 8385, in Jean-Jacques Arnaldez, Yves Derains and Dominique Hascher (eds), *Collection of ICC Arbitral Awards 1996–2000* (Kluwer 2003) 474

Agent (US) v Principal (Russian Federation), Final award, ICC Case No. 13756, 2008 in Albert Jan van den Berg (ed.), *Yearbook Commercial Arbitration*, XXXIX (ICCA 2014) 118

Arbitral Institutions' Challenge Decisions

LCIA Court Decision on Challenge to Arbitrator, LCIA Reference No. UN152998, Decision rendered on 22 June 2015

LCIA Court Decision on Challenge to Arbitrator, LCIA Reference No. 81160, 28 August 2009 (2011) 3 *Arbitration International* 442

Court of Justice of the European Union

Case C-126/97, *Eco Swiss China Time Ltd v Benetton International NV*, ECLI:EU:C:1999:269

Case C-185/07, *Allianz SpA and Generali Assicurazioni Generali SpA v West Tankers Inc.*, ECLI:EU:C:2009:69

Case C-536/13, *"Gazprom" OAO v Lietuvos Respublika*, ECLI:EU:C:2015:316

European Court of Human Rights

Golder v. the United Kingdom, 21 February 1975, application no. 4451/70

Tabbane v Switzerland, 1 March 2016, application no. 41069/12

National Courts

Australia
Supreme Court of Queensland, 29 October 1993, *Resort Condominiums International Inc. v Bolwell*, (1994) 10(2) *Arbitration International* 385

Austria
Austrian Supreme Court, 6 February 2018, OGH 18 ONc 4 / 17h

Belgium
Court of Appeal of Brussels, *République de Pologne c. Eureko B.V. et Schwebel Stefen M.*, R.G.No 2007/AR/70

Brazil
Paranapanema, São Paulo State Court, 2 May 2013

Canada
Rampton v Eyre, Ontario Court of Appeal [2007] ONCA 331
Librati v Barka Co. Ltd, Superior Court of Quebec [2007] QCCS 5724
Tusculum BV v Louis Dreyfus Holding SAS, Superior Court of Quebec [2008] QCCS 5904

England and Wales
Henderson v Henderson (1843) 3 Hare 100
Margulies Brothers Ltd v Dafris Thomiades and Co (UK) Ltd [1958] 1 Lloyd's Rep 205
Bremer Handelsgesellschaft mbH v Westzucker GmbH (No.2) [1981] 2 Lloyd's Rep. 130
British Airways Board v Laker Airways Ltd, House of Lords [1985] A.C. 58
Ashville Investments Ltd v Elmer Contractors Ltd, Court of Appeal [1989] Q.B. 488
Arnold v Nat'l Westminster Bank [1991] 2 A.C. 93 (H.L.)
Channel Tunnel Group Ltd v Balfour Beatty Construction Ltd and others [1992] 1 Q.B. 656; [1993] 2 WLR 262
Johnson v Gore Wood & Co [2000] UKHL 65
Director General of Fair Trading v Proprietary Association of Great Britain [2001] EWCA Civ. 1217
Porter v Magill [2001] UKHL 67
Lawal v Northern Spirit Ltd [2003] UKHL 35
Peterson Farms Inc. v C&M Farming Ltd [2004] EWHC 121 (Comm)
Republic of Kazakhstan v Istil Group Inc. [2006] EWHC 448 (Comm)
Fiona Trust & Holding Corp v Privalov, Court of Appeal [2007] EWCA Civ 20.
Premium Nafta Products Limited and others v Fili Shipping Company Ltd, House of Lords [2007] 4 All ER 951
Emmott v Wilson & Partners Limited [2008] EWCA Civ 184
Emmott v Wilson & Partners Limited [2008] EWCA Civ 184
Habas Sinai Ve Tibbi Gazlar Isthisal Endustri AS v Sometal SAL [2010] EWHC 29 (Comm)

Continental Transfert Technique Ltd v Federal Government of Nigeria [2010] EWHC 780 (Comm)
Jivraj v Hashwani [2011] UKSC 40
Sulamérica v Enesa Engenharia [2012] EWCA Civ 638
West Tankers Inc v Allianz SPA & Generali Assicurazioni SpA [2012] EWCA Civ 27
Diag Human Se v Czech Republic [2014] EWHC 1639 (Comm) (22 May 2014)
BDMS Ltd v Rafael Advanced Defence Systems [2014] EWHC 451 (Comm)
A v B [2017] EWHC 3417 (Comm)
Ekran OAO v Magneco Metrel [2017] EWHC 2208 (Comm)
Michael Wilson & Partners Limited v John Forster Emmott [2018] EWCA Civ 51

France

French Court of Cassation, 14 December 1983, *Epoux Convert c/ Droga* (1984) *Revue de l'arbitrage* 483
Court of Appeal of Paris, 14 February 1985, *Tovomon c/ Amatex* (1987) *Revue de l'arbitrage* 325
French Court of Cassation, *Siemens v BKMI and Dutco*, 7 January 1992
Court of Appeal of Paris, 24 March 1994, *Deko c/Dingler* (1994) *Revue de l'arbitrage* 515
French Court of Cassation, 23 March 1994, *Société Hilmarton Ltd v Société Omnium de traitement et de valorization (OTV)*
Court of Appeal of Paris, 7 February 2002, *SA Alfac c/ Société Irmac Importacão, comércia e industria LTDa* (2002) *Revue de l'arbitrage* 413
French Court of Cassation, 7 July 2006, *Cesareo*
Société Dansk Eternit Fabrik 1994 c Société Copernit & C SpA, Court of Appeal of Angers, 16 September 2008, No. 07/01636
Court of Appeal of Paris, 17 January 2012, *Planor Afrique SA v Société Emirates Télécommunications corporation "Etisalat"* (2012) 3 *Revue de l'Arbitrage* 569

Germany

German Bundesgerichtshof, 27 February 1970 (1990) 6 *Arbitration International* 79
Oberlandesgericht Dresden, 5 December 1994, in Albert Jan van den Berg, *Yearbook Commercial Arbitration*, XXII (ICCA 1997) 266
Kaammergericht Berlin, 15 October 1999, in Albert Jan van den Berg (ed), *Yearbook Commercial Arbitration*, XXVI (ICCA 2001) 328
Hanseatisches Oberlandesgericht, Hamburg, 24 January 2003, in Albert Jan van den Berg (ed.), *Yearbook Commercial Arbitration*, XXX (ICCA 2005) 509
Oberlandesgericht Hamm, 27 September 2005, in Albert Jan van den Berg (ed), *Yearbook Commercial Arbitration*, XXXI (ICCA 2006) 685
German Bundesgerichtshof, 25 January 2007, VII ZR 105/06
Oberlandesgericht München, Germany, 23 February 2007, 34 Sch 31/06
Oberlandesgericht München, 3 February 2010 (2010) *SchiedsVZ* 336

Hong Kong

Guangdong v Conagra [1993] HKCU 0578
Lucky-Goldstar Int'l (HK) Ltd v Ng Moo Kee Eng'g Ltd - [1993] 1 HKC 404
Wuzhou Port Foreign Trade Dev. Corp. v New Chemic Ltd [2001] 3 HKC 395
Kenon Engineering Ltd v Nippon Kokan Koji Kabushiki Kaisha [2004] HKCA 101
Grandeur Electrical Co. Ltd v Cheung Kee Fung Cheung Construction Co. Ltd [2006] HKCA 305
VK Holdings (HK) Ltd v Panasonic Eco Solutions (Hong Kong) Company Ltd [2014] HKCFI 2358

India

Supreme Court of India, *M/s Centrotrade Minerals & Metal Inc. v Hindustan Copper Ltd.*, Civil Appeal No. 2562 of 2006

Ireland

Kastrup Trae-Aluvinduet A/S (Denmark) v Aluwood Concepts Ltd (Ireland), case no 129 MCA, 13 November 2009

Italy

Italian Court of Cassation, Judgment no. 12616 of 17 December 1998

Jamaica

National Housing Trust v YP Seaton & Associates Co Ltd [2015] UKPC 43

Netherlands

District Court of Amsterdam, *SPP (Middle East) Ltd. v The Arab Republic of Egypt*, 12 July 1984 in Pieter Sanders (ed.), *Yearbook Commercial Arbitration*, X (ICCA 1985) 487–489
Court of Cassation, *Nikolay Viktorovich Maximov v Open Joint Stock Company "Novolipetsky Metallurgichesky Kombinat"*, 24 November 2017, ECLI:NL:HR:2017:2992

Singapore

WSG Nimbus Pte. Ltd v Board of Control for Cricket in Sri Lanka [2002] SGHC 104
P. T. Tri-M.G. Intra Asia Airlines v Norse Air Charter Limited [2009] SGHC 13
Insigma Technology Co. Ltd v Alstom Technology Ltd [2009] SGCA 24

South Africa

Cape Pac. Ltd v. Lubner Controlling Inv. Pty Ltd, South Africa Supreme Court of Appeal [1995] (4) SA 790 (AD)

Spain

Camimalaga, S.A.U. v DAF Vehiculos Industriales S.A.U., Madrid Audiencia Provincial Civil, Decision No. 147/2013

Sweden

Swedish Supreme Court, 19 November 2007, Case No. T 2448–06
Swedish Supreme Court, 7 April 2017, Case No. Ö 1096–16

Switzerland

Swiss Federal Tribunal, 7 February 1991 (1991) 9 ASA Bulletin 269
Swiss Federal Tribunal, 14 May 2001 (2001) 19 ASA Bull 555
Swiss Federal Tribunal, 21 November 2003, DFT 130 III 66
Swiss Federal Tribunal, 8 July 2003, DFT 129 III 675
Swiss Federal Tribunal, 19 May 2003 (2004) 22 ASA Bull. 344

United States

Hoosac Tunnel Dock & Elevator Co. v O'Brien, 137 Mass. 424 (Mass. 1884)
Commonwealth Coatings Corp. v Continental Casualty Co., 393 US 145, 89 S.Ct. 337, 21 L.Ed.2d 301 (1968)
Lea Tai Textile Co. v Manning Fabrics, Inc., 411 F.Supp. 1404, 1407 (S.D.N.Y. 1975)
Shuffman v Rudd Plastic Fabrics Corp., 407 N.Y.S.2d 565, 566 (N.Y. App. Div. 1978)
Astra Footwear Indus. v Harwyn Int'l, Inc., 442 F.Supp. 907 (S.D.N.Y. 1978)
Fertilizer Corp. of India v IDI Management, Inc., 517 F. Supp. 948 (S.D. Ohio 1981)
Morelite Construction Corp. v New York City District Council Carpenters Benefit Funds, 748 F.2d 79, 84 (2d Cir. 1984)
Mitsubishi Motors Corp. v Soler Chrysler-Plymouth, Inc., 473 US 614 (1985)
Apple v Jewish Hosp. & Med. Ctr., 829 F.2d 326, 332–333 (1987)
United States v Panhandle Eastern Corp., 119 F.R.D. 346 (D.Del.1988)
Tennessee Imp., Inc. v Filippi, 745 F.Supp. 1314 (M.D. Tenn. 1990)
Third Nat. Bank In Nashville v WEDGE Group, Inc., 749 F.Supp. 851 (M.D.Tenn., 1990)
Warnes SA v Harvic Int'l Ltd, 1993 WL 228028 (S.D.N.Y. 1993)
Rosgoscirc v Circus Show Corp., 1993 U.S. Dist. LEXIS 9797 (S.D.N.Y. 1993)
Mastrobuono v Shearson Lehman Hutton, Inc., 514 U.S. 52 (1995)
In re HZI Research Center v Sun Instrument Japan, (1995) WL 562181 (S.D.N.Y. 1995)
Aviall, Inc. v Ryder Sys., 110 F.3d 892 (2d Cir. 1997)
Norton v AMISUB St. Joseph Hosp., 155 F.3d 1040 98th Cir. (1998)
Karaha Bodas Co., LLC v Perusahaan Pertambangan Minyak Dan Gas Bumi Negara, 190 F.Supp.2d 936, 945 (S.D. Tex. 2001)
Larry's United Super, Inc. v Werries, 253 F.3d 1083 (8th Cir. 2001)
Gulf Guar. Life Ins. Co. v Connecticut Gen. Life Ins. Co., 304 F.3d 476 (5th Cir. 2002)
HIM Portland, LLC v DeVito Builders, Inc., 317 F.3d 41, 42 (1st Cir. 2003)
Arrowhead Global Solutions, Inc. v Datapath, Inc., 166 F.Appx. 39, 44 (4th Cir. 2006)
Applied Indus. Materials Corp. v Ovalar, 492 F.3d 132 (2d Cir. 2007)

New Regency Productions Inc. v Nippon Herald Films Inc. C.A.(CAL.), 2007

ITT Educational Services v Arce, 533 F.3d 342 (5th Cir. 2008)

HT of Highlands Ranch, Inc. v Hollywood Tanning Sys., Inc., 590 F.Supp.2d 677, 684 (D.N.J. 2008)

Ometto v Asa Bioenergy Holding A.G., 12–4022(L) (2d Cir. 2014)

Thai-Lao Lignite (Thailand) Co., Ltd v Government of the Lao People's Democratic Republic, No. 14–597

(2d Cir. 2017)

Albtelecom SH.A v UNIFI Communications, Inc., 16 Civ. 9001 (PAE) (S.D.N.Y.), 30 May 2017

Transocean Offshore Gulf of Guinea VII Limited et al. v Erin Energy Corporation (f/k/a CAMAC Energy Inc.), United States District Court, Southern District of Texas, Houston Division, Civil Action No. H-17–2623, 12 March 2018 in Albert Jan van den Berg (ed.), *Yearbook Commercial Arbitration*, XLIII (ICCA 2018) 722

INTRODUCTION

The structure and drafting of this book have been directed by one of the most distinctive features of international commercial arbitration, and one that makes arbitration such a fascinating and enjoyable field to be part of: arbitration is fundamentally about ideas. That is, the one thing that everyone knows about arbitration is that it is flexible: you can arbitrate in almost any way you want. But the flipside of that freedom is a lack of structure. There are almost no rules on how arbitration operates. There are no universal "civil procedure rules" dictating how arbitral proceedings should function. There are no universal professional qualifications that dictate who can and cannot work as an arbitrator, or as counsel. Moreover, even when there are rules, those rules are consistently drafted in ways designed to protect arbitration's flexibility, and so impose only minimal constraint.

The important consequence of this is that arbitration is ultimately a field of legal practice dominated by ideas. Arbitration conferences and journals certainly include technical discussions of national laws and of which procedures work best, but also routinely include theoretical discussions, led by practitioners, on what arbitration really is, what an arbitrator's proper function is, how arbitration should or should not interact with national legal systems, and more. In essence, the lack of binding rules has turned arbitration into a field of practice-makers, combining a focus on winning disputes for their clients or deciding disputes as arbitrators, with convincing others in the community to approach arbitration in the way that they think is correct. In short, the way that you practice arbitration is determined to a large extent by your own idea of what arbitration is, and how it should function.

For that reason, this book takes as its foundation the ideas underlying arbitration. While the many books that discuss the law and practice of arbitration are an essential support for anyone with an interest in the field, they can only ever be part of an arbitration education. You can be informed about how certain things are generally done, but unless you understand why they are done that way, you cannot really engage with arbitration practice, even if only to convince a tribunal to do things in a different way.

The goal of this book, then, is not to replace or supersede the excellent general discussions of arbitration that are already available. It is, rather, to supplement them, by focusing not on the technical details of how arbitration is practiced in certain jurisdictions, but on the reasons why arbitration practice has evolved the way it has, on the issues that arise in arbitration, and on how they can be thought about.

At times, of course, you will also read the view of one or both of the authors of how an issue is best approached, but these are only ever suggestions. There are no views expressed in this book with which you cannot quite legitimately disagree. Our goal as authors is to facilitate you in starting to think about arbitration, not to dictate certain views that you should have. But whether your goal in learning about arbitration is to work in the field, pass a course, or even just understand what your company has agreed to do, you will be better placed to achieve that goal once you have grappled with the issues that motivate how arbitration is practiced.

There are certain methodological features of this book that should be emphasised. Firstly, each chapter is divided into two sections. It opens with a set of "Rules". These are simple, one-sentence statements of a fundamental principle, each rule followed by a short explanation. Learning these rules will give you a solid foundation in arbitration, and if you are new to the field, they can give you a useful anchor. However, the essential reality of arbitration is that there simply are no fixed rules; any listing of the "rules of arbitration", hence, will unavoidably be incomplete and even misleading. For that reason, the second part of each chapter provides a more detailed discussion of each rule, introducing the ideas behind the rule and highlighting the complexities that the simple statement of the rule unavoidably hides.

Secondly, we took the decision to try to "personalise" the discussion of arbitration, as a way of helping people not yet involved in mainstream arbitration connect more immediately to the ideas under discussion. That is, books on international commercial arbitration normally use examples involving large companies in cross-border disputes. That makes sense, because that is the standard context of international commercial arbitration. However, it also abstracts arbitration from the experience we have of our own lives. It makes us think of arbitration as something "they" do, rather than something we might be involved in ourselves. For that reason, we have used "human-sized" examples, in which two people are in a dispute, rather than two large companies. This makes no substantive difference to the example, but we believe that it helps make the situation more understandable, and so enhances the engagement with the ideas. It is easier to think "What would I want to do in this situation?" than it is to think "What would a major multinational want to do in this situation?". For the same reason, we have excluded investor – State arbitration from the scope of the book. While treaty-based cases between private investors and States constitute an important field of arbitration practice, it was our intention to introduce the basics of arbitration in the simplest possible setting, rather than exploring the further complexities arising out of the use of arbitration in the area of international investments. Readers interested in these matters will find many useful textbooks and treatises focusing specifically on investor – State arbitration.

Thirdly, we have self-consciously "diversified" the discussion of arbitration in terms of nationalities. It is unavoidable that when we refer to case-law or institutional rules, we will often rely upon the major arbitration jurisdictions and arbitral institutions. However, we have attempted to add additional references to a broader range of laws and institutions, to reflect the reality that arbitration extends far beyond the major jurisdictions of England, France, and so on. Moreover, we have consciously constructed examples around individuals from a wide range of countries, many little known for their involvement in international commercial arbitration. We think recognition of the geographical diversity of arbitration is important.

Finally, you will notice that every arbitrator in this book is a woman. There is a reason for this: arbitration has a diversity problem. Not just with respect to gender, but gender is the one issue we can directly confront just through the choice of a particular pronoun. To the credit of those in the field, this diversity problem is now being acknowledged, but there remains a long way to go, and one of the simplest steps that we can achieve is that when we imagine an arbitral tribunal, we don't imagine three white men sitting behind a table. Getting used to the idea of referring to arbitrators as "she" rather than "he" is a trivial act that can help substantially in achieving this goal.

Perhaps the best approach to using this book, then, is to initially read through the Rules at the beginning of a chapter. This will give you a clear basic idea of the primary ideas guiding the aspect of arbitration discussed in the chapter. Then, instead of simply reading through the remainder of the chapter, alternate between the two sections. Read a rule in part one, then read the discussion of the rule in part two. Then, importantly, think about it for yourself. Consider what you have read, and decide what you think about the issue under discussion. Then move on to the next rule, following the same process. By the end of the chapter, you won't be an expert in that area of arbitration, but you will have started to think about it seriously, so that when you do further research on the specific rules and laws that you will find discussed in other books, you will understand better why those particular approaches have been adopted, and be better positioned to critique whether they are good or not.

Ultimately, remember that arbitration is a field based on ideas. The more you think about how arbitration operates, why it operates that way, and how it should operate, the better you will understand it, and the better you will be at it.

1 What is arbitration?

Rules

1. Arbitration is a private, third-party mechanism of rule-based adjudicatory dispute resolution

Arbitration is private in nature: proceedings need not take place in public, arbitrators do not act as government officials, and the parties have the power to decide how they want to arbitrate. Arbitrators perform an adjudicatory function: they hear the opposing parties' arguments and apply agreed rules to decide the disputed issues, binding the parties with their decision, rather than merely advising them.

2. Party autonomy is central to arbitration

Parties cannot be forced to arbitrate, but must agree to do so. The rules governing an arbitration are ultimately determined by the contents of the parties' agreement to arbitrate.

3. Arbitration precludes litigation

If parties have agreed to arbitrate a dispute, that dispute can only be taken to court if both parties agree to do so.

4. Arbitral awards are final and binding

A decision in which arbitrators resolve one or all of the substantive issues submitted to arbitration is called an "award". Arbitration is fundamentally a "one-stop shop": once an award has been delivered, there are very few grounds on which it can be challenged (simply being wrong is not enough). Parties must comply with an award, and if they refuse to do so, it can be enforced through the courts.

5. Not all disputes can be submitted to arbitration

National laws place limits on the types of disputes that can be submitted to arbitration. If parties arbitrate a dispute that is not "arbitrable" under the law governing the arbitration, courts applying that law will refuse to assist the arbitration or enforce any resulting award. Courts elsewhere in the world may refuse to enforce awards arising from that arbitration as well.

6. Arbitration can be domestic or international

Arbitration can be used to resolve both domestic and international disputes. Local law will determine whether an arbitration qualifies as "international", and in some jurisdictions different laws will apply to an "international" arbitration, than apply to a "domestic" arbitration.

7. Arbitration is not always between private parties

Although arbitration is private in nature, the parties to it are not necessarily private themselves, and States and State entities now regularly use arbitration.

8. Arbitration comes in different varieties

Arbitration can be used to resolve different types of disputes, and different laws may apply depending on the type of arbitration in question.

9. Arbitration can be institutional or **ad hoc**

Parties who have agreed to arbitrate can do so with the assistance of an arbitral institution, which will provide administrative support and rules to assist their arbitration. However, use of an arbitral institution is voluntary, and parties can also arbitrate *ad hoc*, or without the involvement of an arbitral institution.

10. Arbitration offers potential advantages

Arbitration can offer significant advantages over other forms of dispute resolution. In particular: (i) neutrality, (ii) speed, (iii) finality, (iv) enforceability, (v) expertise, (vi) flexibility, and (vi) confidentiality.

11. Arbitration has potential drawbacks

Arbitration also has drawbacks that can make it less desirable for a particular dispute than other forms of dispute resolution: (i) cost, (ii) limits to arbitral jurisdiction, (iii) limits to arbitral power, (iv) lack of appeal, and (v) lack of expertise of arbitrators in arbitration.

Analysis

1. Arbitration is a private, third-party mechanism of rule-based adjudicatory dispute resolution

One of the first difficulties faced by anyone encountering arbitration for the first time is getting a clear idea of what exactly "arbitration" is. That is a significantly harder task than it might seem to be, as there really is no such "thing" as arbitration. It is a mechanism for resolving disputes, but what exactly that mechanism is, it is very hard to say. Rather, there are just many things that are <u>not</u> arbitration. "Litigation" is not arbitration. "Mediation" is not arbitration. Flipping a coin or engaging in armed combat are not arbitration. But beyond this process of gradually setting limits to arbitration by listing things that are not arbitration, it is virtually impossible to describe with any precision what arbitration actually is.

One reason for this is that "arbitration" is a very old and widely used label, and it has been used and still is used to describe a very wide range of approaches to dispute resolution. "Arbitration", that is, has often served as a label that means little more than "the resolution of a dispute through recourse to a third party, other than a court".

Even this very basic definition, though, does give us some important insight into what arbitration is. Firstly, <u>arbitration is a third party dispute resolution mechanism</u>. Flipping a coin or engaging in armed combat might qualify as arbitration if you believe that a god or other higher power will determine the winner. But so long as you believe that the coin toss will be decided by luck, and the armed combat by whoever fights better, then there is no third party involved, and hence there is no arbitration. Similarly, then, negotiation between two parties is not arbitration – and even if a settlement agreement is reached, it cannot be enforced in court as an arbitral award.[1]

Notably, though, both litigation and mediation involve a third party – yet they are not arbitration. Clarifying why they are not gives us additional details about arbitration.

Litigating in national courts is, by its very nature, an unusual activity, a departure from the way that people normally interact with one another. It is a dispute resolution mechanism created by a State,[2] and used by people when either they do not have a relationship, or when that relationship has broken down so badly that they want formal, governmental validation of their position and enforcement of their rights.

Arbitration, on the other hand, is far more intimately connected to human relationships. It is a form of dispute resolution that is controlled by the parties to the dispute, and so can occur in almost any form that they wish to use. It varies in its form, in accordance with variations in the identities of the parties in the dispute.

Litigation, that is, involves a government effectively saying: "I will resolve your dispute, but I can't make up new rules for every new case, so you need to use the same procedures as everyone else." It is a "one size fits all" dispute resolution mechanism. Arbitration, on the other hand, has no rules, only limits. As long as the parties stay within those limits, they can resolve their dispute in any way they wish, and it still constitutes arbitration. The second principle, then, is that <u>arbitration is a private dispute resolution mechanism</u>. It need not be "confidential", as some arbitrations are held in public. But it is "private" in the sense that it is controlled by the parties to the dispute, and can vary its form to match their wishes and needs.

Mediation, though, is also private in this way. Distinguishing mediation from arbitration, then, gives us our third basic principle: <u>Arbitration is an adjudicatory dispute resolution mechanism</u>. In other words, while mediation involves a third party (the mediator), and is controlled by the parties (and so is private), it is based on the idea that the third party should help the disputants to reach an agreement. The mediator does not decide the dispute: she facilitates settlement, but it is up to the disputing parties to decide whether they want to settle, and on what terms. In arbitration, on the other hand, an arbitrator is appointed to consider the arguments and evidence presented by the parties and then deliver a decision (called an "award"), just as does a judge in litigation. One or even both parties may be unhappy with that decision, but by agreeing to arbitrate their dispute they agreed to allow the arbitrator to decide the dispute on their behalf. Consequently, if their procedure is to count as arbitration, they are bound by that decision even if one of them disagrees with it.

There is one final basic principle that is always true of arbitration: <u>Arbitration is a rule-centered dispute resolution mechanism</u>. That is, while an arbitrator will have to make decisions on facts when resolving a case, if the dispute is resolved purely on the facts, it is not arbitration. So, for example, suppose that Ezra and Sufyaan agree that under their contract the wood used to build a house had to come from a particular species of tree, and they hire a third party to determine whether the wood actually used to build that house was the correct type. This is a dispute that can be resolved entirely by a decision on the facts. The decision on the facts has legal consequences, but the third party has only been asked to make a decision on the facts, not on the law. In many jurisdictions this procedure is known as "expert determination", and it serves as another boundary to what constitutes arbitration. An arbitrator need not actually base her decision on the law, and can for example be authorised by the parties to decide *ex aequo et bono*, or on the basis of her own perception of rightness and fairness. However, whether the arbitrator is applying the law or making a judgement of fairness, a dispute resolution procedure can only qualify as arbitration if it involves a decision-maker applying a guiding rule to the facts of a dispute.

We have, then, four basic principles that can serve as guidelines as to what arbitration actually is: (1) Arbitration is a third party dispute resolution mechanism; (2) Arbitration is a private dispute resolution mechanism; (3) Arbitration is an adjudicatory dispute resolution mechanism; (4) Arbitration is a rule-centered dispute resolution mechanism.

Within the boundaries of these four principles, arbitration can be anything that the parties want it to be. In this way, arbitration is the essence of "private justice".

2. Party autonomy is central to arbitration

Perhaps the most commonly used expression in discussions of arbitration is "party autonomy". It is invoked on a regular basis to describe how arbitration operates, to justify procedural decisions taken in arbitration, and to praise or criticise governments and courts for actions they take relating to arbitration. "Party autonomy" refers to the idea that arbitration is characterised by the freedom of the parties to control almost every aspect of the arbitral process, so that they can design their own dispute resolution procedure that will meet their particular needs and preferences. It has arguably become the central doctrine in arbitration, routinely invoked to justify interpretations of how arbitration should operate, and is almost never criticised.

When trying to understand the place of party autonomy in arbitration, it is important to draw a distinction between what can be called "independent" and "supported" conceptions of party autonomy. The independent conception of party autonomy arises naturally from the basic fundamentals of arbitration, as discussed in the previous section. Arbitration is essentially a form of private justice, in which two parties agree to resolve their dispute through an adjudicatory dispute resolution mechanism they set up themselves. The independent conception of party autonomy in arbitration, then, is purely descriptive: it simply recognises that arbitration, by its private nature, delivers significant power to the parties to create their own dispute resolution process. Arbitration, as an idea, inherently includes this independent notion of party autonomy: it is the parties' procedure, so they can shape it as they prefer.

Importantly, though, the independent conception of party autonomy relies upon a notion of arbitration as an entirely free-floating process, separate from government-run dispute resolution systems. The type of autonomy it involves is the same type of autonomy that you have when you are deciding where to eat your dinner if you are home alone. When your family is home they may perhaps expect you to eat with them at the dinner table, but if you are alone you can eat on the couch, in your bedroom, or anywhere else. The autonomy involved in the independent conception, hence, is the autonomy that comes from isolation. Because an arbitration is private, it can be run without the involvement of anyone but the disputing parties, and so can be run however they want to run it.

The problem with this picture of arbitration, though, is that while it describes a form of arbitration, it doesn't describe a form of arbitration that many people find attractive. After all, the other side may not turn up at the time you agreed to arbitrate; the arbitrator may take a bribe; the loser may refuse to pay what the arbitrator decides they owe. The autonomy of this basic form of arbitration, that is, brings with it the autonomy of everyone involved in the process not to cooperate with it.

What parties actually want from arbitration is not this free-floating form of arbitration that the independent conception of party autonomy describes. Instead, as much as arbitration is constantly described as a private procedure, operating as an alternative to national court systems, what parties most want is arbitration connected to national laws and national courts. This way, when parties refuse to fulfil their agreement to arbitrate, they can be made to do so; when arbitrators act corruptly, they can be removed; when losing parties refuse to pay what they owe, the debt can be collected against their will.

The problem this creates is that governments are also free. There is no inherent obligation on any government to support a private arbitration. It is now standard that they do so, but that is because they have decided that the use of arbitration is desirable for the achievement of their own goals. This means, however, that governments are able to condition their support of arbitration. They have every legitimate right to say: "Yes, I will support your private dispute resolution procedure, but only if you run it in accordance with these rules". This would not violate the independent conception of party autonomy, as disputing parties would still have the freedom to arbitrate in a way that violated the government's rules, if they were willing to do so without government assistance. Yet it creates a potential problem for arbitration, as if governments impose too many regulations, arbitration begins to lose its value as an alternative to court litigation.

This is where the supported conception of party autonomy comes in. The supported conception is not purely descriptive, as is the independent conception. It is instead a normative view of the role of party autonomy in arbitration: it posits that party autonomy is so important in arbitration that it creates rules for how arbitration can be regulated; that States unquestionably have the legitimate power to lay down detailed rules on how arbitrations can operate, but that they are wrong to do so. According to the supported conception, party autonomy does not just describe arbitration, but constitutes its central core. Consequently, governments should legislate in ways that assist arbitration, as this supports the parties' exercise of their autonomy. They should also exert control over arbitration to the extent necessary to ensure that each arbitration operates fairly, as this guarantees that the autonomy of one party is not overruled by the autonomy of another, more powerful party. But the supported conception of party autonomy also entails that a State should not insist that arbitrations operate in accordance with any particular rules, or obey particular social conceptions of how disputes can be resolved. To do so would impose on the parties the views of individuals and entities not themselves involved in the arbitral process. As a result, it would constitute a violation of the principle of party autonomy.

It is, beyond question, the supported conception of party autonomy that has come to dominate international arbitration, both in terms of how it is approached by practitioners, and in terms of how it is overwhelmingly viewed by governments. By creating a structural support for party autonomy, States do not limit the ability of parties to shape arbitration in accordance with their needs and preferences, but rather offer an infrastructure which ensures that party autonomy can operate effectively. Nonetheless, it is important to consider the consequences for arbitration of the centrality of party autonomy.

Firstly, one of the most important differences between arbitration and State court litigation is that the latter constitutes an expression of national sovereignty, while the former does not. In other words, the power of State courts to resolve disputes derives from the inherent authority of the State to govern actions subject to its jurisdiction. It constitutes a service provided by the government to individuals, and is made available to all. Consider, for example, one of the most basic forms of dispute, based on a contract between two parties: if a dispute arises, either of the parties can commence proceedings before the competent State court, even if the contract made no reference to the possibility of bringing a claim in court. The right to bring a claim against another contracting party is simply a right given by the State to everybody under its jurisdiction.

By contrast, the centrality of party autonomy to arbitration means that no-one can be forced to arbitrate. Every arbitration must be based upon an agreement to arbitrate. This does not mean that both parties must wish to arbitrate when the arbitration commences, let alone throughout the entire course of the arbitral process. But they must both have bound themselves to arbitrate at some point. Parties cannot be forced to arbitrate, but they can be forced to fulfil their agreement to arbitrate: this does not violate party autonomy, as it merely enforces a party's prior autonomous choice to bind her future self.

This leads to a second important consequence: Arbitrators only have the powers that the disputing parties have given them. Judges receive their power from the State, and so have whatever powers the State has decided to give them. Consequently, they may have, and use, powers that neither party in a dispute wants them to have. An arbitrator, though, can do nothing that the parties have not mutually agreed she can do. If the parties have only agreed to arbitrate certain types of disputes, an arbitrator has no power to make decisions on other disputes between the parties. If the parties have agreed that the arbitrator cannot perform a certain action (e.g. order certain types of documents to be handed over to the other party), then she cannot do it – even if this involves a standard feature of arbitration.

Importantly, even if an arbitrator believes that the arbitration cannot be successful if a certain action is not taken, she cannot order that action to be taken if she has not been given the power to do so. The centrality of party autonomy to arbitration means that the parties not only have the freedom to decide whether or not to arbitrate, but also the freedom to decide how to arbitrate – even if this means arbitrating badly.

This idea that the arbitrator only receives her powers from the parties links to another central aspect of party autonomy in arbitration: unlike in court litigation, where a judge is appointed to each case through a process decided by the State, the parties to an arbitration select their own arbitrator. It is easy to see why this is such a central component of arbitration, as the right to arrange your own dispute resolution proceedings would mean little if the individual making the decision in your case was still being imposed on you by the government. But it is important to recognise how far this notion has been embraced in contemporary arbitration. There are still some jurisdictions in which constraints are placed upon who can be appointed as an arbitrator, if the parties wish their award to be subsequently enforceable through national courts. Overwhelmingly, however, States around the world have now embraced the idea that the parties to a dispute should have full autonomy in selecting their arbitrator. An arbitrator need not be a lawyer, need not be on a government-controlled list of permissible arbitrators, and indeed need know nothing whatsoever about arbitration. So long as she has been appointed through the process agreed to by the parties, then she can act as an arbitrator. Of course, even in the most developed arbitration jurisdictions some constraint remains, and the arbitrator must at least have the mental capacity to perform the role, or else the resulting award would be open to be challenged. But within this very minor constraint, parties generally have absolute freedom to select their own arbitrator. The usual mechanisms through which the arbitrators are selected will be discussed in detail in Chapter 4.

Finally, as has already been suggested above, one of the core benefits that arbitration can provide to parties is the ability for them to design their own dispute resolution procedure, rather than having to adhere to the procedures used in any particular national court system. Earlier in arbitration's history it was not uncommon for States to refuse to enforce arbitral awards if the arbitration had been conducted in ways that differed substantially from national court procedures – after all, these procedures were regarded as essential for ensuring justice. It has, however, now been almost uniformly accepted that so long as the procedures agreed by the parties ensure the fundamental fairness of the arbitration, then the parties should be allowed to use whatever procedures they see as most appropriate for the resolution of their dispute. Arbitral procedure will be discussed in Chapter 5.

Of course, if the parties adopt procedures that result in an unfair process, such as by not allowing one of the two parties to present its case adequately, even courts in the most "arbitration friendly" jurisdictions will refuse to enforce any resulting arbitral award. Hence, in no jurisdiction is the embrace of party autonomy in arbitration absolute. But the very minor limits that are placed on party autonomy in contemporary international arbitration justify regarding party autonomy as indeed the central characterising feature of modern international arbitration.

3. *Arbitration precludes litigation*

Access to justice is a fundamental right, enshrined in many international instruments and national constitutions.[3] Consequently, anyone who has suffered the violation of a legal right must be able to seek a remedy through litigation in State courts. However, any party who agrees to arbitrate loses the right to have his/her dispute heard by State courts: it is now accepted that when parties conclude an arbitration agreement, they simultaneously waive their right to access State courts. This is why parties cannot be forced to arbitrate without their consent. Arbitration entails the waiver of a fundamental right, and so parties can only be obligated to arbitrate if they have freely chosen to waive that right.

Note, though, that in the modern world this situation is not unproblematic, as many contemporary legal systems have adopted a very generous and often formalistic approach to determining whether an agreement to arbitrate exists. A commercial party may, for example, sign a long and complex contract, not noticing the existence of an arbitration agreement within it. Similarly, a party may agree to standard terms and conditions that include an arbitration agreement, without reading the text. In these cases, courts in jurisdictions supportive of arbitration will generally find that an agreement to arbitrate has been formed, and the right to access State courts waived.

Consent to arbitration, that is, does not generally have to be knowing or informed, and once consent has been given, the fundamental right to access State courts has been waived.

Moreover, once this waiver has been given, it cannot be unilaterally retracted. An arbitration agreement can be terminated, allowing both parties to access State courts, but only with the consent of both parties. If either party wishes to keep the arbitration agreement in force, then it will remain effective, despite the objections of the other party.

Understanding arbitration through case-law

Incorporation by reference: an example from practice

Case details: *Habas Sinai Ve Tibbi Gazlar Isthisal Endustri AS v Sometal SAL* [2010] EWHC 29 (Comm)

Authority deciding the case: Queen's Bench Division (Commercial Court)

Facts of the case: The parties concluded a series of fourteen contracts. Some of the contracts included an agreement to arbitrate, providing for arbitration in London. By contrast, other contracts did not expressly include an arbitration clause, but provided that "The rest will be agreed mutually", or "The rest will be as per previous contracts", or "All the rest will be same as our previous contracts". A dispute arose out of the fourteenth contract, which did not include an arbitration agreement, but stated that "All the rest will be same as our previous contracts".

One of the parties commenced arbitral proceedings in London, seeking compensation. The other party objected that the arbitral tribunal did not have jurisdiction, because the fourteenth contract did not contain an arbitration clause and did not make express reference to the clause included in other previous contracts. The arbitral tribunal issued an Interim Final Award on Jurisdiction and Costs, deciding that it had jurisdiction because the arbitration clause present in the previous contracts had been

> incorporated in the fourteenth contract by virtue of the "All the rest" clause. The award was challenged before the Commercial Court in London.
>
> **Decision:** The Court found that the arbitral tribunal had jurisdiction. English law generally allows the incorporation of standard terms, including arbitration agreements. The contract which gave rise to the dispute contained a very broad reference, encompassing "All the rest"; therefore, the agreement to arbitrate contained in the previous contract must be deemed to be incorporated in the fourteenth contract as well.

But what happens if a party brings a claim to court, despite the existence of an arbitration agreement? The precise details will differ from one legal jurisdiction to another, but in essence, once the existence of the arbitration agreement has been pointed out to the court, the court is obligated to refuse to allow the litigation to continue, and must direct the parties to arbitrate their dispute. Indeed, as will be discussed in Chapter 3, often the court will not even decide for itself whether a binding agreement to arbitrate exists, but will instead also leave that decision to be made by the arbitrator. As Chapter 3 will discuss in detail, the enforcement of arbitration agreements in State courts is regulated by a particularly important instrument of international law, the 1958 New York Convention on the Recognition and Enforcement of Foreign Arbitral Awards (New York Convention).

4. Arbitral awards are final and binding

Not only are agreements to arbitrate binding, but once an arbitral award has been rendered, it also is binding on the parties. The waiver of access to court litigation contained in an arbitration agreement is nearly absolute. Not only may parties not ignore an agreement to arbitrate and take their claim to court, but once the arbitrator has rendered her decision, the parties have very limited possibilities to challenge it.

This is an important point to understand about arbitration, as it is a fundamental way in which arbitration differs from litigation. A standard feature of court systems is the ability to appeal an initial court judgement to a higher court, arguing that the initial judge was mistaken in his/her ruling, either on the facts or the law. By contrast, while national laws and practices on the issue vary (see Chapter 7), the dominant approach to arbitration around the world allows very little scope for court challenges to an arbitral award.

This character of arbitral awards is generally referred to as "finality": when the arbitrators have made a decision, it is final, and should not be overturned by courts, except in rare circumstances usually relating solely to procedural fairness. The arbitral award, in other words, normally constitutes the final word on the matters in dispute. Even if a judge believes that the award was wrong on the facts or misinterpreted the law, the award should generally remain in place. By agreeing to arbitrate, parties opted for a dispute resolution system in which they could select their own decision-maker, and as a result determine for themselves what views and expertise should be used to decide the case. If they selected poorly, and receive an award that is questionable, or even demonstrably wrong, this was a risk they took when they opted for arbitration. Consequently, so long as the arbitral process was fundamentally procedurally fair, courts will not assist parties who believe they have received a mistaken arbitral award – even if the court agrees.

In addition to being "final", arbitral awards are also "binding" as soon as they are issued by the arbitrator: the losing party must comply with the decision. In this respect, the role of arbitrators is very different from that of mediators: mediators merely propose a solution to the parties, and each party has the right to reject the proposal if they do not like it. Arbitrators, by contrast, have the power to impose a ruling which the parties must respect even if they do not agree with it.

The winning party can rely upon the assistance of national courts in enforcing the award if the losing party refuses to obey it. Again, courts will offer this assistance even if they believe the award to be incorrect. This is one of the fundamental risks of arbitration: unless you choose your arbitrator carefully, you may be bound by an award even though it is demonstrably incorrect.

5. *Not all disputes can be submitted to arbitration*

Because of the fundamentally private nature of arbitration, there have always been certain types of disputes that could not be taken to arbitration. Parties could agree to appoint an individual to resolve their dispute, much as in arbitration, but neither party would be bound by that agreement, and the appointee's decision would not be legally binding, leaving either party free to re-litigate the dispute in court. The notion of "arbitrability" expresses this concept: it is only possible to submit a dispute to arbitration if the dispute is arbitrable.

The reason for these limitations is well illustrated by the classic example of a non-arbitrable legal claim, namely criminal acts. It is theoretically possible for the victim of a crime and a criminal actor to appoint a third party to decide guilt and appropriate punishment. However, even though criminal acts involve private individuals, crime is not regarded as a purely private matter: it raises considerations of broader public importance, including both the right to protect others from subsequent criminal acts by the wrongdoer and the right of the State to punish individuals for committing certain acts. As a result, even those States that are most supportive of arbitration have retained the right to ignore any private settlement or decision relating to a criminal act and bring criminal proceedings.

What sorts of disputes may and may not be arbitrated varies among national jurisdictions, but this notion of "public interest" characterises the boundaries of arbitrability well. Nonetheless, it is necessary to interpret "public interest" broadly, as arbitrability restrictions can extend well beyond criminal matters. In some jurisdictions, for example, restrictions are placed on the arbitrability of disputes between consumers and traders – on the ground that a significant power imbalance exists between the consumer and trader, which can be used to create an unfair arbitration, conflicting with the "public interest" in ensuring the fair resolution of consumer disputes. Other examples of arbitrability restrictions include arbitrations involving governmental bodies, bankruptcy, patents, securities, family law, and other categories of disputes that have been argued to involve a "public interest" that will not be properly served by allowing such disputes to be taken to private arbitration.

Nonetheless, while there still remain arbitrability restrictions in even the States most supportive of arbitration, the boundaries of arbitrability have progressively expanded over time, with an increasing range of disputes being allowed to be submitted to arbitration. Chapter 3 will discuss arbitrability in more detail.

6. Arbitration can be domestic or international

Arbitration can be used to resolve both domestic and international disputes. National laws will determine whether an arbitration qualifies as "domestic" or "international", but as a general guideline, a dispute will be treated as domestic if all of its elements, including the identities of the parties and the physical location of the actions underlying the dispute, relate to a particular State. Take the example of a contract concluded between two French nationals and residents, governed by French law and to be performed entirely in France: a dispute arising out of such a legal relationship can unmistakably be labelled as "domestic". When arbitration is used to resolve this type of case, it is referred to as a "domestic arbitration". By contrast, a dispute between a German and a Brazilian company is not purely domestic, as it involves nationals of two different States. Depending on the national law involved, even a slight level of "international" context can suffice to qualify an arbitration as international.

The importance of this distinction goes far beyond mere labelling, as in many States domestic and international arbitration are subject to very different legal rules. While international arbitrations are routinely treated with great deference by national courts, States have traditionally regarded domestic arbitration as a legitimate topic of national interest. As a result, in some States courts are willing to intervene in and even control domestic arbitrations, and can be far more willing to grant challenges to domestic arbitral awards than is the case for international arbitrations.

In addition to this formal difference, the practices of domestic and international arbitration can vary significantly within the same State, even where the same lawyers and arbitrators are involved. Domestic arbitration closely resembles court litigation in some States, with both arbitrators and lawyers merely using standard litigation practices in a different setting. By contrast, practitioners and arbitrators operating in the field of international arbitration have progressively developed a body of practices, guidelines and standards which distinguish international arbitration from its domestic counterpart. International arbitration practice can still be seen to vary from State to State, with local customs and preferences influencing how even international arbitrations are conducted, but the variations are less stark than in domestic arbitration, and occur around a core of shared international arbitration procedural standards. Because of this, even in the absence of a formal distinction in the applicable procedural law, international and domestic arbitration are often conducted in different ways.

7. Arbitration is not always between private parties

Arbitration has become most prominent in the form of commercial arbitration, in which businesses engaged in a commercial transaction agree to resolve their dispute through arbitration, rather than by litigating in court. Indeed, it may seem odd for a State to use arbitration, given that arbitration serves as an alternative to courts, and courts are provided by States.

12 *What is arbitration?*

Nonetheless, there is nothing about the private nature of arbitration that entails that the parties themselves must be private entities, and States and State entities now regularly use arbitration, whether in the form of standard commercial arbitration, or in a version of arbitration expressly designed for the involvement of States.

8. Arbitration comes in different varieties

As discussed at the beginning of the chapter, arbitration is a supremely flexible form of dispute resolution, with very few rules about how it must be done. As a result, arbitration is easily adaptable for a wide range of disputes. One of the things that is important to recognise, however, is that while each of these forms of arbitration is indeed arbitration, there are nonetheless often significant differences in how each form operates, with adaptations made according to the type of dispute, the parties involved, and even the specific communities of arbitrators and practitioners who work on such arbitrations. This section will give examples of some of the most prominent forms of arbitration, but it is by no means exhaustive.

8.1 Domestic commercial arbitration

Commercial arbitration is arguably the most well-known form of arbitration, and involves a dispute between two commercial entities, relating to a transaction between them. Whether because of concerns about the slowness of local courts, the desire for a trusted industry specialist to serve as arbitrator, or another reason relating to potential benefits that arbitration can offer, arbitration has come to play a central role in commercial dispute resolution in many States around the world.

Indeed, it is in the context of the resolution of commercial disputes that contemporary international arbitration, and the ideas on which it is built, was developed. This is because operating an effective arbitration takes both the resources needed to pay the costs involved (costs which are often paid by the government in court litigation), and enough understanding of arbitration to structure an effective and efficient arbitral process. For these reasons, ordinary citizens have traditionally been happy to take their disputes to courts, leaving businesses to develop arbitration as a form of dispute resolution.

8.2 International commercial arbitration

It is, however, with the rise of cross-border commerce in the late 20th Century that arbitration came to particular prominence. Indeed, for most of the 20th Century arbitration remained a "niche" form of dispute resolution, used mainly within the context of specialised industries, or in significant cross-border transactions. The rise in the volume of cross-border transactions beginning in the final quarter of the 20th Century, however, led to a boom in arbitration, and to the prominence that it holds today. The international context is particularly appealing for arbitration because international transactions raise concerns about two issues arbitration is particularly good at dealing with: bias and procedural flexibility.

For example, a company from Brazil and a company from China may enter into a sales contract for goods manufactured in China, and to be delivered in Brazil. In any contract there is always the risk that a dispute will arise. However, the Brazilian party does not wish to have to litigate any such dispute in Chinese courts for several reasons: (1) China is far away, so that bringing executives, witnesses, etc. to China for a litigation will be expensive; (2) Litigating in China requires hiring Chinese lawyers, but the Brazilian party has no idea which Chinese lawyers are or are not good; (3) The Brazilian party is worried that Chinese courts may favour the Chinese party against a foreign party; (4) The Brazilian party has no idea how a Chinese court will interpret the contract; (5) The Brazilian party does not know the procedural rules of Chinese courts, or knows them but finds them "alien", and perhaps inconsistent with a Brazilian sense of procedural justice. Similarly, though, the Chinese party does not wish to have to litigate in Brazilian courts, for precisely the same reasons. In the international context, therefore, arbitration becomes important as a "defensive" manoeuver: a way of avoiding potential undesirable aspects of foreign courts.

The very different reasons that often motivate the use of arbitration in the domestic and international contexts explain why it is important to distinguish domestic and international commercial arbitration. Both are arbitration, and both are commercial arbitration. However, the very different contexts in which the parties are operating in the domestic and international commercial spheres means that the attractiveness of arbitration arises from very different considerations. As a result, domestic and international arbitration can differ considerably in form, and are sometimes even practiced by distinct communities of arbitration specialists.

8.3 Investment arbitration

The cross-border nature of contemporary commerce does not only mean that businesses may find themselves in dispute with businesses from other States. It also means that businesses will often need to subject themselves to the power of a foreign government, particularly if they choose to set up a long-term investment abroad, rather than merely entering into a sales transaction with a foreign party. Think, for example, of a US manufacturer of electronics opening a new production facility in India. In general terms, this phenomenon can be understood as a flow of resources: an entrepreneur decides to deploy some of her assets and invest them in a venture to be conducted in a foreign State. The foreign State where the investment is conducted (India, in the preceding example) is commonly referred to as the "Host State".

The risk this situation creates is that the Host State may take actions that harm or destroy the foreign investor's investment. There may be mechanisms under the law of the Host State through which the foreign investor could attempt to seek compensation, but in many States these mechanisms remain relatively undeveloped. In addition, the investor may be concerned that the domestic courts of the Host State will be biased in favour of the Host State's government. In such cases, foreign investors may be able to rely upon certain provisions of international law and bring their claim directly against the State in an investor – State arbitration – so long as the State has agreed to arbitrate such claims. As in all forms of arbitration, consent by both parties is necessary, and a State cannot be obligated to arbitrate even international law claims if it has not agreed to do so. Although investment arbitration is closely related to commercial arbitration, both in terms of its procedures and the practitioners involved, the laws involved and the fact that one of the disputing parties is a State have a significant enough impact on how it functions that it is appropriate to treat it as an independent form of arbitration.

8.4 Consumer arbitration

While historically arbitration was primarily a mechanism for the resolution of commercial disputes, the increasingly supportive approach to arbitration taken by courts and governments around the world has also led to many businesses choosing to incorporate arbitration agreements into consumer contracts. In some ways arbitration is an ideal dispute resolution mechanism for consumer disputes, as the procedural freedom contemporary arbitration involves allows arbitrations to be conducted more quickly and even more cheaply than is possible in many court systems. However, the unbalanced nature of the relationship between the consumer and the business, which often involves the business insisting upon the use of an arbitration provider and arbitration rules that it has unilaterally selected, raise concerns of fairness that are less common in the commercial context. For these reasons the ability of consumers to be bound by arbitration agreements is in some States strongly limited, or even completely eliminated.

8.5 State – State arbitration

One final variety of arbitration is also worth covering here, given its historical importance. One of the significant limitations to court litigation is that court systems are controlled by national or sub-national governments. This creates a problem when two States are in dispute, as neither State will be willing to subject itself to the powers and judgements of the courts of the other State, or any third State. Historically, the most common way of solving such disputes was through either military action or trade sanctions.

However, there has also been a third mechanism that States have used to resolve their disputes: arbitration. Arbitration, after all, is a private dispute mechanism, and yet as discussed above, this does not mean that the parties themselves must be private entities, but only that it is controlled by the parties to the dispute. There is, hence, no reason why those parties cannot themselves be governments, so long as the dispute resolution mechanism itself is not part of any government's court system. State – State arbitrations are known to have occurred, for example, in Ancient Greece, as early as the 7th Century BC. In 1899, the Permanent Court of Arbitration (PCA) was established, a specialised arbitral institution devoted to arbitrations involving States that remains active to this day. Note, however, that as it is an arbitral institution, the tribunals established by the PCA are not "courts", and none of them is "permanent" – such are the wonders of naming.

Currently, many State – State disputes are resolved at the International Court of Justice, but this does not mean that State – State arbitration has lost its practical relevance. For instance, according to Article 287(3) of the United Nations Convention on the Law of the Sea (UNCLOS), if the State parties have not expressed any preference concerning the resolution of disputes arising out of the interpretation or application of the Convention, the default rule is *ad hoc* arbitration under Annex VII of UNCLOS.

State – State arbitration is heavily influenced by the public international law nature of the disputes it typically aims at resolving. State – State arbitrations are often far more formal than commercial arbitrations, reflecting the involvement of governments on both sides, and while some commercial arbitration practitioners are also involved in State – State arbitrations, the latter have their own group of specialised practitioners.

9. *Arbitration can be institutional or* ad hoc

Courts are permanent institutions: they are part of the institutional architecture of a State, and the same court is involved in the resolution of a number of unrelated disputes involving many different parties. Take the example of a court case between Deon (claimant) and Janice (respondent): the court already existed before Deon commenced the litigation, and will still exist once the case has been decided.

Arbitral tribunals, by contrast, are part of a dispute resolution process that has been set up to address a particular dispute. As a consequence, arbitral tribunals are by their nature temporary. Arbitrators are appointed to the tribunal to address particular issues between the parties, and once those issues have been finally resolved, the tribunal's mandate ends, and the tribunal ceases to exist.

One important consequence of this temporary nature of arbitral tribunals is that arbitrations can be pursued without the long-term institutional framework that is necessary for a functioning court system. If courts are to be able to operate effectively across a wide range of cases and a wide span of time, they require an administrative framework that allows them to move effectively from one case to the next, employees to provide the background work necessary to allow this transition to occur, and so on. On the other hand, as an arbitral tribunal will cease to exist as soon as it has delivered its final award, all that is required for an effective arbitration is an arbitrator.

Nonetheless, while arbitration can occur without any supporting institutional framework, and large numbers of arbitrations use this model every year, the absence of an institutional framework can create difficulties. After all, an arbitration is still a legal process, so there will need to be rules regarding how the procedure will operate, materials will need to be exchanged between the parties, if hearings are needed then hearing rooms must be booked, transcripts of hearings may be needed, arbitrators must be paid, and so on. But whereas in the context of a court system all of these issues will be handled by the court's supporting institutional framework, in arbitration they must be handled by the parties themselves. The parties, however, may have no experience with arbitration, and so have no idea what must be done. Moreover, the parties are currently in dispute, and so may be highly antagonistic to one another and unable to agree on even minor details.

"Arbitral institutions" are the solution that has evolved over time to deal with this issue. Arbitral institutions are permanent bodies, often private businesses but sometimes government entities, which take on the role of providing support to arbitrations: they offer professional secretarial staff, often provide hearings rooms, and so on. In addition, they will usually have a set of institutional rules describing how arbitrations administered by the institution must operate, thereby freeing the parties from the requirement to make up their own rules. It is important to emphasise, however, that arbitral institutions are not decision makers: they assist in the organisation of the arbitral proceedings, but they play no role in deciding the dispute. Decision-making is entirely performed by the arbitral tribunal.

Arbitral institutions, that is, provide to arbitrations the same type of institutional framework from which national courts benefit. However, unlike the institutional framework that supports national courts, which is a mandatory system for any case heard by the court, parties must agree to use an arbitral institution, and remain free not to use any arbitral institution at all. Parties may choose not to use an arbitral institution, for example, if they are already familiar with arbitration, if they want to avoid the constraints deriving from the involvement of an arbitral institution, or if they want to prevent anyone other than the parties and the arbitrators from knowing the details of the dispute.

Moreover, national laws allow parties only limited freedom to choose their court, generally allowing the litigants to select the location in which they wish their case to be heard, but then mandating that any cases heard in a given location must be submitted to a particular court. By contrast, parties involved in arbitration retain absolute freedom in their choice of arbitral institution. Not only can they choose not to use an institution at all, but they can choose to use any institution from anywhere in the world, no matter where their arbitration is taking place (so long as the institution itself is willing to take their case). As a result, the mere fact that a given arbitral institution is located in France, for example, does not mean that it only handles arbitrations located in France – it can, in fact, handle arbitrations located anywhere in the world.

There are literally thousands of arbitral institutions around the world, although many handle few, and often no, arbitrations. Moreover, while there are substantial similarities in the types of support that arbitral institutions offer to arbitrations, significant differences do exist. As a result, it is always important to examine the rules and approach to arbitration offered by an institution to determine if it is appropriate for the parties and the dispute. The role of institutional rules in regulating the conduct of arbitration will be described in detail in Chapter 2.

As the institutional framework of arbitration, arbitral institutions have also come to play a broader role within arbitration, often taking on the task of promoting understanding of arbitration amongst businesses, legislators and judges. In addition, because arbitral institutions often have the role of appointing arbitrators when the parties in a dispute cannot agree on an arbitrator, or when one party has failed to appoint an arbitrator, arbitral institutions also play an important role in helping develop arbitration as a profession, giving opportunities to new arbitrators, and providing training and networking opportunities to those interested in a career in arbitration.

When arbitration is conducted under the auspices of an arbitral institution, it is referred to as "institutional arbitration". By contrast, if there is no arbitral institution administering the arbitration, the proceedings are called "*ad hoc*".

10. Arbitration offers potential advantages

Given that parties cannot be forced to arbitrate, arbitration can only succeed if it is seen as providing benefits over other forms of dispute resolution. This section will highlight certain features of arbitration that are often argued to make it preferable to other dispute resolution mechanisms.

10.1 Neutrality

One of the most important features of any dispute resolution mechanism is that it provides a neutral forum, in which the dispute between the parties can be addressed fairly and without bias. Arbitration is certainly not alone in being able to provide this forum, and one of the primary virtues of court litigation is precisely the neutrality of judges and the State-controlled litigation process.

There are situations, however, in which the neutrality of court litigation can come into question, and questions concerning court neutrality in international disputes have been a primary factor in the rapid growth of international arbitration since the middle of the 20th Century. Specifically, when a dispute involves parties coming from different States, both parties are likely to be concerned about having to litigate their dispute in the other party's "home" court system.

Firstly, parties sometimes fear that they will be treated unfavourably by the other party's "home" court system simply because they are from another State. This problem is often referred to as "home bias", and refers to an alleged tendency of some State courts to favour the interests of local disputants over those of foreigners. Sometimes such favouring can be explicit, and constitute actual bias of courts against foreign parties, but at other times it can merely reflect cultural differences, with courts from a State more likely to approve of behaviour in accordance with its own cultural norms.

Of course, the risk of home bias is particularly high when the dispute involves a State or a State-controlled entity. In such cases, local courts may feel that national interests should override private commercial interests, or may even be placed under direct pressure from governmental authorities. Moreover, judges may have been appointed to their position by the very government whose actions are being challenged, and their career advancement may depend on government officials having a positive view of their actions.

Nonetheless, even when a State's national courts are trusted to act impartially, other neutrality concerns can be raised by cultural differences relating to the proper means of resolving legal disputes. In some States, for example, witnesses are not expected to testify against their employer, while in other States such testimony is regarded as essential if a case is to be resolved fairly. Similarly, in some States parties in litigation have the ability to request large amounts of documentation regarding the dispute from the other party, as a means of helping to substantiate their claim or defence; in other States such "disclosure" is much more limited, in order to preclude "fishing expeditions" in which claims are brought without proof, in the hope that proof will be found in disclosed documents. Because of the significant differences that can exist between national court systems, foreign parties can have concerns about the legitimacy of the processes used in a State's courts, even if they concede that the courts themselves show no home bias.

Arbitration is seen as providing an important alternative to court litigation in such contexts, as it is perceived as providing a neutral forum over which both parties have control. It is important to understand, however, the manner in which arbitration's neutrality works. Unlike courts, which are (ideally) expressly designed to provide a neutral forum, an arbitration is constructed by the parties to the dispute – each of which will usually be only too happy to have the arbitral process biased in its favour. Selection of arbitrators, selection of procedural rules, and all the other aspects of the arbitral process, then, are not done with an eye to neutrality, but are instead often approached by the parties as part of the "conflict", with each attempting to secure an advantage.

That arbitration provides a neutral forum despite being subject to active attempts to bias it results from the balance of biases that it secures, rather than any inherent neutrality. That is, arbitration's procedural flexibility means that arbitration is easily biased. However, so long as both parties are active in the design of the arbitration, and have roughly equivalent power over it, their respective efforts to secure advantages will counteract one another, and produce a genuinely neutral process. The parties can agree on an arbitrator, or each party can ensure that its own preferred arbitrator sits on a tribunal of three arbitrators; parties can agree on mutually acceptable procedures, or those procedures can be set by a tribunal reflecting their respective viewpoints; and so on.

This, then, is the neutrality of arbitration in a nutshell. Arbitration is not inherently neutral, and indeed is easy to bias. However, a balanced arbitral process will provide a more assuredly fair and neutral dispute resolution forum than any court system.

10.2 Speed

One of the common conceptions of arbitration is that it is a "speedy" form of dispute resolution, providing a faster resolution of disputes than is usually available from national courts. Speed of resolution can be particularly important in the context of commercial disputes, as disputing parties wish to be able to move forward, but may not be able to do so until their dispute is resolved.

Speed is indeed a valuable feature offered by arbitration, but it is important to recognise the complexity in arbitration's connection with "speed". Firstly, there is nothing inherently fast about arbitration. Indeed, in a 2014 survey of European arbitration practitioners, 46% stated that most domestic arbitrations in which they had been involved in the past five years took over one year to conclude. The situation was even more extreme in international arbitration, with 84% stating that most arbitrations took over a year to conclude, and 28% stating that most arbitrations took over two years to conclude.

Arbitration, then, is not inherently fast; this is particularly true for international commercial arbitration, which is likely to involve more complex transactions and greater scheduling obstacles than domestic arbitration. Nonetheless, 82% of the same respondents reported that arbitration was "faster" than the national courts in their home State, and 48% stated that it was "much faster". Arbitration, then, may not be "speedy" in absolute terms, but it is "*comparatively* speedy". Resolving a complex dispute through arbitration will still take a significant amount of time, but it will usually take less time than would be required to resolve the same dispute through litigation.

The reasons for this situation are important to understand. Firstly, there are certain aspects of arbitration that unavoidably create short-term delays. State courts and judges are already in place before parties have a dispute: as a result, commencing litigation simply involves bringing a claim through the appropriate process. Arbitration, by contrast, requires that one or more arbitrators be appointed, either by agreement of the parties or through a process allowing each party to nominate an arbitrator to the tribunal. In either case, a party wishing to hinder arbitration can do so by delaying agreement on or appointment of an arbitrator. Similarly, courts supply buildings, administrators, procedural rules and full-time judges whose only job is usually to preside over litigations. In arbitration, on the other hand, all these elements must be either agreed between the parties or decided by a tribunal (once appointed), and must then be arranged.

On the other hand, however, there are aspects of arbitration that facilitate the fast resolution of disputes. Court litigation is often delayed by the need to compete against other disputes for the court's time, with overloaded courts struggling to coordinate the demands on their limited time. By contrast, so long as both parties in an arbitration wish their dispute to be resolved quickly, they have the freedom to arrange their arbitration so that it concludes in a time convenient for them. If one party wishes to delay resolution of the dispute, this can slow the arbitral process, but the same is true of litigation.

A useful image for the comparison of arbitration and litigation, then, might be that of a human (litigation) racing a car (arbitration). Cars take longer than humans to start moving – however, once the car is moving, it can pass the human and leave it behind with no difficulty at all. Similarly, then, arbitration starts slowly, but the control the parties have over the process means that once it is moving, a properly functioning arbitration can always be faster than litigation, if that is what the parties want.

10.3 Finality

The preceding discussion does not even consider one of the most important reasons why arbitration is often viewed as faster than litigation: arbitral awards cannot usually be appealed.

One of the greatest delays involved in litigation is the ability of a losing party to appeal unfavourable decisions to a higher court. Because of the availability of appeal, even winning in litigation does not guarantee that the dispute has concluded. Instead, a losing party may re-litigate the dispute in one or more successively higher courts. In some jurisdictions this process can result in parties waiting a decade or more for their dispute to be finally resolved. Arbitration, conversely, usually involves very limited opportunities for appeal. An award is final, and can be immediately enforced against the losing party. Moreover, while it is possible for a losing party to attempt to challenge an arbitral award or resist its enforcement, the grounds on which this can be done in most jurisdictions are so limited that such attempts are rarely successful.

Arbitration, then, can not only be faster than litigation, but provides a "one-stop" forum, in which the decision of the arbitrator will almost always finally resolve the dispute – thereby avoiding the risk of years of protracted litigation in appellate courts.

10.4 Enforceability

An arbitral award in itself has little value. An arbitrator is not an agent of a State, and so cannot compel a losing party to obey the terms of the award. In itself, that is, an arbitral award is just the view of a private individual on how a dispute should be resolved, and has no greater value than the view of any other private individual.

If this were the end of the story, then arbitration would be rarely used. The arbitral award would be no more than a recommendation to the parties on how their dispute should be resolved, and the losing party could simply ignore it. As a result, there would be little value in arbitration in most cases. Arbitration, however, has been widely embraced and supported by States, who have accepted the view that it provides an important alternative to court litigation. As a result, most contemporary States have laws allowing rapid enforcement of arbitral awards, while providing only very limited grounds on which enforcement can be challenged. Moreover, States have entered into international treaties, most famously the New York Convention on the Recognition and Enforcement of Arbitral Awards, in which they have agreed to enforce arbitral awards delivered in other States, while again providing only very limited grounds on which enforcement can be challenged.

As a result, while arbitration is a private process, it has been endorsed so strongly by States that an arbitrator's decision has at least as much power as that of a judge. Indeed, given the limited grounds on which arbitral awards can be challenged, and the treaties that allow arbitral awards to be enforced abroad more easily than court judgments,[4] there is good reason to state that an arbitrator's decision is actually significantly more powerful than that of a judge.

Recognition and enforcement of arbitral awards will be discussed in detail in Chapter 7.

10.5 Expertise

One of the greatest benefits that arbitration provides to parties is the power to select the arbitrator(s). The identity of the decision-maker is arguably the most important feature of any adjudicative dispute resolution process, as it has a major impact not only on how the law is interpreted and applied, but also with respect to many procedural decisions that will be taken in the course of the process.

In litigation, parties must simply accept the judge who is allocated to hear their case. This may mean, though, that the judge lacks the expertise necessary to understand fully certain technical elements of the parties' arguments, or the business context in which a transaction occurred. Some types of disputes hinge on industry-specific problems and therefore require a special technical expertise: a complex construction contract, for example, may be best resolved by an arbitrator with a strong background in engineering. In other cases, the parties may want their dispute resolved by someone with a strong commercial sensitivity, e.g. someone who understands the realities of international business relations.

In arbitration, parties are able to ensure that the arbitrator(s) possesses the technical knowledge or contextual understanding necessary to decide the case correctly. Moreover, as both parties are involved in arbitrator selection, each party can prioritise something of particular importance to its own case.

Unfortunately, too often parties fail to take advantage of this opportunity, and appoint someone merely because they are an experienced arbitrator, or are recommended by their counsel or by an acquaintance. Ultimately, however, it is up to the parties to select the right arbitrators, and thereby ensure a high quality final award. If they fail to make the effort necessary to select an arbitrator who is right for their particular arbitration, they have wasted one of the greatest benefits that arbitration provides.

10.6 Flexibility

Whereas in litigation parties must conform to the procedural rules and the schedule of the court, arbitration can take almost any form agreed to by the parties, restricted only by the need for the process to be fundamentally fair to both of them. By way of example, the parties can agree on which documents they should and should not have to disclose to the other side; on whether witness testimony should be allowed, and in what form; on what languages should be used; on the rules of evidence to be applied; ultimately, on every aspect of the arbitral process.

Arbitration, hence, is best understood as a bespoke dispute resolution mechanism, which gives the parties to a dispute the power to design their own process, to have no procedural rules at all, or even just to mimic the procedures of their preferred court system. While court litigation is fundamentally a standardised service provided by the State, arbitration belongs to the parties to the dispute, and leaves them free to decide how they wish to resolve that dispute.

10.7 Confidentiality

Arbitration is a private, third-party dispute resolution mechanism. It is, however, not necessarily confidential.

This is an important point to emphasise, as many people unfamiliar with the details of arbitration make the mistake of confusing arbitration's privacy with confidentiality. Arbitration is private in that it is controlled by the parties, who can therefore usually preclude all other parties, including the State, from involvement in the process. There is, however, nothing essentially confidential about arbitration, and whether information revealed in an arbitration can be repeated to third parties varies from one State to another. Parties seeking confidentiality, therefore, must examine the applicable law(s) in order to determine if there are specific acts they must undertake, such as signing a confidentiality agreement, to ensure the confidentiality of the process.

Nonetheless, while arbitration is not inherently confidential, it provides an opportunity for confidentiality that court litigation cannot provide. The privacy of arbitration means that as long as the parties and other participants in the arbitration maintain confidentiality, it is possible for an arbitration to take place without third parties even knowing of its existence, let alone of the subject matter of the dispute. There is, for example, no obligation to record the existence of an arbitration in public records, or to deposit any documents from the arbitration in a publicly accessible repository, both of which may be required by court litigation. Indeed, so long as both parties willingly conform to the award, taking the actions that it directs them to take, there is usually no obligation to deposit an award with the State, or even notify the State that the arbitration has taken place.

Arbitration, then, is not inherently confidential, but it provides an opportunity for confidentiality that even the most confidential court litigation cannot provide.

11. Arbitration has potential drawbacks

While arbitration has many virtues, no dispute resolution process is perfect, and arbitration has some important drawbacks as well.

11.1 Cost

One of the greatest benefits provided to parties involved in litigation is the subsidisation of public courts by governments. While court systems vary in the costs they impose on users, court litigation is ultimately a service provided by governments to assist individuals resolve their disputes. To achieve this goal, judges must be paid, buildings must be provided, court employees must be paid, jurors must be recruited, and so on. There are many expenses involved in providing court litigation, and traditionally parties have had to pay very little of that cost (although this situation is increasingly changing, and the costs of litigation can vary significantly from jurisdiction to jurisdiction).

Arbitration, however, while encouraged by many governments, is not provided by the government. It is a private process, voluntarily undertaken by the parties, as an alternative to using the government-provided court system. As a result, even those governments most supportive of arbitration have seen no reason to provide financial support to those using arbitration instead of court litigation. The consequence, of course, is that all the expenses connected with arbitration must be paid by the parties themselves.

Importantly, the flexibility of arbitration means that parties who want an inexpensive dispute resolution process can ensure that arbitration is actually cheaper than litigation, by choosing to eliminate aspects of the process that would normally be expensive, or just by choosing cheaper options than they might have used in court. But unless such cost-cutting efforts are made, an arbitration that matches precisely litigation in a given court system will unavoidably cost more for the parties than court litigation.

This said, however, it must be remembered that there are "costs" to a dispute resolution process that may not be as obvious as out-of-pocket expenses, but must nonetheless be taken into account. By way of example, a State court system charging very low court fees but requiring several years to resolve a case may be formally cheaper than a corresponding arbitration, but those benefits may rapidly be lost in opportunities that must be foregone while the litigation continues, and in the reputational damage that may be suffered before a decision is finally reached.

11.2 Limits to arbitral jurisdiction

Courts are based upon the power of the State to control the people and activities within their jurisdiction. As a result, courts have the power to compel individuals to assist a court case, even if they are not themselves parties to the dispute, and even if they have no wish to do so. In general, courts draw upon the power of the State to compel individuals to perform certain actions.

Arbitration, by contrast, is based upon the consent of the parties, not upon the power of the State. Consequently, arbitrators only have the powers given to them by the parties, and can only be given powers that the parties are able to give. The parties to a dispute, in particular, have no legal power to compel unconnected third parties to do anything; consequently, they cannot give this power to an arbitral tribunal. Similarly, the tribunal only has the power to make decisions over those aspects of a dispute that have been submitted to arbitration – there may be other aspects of the same dispute that are not covered by the arbitration agreement, and so the arbitrators have not been given the power to decide them.

As a result, the jurisdiction of an arbitral tribunal is limited: it normally only covers the parties to the arbitration agreement, and only those subject matters the parties agreed to refer to arbitration. This may in some cases create problems: a dispute, for example, may require that evidence be provided by an entity which was not a party to the arbitration agreement; or the dispute may be closely related to another dispute between the same parties, but that is not covered by the arbitration agreement. An arbitral tribunal has no power to address these situations unless given it by the applicable law, and so parties must usually rely on local courts to offer support to the arbitration, such as by compelling non-parties to participate in the arbitration.

These problems are less significant than they used to be, as the strong support States have given to arbitration means that courts often interpret arbitration agreements broadly, as covering things not expressly referenced in the language of the agreement, while arbitration laws often obligate courts to provide assistance to arbitrations. Nonetheless, national laws and the views of courts regarding arbitration still vary around the world, and so these limitations to arbitral jurisdiction can still constitute an obstacle if the arbitration is taking place in a less supportive State.

11.3 Limits to arbitral power

Another consequence of the fact that arbitrators only have the powers that they are given by the parties, and so only have the powers that parties are able to give them, is that there are sometimes limitations placed by the State on the powers of arbitrators. In other words, sometimes States do not allow parties to give arbitrators certain powers.

The most prominent example of such limitations is that of arbitrability, which refers to whether or not the law allows a certain type of dispute to be submitted to arbitration. If the applicable law, for example, does not allow disputes relating to gambling to be submitted to arbitration, then such disputes must be taken to court litigation, even if both parties wish to use arbitration. Any tribunal appointed to such a dispute must hold that it does not have the power to hear the dispute, or risk its award being unenforceable in the jurisdiction in question – as the parties did not have the power to submit the dispute to arbitration, and so could not give the arbitrators the power to hear it.

These limitations also sometimes relate to specific powers, rather than to the broader question of the right to arbitrate a dispute at all. Historically, for example, many legal systems precluded arbitral tribunals from ordering interim/provisional measures, such as requiring that a party not sell property the ownership of which was the subject matter of the arbitration. Instead, parties were required to make an application for interim/provisional measures to a local court, which would issue the order in support of the arbitration. Contemporary State support for arbitration means that such limitations are now becoming less common, and interim/provisional measures is one area in which significant changes have indeed occurred. Nonetheless, limitations of this nature still do exist in many jurisdictions, and so must be considered when choosing a jurisdiction in which to arbitrate.[5]

Finally, even when arbitral tribunals are not formally denied a power, courts have sometimes adopted doctrines presuming that the parties did not wish to give a particular power to arbitrators, unless they stated explicitly that the arbitrators should have that power. Many courts, for example, deny that arbitrators have the right to impose financial sanctions on parties who refuse to produce requested evidence, or otherwise refuse to cooperate with the arbitration. While such sanctions are standard in many systems of court litigation, they will often be struck down by courts if issued by arbitrators. As a result, arbitrators are forced to use "softer" versions of compulsion, such as adopting a presumption that evidence not produced by a party was unfavourable to that party. Such presumptions are less effective than the sanctions that could be imposed by a court, but nonetheless give arbitrators some power over uncooperative parties.

11.4 Lack of appeal

As noted above, one of the most beneficial features of arbitration is the lack of appeal from an arbitrator's award. This lack of appeal means that an arbitration is final, and parties do not need to be concerned about continued re-litigation of their dispute in appeals courts years after the original decision was issued.

There is, though, also an important negative aspect to the lack of appeal in arbitration. While it is possible to challenge an arbitral award in court, in even the most pro-arbitration jurisdictions, few contemporary legal systems allow such challenges to be made to the substantive decision of the arbitrators. As a result, so long as the procedures used in the arbitration were fundamentally fair to both parties, courts will enforce an arbitral award – even if they believe that it was clearly wrong on either the facts or the evidence.

The lack of appeal in arbitration, that is, provides certainty to the parties and a quick resolution of their dispute – but it also means that if they receive a poor decision, or even one that is demonstrably wrong, there is often nothing they can do about it, and that decision will be enforced by courts around the world.

11.5 Lack of expertise of arbitrators in arbitration

One final consideration must also be kept in mind: despite the lack of formal rules, arbitration is very technical, especially because it often needs to interact with national legal systems and national courts. Arbitration, after all, is based upon the consent of the parties, and arbitrators only have the powers that the parties have given them. Moreover, national arbitration laws do vary, and courts may refuse to enforce an award that was given in an arbitration that did not conform to local arbitration law. This means that while parties are largely free to arbitrate however they wish, arbitrators must be careful to adhere to applicable local law, and to demonstrate in their award that they have at all times remained within the powers legitimately given to them by the parties.

Unfortunately, while the lack of formal requirements in most jurisdictions for serving as an arbitrator enhances the ability of the parties to select an arbitrator they believe is most suitable for their dispute, it can also lead parties to select arbitrators with inadequate knowledge of the technicalities of arbitration. As a result, while most arbitrations produce enforceable awards, and arbitration has become a highly effective dispute resolution mechanism, it is far from unknown for parties to end up with an unenforceable award simply because they did not select an arbitrator who genuinely understood arbitration.

Notes

1 The enforcement of settlement agreements is traditionally regulated in different ways by several national laws. However, on 20 December 2018, the United Nations Commission on International Trade Law (UNCITRAL) adopted a Convention on the enforceability of settlement agreements

2 Some readers may be initially confused by the use of the word "State" in this book. In the United States of America and some other countries, the word is often used to designate the US states, such as California or Florida. In this book, however, the word is used in a different and more general meaning, to indicate all sovereign States around the world, such as for instance France or Japan. To mark this difference, "State" is spelt with a capital "S".

3 The right of access to court is an inherent aspect of the right to a fair trial under Article 6 of the European Convention on Human Rights: see European Court of Human Rights, *Golder v. the United Kingdom* (21 February 1975, §§ 28–36, Series A no. 18). Furthermore, Article 13 of the Convention enshrines the right to an effective remedy. Along similar lines, Article 47 of the Charter of Fundamental Rights of the European Union recognises the right to an effective remedy and to a fair trial. Article 8 of the American Convention on Human Rights also guarantees the right to a fair trial. For a landmark theorisation of access to justice grounded in comparative law see B.G. Garth and M. Cappelletti, "Access to Justice: The Newest Wave in the Worldwide Movement to Make Rights Effective" (1978) 27 *Buffalo Law Review* 181.

4 The recognition and enforcement of foreign court judgments is not impossible, but it is made more difficult by the absence of an international convention as successful as the 1958 Convention on the Recognition and Enforcement of Foreign Arbitral Awards (commonly known as "The New York Convention"). Things, however, may change in the future: on 2 July 2019, the Hague Conference on Private International Law concluded a Convention on the recognition and enforcement of foreign judgments in civil or commercial matters. The instrument is currently open for ratification.

5 For instance, Article 818 of the Italian Code of Civil Procedure still prevents arbitrators from issuing interim measures.

2 The laws and rules applicable to arbitration

Rules

1. Different laws can govern different aspects of an arbitration

While those unfamiliar with international commercial arbitration often think of it as providing an alternative to the strictly law-focused approach of court litigation, arbitration is intimately entwined with the law. Indeed, a single arbitration may have several applicable laws, each governing one or more aspects of the arbitral process or the parties' dispute.

2. The procedure of an arbitration is regulated by the law of the seat of the arbitration (lex arbitri) and by any applicable arbitration rules

Arbitrations are regulated by the law of the "seat" of the arbitration, often referred to as the *lex arbitri*. The "seat" is where the arbitration is *legally* taking place, and may be different from where the arbitral proceedings are *physically* taking place. Contemporary arbitration laws are usually designed to support arbitrations, rather than control them, and so largely leave parties free to decide the rules for their own arbitration. Parties may design their own procedural rules, but can also agree to use pre-designed arbitration rules, such as those created by an arbitral institution.

3. The tribunal must decide the parties' dispute in accordance with the applicable law

An arbitral tribunal must decide the parties' dispute by applying the law applicable to that dispute, even if it dislikes the result that the law produces.

4. Parties are largely free to choose the substantive law to be applied in resolving their dispute

Parties are generally free to choose the law governing their dispute, and can most effectively do so by incorporating a "choice of law" agreement into their original contract. Parties can also agree to have their dispute resolved in accordance with rules other than those of a national or sub-national legal system, including in accordance with custom or *lex mercatoria*. They can also authorise an arbitrator to decide their dispute *ex aequo et bono*, or in accordance with the arbitrator's own sense of justice and fairness. However, whatever laws or rules parties select, arbitrators should also apply any public policies or mandatory rules of the seat of the arbitration.

5. *If the parties have not chosen the substantive law to be applied in resolving their dispute, the arbitral tribunal must make this choice*

As arbitrators must decide a dispute by applying laws/rules to facts, if the parties have not agreed on the law or rules to be applied, this decision must be made by the arbitrators. The law of the seat of the arbitration will usually specify the approach arbitrators should take in identifying the applicable law. However, contemporary arbitration laws often specify an approach that leaves arbitrators with a great deal of discretion.

6. *The law governing the agreement to arbitrate may differ from the law governing the contract in which the agreement to arbitrate is contained*

Even if parties have included a "choice of law" clause in their contract, the doctrine of "separability" means that this choice may not apply to an arbitration clause included in the contract. There is no uniformly accepted approach to determining what law should be applied to an arbitration agreement. The guiding principle, however, must always be to determine and apply the intention of the parties.

Analysis

1. *Different laws can govern different aspects of an arbitration*

1.1 Arbitration is closely intertwined with the law

People new to arbitration often view arbitration as an informal alternative to court litigation, which allows parties to avoid the technicalities of legal rules and concentrate instead on developing a procedure that matches their specific needs and preferences. This is an illusion. As with many illusions, though, it contains a kernel of truth.

Fundamentally, arbitration is like a swan. A swan is a remarkably graceful swimmer that seems to almost glide across the water. Yet it can only do this because under the water its feet are paddling furiously. Arbitration is the same. In an effective arbitration the parties can address their dispute in a way that is well-designed for their own personal needs and preferences, avoiding if desired the technical rules of court litigation – but it can only do this if the arbitrators are so in command of the applicable law that the parties don't need to worry themselves with it.

The consequence of this situation, though, is obvious. If the arbitrators aren't in command of the applicable law, then the parties will ultimately discover, to their great unhappiness, just how intertwined with law arbitration is. To conclude the metaphor: if your swan doesn't know how to paddle, its legs will rapidly tangle and it will very ungracefully tip over head-first into the water.

This chapter will not attempt to address every way in which the law might potentially interact with an arbitration, but it will clarify the primary ways in which this interaction occurs. Unless the participants in an arbitration understand the reality of arbitration's intimate relationship with the law, even an apparently straightforward arbitration runs a serious risk of failure.

1.2 Substantive versus procedural law

To understand the relationship between arbitration and the law, it is useful to start from the distinction between "substance" and "procedure". Every legal relationship between two or more parties is regulated by certain laws: a contract, for example, will be regulated by a certain jurisdiction's contract law, while a non-contractual claim between the same parties might be governed by the same or a different jurisdiction's tort law. These bodies of rules, regulating the legal relationships of parties, are usually referred to as "substantive law". If any dispute arises between two or more parties, a legal decision-maker (whether an arbitral tribunal or a State court) will examine the applicable substantive law to determine how the case should be resolved, i.e. which of the disputing parties should win, and how much they should win.

This is the obvious way in which law will usually apply to a dispute, including a dispute that is taken to arbitration: the parties to the dispute each have certain legal rights and obligations, and the decision-maker's role is to examine the law and the facts, and deliver a decision applying the law as she interprets it to be, to the facts as they have been established to her satisfaction.

There is, however, another aspect of the law that is important for any dispute resolution process, as it assures the parties to a dispute that the substantive law will be applied to their dispute in a predictable and fair way. This is what is called "procedural law", and it identifies the specific procedures that a tribunal or court will use to resolve the parties' dispute, addressing such things as when documents must be submitted by the parties, whether witnesses can be used and how they can be questioned, what language is to be used in any hearing, and so on.

Procedural law may initially seem to be less truly "law" than substantive law, and instead just a set of rules about how disputes will be resolved. But the crucial role of procedural law in any legal system is clear if you consider what it would be like to be told that the substantive law says you have a right to compensation for something that has happened, but that to actually receive that compensation you must convince a judge that you took certain actions – however, whether or not the judge will actually look at your evidence, or listen to your testimony, is entirely up to her. That is, substantive legal rights only have value to the extent that procedural law gives parties the ability to enforce them. Procedural law may seem to be less truly "law" than substantive law, but without both types of law there is nothing that can properly be called a legal system.

The traditional method through which substantive legal rights have been enforced is, of course, court litigation, and the procedural rules in accordance with which courts will operate is often formally laid out in a statutory code of civil procedure. Arbitration, however, just like court litigation, is a procedure: it is an orderly sequence of activities, at the end of which a decision-maker will deliver a decision applying the substantive law to the facts of the parties' dispute.

Just like litigation, that is, arbitration attempts to go beyond merely having an individual decide a dispute, and instead aims at producing a decision that is genuinely "legal": that evaluates the evidence produced by the parties and the arguments made by the parties, through a procedure that is designed to ensure fairness to both sides. That procedure might differ fundamentally from the procedure used in the courts of the jurisdiction in which the arbitration is taking place, and it will often be much less formal than most court procedures, with the arbitrators merely deciding procedural issues as they arise rather than adopting a set of pre-existing procedural rules. But nonetheless arbitration is a "procedural" dispute resolution mechanism – it involves adjudicators making their decision at the end of a formalised process, which was adopted as it was believed to be an effective means of identifying and enforcing each party's legally valid rights and obligations.

2. The procedure of an arbitration is regulated by the law of the seat of the arbitration (lex arbitri) and by any applicable arbitration rules

2.1 The seat of arbitration

The idea of the "seat" of an arbitration is one of the most surprising aspects of arbitration to anyone new to the subject. After all, we would all find it ridiculous to be told that someone sitting in a café in Paris drinking coffee was in fact actually drinking coffee in Berlin, simply because they said they were. Yet that is almost the consequence of the concept of the "seat" of an arbitration – it means that an arbitration may not *legally* be occurring where it is *physically* occurring. That is, that arbitrators, parties and lawyers involved in an arbitration hearing taking place in Paris, may actually be participating in an arbitration that is legally occurring in an entirely different jurisdiction. This notion of the *legal* location of an arbitration, as opposed to its *physical* location, is the essence of the "seat" of an arbitration.

The notion of an arbitral "seat" derives from the fact that although arbitration is a private mechanism of dispute resolution, it relies for its success on the willingness of States to support arbitrations as they are occurring, and to enforce arbitral awards when they are delivered. The mechanism that States have adopted to enable this support is the arbitral "seat". In essence, while arbitration is private, it does not happen in a vacuum. Every arbitration is linked to the legal system of a particular State, which is then referred to as that arbitration's "seat".[1]

In broad terms, the seat of the arbitration is where, as a matter of law, an arbitration is recognised as occurring. Individual parts of the arbitration, such as hearings, may occur in other jurisdictions, but unless the parties specifically agree to change the seat, even those parts of the arbitration *physically* occurring in other jurisdictions are treated as having *legally* occurred at the arbitration's seat. By way of example, an arbitration may be seated in State X, with the hearings held in State X. However, because certain witnesses live in State Y, a single day-long hearing is also held in State Y. Although that hearing physically takes place in State

Y, it will legally be treated as occurring in State X – meaning that if the assistance of courts is needed for that hearing, it will usually have to be sought from the courts of State X, unless the law of State Y allows the courts of State Y to assist foreign arbitrations.

Of course, this example also points to one of the serious risks in separating the legal and physical locations of an arbitration: courts have jurisdictional limits to their powers, and the parties in this example may well find that the courts of State Y are unwilling or unable to assist their arbitration because it is "foreign", while the courts of State X are willing to assist but unable do so because the courts of State X have no jurisdiction in State Y.

Notably, the separation between the physical location and the legal location of an international commercial arbitration has become so widely accepted that many national arbitration laws do not require that even a single element of an arbitration physically occur in a State for that State to be the arbitration's seat. All that is required is that the parties have agreed that the State in question is the arbitration's seat.[2]

The fact that every international commercial arbitration is seated in a particular State has a fundamental practical consequence: every arbitration is regulated by the law of its seat. Arbitration is private, but just as your own government can legitimately tell you what you can and cannot do in the privacy of your own home (you can't avoid a murder prosecution by pointing out that you committed the murder in your bathroom, rather than in public), so the State can legitimately control how arbitrations can and cannot be undertaken when they occur within that State's borders. Consequently, by selecting a certain jurisdiction to be the seat of an arbitration, the parties have thereby subjected their arbitration to whatever laws apply to arbitration in that jurisdiction.[3]

The arbitration laws of the seat are often referred to as the *lex arbitri*, and the *lex arbitri* plays a fundamental role in arbitration. Firstly, it provides the legal framework within which the arbitration operates: many aspects of an arbitration, from the constitution of the tribunal to the conduct of the proceedings, are regulated by the *lex arbitri*.

Secondly, the seat determines the nationality of the award for the purpose of international recognition and enforcement: if an arbitration is seated in State X, then the resulting award will usually be treated as "from" State X for the purpose of recognition and enforcement. As a result, even if all the hearings and other elements of the arbitration physically occurred in State Y, if the winning party attempts to enforce the award in State Y it will usually be treated by the courts of State Y as a "foreign" award – even though the arbitrators and the parties never set foot outside State Y at any point in the arbitral process, and even though the arbitrators applied the substantive law of State Y to resolve the dispute.

2.2 Nature and content of the lex arbitri

Arbitration is, of course, not the only dispute resolution procedure regulated by national law. Litigation before State courts, for example, is usually regulated by very detailed procedural rules. For this reason, one might initially be inclined to think that a State's *lex arbitri* will roughly parallel the civil procedure rules the State has adopted to regulate court litigation, in both level of detail and content.

Such an assumption, however, will very rarely be correct, as there is a fundamental difference between the goals States are attempting to achieve with their arbitration laws and those they are attempting to achieve with their civil procedure rules. Litigation, after all, is a State-controlled process, supplied by the government and built on the power and authority of the State. States understandably take great concern in how litigation functions and adopt detailed rules to ensure that litigation procedures are transparent, predictable, and correlate with widely held views on the nature of a fair dispute resolution procedure. International commercial arbitration, on the other hand, is a private procedure that rarely has significant direct consequences for anyone not a party to the arbitration. As a result, States are not responsible for the conduct of arbitrations in the way they are for litigations, and also rarely need to protect non-parties from possible negative consequences of a poorly run arbitration.

For this reason, while States have adopted civil procedure rules in order to <u>control</u> litigation, and ensure that it operates in a way acceptable to the government and the broader populace, they adopt the *lex arbitri* to <u>assist</u> private parties resolve their disputes in accordance with their agreement. It is this difference in motivation that explains why although civil procedure rules control litigation proceedings in detail, a State's *lex arbitri* will usually just set forth a minimal infrastructure of rules, upon which parties are largely left free to elaborate.

In other words, *lex arbitri* overwhelmingly focus on ensuring that legal mechanisms are available to support arbitrations if needed, while keeping to a minimum the limitations placed on how parties can run their arbitration. This approach is commonly referred to as a State attempting to be "arbitration-friendly".

One obstacle States traditionally faced in developing an effectively supportive *lex arbitri* was the simple fact that while States had been regulating litigation for decades or even centuries, few had any real experience with legislating for international commercial arbitration. A major development in addressing this problem was the adoption by the United Nations Commission on International Trade Law (UNCITRAL) in 1985 of the "Model Law on International Commercial Arbitration". As its title indicates, the Model Law is not actually a law, and so is not binding on anyone. It is, rather, a "model" – it is the text of a complete arbitration law that can simply be copied into the domestic law of any jurisdiction wishing to improve its arbitration law, with adjustments made where desired. It is, in effect, nothing more than a statement equivalent to "Here is UNCITRAL's view of what a well-designed and effective arbitration law should say." The Model Law has unquestionably been very successful, and as of July 2019, 80 States have based their national arbitration laws directly on the Model Law (these States often being referred to as "Model Law countries"). Moreover, the Model Law is now accepted as representing the "gold standard" for the regulation of arbitration, and is regularly cited in discussions of arbitration law even in States that have not themselves adopted the Model Law.

The *lex arbitri* supports arbitration in two main ways: by providing positive assistance, and by providing fall-back mechanisms.

An arbitration may require the positive assistance of the State, for example, because one of the parties to the arbitration agreement no longer wishes to arbitrate and so is not cooperating with the arbitration, or because the cooperation is required of someone who is not bound by the arbitration agreement (e.g. an independent witness). If a party to an arbitration agreement is refusing to arbitrate, the *lex arbitri* will usually provide that courts may not allow a party to an arbitration agreement to commence litigation as long as a valid arbitration agreement remains in place, thereby preventing the non-cooperative party taking their dispute to court. Alternatively, the non-cooperative party may have refused to appoint an arbitrator, thereby preventing the formation of the arbitral tribunal; *lex arbitri* normally address this situation by allowing a court to appoint an arbitrator if a party has failed to do so.

With respect to non-parties to the arbitration agreement, an arbitrator will usually not have the power to order a non-party to assist the arbitration. After all, an arbitrator is just a private individual, whose power depends entirely on the consent of certain individuals (i.e. the parties) to take part in a dispute resolution procedure, and in doing so to follow any legitimate orders of the arbitrator. But a non-party has never consented to follow any orders the arbitrator may issue. As a result, a non-party has no more obligation to do what an arbitrator says than you would have an obligation to take off your shoes simply because someone walked up to you in the street and said "I don't like your shoes, take them off".

Lex arbitri often address this issue by allowing courts to order non-parties to cooperate with the arbitration. For example, the law may allow an arbitrator to request a court to issue an order to a non-party to the arbitration agreement, requiring him to provide evidence to the arbitration, or otherwise assist the arbitration. Once such an order is issued, the non-party can now be sanctioned by the court if he fails to assist the arbitration in the way he has been ordered to do so by the court – not because he has continued to defy the orders of the arbitrator, but because he is now defying the order of a court.

By providing these types of positive assistance the *lex arbitri* ensures that arbitrations can operate effectively even though the private nature of arbitration means that arbitration tribunals do not possess many of the powers possessed by courts.

Not all assistance provided by the *lex arbitri* requires positive actions by the State, however, and a well-designed *lex arbitri* will also contain fall-back mechanisms designed to ensure the effectiveness of an arbitration even when the parties have not themselves adequately designed the arbitral procedure. For example, the arbitration agreement may not specify the number of arbitrators to be appointed, resulting in a dispute between the parties as to whether one or three arbitrators is required. The *lex arbitri* will standardly address this problem by providing a default number of arbitrators whenever the parties cannot agree.[4] Similarly, the *lex arbitri* may also provide certain basic procedural rules to be used in an arbitration if the parties have not agreed otherwise – the parties usually retaining the power, however, to adopt rules inconsistent with these default rules if that is their preference.

Nonetheless, it has to be remembered that while the fundamental purpose of a contemporary *lex arbitri* is to facilitate international commercial arbitration, rather than to control it, States ultimately retain the power to require that arbitrations be performed in a certain way. Indeed, even the most "arbitration-friendly" States have certain "mandatory rules", which the parties to an arbitration are not permitted to depart from even if both parties wish to. A typical example in this respect relates to the ability of a party to apply for annulment of the arbitral award (see Chapter 7) – an ability which can in some cases be limited by the parties, but usually cannot be completely excluded.[5] These instances of mandatory rules, however, must be seen as exceptions to the general approach of a contemporary *lex arbitri*: they are restricted to issues that involve the most fundamental values of the State, as a way of ensuring that arbitrations operate fairly and that they do not inhibit legitimate interests of non-parties. Such rules do not undermine the essential goal of a contemporary *lex arbitri*, namely facilitating the conduct of international commercial arbitrations in accordance with the agreement of the parties.

2.3 The role of institutional rules

As has just been discussed, most national arbitration laws leave the parties to an arbitration agreement free to determine, to a large extent, the rules in accordance with which their arbitration will function.[6] This helps achieve one of the primary benefits of arbitration, namely the ability to design an arbitral procedure suitable for the specific parties to the arbitration agreement and for the specific dispute being addressed.

This sounds wonderful. In reality, of course, relatively few parties have enough experience with arbitration that they are able to design their own procedure effectively. Most arbitration agreements are very brief and do little more than express the agreement of the parties to resolve their disputes through arbitration. Moreover, once an arbitration has commenced, the parties are in a dispute and likely want different things from the procedure.

One way this problem has been addressed is through the adoption by arbitral institutions of their own procedural rules. These rules apply by default to all arbitrations an institution administers, although they usually allow many elements of the rules to be varied by party agreement or by decision of the arbitral tribunal.

Nonetheless, as noted in Chapter 1, many arbitrations are conducted *ad hoc*, and so cannot benefit from the availability of institutional rules. This issue was addressed in 1976, when the United Nations Commission on International Trade Law (UNCITRAL) adopted the first edition of its Arbitration Rules, providing a coherent set of procedural rules that can be used by parties even in *ad hoc* arbitration.

Realistically, of course, many parties who enter into arbitration agreements have not even considered the need for procedural rules, and are entirely unaware that pre-designed arbitral rules exist. Nonetheless, while parties can only use the UNCITRAL Arbitration Rules if they expressly refer to them in their arbitration agreement, or agree later to use them, it is clearly established that an agreement to arbitrate under the auspices of a particular arbitral institution also constitutes an agreement to use that institution's arbitration rules, unless the institution itself specifies otherwise. As a result, as long as the parties to an arbitration agreement have included within their agreement a reference to an arbitral institution, they will usually thereby also gain access to a set of rules that have been designed by individuals experienced in arbitration, and are known from experience to provide an effective support to arbitration – unless, of course, they have selected their institution badly, and the institution either has no procedural rules, or its procedural rules are poorly designed.

A more complex question is whether the parties can choose *ad hoc* arbitration but still choose to use a certain set of institutional rules. For example, the parties may have heard of the International Chamber of Commerce's International Court of Arbitration (ICC), a leading arbitral institution. They decide that it surely must have effective arbitration rules, and so agree to arbitrate in accordance with the ICC's rules, even though they wish to arbitrate *ad hoc*. That is, they do not wish to use the ICC itself, but only to use the ICC's rules. The problem this creates is that institutional rules are expressly designed to be used for arbitrations administered by a particular institution, and so will often specify that certain actions will be undertaken by that institution. Yet if the rules are used in an *ad hoc* arbitration, the institution will not be involved, and as a result those actions cannot be performed in accordance with the rules to which the parties have agreed to arbitrate (since they cannot be performed by the institution the rules specify they must be performed by). As a result, one of the parties may object that the arbitration is not taking place in accordance with the rules both parties agreed would be used.

A similar problem exists if parties attempt to use the rules of one institution in an arbitration administered by a second institution. They might, for example, want their arbitration to be administered by a local institution, staffed by individuals they know and trust, but nonetheless believe that the local institution's procedural rules are inadequate in some way. As a result, in their arbitration agreement they agree to arbitrate under the auspices of their local institution, but using the rules of, for example, the ICC. The same problem arises here as in the previous case: the ICC's rules will require that certain actions be undertaken by the ICC, but the ICC is not administering the arbitration, and so cannot perform those actions.[7] The obvious solution would be for the local institution to perform all the acts that the rules require be performed by the ICC, but that is ultimately not what the parties agreed would happen – by adopting the ICC's rules, the parties agreed that the ICC would perform the actions that the rules say it must perform; the parties could now agree to let the local institution perform those actions, but one party may no longer wish to arbitrate and so refuse to agree.

Ultimately there have been diverging views on how these two situations should be resolved. As a result, until the situation becomes clearer parties should avoid agreeing to use an institution's arbitration rules if they do not also want to have their arbitration administered by that institution.

Understanding arbitration through case-law

Arbitration administered by one institution under the rules of a different institution

Case details: *Insigma Technology Co. Ltd v Alstom Technology Ltd* [2009] SGCA 24

Authority deciding the case: Singapore Court of Appeal

Facts of the case: Insigma and Alstom concluded an arbitration agreement according to which all disputes should be resolved "by arbitration before the Singapore International Arbitration Centre [SIAC] in accordance with the Rules of Arbitration of the International Chamber of Commerce". In other words, the parties agreed to have their arbitration administered by the SIAC, but under the ICC rules.

Alstom commenced arbitration at the ICC; Insigma, however, objected to the jurisdiction of the ICC tribunal, on the ground that the arbitration clause specified that SIAC would administer the arbitration. Alstom discontinued the ICC arbitration and commenced SIAC proceedings. SIAC agreed to administer the arbitration in accordance

> with the ICC rules. Insigma, however, objected to the jurisdiction of the SIAC tribunal as well, arguing that the clause was null and void because of the uncertainty created by its wording.
>
> After the conclusion of the arbitration, Insigma commenced annulment proceedings before the courts of Singapore, where the arbitration was seated. Insigma argued that the award had to be annulled on grounds of invalidity of the agreement to arbitrate.
>
> **Decision:** The Singapore Court of Appeal refused to annul the award and held that an arbitration agreement whereby the parties select an arbitral institution, but provide for the application of a set of rules belonging to a different institution, is not invalid. The Court adopted an arbitration-friendly approach, in accordance with which the parties' choice to use arbitration should be given effect whenever possible. The unusual wording of the clause was not considered to be a source of serious uncertainty, and the Court held that any difficulties arising out of the application of the clause could be overcome with the help of the arbitral institutions, arbitrators and State courts.
>
> The decision to uphold the validity of this type of arbitration clause has been met with a mixed reaction from arbitration specialists. While enforcing the parties' agreement to arbitrate is undoubtedly a fundamental policy goal for any arbitration-friendly jurisdiction, the selection of a set of arbitration rules other than the one issued by the administering institution raises numerous practical problems. The ICC's current arbitration rules try to limit this phenomenon by providing, at Article 1(2), that "(t)he Court [i.e. the ICC] is the only body authorized to administer arbitrations under the Rules". The ICC rules, however, do not bind other institutions.
>
> **Read more:** Jennifer Kirby, "Insigma Technology Co. Ltd v. Alstom Technology Ltd: SIAC Can Administer Cases under the ICC Rules?!?" (2009) 25(3) *Arbitration International* 319

A further question that arises with respect to the role of institutional rules, given the preceding discussion of the role of a contemporary *lex arbitri* in supporting international commercial arbitrations, is how a conflict between the *lex arbitri* and institutional rules should be resolved. The traditional view, of course, is that the law is superior to and overrules private agreements, and indeed that is the rule that applies in this situation. Parties cannot, therefore, avoid applicable mandatory rules of law by selecting institutional rules which conflict with them.

An important qualifier arises, however, from the nature of most contemporary *lex arbitri*. As noted above, contemporary *lex arbitri* are designed to assist parties in arbitrating in accordance with their agreement, not to control how they arbitrate. Consequently, while it is true that the *lex arbitri* is always superior to and will overrule institutional rules, in most jurisdictions the two will very rarely come into conflict. Rather, with the exception of a limited number of mandatory rules, the *lex arbitri* will usually expressly allow the application of any of its provisions to be altered or even completely excluded by agreement of the parties in an arbitration.[8]

Importantly, however, one mechanism by which parties to an arbitration can decide to alter or exclude provisions of the *lex arbitri* is by agreeing to arbitrate using institutional rules that are inconsistent with non-mandatory provisions of the *lex arbitri*. The parties, that is, need not consciously decide to alter or exclude provisions of the *lex arbitri*, or even know that by adopting the institutional rules in question they have done so. But as a matter of the *lex arbitri* itself, consistent with its underlying goal of facilitating the parties arbitrating in accordance with their agreement, if the parties have agreed to use institutional rules, then those are the rules that the *lex arbitri* requires be applied (absent any further agreement by the parties to vary or exclude certain of the institutional rules).

3. The tribunal is obligated to decide the parties' dispute in accordance with the applicable law

One of the most important constraints on an arbitral tribunal is its obligation to resolve the parties' dispute by applying whatever law or rules the parties have selected for the resolution of their dispute. Indeed, while there are usually very few grounds on which an arbitral award can be annulled, or its enforcement refused, the failure of the tribunal to apply the applicable law is standardly recognised as one of them.

Ultimately the arbitral tribunal are employees of the parties. They have been hired to resolve the parties' dispute through the application of certain laws or rules, and they do not have the authority to reject those laws or rules, even if they dislike the result that they produce.

4. Parties are largely free to choose the substantive law to be applied in resolving their dispute

4.1 The prevailing role of party autonomy

In the context of international commercial arbitration, arbitrations usually arise through a transaction based upon a contract (although this need not always be true). In such a case, the law the arbitral tribunal must apply when deciding the case on the merits is the law governing that contract. Importantly, this is true even if the law governing the contract is not the law of the seat of the arbitration. By way of example, in an arbitration arising out of a joint venture contract governed by German law, an arbitral tribunal seated in England must resolve the substance of the dispute by applying German law, not English law.

One question that may arise is what arbitrators should do if the substantive law applicable to the dispute contradicts a mandatory provision of the *lex arbitri*. The tribunal has, after all, been hired to decide the dispute in accordance with the substantive law in question; but the tribunal has also been hired by the parties to operate the arbitration in accordance with the *lex arbitri*. Views on this question differ, with some practitioners and commentators arguing that the primary obligation of the tribunal is to the parties, not to the legal system of the seat, and this obligation is better fulfilled by adhering to the substantive law governing the parties' transaction than to the *lex arbitri*. The better view, however, acknowledges that the tribunal ultimately functions under the terms of the *lex arbitri*, and only has the powers that the *lex arbitri* permits it to have. Consequently, if a mandatory provision of the *lex arbitri* conflicts with the substantive law chosen by the parties, the tribunal is obligated to apply the provision of the *lex arbitri*. After all, if both parties dislike this result, they have the power to mutually agree on changing the seat of the arbitration – absent such an agreement, however, the mandatory terms of the *lex arbitri* must prevail.

With this limitation, however, any choice made by the parties regarding the substantive law applicable to their relationship must be respected by the tribunal, and indeed it is common for parties entering into an international commercial contract to include in that contract a specific provision identifying the applicable substantive law. This provision is commonly referred to as a "choice of law clause", "applicable law clause" or "choice of law agreement".

National laws around the world now accept the desirability of allowing parties to an international commercial transaction to choose the law to be applied to their relationship, and such choices will usually be respected by courts. The argument for respecting such a choice in the context of international commercial arbitration is even stronger than in litigation, given that the goal of contemporary arbitration laws is to assist the parties to arbitrate in accordance with their arbitration agreement, rather than to mandate how they must arbitrate. Indeed, the UNCITRAL Model Law is fully consistent with this approach, specifying in Article 28(1) that the tribunal "shall decide the dispute in accordance with such rules of law as are chosen by the parties as applicable to the substance of the dispute".

The reason parties to an international commercial transaction might want to specify the applicable substantive law is simple: if they do not do so, then the arbitral tribunal must itself determine the applicable law before making any decision on the merits of the dispute.[9] This means, however, that the tribunal may well decide that the parties' rights and obligations in their transaction are actually governed by a law different than the one either or indeed both of the parties believed governed their relationship. As a result, even parties that have been attempting to act in accordance with their contractual obligations may find that they have breached their contract simply because they did not realise which jurisdiction's law would be applied by the tribunal.

4.2 Contents of choice of law agreements

It might seem that a choice of law clause is a relatively simple thing to draft. After all, it just requires saying "This contract is governed by the law of . . .". In the context of international commercial transactions, however, choice of law clauses can become quite complex. This partially reflects the often-complex nature of international commercial transactions themselves. However, it also often results from a fundamental disagreement between the parties over the substantive law that should govern their relationship, resulting in a compromise solution that is designed to favour neither party. While this is not a problem unique to arbitration, the regularity with which disputes brought to international commercial arbitration require interpretation of a choice of law clause means that it is an issue that must be understood by anyone engaged in international commercial arbitration. For that reason, some of the most common examples of complex choice of law agreements will be analysed in this section.

Agreements selecting more than one national law

The most straightforward form of "complex" choice of law clause simply adopts more than one law as the governing law of the parties' relationship. By way of example, a choice of law clause could read as follows: "This contract shall be governed by the laws of Venezuela and of Honduras". A clause of this nature is likely to have resulted from a compromise between the two parties, one familiar with and wanting to conform to the law of Venezuela, and the other familiar with and wanting to conform to the law of Honduras. Neither was willing to agree to apply the law preferred by the other party, and there was no agreement on an acceptable third law, so the parties took the apparently reasonable course of effectively saying "Well, neither of us has any intention of breaking the law of either Venezuela or Honduras, so let's just agree to conform to both laws." On its face, not an unreasonable thing to do.

Most legal systems and arbitral tribunals will treat a clause of this type as valid, even though it selects more than one applicable law. There is, though, a clear problem that can, and often does, arise: what if the two laws contradict one another? That is, there is no particular problem if the laws merely require different things: Venezuelan law specifies that the parties must do X; Honduran law specifies that the parties must do Y; so the parties just do both X and Y.

But consider this situation: Venezuelan law specifies that the parties must do X *and may not do Y*; Honduran law specifies that the parties must do Y *and may not do X*. In such a situation there is literally no way that the parties can perform their transaction while not violating one of the applicable laws.

The problem faced by an arbitral tribunal in this situation is clear: the parties did not enter into their contract with the intention that it would be impossible to perform legally; and yet that is the unavoidable consequence of respecting the clear language of the contract's choice of law clause. The tribunal may "creatively" interpret the choice of law clause to avoid the conflict, but in doing so it will unavoidably benefit one party over the other – and without having a clear textual justification for doing so.

Understanding arbitration through case-law

Choice of law clause referring to principles common to two legal systems

Case details: *Channel Tunnel Group Ltd v Balfour Beatty Construction Ltd and others* [1992] 1 Q.B. 656; [1993] 2 WLR 262

Authorities deciding the case: English Court of Appeal; House of Lords

Facts of the case: The case arose out of a construction contract regarding the Channel Tunnel, which connects France and the United Kingdom. The contract contained an ICC arbitration clause.

Unable to agree on any single national law, the parties inserted in their contract a choice of law clause which read as follows: "The construction, validity and performance of the contract shall in all respects be governed by and interpreted in accordance

> with the principles common to both English law and French law, and in the absence of such common principles by such general principles of international trade law as have been applied by national and international tribunals. Subject in all cases, with respect to the works to be respectively performed in the French and in the English part of the site, to the respective French or English public policy (*ordre public*) provisions".
>
> The clause created several practical problems. First of all, it required a complex comparative law exercise: the tribunal had to analyse the contents of both English and French law, in order to determine whether any principles common to both legal systems existed in a specific case. Secondly, in cases in which English and French law diverged to such an extent that it was not possible to identify any common principles, the clause required the application of general principles of international trade law. However, "general principles" are by their nature vague, and so the reference to international trade law was unlikely to help the tribunal identify the substantive rules according to which the dispute was to be decided. Thirdly, the application of substantive law was further complicated by the circumstance that the clause required the application of either French or English public policy provisions, depending on which part of the site the dispute related to.
>
> **Decision:** The validity of the choice of law clause was undisputed in the case at hand: while not easy to apply, the contractual provision was surely valid. The dispute dealt with different matters, which did not directly involve the validity of the clause. Nonetheless, one of the Court of Appeal judges noted that entering into such a complex choice of law agreement was likely to generate long and expensive disputes, given the uncertainties unavoidably arising out of the cumulative reference to more than one legal system.

Split clauses or depeçage

Unlike clauses selecting two laws to govern the parties' entire relationship, split clauses select different laws to govern different parts of the parties' relationship. By way of example, Arielle and Milly may enter into a contract giving rise to two distinct obligations: Arielle's obligation to deliver certain goods and Milly's obligation to pay an amount of money. The contract may contain a split clause, providing that rights and obligations relating to the delivery of goods will be governed by the laws of Mauritania, while rights and obligations relating to payment will be governed by the laws of Australia.

Split clauses are generally held to be valid in most legal systems, and will usually be upheld by arbitral tribunals. Moreover, they do not create the same problem of legal uncertainty as is created by selecting two laws to govern the parties' entire relationship: even if the two selected laws conflict in certain ways, the tribunal has been given a method for determining which law to apply in which context.

Nonetheless, this does not mean that split clauses are entirely unproblematic. In particular, there may be issues that do not obviously fall into one or the other of the two categories identified in the choice of law clause, but are instead inextricably intertwined with both. In such cases, the tribunal will again be required to interpret the agreement in a way that allows identification of an applicable law, despite not having clear textual justification for its choice. However, while split clauses may not completely avoid problems of legal uncertainty, they are considerably more functional than choice of law clauses selecting two laws to govern the parties' entire relationship.

Floating choice of law clauses

In a floating choice of law clause the parties do not specifically identify the law applicable to their relationship, but instead identify a mechanism for selecting it. A classic example of such a clause is one in which the parties provide that in the event of an arbitration being commenced by either party, the substantive law to be applied to the parties' agreement will be the national law of the respondent, i.e. the party against whom the claim is being brought. In such a clause, the choice of law is not fixed: the term "floating" refers to the fact that the applicable substantive law changes depending on which of the parties commences the arbitral proceedings.

The purpose of a floating choice of law clause is generally to achieve a goal other than providing the parties with certainty regarding the law to be applied to their relationship – in the example given, the goal is to encourage parties to resolve disputes amicably, rather than through arbitration, as whichever party commences arbitration will not have its preferred substantive law applied to the dispute. The cost in legal certainty is high, as until an arbitration is commenced the parties have no way of knowing whether they have been fully conforming with the applicable law or not. However, it is precisely this cost which makes use of a floating clause appealing to parties who wish to avoid the total breakdown in a relationship that often results from arbitration or litigation.

4.3 Interpretation of choice of law clauses

A choice of law clause represents an agreement between the parties, just as does every other element of a contract. As a result, even though the purpose of the choice of law clause is to guide a tribunal in its interpretation of the contract, it too must be interpreted. Problems might arise, for example, where the parties have not clearly identified the law they have agreed to apply, or have even done so inaccurately, such as by referring to "the laws of the United Kingdom" – even though the United Kingdom actually includes three jurisdictions, so that this reference could mean English Law,[10] Scots Law, or Northern Ireland Law.

One particular interpretative issue is worth highlighting here, as it results not from poor drafting by the parties, but from a complexity inherent to all legal systems of which few non-lawyers are aware. In addition to provisions of substantive law, every contemporary legal system includes rules relating to what is termed "private international law" or "conflict of laws". These provisions are not themselves intended to establish any substantive legal rights or obligations, but rather to identify the rules that courts and other tribunals operating within a given legal system must use to determine the substantive law applicable to a dispute. For example, under Article 4(1)(a) of the Rome I Regulation,[11] in the absence of an agreement by the parties on the applicable law, a contract for the sale of goods will be governed by the law of the State in which the seller has his habitual residence.

Rules of this nature are clearly necessary for any legal system, as without standardised rules for selecting the applicable substantive law, the law applied to a dispute will vary depending on the court before which the parties appear, and legal certainty will be undermined. Nonetheless, while conflict of laws rules are necessary, they create a difficulty that can end up frustrating the attempt of parties to select a particular substantive law to be applied to their dispute, even when they have accurately identified that law and drafted their choice of law clause clearly.

By way of example, a choice of law clause that States "This contract is to be governed by the law of Hong Kong" appears simple and clear. The parties wish their contract to be interpreted in accordance with Hong Kong law. Few non-lawyers would see any lack of clarity in this clause.

The problem that exists is that, as just noted, all contemporary legal systems include conflict of laws rules that are to be used to determine the applicable substantive law. In the context of the preceding example, this raises the question: "When the parties chose Hong Kong law, did they just mean substantive Hong Kong law, or did they mean Hong Kong law including Hong Kong conflict of laws rules?"

This is an important question because if Hong Kong conflict of laws rules would identify Seychelles law as applicable to the dispute, then a court applying "Hong Kong law including Hong Kong conflict of law rules" would actually apply Seychelles law to the parties' dispute – even though the parties only ever expressly referred to Hong Kong law. The obvious problem this creates is that the parties incorporated a choice of law clause into their contract precisely to reduce legal uncertainty and clarify the substantive law that should be applied to determine their respective rights and obligations – and yet despite agreeing on an applicable law and drafting their choice of law clause carefully, they nonetheless have ended up with a completely unexpected law being applied to their dispute.

Sophisticated parties who are experienced in international commercial transactions are able to address this issue by expressly excluding conflict of laws rules from their choice of law clause, e.g. "This contract is to be governed by Hong Kong law, excluding its conflict of laws rules". However, it remains a risk for less experienced parties.

Nonetheless, this point being made, it must be emphasised that it is a risk that is now less significant than it once was, as the conflict of laws rules of some national legal systems now expressly exclude consideration of the conflict of laws rules of other States.[12] Indeed, the UNCITRAL Model Law on International Commercial Arbitration adopts a similar approach, providing at Article 28(1) that unless the parties have expressly agreed otherwise, a choice of law agreement should be construed as directly referring to the substantive rules of the chosen national legal system and not to its conflict of law rules. Nonetheless, this sort of legal rule is by no means universal, and parties who have not expressly excluded the application of conflict of laws rules in their choice of law clause run a risk of having a law applied to their relationship that neither party expected.

4.4 A-national substantive rules

While the discussion up to this point has focused on the application of national laws, parties can also provide for the application of substantive rules that do not form part of any national or sub-national legal order. Although courts in some States will refuse to apply such a choice in litigation, it is an accepted option in the context of international commercial arbitration and such a choice by the parties will usually be respected by an arbitral tribunal. Indeed, many national arbitration laws leave the parties free to make such a choice if that is what they wish to do.[13] Such systems of a-national rules are often referred to as "transnational law" or "stateless law", although the use of the term "law" in this context is controversial.[14]

By far the most famous example of system of a-national substantive rules is what is referred to as *lex mercatoria*. Literally translated as "law merchant", *lex mercatoria* refers to a set of rules allegedly followed as a matter of custom by parties involved in international business transactions. There is, however, significant disagreement amongst commentators as to which rules are and are not included within *lex mercatoria*, and even as to whether such a thing exists at all.

However, perhaps the most well-developed approach to *lex mercatoria* argues that it is best understood as fundamentally different in nature from State law: rather than being a list of rules regulating commercial relations, *lex mercatoria* is instead best understood as a method of decision-making.[15] Specifically, when applying *lex mercatoria* an arbitral tribunal should examine various national laws to determine the possible solutions to the dispute, and thereby distil a "transnational" rule, identified as being the solution which best suits the needs of the international business community.

Possibly reflecting concerns about the ability of arbitrators to make such a determination accurately and predictably, the available empirical evidence indicates that parties to international commercial transactions very rarely expressly select *lex mercatoria* as the substantive law applicable to their relationship.[16] Nonetheless, this being acknowledged, it has also been argued that even when arbitral tribunals apply State law they will standardly do so in a different way than would a domestic court, taking into consideration the needs of international business, even when those needs are not referred to in the applicable law.[17]

In other words, while the application of *lex mercatoria* as a governing law may be very rare even in international commercial arbitration, the primary goal of *lex mercatoria*, of ensuring that international commercial disputes are resolved with a sensitivity to the realities of international business, has been strongly embraced by many international commercial arbitrators, resulting in parties receiving a different interpretation of applicable national laws than they would have received had they taken their dispute to court – an interpretation intended to reflect "commercial reasonableness", rather than strict application of the applicable law.

4.5 Ex aequo et bono *and* amiable compositeur

While overwhelmingly parties in international commercial arbitration prefer to have their dispute decided in accordance with an agreed or otherwise applicable law, it is nonetheless possible for parties to agree instead that the arbitral tribunal should resolve their dispute by applying principles of equity and fairness. This is referred to as authorising the tribunal to decide *ex aequo et bono* or as an *amiable compositeur*.

It may initially be surprising that such an approach is acceptable, given the fundamentally "legal" nature of arbitration. Few people would, for example, expect to turn up at court and be told that rather than applying the law, the judge will instead merely decide based on what he personally feels is right and wrong. Such an approach just seems inconsistent with the very nature of legal dispute resolution.

However, *ex aequo et bono* decision-making has a long tradition in arbitration, and is easily reconciled with arbitration's legal nature by emphasising that an arbitrator is only permitted to act as an *amiable compositeur* with the agreement of the parties. That is, a decision *ex aequo et bono* retains its "legal" status because it is merely manifesting the contractual agreement of the parties. An award that has been decided *ex aequo et bono* without the approval of the parties can be annulled or have recognition and enforcement refused. Similarly, while to some degree allowing an arbitrator to decide *ex aequo et bono* enables her to lay aside rules of law, the arbitrator must still take into account any applicable public policy or mandatory rules of law, as failure to do so may result in the award being annulled or denied recognition and enforcement.

Most arbitration laws allow parties to provide for an arbitrator to decide their dispute *ex aequo et bono*.[18] However, this option is rarely exercised in practice, as parties are often uncomfortable with the unpredictability such an approach brings.

4.6 Public policy and mandatory rules

While arbitration laws standardly allow the parties to agree on the substantive law to be applied to their dispute, public policy and mandatory rules can nonetheless impose constraints on this choice: such rules imposed by the seat of the arbitration should be applied by the tribunal even if they are not part of the substantive law the parties have chosen to be applied to their dispute.

By way of illustration, Aariz and Nadine have agreed to arbitrate their dispute in Equatoriana. The arbitration law of Equatoriana allows the parties in an arbitration to select the substantive law to be applied by the tribunal. However, Equatoriana also has a public policy preventing certain types of damages to be awarded in the type of dispute Aariz and Nadine are taking to arbitration. By contrast, the substantive law agreed upon by Aariz and Nadine has no such restrictions. In such a case, the *lex arbitri* precludes the arbitral tribunal awarding those damages not permitted by the public policy of Equatoriana, even though they are permitted by the substantive law agreed upon by the parties. If the tribunal awards the precluded types of damages, that award may be annulled by the courts of Equatoriana.

While the concepts of public policy and mandatory rules are similar, they are not the same. "Public policy" refers to basic, fundamental principles of a jurisdiction, which cannot be ignored even in the context of a private dispute resolution procedure such as arbitration. If a tribunal does ignore a jurisdiction's public policy, it cannot expect the courts of that jurisdiction to support the arbitration or to enforce any resulting award.

Although it is now almost uniformly agreed that public policy restrictions should be applied in the context of international commercial arbitration only in exceptional cases, not all jurisdictions adopt the same understanding of what those cases are. Many States now adopt a very restrictive interpretation of public policy in the context of international commercial arbitration, applying the concept only to certain basic guarantees of due process recognised internationally as required for a fair dispute resolution procedure. As a result, they apply a more restrictive concept of public policy than they would apply to precisely the same dispute brought in domestic litigation. Such an approach is seen as consistent with the needs of international commercial transactions, as one or more of the parties may have no prior knowledge of the culture and values of the jurisdiction whose public policy is now being applied. This approach to public policy does not constitute a significant obstacle to party autonomy in the determination of the applicable substantive law.

The situation is more complex, however, in jurisdictions in which public policy is seen to encompass not only important procedural guarantees, but also substantive values, such as core constitutional standards. In such cases, a conflict may exist between the public policy of the seat of arbitration and the substantive law chosen by the parties to be applied to their dispute. Conflicts of this nature are now rare, but a tribunal must be aware of them if challenges to the award are to be avoided.

While "public policy" refers to a jurisdiction's fundamental values, "mandatory rules" refers to specific legal provisions that must be applied even if both parties in an arbitration agree that they should not be applied. By way of example, rules of employment law are often mandatory, as a means of ensuring that employees are not forced to give away valuable protections in order to secure employment. Where a mandatory rule applies in an arbitration the tribunal must apply it, or else the award may be annulled by the courts of the seat.

5. If the parties have not chosen the substantive law to be applied to their dispute, the arbitral tribunal must identify the applicable law

5.1 Implicit choice of law through adoption of arbitration rules

Many arbitration rules include a conflict of laws provision. As a result, even if parties to an arbitration have not themselves agreed on an applicable substantive law, because they have agreed to arbitrate in accordance with particular arbitration rules they have thereby agreed on the method by which the tribunal is to select the applicable substantive law.

The arbitration rules of many leading arbitral institutions, however, merely specify that the tribunal itself may select the applicable substantive law. By way of example, according to Article 21(1) of the 2017 ICC Rules of Arbitration, in the absence of a choice of law agreement the arbitral tribunal "shall apply the rules of law which it determines to be appropriate".[19]

Of course, as already discussed, national laws also have conflict of laws provisions, intended to be applied by tribunals when the parties have not entered into a valid choice of law agreement. The question this raises is whether the conflict of laws provision in a set of arbitration rules agreed upon by the parties will prevail over the conflict of laws rules of the seat of the arbitration. In principle, the answer would seem to be yes, as while the parties have not agreed on a specific substantive law, they have agreed on a method for that substantive law to be chosen.

Nonetheless, this solution is not uniformly accepted, and some tribunals have held that unless the parties have agreed on a specific substantive law to be applied to their dispute, the conflict of laws rules of the seat of the arbitration must be used to identify the applicable substantive law. In other words, under this approach, the State's conflict of laws rules cannot be trumped by a provision in arbitration rules agreed upon by the parties.[20]

5.2 Standard approaches to determination of the applicable substantive law in the absence of a choice of law agreement

In the absence of a choice of law agreement, it is up to the arbitral tribunal to determine the applicable substantive law. Nonetheless, the tribunal is rarely completely unrestrained in this respect, and many arbitration laws set forth rules in accordance with which the applicable substantive law is to be identified. Indeed, even the Model Law, which generally maximises the autonomy of tribunals so long as they remain within any limits on their powers set by the parties, specifies in Article 28(2) that "[f]ailing any designation by the parties, the arbitral tribunal shall apply the law determined by the conflict of laws rules which it considers applicable", thereby allowing the tribunal the freedom to determine which conflict of laws rules to apply, but requiring that the tribunal use formal rules, instead of merely selecting a law based on personal preference.

Broadly speaking there are four primary approaches that national arbitration laws have taken to the identification of the applicable substantive law in the absence of a choice of law agreement. These four options will be addressed below, although it must be emphasised that these four options are not exhaustive of the possible approaches tribunals may adopt.

Application of the conflict of law rules of the seat

Traditionally, many national arbitration laws reflected a view that arbitral tribunals were fundamentally merely private courts. As a result, the law would require that when determining the applicable substantive law, arbitration tribunals seated in a State must use the same conflict of law rules as were used by that State's courts. This approach was, for example, adopted in as prominent an arbitration jurisdiction as England prior to the Arbitration Act 1996.

This approach has been subjected to significant criticism on the ground that it fails to recognise an appropriate distinction between international commercial arbitration and domestic litigation, the former indeed often being chosen by the parties specifically to avoid the formalities of the latter.[21] As a result, this approach is now far less common.

Specific conflict of laws rules for international arbitration

Acknowledging the fundamental differences between court litigation and international arbitration, some jurisdictions set forth specific conflict of laws rules for the latter. However, while traditional conflict of laws rules adopted for litigation will usually point rigidly towards a particular result, these arbitration-tailored rules are often characterized by the degree of flexibility they afford the tribunal.

An example in this respect is Article 187(1) of the Swiss Private International Law, according to which, in the absence of a choice of law agreement, the tribunal must apply the law with which the dispute has the closest connection. While this rule does specify the approach the tribunal must take in determining the applicable substantive law, the vagueness of the rule it adopts nonetheless grants the tribunal a significant degree of freedom, as the tribunal is not even told the criteria by which it must determine how closely a law is connected to the dispute. As a result, this approach constrains the tribunal in the sense that the tribunal may not simply choose a law based on personal preference, but nonetheless ensures that the tribunal is able to take into account any consideration it believes appropriate when making its determination.

Autonomous selection of a conflict of laws rule

Other national laws adopt yet another solution, requiring that the arbitral tribunal adopt a conflict of laws rule, but allowing the tribunal the freedom to select the conflicts of laws rule that it believes to be appropriate. As already noted, this approach is incorporated into the UNCITRAL Model Law, and so is standard for Model Law jurisdictions. It is, however, also found in non-Model Law jurisdictions, including in the English Arbitration Act 1996.[22]

On its face, such an approach might not seem to impose any serious restriction on an arbitral tribunal, as a tribunal could simply examine a range of conflict of laws rules and then just select one that identifies precisely the law the tribunal always wanted to apply. However, while any rule is open to abuse, by emphasising to the tribunal that it must adopt a conflict of laws rule, rather than merely choosing its preferred substantive law, this approach does impose discipline on any tribunal performing its function in good faith. Such a tribunal will, therefore, not merely select a rule based on the result the rule generates, but will instead take all relevant factors into account to enable it to select the most fitting conflict of laws rule for the case it is addressing. This approach, then, facilitates an effective tribunal in its attempts to tailor the arbitral process to the dispute and to the parties, while nonetheless emphasising the need for arbitration to remain a rule-bound dispute resolution procedure.

Autonomous selection of the substantive law

Finally, some national arbitration laws empower the arbitral tribunal to select and apply the substantive law it considers appropriate. This approach is adopted, for example, by the French Code of Civil Procedure with respect to international arbitration.[23]

The difference between this approach and the previous one (autonomous selection of a conflict of laws rule) is that the tribunal need not adopt any formal rule for selecting the applicable substantive law, but may simply select the law it believes to be appropriate. This approach thus maximises the discretion of the tribunal, which is usually not even required to justify its choice, but merely to state what that choice is. As with the previous approach, therefore, it relies significantly upon the good faith and good judgement of tribunals. It is, however, more problematic than the previous approach, in that it imposes no discipline upon the tribunal at all, creating a situation in which parties have less ability to predict the substantive law that will be applied to their dispute.

6. The law governing the agreement to arbitrate may differ from the law governing the contract in which the agreement to arbitrate is contained

Perhaps the most unique aspect of applicable law in the context of arbitration results from what is known as the "separability" of an arbitration clause from the contract in which it is contained. This doctrine will be discussed in more detail in Chapter 3, but in essence it provides that any contract containing an arbitration clause is in fact two separate contracts: one relating to the substantive matters addressed in the contract, and then a second one consisting solely of the arbitration clause itself.

The fundamental goal of "separability" is to ensure that the parties' agreement to arbitrate survives no matter what happens to the contract in which it is contained. However, it also has an important consequence in terms of the applicable law: because the arbitration contract is a separate contract from the contract in which it is contained, it may be governed by a different law than the one governing the contract in which it is contained.

An example will make this clearer. Miyah and Chris are parties to an international commercial contract, and have included an arbitration agreement within their contract, agreeing to arbitrate any disputes in Taiwan. In addition, they have agreed that they want their transaction to be governed by the law of Belize, and so have included in their contract a choice of law clause clearly stating that all matters addressed in the contract are to be resolved in accordance with the law of Belize. A dispute indeed arises, and Miyah argues that the dispute is not covered by the arbitration agreement.

What law will an arbitrator or judge apply to determine if the dispute is covered by the arbitration agreement? The obvious answer might seem to be the law of Belize, given the very clear choice of law clause. The consequence of "separability", however, is that the parties have actually entered into two separate contracts: (i) the substantive contract and (ii) the arbitration agreement. The problem this creates is that although the choice of law clause agreed by the parties states that all matters addressed in the contract should be resolved in accordance with the law of Belize, that choice of law clause is only included in contract (i) – it is not included in contract (ii), and so does not directly apply to interpretation of the arbitration clause.

However, although "separability" entails that a choice of law clause in a contract does not directly determine what law will be applied to an arbitration clause in that contract, this does not mean that parties are unable to select the law to be applied to their arbitration agreement. They could, for example, specifically state in their choice of law clause that the law chosen is intended to apply to the arbitration clause as well as to the remainder of the contract in which it is contained. Alternatively, they could insert a second choice of law clause within the arbitration agreement itself, either selecting a different law to be applied to their arbitration agreement than is applied to the contract in which the agreement is contained, or reaffirming the selection of the same law.

The impact of "separability" on the applicable law, then, has both positive and negative aspects. The positive aspect is that it enhances the power of the parties to design their own arbitral process – they can, for example, select the substantive law of State X because it is desirable for their substantive transaction even though State X has a very poor arbitration law; in turn, they can then select the law of State Y to be applied to their arbitration agreement, avoiding State X's poor arbitration law, while retaining the benefits of its desirable substantive law.

The negative aspect is that no-one who is not experienced in international arbitration has ever heard of "separability", or would be likely to expect that a single clause in their contract will in fact be treated by arbitral tribunals and courts as an entirely separate contract. As a result, they may find that their arbitration agreement is being interpreted in accordance with the law of Yemen, even though their contract contains a clear choice of law clause applying the law of Israel to every element of that contract. "Separability", that is, can frustrate the legitimate expectations of even sophisticated parties if they are not already familiar with international commercial arbitration.

How, then, will an arbitral tribunal, or a court in one of the many jurisdictions that adopts "separability", determine what law is applicable to an arbitration agreement? There is no clear answer to this question, but as with many things in international commercial arbitration, the best guide is the principle of party autonomy.

For example, the freedom of the parties to an arbitration agreement to agree on the law to be applied to that agreement is enshrined in Article V(1)(a) of the 1958 New York Convention: an arbitral award may be denied recognition and enforcement if the arbitration agreement on which it is based is not valid "under the law to which the parties have subjected it". That is, the parties to an arbitration agreement have the power to select the law to be applied to that agreement, either directly through the adoption of a choice of law clause specifically applicable to the arbitration agreement, or indirectly through some other choice they have made.

Consistent with this emphasis on party autonomy, then, the proper goal of any tribunal or court is to determine and apply the intention of the parties. It is no more precise than that. Some tribunals favour application of the substantive law of the contract, on the rationale that at least this was a law expressly chosen by the parties, and in recognition of the fact that many parties will not have heard of "separability", and so will likely have expected their choice of substantive law to apply to their arbitration agreement. Alternatively, other tribunals favour application of the law of the seat of the arbitration, on the rationale that this is the law that the parties have expressly agreed should govern their arbitration, even if they have selected a different law to apply to their substantive transaction. A smaller number of tribunals will adopt other approaches, including simply applying whichever law amongst those plausibly applicable will lead to the arbitration agreement being upheld.[24] There is, quite simply, no uniformly accepted approach. The guiding principle, however, must always be to determine and apply the intention of the parties.

Notes

1 References are sometimes made to the "place of arbitration" or to the "arbitral forum". While "arbitral forum" is an acceptably clear term, "place of arbitration" should be avoided, as it is an ambiguous term that can easily be understood to be referring to the physical location in which arbitration hearings are held.

2 Article 20 of the UNCITRAL Model Law adopts this approach, providing that while the parties or the arbitrators are free to determine the seat, the tribunal remains free to meet at any other location for consultations, hearings or inspections. Furthermore, pursuant to Article 31(3) of the Model Law, the award is deemed to have been made at the seat of the arbitration, even if it was actually drafted or signed somewhere else. Similar rules are contained in numerous national arbitration statutes: see, for instance, in Article 1037 of the Code of Civil Procedure of the Netherlands, Article 31 of the Portuguese Voluntary Arbitration Law, article 35 of the Peruvian Arbitration Act, and Article 28 of the Japanese Arbitration Law.

3 The mechanism of selection of the seat of arbitration will be analysed in detail in Chapter 5.

The laws and rules applicable to arbitration 49

4   For instance, Article 12 of the Spanish Arbitration Act provides that the dispute will be decided by a sole arbitrator, if the parties have not provided otherwise; by contrast, Article 1227 of the Luxembourgish Code of Civil Procedure provides for three arbitrators.
5   For a discussion of the annulment of arbitral awards at the seat of arbitration see Chapter 7.
6   See e.g. Article 1184 of the Polish Code of Civil Procedure, or Section 34 of the English Arbitration Act.
7   See, for instance, Article 13(2) of the ICC Rules, according to which the ICC Secretary-General confirms as arbitrators persons nominated by the parties, or pursuant to the parties' agreement. If the ICC is not involved as an institution, it is of course impossible for the Secretary-General to perform this function, unless special arrangements are made.
8   See e.g. Article 19 of the UNCITRAL Model Law, or Section 34 of the English Arbitration Act, granting the parties wide discretion in the determination of the rules of procedure.
9   See the discussion of Rule 5.
10 The status of Welsh law as independent from English law is a somewhat complex question that goes beyond the purposes of the present book. As a result, while this book will only refer to English law, as this is the standard term used, it is nonetheless worth noting that some matters will be covered by different laws in Wales than in England – although these matters are unlikely to be central to an international commercial dispute.
11 Regulation {EC} No 593/2008 of the European Parliament and of the Council of 17 June 2008 on the law applicable to contractual obligations.
12 US Restatement {Second} of Conflict of Laws § 8; Rome I Regulation {n 5}, Article 20. While the Rome I Regulation is not applicable to arbitration, it does constitute an important indicator of the tendency to avoid this problem in order to enhance predictability and legal certainty.
13 By way of example, Article 28(1) of the UNCITRAL Model Law refers to "rules of law" chosen by the parties, thus implicitly encompassing not only national legal systems, but also other normative systems. A similar wording is adopted for instance by Article 1511 of the French Code of Civil Procedure and Section 27a of the Swedish Arbitration Act.
14 For a critique of this use of the term "law" see Thomas Schultz, *Transnational Legality: Stateless Law and International Arbitration* (OUP 2014).
15 Emmanuel Gaillard, "Transnational Law: A Legal System or a Method of Decision Making?" (2001) 17(1) *Arbitration International* 59.
16 Christopher R Drahozal, "Contracting Out of National Law: An Empirical Look at the New Law Merchant" (2005) 80(2) *Notre Dame Law Review* 523.
17 Joshua D H Karton, *The Culture of International Arbitration and The Evolution of Contract Law* (OUP 2013). The UNCITRAL Model Law adopts a similar approach by providing, at Article 28(4), that the tribunal must in all cases "take into account the usages of the trade applicable to the transaction". Article 1511 of the French Code of Civil Procedure contains an analogous specification.
18 See e.g. Article 1194 of the Polish Code of Civil Procedure and Article 327–18 of the Moroccan Code of Civil Procedure. See also the analogous provisions contained in most arbitration rules, e.g. Article 42(3) of the NAI Rules; Article 3(1) of the Milan Chamber of Arbitration Rules; Article 36(2) of the Hong Kong International Arbitration Centre (HKIAC) Rules.
19 Similar rules are contained in most sets of arbitration rules: see e.g. Article 3(3) of the Milan Chamber of Arbitration Rules, Article 42(2) of the Netherlands Arbitration Institute Rules, or Article 27(1) of the Stockholm Chamber of Commerce Rules.
20 For a recent example of an ICC award in which the arbitrator chose to apply the conflict of laws rules of the seat of arbitration (Sweden), rather than using a discretional power provided by the ICC rules to determine the applicable law, see *Agent (US) v Principal (Russian Federation)*, Final award, ICC Case No. 13756, 2008 in Albert Jan van den Berg (ed.), *Yearbook Commercial Arbitration*, XXXIX (ICCA 2014) 118.

21 Berthold Goldman, "Les conflits de lois dans l'arbitrage international de droit privé" (1963) 109(2) *Recueil des cours* 347.
22 See Section 46(3) of the English Arbitration Act 1996.
23 See Article 1511 of the French Code of Civil Procedure. See also Section 27a of the Swedish Arbitration Act, simply stating that, if the parties have not chosen the applicable law, "the arbitrators shall determine the applicable law", without referring to any criterion or standard guiding such determination.
24 See Article 178(2) of the Swiss Federal Statute on Private International Law.

3 The agreement to arbitrate

Rules

1. Arbitration is consensual, but requires that agreements to arbitrate be enforceable

Arbitration is based on the consent of the parties, but by the time a dispute has arisen, one party will often no longer wish to arbitrate. As a result, arbitration can only be effective as a dispute resolution mechanism if parties can be compelled to arbitrate once they have agreed to do so.

2. Not all disputes can be referred to arbitration: there are limits to "arbitrability"

Even those jurisdictions most supportive of arbitration place limits on what types of disputes can and cannot be arbitrated. Legal systems around the world have progressively enlarged the boundaries of arbitrability, so that many types of disputes once argued to be inappropriate for arbitration, can now be arbitrated.

3. Arbitration agreements can be concluded before a dispute arises (pre-dispute arbitration agreements) or after one has arisen (post-dispute arbitration agreements)

Many legal systems once placed strict limitations on agreements to arbitrate future disputes, on the ground that the right to access court is so fundamental that a party cannot give it up without knowing the specific dispute it is agreeing to arbitrate. However, it is now accepted in jurisdictions around the world that parties can legitimately agree to arbitrate all future disputes relating to a particular contract, transaction, or relationship, without knowing the specific dispute that will be arbitrated.

4. An arbitration agreement is a separate contract from a contract in which it is contained: the doctrine of separability

Even if an agreement to arbitrate is only a clause in a larger contract, the doctrine of separability requires that it be treated as a separate contract from the contract in which it is contained.

This ensures that an arbitration agreement generally remains binding on the parties to a contract even if the contract itself is no longer binding.

5. Both courts and arbitrators may rule on the existence and validity of an arbitration agreement: the doctrine of competence-competence

Different legal systems have different rules regarding when courts and arbitral tribunals may rule on the existence and validity of an arbitration agreement. However, it is now generally accepted that in most cases an arbitral tribunal should first be allowed to decide this question, rather than a court. This is the doctrine of "competence-competence".

6. Parties may agree the law to be applied to their arbitration agreement

Although parties are only bound by an arbitration agreement if it is valid, it is now accepted that parties can state in their arbitration agreement which law should be applied when determining its validity or scope, and that this choice should be respected. There is no uniformly accepted approach to be taken when the parties have not reached agreement, but the better approach is to apply the law of the seat of the arbitration.

7. The standards to be used in determining the existence and validity of an arbitration agreement will be decided by the applicable law, and can vary from one jurisdiction to another

An arbitration agreement will be interpreted in accordance with the law applicable to it, and the consequences of a finding that an arbitration agreement is invalid or otherwise not binding can be significant. However, jurisdictions around the world have adopted increasingly supportive approaches to the interpretation of arbitration agreements, and in many jurisdictions the intent of the parties to arbitrate will be respected even if the language of the arbitration agreement is formally inadequate.

8. Even if an arbitration agreement is valid, its scope may be unclear

The wording of an arbitration agreement may be sufficiently unclear that the parties disagree whether a particular dispute is covered by the agreement, even though they both acknowledge that there is an arbitration agreement between them. Many jurisdictions now adopt generous approaches to the interpretation of the scope of arbitration agreements. However, careful drafting of the language of an arbitration agreement is nonetheless essential, to ensure that it will be found to cover those disputes the parties wish it to cover.

9. An agreement to arbitrate can be viewed as both a procedural agreement and as a substantive contract

On its face, an agreement to arbitrate is merely a procedural agreement between the parties to resolve their disputes in a certain way, namely through arbitration. However, as the doctrine of separability entails that an arbitration agreement is a contract between the parties, it can also be viewed as giving rise to substantive rights and obligations. Legal systems vary in their views on this issue, and these differences can have important impacts on the consequences of the breach of arbitration agreements, and on the mechanisms available for their enforcement.

10. An arbitration agreement is technically only binding between the parties to the agreement, but non-parties can be bound under limited circumstances

Because arbitration is based on consent, non-parties to an arbitration agreement usually have no obligation to participate in an arbitration, as they have never consented to do so. There are, however, limited circumstances in which a non-party to an arbitration agreement can be held to be obligated to arbitrate with a party to the agreement, or to have the right to commence an arbitration against one of the parties to the agreement.

Analysis

1. Arbitration is consensual, but requires that agreements to arbitrate be enforceable

Without question the most important difference between international commercial arbitration and court litigation is captured in the phrase "arbitration requires consent". If someone brings a lawsuit against you in a competent State court, you don't have the option to just ignore it, or to turn up to the court and say "Sorry, I just don't feel like being sued, please dismiss it." If you fall within the jurisdictional limits of that court, then the court has the power to conduct proceedings involving you – whether or not you consent is simply irrelevant.

One of the defining features of international commercial arbitration, however, has always been that only parties who have agreed to arbitrate a specific dispute before a specific tribunal can be made to do so.[1] Arbitration, as the saying goes, "requires consent".

It is, however, important to understand what this means, and in particular to recognize that the "consensual" nature of international commercial arbitration should not be confused with the idea that international commercial arbitration is fundamentally detached from local legal systems. By way of comparison, if you get into a disagreement with a friend, you can both agree that a third friend should decide which of you is right – that is a truly consensual dispute resolution process. Neither disputing party was forced to agree to use it, either party can simply walk out of the process at any time, and either party can simply ignore the third friend's decision if they don't like it. Every aspect of the process requires the consent of both disputing parties at all times.

There is, however, no question that if international commercial arbitration relied upon this level of consent, it would rarely be used. There will be arbitrations which operate so harmoniously that no level of compulsion is required, but fundamentally international commercial arbitration has become a central mechanism for the resolution of cross-border disputes precisely because it is not completely consensual. In other words, "consent of the parties" forms the foundation of arbitration, but ultimately if compulsion is required, it is available: if a party has agreed to arbitrate a dispute but then attempts to commence court litigation on that same dispute, the court will usually refuse to hear the case; if a party has commenced arbitration but then stops participating, the arbitration can continue without that party, and the resulting award will still be enforceable; if a party is unhappy with an award and refuses to pay the other party what the award says it must pay, the other party can take the award to a court and the court will compel the first party to pay what the award says is owed.

In short, consent forms the foundation of international commercial arbitration, and considerations of "party consent" are the guiding factor in many aspects of how arbitrations function, but what makes international commercial arbitration effective and attractive to parties is actually not its foundation on consent, but rather the way that it combines consent with compulsion.

That distinctive combination of consent and compulsion is the core of this Chapter, which focuses on the nature and consequences of an agreement to arbitrate. Arbitrators, after all, are private individuals – unlike judges, they do not exert any sovereign power and hence they can only decide disputes if the parties have agreed to let them do so. The consequence of this is that understanding the contents and boundaries of the agreement to arbitrate is essential to understanding any arbitration: the arbitration agreement both reflects the consent of the parties to arbitrate, and also determines the situations in which national courts will and will not support the arbitration, including the situations in which they will and will not compel the parties to take actions necessary for the arbitration to succeed.

2. Not all disputes can be referred to arbitration: there are limits to arbitrability

2.1 The notion of arbitrability

While contemporary societies around the world increasingly respect the right of individuals to make decisions about their own lives, every society retains some limitations on the power of consent to legitimise behaviour. In some cases these limitations reflect concerns about an individual's ability to make proper decisions for herself (e.g. children or individuals with a mental disability) or to make a genuinely free decision (e.g. an employee threatened with losing her job if she rejects her supervisor's sexual advances), in other cases that one individual's choices can have serious impacts on other people (e.g. speed limits on roads), and in others that there are simply some personal decisions in which it is believed that society as a whole has a legitimate interest (e.g. limitations on assisted suicide).

It should be unsurprising, therefore, that the same limitations occur in the context of international commercial arbitration. Parties are free to agree to arbitrate their disputes, but sometimes governments will simply say "No, you can't arbitrate that one". In the context of international commercial arbitration these limitations are referred to as "arbitrability".

That limitations exist on the ability of parties to agree to arbitrate their disputes follows naturally from the combination of consent and compulsion that characterises international commercial arbitration. That is, "arbitrability" does not actually mean that there are certain types of dispute that parties cannot take to arbitration. Arbitrating a dispute that is regarded as "non-arbitrable" in the seat of the arbitration is not usually a criminal act for which the parties will be punished by the government. Rather, it simply means that the dispute in question is not the sort of dispute that the government believes should be taken to arbitration, rather than to court litigation, and so parties who "consent" to such an arbitration cannot expect the government to use its powers of "compulsion" to help them arbitrate. The parties can go through a complete arbitral process, including having the tribunal deliver an award, but the court will not prevent either party from ignoring the arbitration agreement and commencing court litigation; if there are problems with the arbitration, the courts will not assist it; and if an award is delivered, the courts will not enforce it.

Arbitrability, that is, respects the "consent" of the parties, as it does not prevent them arbitrating. But it withdraws the "compulsion" of the government – since the government believes that this is not the sort of dispute that should be resolved by a private dispute resolution process, it has no obligation to assist the parties in their arbitration, and will not do so.

Notably, while the most important legal text in international commercial arbitration, the New York Convention, is fundamentally designed to support arbitration, rather than regulate it, the Convention nonetheless itself endorses limitations on arbitrability, providing at Article II(1) that the obligation to recognise an agreement to arbitrate only extends to agreements "concerning a subject matter capable of settlement by arbitration". Similarly, under Article V(2)(a) of the Convention, recognition and enforcement of an arbitral award can be refused by the courts of a State if "the subject matter of the difference is not capable of settlement by arbitration" under that State's law. Limitations on arbitrability, then, are unquestionably a mainstream reality of international commercial arbitration, rather than characteristic only of States that are not "arbitration friendly".

This being said, while limitations on arbitrability may be found everywhere, there is no universally accepted standard regarding what can and cannot be arbitrated. Instead, this is left entirely for each jurisdiction to determine in accordance with its own values. Many jurisdictions adopt a very broad approach to arbitrability, allowing arbitration of any dispute that is legally allowed to be settled privately between the parties,[2] or of any dispute relating to substantive rights the parties are permitted to dispose of.[3] Such an approach avoids any negative view of arbitration, and accepts that if parties are not obligated to allow courts or other governmental bodies to resolve their dispute, then there is no reason why they cannot have their dispute resolved through arbitration. Some States, however, retain more significant limitations on arbitrability, precluding the arbitration of disputes in such areas as bankruptcy, securities, employment, and family law.

Fundamentally, the rationale behind restrictions on arbitrability is that the role of State courts in ensuring the proper delivery of justice cannot properly be performed in certain cases through private adjudication. In such cases, State courts retain a monopoly in dispute resolution.

However, that non-arbitrability is an exception, rather than the rule, is important to recognise. Parties wishing to arbitrate a dispute do not need to prove that their dispute falls on the list of those that can be arbitrated. Rather, the presumption falls in the other direction, even in less "arbitration friendly" jurisdictions: any dispute can be arbitrated, unless it can be shown to be one of a limited category of disputes in which arbitration is not possible.

2.2 The progressive enlargement of the boundaries of arbitrability

Not only are disputes presumptively arbitrable, but the boundaries of arbitrability have been progressively expanding in jurisdictions throughout the world. As a result, many types of disputes that historically were not permitted to be taken to arbitration, are now viewed as arbitrable.

Competition/antitrust disputes are a classic example in this respect. Such claims were often regarded as non-arbitrable because a fundamental goal of competition law is the protection of consumers or competitors, and neither of these groups will usually be directly represented in a private arbitration. As a result, it was argued that allowing competition disputes to be arbitrated would undermine the effectiveness of competition law, as there was no assurance that the arbitration would give effective voice to the interests of non-parties – precisely the interests competition law is intended to protect. Nonetheless, over the past four decades an increasing number of legal systems have come to regard competition disputes as arbitrable, including both the United States of America[4] and the European Union.[5]

Understanding arbitration through case-law

Arbitrability of competition law disputes: the US perspective

Case details: *Mitsubishi Motors Corp. v Soler Chrysler-Plymouth, Inc.*, 473 US 614 (1985)

Authority deciding the case: United States Supreme Court

Facts of the case: Soler, a Puerto Rican car dealership, concluded a contract with Chrysler and Mitsubishi. Under the contract, Soler was to sell on the Puerto Rican market the cars that Mitsubishi manufactured. The contract contained a clause providing for arbitration at the Japan Commercial Arbitration Association (JCAA).

After some years, a complex dispute arose between the parties. Initially Mitsubishi commenced court proceedings in Puerto Rico against Soler, arguing that the contract had been breached. Soler brought a counterclaim before the Puerto Rican court, alleging not only that Mitsubishi was acting in bad faith, but also that its behaviour was in violation of US antitrust law (the Sherman Act). More specifically, Soler argued that Mitsubishi was trying to divide markets, and to push the dealership out of Puerto Rico, in order to later replace it. At this point, Mitsubishi objected to the jurisdiction of the Puerto Rican court, arguing that the claims put forth by Soler should be referred to JCAA arbitration. Soler, however, contended that the antitrust claims were not arbitrable, as they involved matters of public interest and thus needed to be decided by US Courts, rather than by a private arbitral tribunal which is under no obligation to enforce the legislative policies of the State.

The case was litigated at length before US Courts and eventually both parties brought an appeal to the Supreme Court. Therefore, the Supreme Court had to decide whether the antitrust claims brought by Soler were arbitrable.

Decision: The Supreme Court decided that antitrust claims are arbitrable. It held, in particular, that arbitration is a particularly suitable mechanism for the resolution of international commercial disputes, such as the one between Mitsubishi and Soler, and that freely negotiated arbitration agreements must be protected and enforced. According to the majority, furthermore, while it is true that arbitral tribunals do not have the obligation to enforce the laws of any particular State, they are nonetheless bound to act in accordance with the parties' mandate. Therefore, if the parties submit to an arbitral tribunal a dispute based on US antitrust law, the arbitrators should resolve it in accordance with that law. The Court also emphasised that courts would retain a supervisory function through their role in the enforcement of arbitral awards (the "second look" doctrine).

Arbitrability of competition law disputes: the European perspective

Case details: Case C-126/97, *Eco Swiss China Time Ltd v Benetton International NV*, ECLI:EU:C:1999:269

Authority deciding the case: European Court of Justice

Facts of the case: In 1986 Benetton, Eco Swiss and Bulova concluded an eight-year licensing agreement. Under that agreement, Benetton granted Eco Swiss the right to manufacture watches bearing the words "Benetton by Bulova". The watches were then to be sold by Bulova in Italy and by Benetton in the other Member States of the European Community (later to become the European Union). The contract included an arbitration clause, providing for arbitration administered by the Netherlands Institute of Arbitrators.

Unhappy with the contract, Benetton gave notice of its termination in 1991, three years ahead of time. Eco Swiss and Bulova commenced arbitration proceedings and claimed compensation for the damages they suffered as a result of Benetton's premature termination. The arbitral tribunal issued a partial final award in 1993, holding that Benetton was liable, and then a final award in 1995, ordering Benetton to pay USD 23,750,000 to Eco Swiss and USD 2,800,800 to Bulova. Benetton commenced annulment proceedings against the final award before Dutch courts.

In the annulment proceedings, a new question arose: Benetton argued that the licensing agreement was void, as it constituted an unlawful market-sharing arrangement. More specifically, it was argued that the arrangement whereby Benetton would not sell the watches in Italy, while Bulova would not sell them in the other Member States, was incompatible with European competition law (Article 81 of the Treaty Establishing the European Community – TEC, currently corresponding to Article 101 of the Treaty on the Functioning of the European Union – TFEU). Importantly, this problem had not been discussed during the arbitration proceedings. Hence, the arbitral award had been rendered on the basis of the assumption that the contract was indeed valid.

The Dutch courts, then, referred a question to the European Court of Justice, asking it to determine, among other things, whether an award must be annulled if it is contrary to a provision of European competition law, such as Article 81 TEC/101 TFEU.

Decision: The Court of Justice held that, if under the applicable arbitration law awards must be annulled when they are against public policy, then they must also be annulled when they are contrary to Article 81 TEC/101 TFEU. The implicit assumption underlying this conclusion is that nothing in European law prevents the arbitrability of

58   The agreement to arbitrate

> competition law disputes, along similar lines as held by the US Supreme Court in *Mitsubishi v Soler*. In addition, by stating that the public policy clause should be applied when an award violates primary EU competition law, the Court of Justice indirectly granted public policy status to this body of law. As a result, if the arbitration is seated in an EU Member State, the arbitral tribunal should refrain from issuing an award incompatible with competition law, lest it be annulled on public policy grounds. That is, not only *can* arbitrators apply competition law – they *must* do so.
>
> **Read more:** Julian DM Lew, "Competition Laws: Limits to Arbitrators' Authority", in Loukas A Mistelis and Stavros L Brekoulakis (eds), *Arbitrability: International and Comparative Perspectives* (Kluwer 2009) 241

A further notable variation in the application of arbitrability occurs with respect to intellectual property rights. While in an increasing number of jurisdictions intellectual property disputes are now fully arbitrable, some jurisdictions retain a distinction between arbitration of intellectual property rights themselves, and arbitration of contractual or commercial rights arising from intellectual property rights. That is, questions of the entitlement to intellectual property rights, such as a dispute between two parties over ownership of a patent, are treated as non-arbitrable, as they will have significant impact on the rights of non-parties to the arbitration. On the other hand, contractual or commercial rights arising from intellectual property rights, such as a dispute over interpretation of a licensing agreement, are accepted as arbitrable, as the broader direct effects on non-parties to the arbitration do not exist.[6]

Overall there is no question that the consistent tendency throughout the world is for the boundaries of arbitrability to continue expanding. It is unlikely that there will ever be a time that all disputes are arbitrable in any jurisdiction, or that it would be desirable for that to happen. However, the continued success of international commercial arbitration to address previously non-arbitrable issues without giving rise to the problems that the non-arbitrability doctrine was intended to avoid ensures that it will continue to be trusted with an ever-broader range of issues. So long as this expansion is done after a careful judgement that arbitration can effectively protect the interests the law is designed to protect, rather than through a blind insistence that arbitration is a desirable way of resolving any dispute, the continued expansion of the boundaries of arbitrability can only be a good thing.

3. Arbitration agreements can be concluded before a dispute arises (pre-dispute arbitration agreements) or after one has arisen (post-dispute arbitration agreements)

3.1 Pre-dispute and post-dispute arbitration agreements

One of the most important developments behind the sharply increased use of international commercial arbitration over the course of the past century was the acceptance by governments that parties should be able to enter into arbitration agreements both before and after a dispute has arisen. Historically, many States had drawn a distinction in this respect, enforcing post-dispute arbitration agreements (or submission agreements, or *compromis*), but refusing to enforce pre-dispute arbitration agreements, on the rationale that enforcing an arbitration agreement prevents parties accessing court, but access to court is a fundamental right and so can only be given up as the result of an informed decision – yet an agreement to arbitrate all future disputes relating to a certain transaction is inherently vague and uncertain, as the parties cannot know in advance precisely what their dispute will be about. As a result, it was argued, pre-dispute arbitration agreements should be unenforceable, in order to avoid parties losing their right to access court for a dispute they would not knowingly have agreed to submit to arbitration.

This distinction has, however, now been solidly rejected by jurisdictions around the world, and there is no longer any question that parties will indeed be bound by a pre-dispute arbitration agreement.[7]

In the context of international commercial arbitration, pre-dispute arbitration agreements are unquestionably the norm, with only a minority of arbitrations arising from post-dispute arbitration agreements. This might appear to undermine the claims of those who argue that arbitration is attractive in the international commercial context – after all, if parties are much less likely to agree to arbitration when they know as a fact that there will be one (i.e. after a dispute has already arisen), that might indicate serious reservations about the desirability of arbitration. A better explanation, however, simply relates to the reality of party decision-making.

That is, prior to a dispute arising, and particularly at the time of agreeing a contract, parties are working together to attempt to construct a successful transaction. At this time the inherent attractions of arbitration will be appealing, and parties will concentrate on the control arbitration will give them over the dispute resolution process, its neutrality, and so on. On the other hand, once a dispute has arisen, the parties will often no longer be communicating with each other in a functional way, and most parties will be focused less on maintaining their relationship with the other party, or on having a fair dispute resolution process, than on triumphing in the dispute. As a result, not only is it unlikely that the parties will reach agreement on something as significant as the mechanism through which their dispute should be resolved, but it will often be the case that neither side is particularly looking for a neutral and fair process. Instead, each side will want to use the dispute resolution process that is most likely to award them victory – most likely their own home courts.

The fact that international commercial arbitrations are overwhelmingly based on pre-dispute arbitration agreements, then, does not undermine claims that it is a desirable and fair dispute resolution process. Indeed, if anything, it supports those claims: the parties most attracted to use arbitration are the ones concentrating on identifying a fair dispute resolution process; it is when fairness is no longer a priority for the parties that they no longer find arbitration attractive.

3.2 Drafting of pre-dispute arbitration agreements

Given this distinction between the attitude of parties at the time of entering into a pre-dispute arbitration agreement and after a dispute has arisen, the drafting of a pre-dispute arbitration agreement is enormously important. After all, the agreement must not only clearly signify the desire of the parties to arbitrate their disputes, but must clearly identify those disputes the parties wish to arbitrate and those they do not, as well as clarifying any important procedural aspects of the arbitration. It is certainly possible for parties to agree to alter or supplement a pre-dispute arbitration agreement after a dispute has arisen – it is their agreement, so the parties can amend it at any time – however the reality is that parties will be less likely to be able to reach agreement once a dispute has arisen. Consequently, if a pre-dispute arbitration agreement is poorly drafted, it can result in an unsuitable or inefficient arbitration process, or even in an agreement that is so dysfunctional that courts will refuse to enforce it.

The primary difficulty with drafting a pre-dispute arbitration agreement, of course, is that the parties have no way of knowing what their dispute will be about. The unavoidable consequence of this situation is that pre-dispute arbitration agreements are standardly very general and very vague, doing little more than expressing the agreement of the parties to arbitrate any disputes that might arise out of a particular transaction or broader relationship.

This is unquestionably problematic. Imagine a situation in which you have met someone and you agree to go on a date the following Tuesday. Tuesday arrives. What have you agreed to do? You have unquestionably agreed to go on a date. But at what time? Where do you meet? Are you going alone, or should you each bring a friend? Are you going to dinner, a movie, something else? Who is paying for what, and how much will you end up having to pay? All you have done, that is, is agree to go on a date – but there is a host of questions that must be answered for that date to occur, and you simply never answered them.

Luckily, you both want to go on the date, so you can probably work them out. But consider now the situation faced by parties with a standard pre-dispute arbitration agreement. It is quite likely that one of the parties doesn't actually want to arbitrate at all. If they do both still want to arbitrate, they may want to arbitrate in completely different ways. Yet all they have done is agree to arbitrate – they have not even considered the host of questions that must be answered for the arbitration to occur.

At this point it might seem that the solution to this problem is simple: include a lot of detail in your pre-dispute arbitration agreement. There is, though, an important problem with this solution. You have no real idea what your arbitration is going to be about. You don't know the amount of money that will be at stake, what aspect of the transaction it will concern, in which parts of the world witnesses and documents might be located, how good or bad the relationship between the parties will be, or even what your own financial situation will be like (full compensation can be less important than speedy partial compensation when a company is facing possible insolvency).

It is, therefore, unquestionably problematic that pre-dispute arbitration agreements are vague. But it could be even more problematic if they were too precise.

International commercial arbitration has, however, developed a generally effective solution to this problem: arbitrators. So long as a pre-dispute arbitration agreement successfully conveys the agreement of the parties to arbitrate the dispute that has arisen, and either directly or indirectly (e.g. by selecting an arbitral seat with an effective arbitration law) provides a mechanism for selecting an arbitral tribunal, then that tribunal is generally acknowledged to have the power to resolve any procedural questions on which the parties have not otherwise agreed. This is assuming, of course, that the parties have selected their tribunal well – many parties have come to regret not being more careful in their selection of arbitrators as their arbitration dragged on for years, costs spiralled, and procedural decisions seemed to reflect little real understanding of the dispute resolution process the parties actually required.

3.3 Types of instruments containing an arbitration agreement

The standard way in which parties will enter into a pre-dispute arbitration agreement is through incorporation of an arbitration clause into a contract, providing that any disputes arising out of or related to the contract will be arbitrated. However, it is important to recognise that pre-dispute arbitration agreements can come in many forms. Indeed, most national arbitration laws place very few restrictions on the contexts in which parties may enter into a pre-dispute arbitration agreement.

Most obviously, the parties may draft an entirely free-standing arbitration agreement, rather than merely incorporating an arbitration clause into another agreement. This arbitration agreement will then function in precisely the same way as would an arbitration clause, so long as it is clear to which other agreement it relates, or which aspects of the parties' relationship it covers.

Moreover, while arbitration clauses are most commonly found in commercial contracts, they are now widely accepted as enforceable even when found in other documents, such as deeds of trust[8] or even a company's articles of incorporation or bylaws.[9] Indeed, while the distinction between pre-dispute and post-dispute arbitration agreements was historically important, it has little impact today on the enforceability of arbitration agreements, and remaining restrictions on the enforceability of pre-dispute arbitration agreements, such as can still be found regarding testamentary wills,[10] reflect broader concerns about the arbitrability of the subject matter of the dispute covered by the arbitration agreement, rather than concerns specifically about the pre-dispute nature of the arbitration clause.

3.4 The binding nature of pre-dispute arbitration agreements

While party consent is often referred to as the foundation of arbitration, the need for consent is limited by the contractual nature of arbitration. That is, just as you are bound to fulfil the terms of a contract to purchase an item or undertake an action, even if you subsequently decide that you no longer think the contract was a good idea, so parties to an arbitration agreement are bound to arbitrate, even if one of them no longer wishes to do so. They may mutually agree to cancel their arbitration agreement, and then both parties are free to resolve their dispute in any appropriate forum. However, so long as either party wants the arbitration agreement to be enforced, both parties remain bound by it.

The simple consequence of this is that when parties have entered into an arbitration agreement, no further consent to arbitrate is required from the parties once a dispute covered by the arbitration agreement has arisen. Indeed, even if one of the parties has changed its mind and no longer wishes to arbitrate, it nonetheless remains bound to do so. If it attempts to commence court proceedings on a matter covered by the arbitration agreement, national arbitration laws and the New York Convention require courts to refuse to allow the litigation to proceed, and to refer the party back to arbitration. If a party refuses to participate in arbitral proceedings relating to a dispute covered by the arbitration agreement, those proceedings can nonetheless continue without that party's involvement, even to the extent of a final award being delivered, which courts will enforce.

In short, an arbitration agreement is the epitome of the classic phrase "Be careful what you wish for, because you just might get it". Arbitration agreements are not to be entered into lightly, because they are not gotten out of easily.

3.5 Drafting of post-dispute arbitration agreements

While the goal in drafting a pre-dispute arbitration agreement is usually to be as broad and inclusive as possible, since the parties do not know what disputes might subsequently arise, the goal in drafting a post-dispute arbitration agreement is usually the exact opposite. A dispute has already arisen between the parties, and they have agreed that this specific dispute is one that they wish to take to arbitration. Realistically this is relatively uncommon, as once a dispute has arisen at least one of the parties is likely to see an advantage in having the dispute heard in the courts of its home State, rather than through arbitration. However, where the dispute has arisen as part of an ongoing relationship, or if both parties see future transactions between them as both desirable and likely, arbitration can be seen as a way of resolving a dispute with a lower risk of serious relationship damage than is likely from court litigation.

For this reason, post-dispute arbitration agreements will typically describe the dispute to be resolved through arbitration in detail, rather than containing a generic formula such as "all disputes arising out or in connection with the contract". In addition, the agreement may name specific individuals to be appointed to the arbitral tribunal, rather than simply setting forth the mechanism whereby the arbitrators will be appointed. Furthermore, the parties will be able to include more specific provisions regarding the procedural and evidentiary rules to be used in the arbitration, rather than leaving such matters to be resolved by the arbitrators.

As a result, post-dispute arbitration agreements give the parties the maximum degree of control over the arbitral process, reducing the need to leave important decisions to be made by arbitrators or negotiated by counsel. As always, however, with that power comes risk: if the parties are not familiar with the technicalities of arbitration, they may design an arbitral process that is inefficient or even inconsistent with the applicable law. It is, therefore, important that even in this context the parties allow the arbitrators the freedom to control the arbitral process, as it is precisely for their expertise in arbitration that the arbitrators have been hired.

4. An arbitration agreement is a separate contract from a contract in which it is contained: the doctrine of separability

4.1 The notion of separability

"Separability" refers to the doctrine that an arbitration clause included in a contract actually constitutes a separate contract from the one in which it is contained – even though neither the clause itself nor any part of the main contract states this is the case. It is one of the areas of arbitration law that is unavoidably most surprising to those new to the field. After all, it seems intuitively obvious that when parties have signed a contract, that is precisely what they have done: they have signed **a** contract. Parties no more expect to be told that by entering into a single contract they have actually unknowingly entered into two contracts, than they expect to be told that by agreeing to ship bananas to France they have also unknowingly agreed to ship oranges to Ecuador. Parties expect their contracts to mean either what the words say ("objective" interpretation) or what the parties meant to say ("subjective" interpretation).

Instead, separability arises as a matter of law. It is interpreted into the parties' agreement even though the language of the main contract does not suggest it is part of that agreement, and even though the parties never considered including it in their agreement.

Nonetheless, it would be a mistake to regard separability as imposed by the legal system against the wishes of the parties. Rather, the development of the doctrine of separability is based on the rationale that such a doctrine is necessary in order to give effect to what the parties have explicitly agreed upon. The parties may not have incorporated separability into their agreement, but if anyone had said to them at the time of contracting "Should you add a clause agreeing to the separability of the arbitration clause?", the parties would admittedly both have initially replied "What? What on earth are you talking about?" But then, once the doctrine of separability had been explained to them, they would have said "Well yes, of course, we certainly both want that in the agreement".

Why, then, would all parties who have entered into an arbitration agreement in good faith want to also include the doctrine of separability in their contract? Because separability will often be essential if an arbitration clause is to have the effect that the parties intended it to have. The role of an arbitration clause in a contract is to resolve disputes between the parties to the contract regarding performance of the obligations in the contract. However, in certain situations a contract can either be terminated by one of the parties, or will terminate automatically as a matter of law. In such a situation one of the parties may be entitled to damages, but neither party is any longer bound by the obligations in the contract.

The problem this creates for an arbitration clause is obvious. The entire point of the arbitration clause is to resolve disputes between the parties relating to the obligations in the contract. Yet if the arbitration clause is part of the main contract, then the obligation to arbitrate is one of the obligations of that contract. As a result, as soon as the main contract is terminated, and its obligations cease to be binding on the parties, neither party any longer has an obligation to arbitrate. The arbitration clause, that is, has ceased to be effective in precisely the situation for which the parties incorporated it into their contract: when a dispute has arisen regarding the obligations in the main contract.

The doctrine of separability, then, has a very practical justification: only by treating the arbitration clause as a separate contract from the main contract in which it is contained, can the parties' agreement to arbitrate their disputes be given full effect.

4.2 The consequences of separability

As will be clear from the preceding discussion, the obvious consequence of the doctrine of separability is that if the contract containing an arbitration clause is null and void or otherwise flawed, these problems do not automatically affect the agreement to arbitrate. The agreement to arbitrate is, after all, a separate contract from the main contract. As a result, problems with the main contract will only affect the arbitration agreement if they directly relate to the arbitration agreement as well.

The primary benefit of separability, then, as suggested above, is that an arbitral tribunal may still have jurisdiction over a dispute between parties to a contract, even though it has held that the main contract in which the agreement to arbitrate was included is itself invalid or otherwise flawed.

Nonetheless, it should be emphasised that this does not mean that arbitration agreements are always valid, and are never affected by problems affecting the agreement in which they are contained. Rather, it simply means that determining whether an arbitration clause is still binding on the parties to a contract requires a separate examination than the one required to determine whether the main contract itself is still binding. It may be that the flaw that is alleged to have resulted in the invalidity of the main contract also applies to the arbitration agreement as a separate contract, such as if one of the parties is alleged to have lacked the capacity to enter into any type of contractual agreements at the time the main contract was signed: Ruby the painting elephant could perhaps have been taught to sign her name on a piece of paper, but this mechanical ability would not have meant she had legal capacity to enter into contracts, and so she should would not have been bound even by an arbitration agreement.

On the other hand, many courts have held that if what a party is alleging is a flaw that applies to the main contract as a whole, rather than specifically to the arbitration clause, the arbitration clause remains binding. By way of example, presume that Antoni finds Moriya's car, which had been stolen. Antoni then contacts Moriya and offers to sell the car back to her, arguing that as he found the car it is actually his now. Moriya disagrees, insisting the car is still hers, but really wants her car back. As a result, she agrees to purchase it from him, and they sign a contract, containing an arbitration agreement, in which Moriya agrees to pay £5,000.00 for the car and Antoni agrees to deliver the car to Moriya. Antoni delivers the car to Moriya, Moriya takes control of the car, but then Moriya refuses to pay the money. Depending on the specific facts of the case, a contract for the sale of a car will usually be void, and so have no legal effect, if the car being purchased was actually already owned by the purchaser. Nonetheless, even though in such a case the law may say that there was never a legally valid contract between Antoni and Moriya, and so no provisions in that contract are legally enforceable, Antoni and Moriya will nonetheless usually be required to arbitrate Antoni's claim that Moriya owes him £5,000.00, rather than litigate it in court. This is because even if the contract between Antoni and Moriya is void, and so never had any legal effect, the reason for its invalidity had nothing to do with Antoni and Moriya's agreement to arbitrate, and so the arbitration agreement, as a separate contract, remains enforceable.

The doctrine of separability has other important consequences as well, arising naturally from the notion that an arbitration clause is a separate contract from the contract in which it is contained. First of all, as discussed in Chapter 2, the main contract and the arbitration clause may be governed by completely different laws. Indeed, even if there is a choice of law clause in the main contract specifically identifying a law to be applied to all parts of that contract, that choice of law clause does not apply directly to the arbitration clause – since the arbitration clause is, after all, not actually part of the main contract. Moreover, even if both the main contract and the arbitration clause are governed by the same law, that law may apply different formal requirements to each of them. By way of example, the applicable law may allow that contracts are binding even if they are created orally (i.e. without being put in writing), but also specify that arbitration agreements must be in writing to be enforceable. In such a case, parties who have entered into a contract orally, and have also orally agreed to arbitrate disputes arising out of that contract, will still have a binding main contract, but will not be obligated to arbitrate disputes arising out of that contract.

5. Both courts and arbitrators may rule on the validity and scope of an arbitration agreement: the doctrine of competence-competence

5.1 Disputes as to the existence and validity of an arbitration agreement

That arbitration requires the consent of the parties is often referenced by those attempting to argue that one of the benefits of arbitration is that it is more harmonious than litigation: parties can be forced to litigate in court, but only have to arbitrate if they have voluntarily agreed to do so, and since arbitration is their chosen method of dispute resolution they can presumably be expected to pursue it in a constructive and positive manner. In reality, of course, as has been discussed above, that a party has "consented" to arbitrate does not actually mean that at the time a dispute arises they are actually "willing" to arbitrate. Consequently, disputes about whether the parties have actually entered into a binding arbitration agreement, or whether an admittedly binding arbitration agreement covers the specific issue being brought to arbitration, are a standard feature of international commercial arbitration. The remainder of this Chapter will address the primary questions that arise in this context, examining first questions arising from disputes relating to the existence and validity of an arbitration agreement, before turning to issues arising from disputes relating to the scope of an arbitration agreement.

5.2 Disputes before State courts

Courts have been created by States to serve as the default mechanism for resolving disputes and enforcing legal rights. It is, therefore, unsurprising that many new to arbitration see courts as the natural forum for any dispute regarding the existence or validity of an arbitration agreement. After all, arbitration requires consent, and if parties have not consented to arbitrate a dispute, then they have no obligation to go to arbitration and they retain their right to go to court. It would seem to follow naturally that if a dispute arises regarding the existence or validity of an arbitration agreement, that dispute would be resolved in court, as the default forum for the resolution of all disputes. As we will go on to see, things are not this simple. Nonetheless, disputes as to the existence or validity of an arbitration agreement can arise before State courts in two different ways: (i) the issue of the existence or validity of an arbitration agreement can be the main subject matter of the proceedings, or (ii) it can be a preliminary question that the court must resolve in order to determine whether it should address the actual main subject matter of the proceedings.

66 *The agreement to arbitrate*

With respect to the first situation, the applicable law may allow parties to bring an action before a court, requesting the court to determine whether or not a valid arbitration agreement exists. Some national arbitration laws specifically allow such an action to be brought: when seised with this type of action, the court will typically render a declaratory judgment, essentially saying whether the parties are bound by a valid agreement to arbitrate or not. In this case, the question of the existence and validity of the arbitration agreement constitutes the main subject matter of the proceedings before the court. The court, in other words, is being asked to determine whether the parties are subject to a binding arbitration agreement; it is not being asked to actually resolve any dispute that is claimed to be covered by that arbitration agreement. A mechanism of this type allows parties to gain certainty regarding the forum in which disputes between them will be heard before those disputes have risen to the level that a legal action has actually been commenced. This information can then be used in ongoing discussions between the parties, and potentially assist the parties reach a consensual solution.

In the second situation, a party may file a claim before a State court against another party, despite the alleged existence of an arbitration agreement between those parties that covers the subject matter of the claim. The respondent must then object to the jurisdiction of the State court, arguing that the matter before the court falls within the scope of a valid arbitration agreement, and that the court must therefore refer the parties to arbitration, either under the applicable arbitration law or as required by Article II(3) of the New York Convention. The claimant, of course, may then respond that the arbitration agreement being invoked by the respondent either does not exist or is otherwise invalid or inapplicable. In this type of case, the proceedings before the court are not primarily about the arbitration agreement itself, as the claiming party has brought a substantive claim before the court. Nonetheless, the court cannot determine whether it has jurisdiction to decide on the merits of the dispute before it until the question of the existence and validity of the arbitration agreement has been resolved.

5.3 Disputes before the arbitral tribunal

Arbitration is based on consent, and so an arbitral tribunal only has the right to exercise any power at all over a party if that party has consented to arbitrate before it. Most, but not all, institutional rules expressly allow arbitrators to determine whether they have jurisdiction over a dispute *sua sponte*, meaning without the issue being raised by either party. Normally, however, questions of the existence or validity of an arbitration agreement will have been raised by one of the parties in the arbitration, if they are raised at all, in the hope of terminating the arbitration.

However, unlike the situation with courts, questions of the existence or validity of an arbitration agreement are in practice typically raised before an arbitral tribunal as a preliminary matter, not as the main subject matter of the proceedings. It would be formally possible for parties to draft an arbitration agreement that allowed a tribunal to issue a declaratory judgement regarding the existence or validity of the arbitration agreement itself, but this is unlikely to be something that would occur to parties when drafting the arbitration agreement. Instead, tribunals routinely issue "partial awards" addressing only their jurisdiction. While in a sense these awards resemble declaratory judgements, as they only address the tribunal's jurisdiction, they are nonetheless only made once a substantive claim has been brought by one of the parties to the arbitration agreement, as a step preceding the tribunal then addressing the substantive claim. They do not arise from an independent arbitral process focused purely on the jurisdiction of the tribunal.[11]

However, it should be emphasised that while questions of the existence or validity of an arbitration agreement will be determined by an arbitral tribunal as a preliminary matter, this is a logical status, not a temporal one. That is, it does not mean that the tribunal must literally determine that it has jurisdiction before it can proceed to address the merits of the parties' dispute. Indeed, in many arbitrations the tribunal will reserve a decision on its jurisdiction to the final award, arguing that many of the issues that must be examined to make a proper jurisdictional determination are also issues that can only be properly examined during a hearing on the merits. This is certainly not an illegitimate position for a tribunal to take, and there are cases in which such an approach is fully justified. However, the best interests of the parties will be served by the tribunal making a jurisdictional determination before any time is spent on the merits of the case whenever it is possible to do so.

5.4 Competence-competence: the idea

That both courts and arbitral tribunals can rule on the existence or validity of an arbitration agreement raises an obvious question: If both of these forums are available, which one should make the decision? That is, if two parties are in a dispute and one denies that there is a valid arbitration agreement between them, should the parties ask a court to determine whether they are obligated to arbitrate before commencing arbitration, or should they commence arbitration and ask the arbitral tribunal to decide whether it has jurisdiction?

The answer to this question might initially seem obvious: Arbitration is based on consent, and if you have not consented to arbitrate then you have no obligation to appear before an arbitral tribunal. As one of the parties denies that he entered into an arbitration agreement, why should he have to argue that point before the arbitral tribunal? After all, if the tribunal decides he is right, and there is no valid arbitration agreement between the parties, then this means it agrees that he never actually had any obligation to appear before them in the first place – even to argue about the existence or validity of the arbitration agreement. The obvious answer, then, is that he can insist that the question be determined by the court with jurisdiction over the issue.

However, while this solution seems intuitively obvious, it also raises a problem. One of the primary reasons parties enter into international commercial arbitration agreements is to avoid local courts, whether because they are slow, non-neutral, or for some other reason. Yet allowing parties to challenge the existence of an arbitration agreement in court undermines this goal, slowing the arbitral process while the parties wait on a decision by the court, and potentially allowing biased or arbitration-unfriendly courts to interfere with an arbitral process that the parties did indeed agree to use.

"Competence-competence" is the doctrine that has been developed to address this problem, and it centres on the fundamental idea that an arbitral tribunal has the "competence" to decide for itself whether it has the "competence" to decide a dispute brought before it. As with

68 *The agreement to arbitrate*

many things in arbitration, the doctrine varies in its details between jurisdictions, but there are fundamentally two primary versions, both of which will be addressed below.

5.5 Competence-competence 1: the compatibility approach

Perhaps the most common approach to competence-competence is one originally derived from German law, according to which both arbitral tribunals and courts are permitted to rule on the existence or validity of an arbitration agreement.[12] Under this approach, if arbitration proceedings have been commenced, but the respondent objects that there is no valid arbitration agreement in existence between the parties, the arbitral tribunal is permitted to decide this question for itself. That is, the question does not need to be referred to the courts of the seat.

In turn, if a party commences litigation and the respondent objects that the subject matter of the litigation is covered by an arbitration agreement, the court may decide for itself whether or not there is a valid arbitration agreement between the parties covering the subject matter of the litigation. In other words, the question does not need to be referred to an arbitral tribunal.

Importantly, however, in many States adopting this approach, the right of a court to determine the existence or validity of an arbitration agreement exists only until an arbitral tribunal has been constituted to address the dispute – that is, until the members of the tribunal have been selected and have accepted their appointment (a process that may not conclude for weeks, at times months, after the claimant has commenced the arbitration). In these States, once an arbitral tribunal has been constituted, a court must refer the question of the existence or validity of the arbitration agreement to the tribunal.

The obvious question this approach gives rise to is whether a ruling issued by a court regarding the existence and validity of an arbitration agreement binds an arbitral tribunal constituted under that agreement. In other words, if a court has held that there is no valid arbitration agreement between the parties, can an arbitral tribunal disagree and proceed with an arbitration? Alternatively, if a court has held that there is a valid arbitration agreement between the parties, can an arbitral tribunal disagree and dismiss the claim on the ground that it has no jurisdiction over the dispute?

Best practice for an arbitral tribunal in such a situation is unquestionably to respect and follow any determination by the courts of the seat of the arbitration regarding the existence or validity of the arbitration agreement. A tribunal only has authority to perform its role in accordance with the agreement of the parties, and the parties have agreed to seat their arbitration in the State in question. A tribunal has no justification for departing from the law of the seat except, perhaps, where both parties agree this should be done. In this context, however, by agreeing to seat their arbitration in that State, the parties have subjected themselves to the jurisdiction of the courts of that State regarding the arbitration. As a result, while the arbitral tribunal may not be directly bound by the court's decision,[13] any decision by a court of the seat regarding the arbitration is binding on the parties themselves, and the parties lack the legal power to authorise the tribunal to reject the court's decision. They may, of course, ask the tribunal to reject the court's decision, but any award issued by a tribunal in this situation will almost certainly be annulled by the courts of the seat, and will also face increased obstacles to international recognition and enforcement.

A subtler question is whether a judgment by a court from a jurisdiction other than the seat of the arbitration regarding the existence or validity of the arbitration agreement is binding on an arbitral tribunal? After all, such a court has no direct legal connection with the arbitration, and while the courts of a State may have the authority to order certain individuals to perform or not perform certain actions while in a third State, those orders do not have automatic legal effect in that third State. Consequently, it might seem clear that a tribunal operating under the arbitration law of State X is simply not bound by any judgment delivered by the courts of State Y regarding the existence or validity of the arbitration agreement under which the tribunal is operating.

It is important to remember, however, that just as arbitral awards can be enforced internationally, so can court judgements, although to a lesser degree. As a result, it may be that under the law of State X, a judgement delivered by a court in State Y regarding the existence or validity of an arbitration agreement will be recognised and enforced by the courts of State X. If this is the case, then that judgement should also be recognised and followed by an arbitral tribunal operating under the arbitration law of State X.[14] Where this is not the case, however, and a judgement by a court in State Y regarding the existence or validity of an arbitration agreement would not be enforced by the courts of State X, then an arbitral tribunal operating under the arbitration law of State X is not bound by that decision, and may disregard it.

One final question is whether a decision by an arbitral tribunal regarding the existence or validity of an arbitration agreement binds a court? It is overwhelmingly acknowledged that the answer to this question is "no". In almost all jurisdictions that adopt the "compatibility" approach, the final decision regarding the existence or validity of an arbitration agreement remains in the hands of the courts of the seat. This decision will usually be given after the final award has been delivered, if an annulment or enforcement proceeding has been commenced, and the court will usually make its decision *de novo*, i.e. without any deference to the decision already reached by the arbitral tribunal. However, in some jurisdictions it is possible to request a ruling from a court as soon as the arbitral tribunal has delivered its own decision on the existence or validity of the arbitration agreement, if it has done so in the form of an award. In this situation the arbitral proceedings are usually permitted to continue while the court examines the question, even to the point of the tribunal delivering a final award.

Importantly, though, the law of the seat may also allow the parties to agree to let the arbitral tribunal make the final decision on its own jurisdiction, which will then only be reviewed by a court under the standards normally applied to review of arbitration awards, i.e. essentially, whether the procedure followed was fair, regardless of whether the court believes the decision is or is not legally correct. Such an approach is rare, most famously being found in the United States of America, and is highly problematic given the reality that the "consent" in many arbitration agreements is purely formal, with one or even both parties often not understanding the full consequences of entering into a binding arbitration agreement.

5.6 Competence-competence 2: the exclusionary approach

The second primary approach to competence-competence derives from French law, and gives a much greater emphasis to the independence of arbitration from national court systems. As is the case under the "compatibility" approach, under the "exclusionary" approach if arbitration proceedings have been commenced, but the respondent objects that there is no valid arbitration agreement in existence between the parties, the arbitral tribunal is permitted to decide this question for itself. With respect to the competence of an arbitral tribunal to rule on the existence or validity of an arbitration agreement, then, or what is often called the "positive" effect of competence-competence, the two approaches are equivalent.

The difference between the two approaches arises from the way that the "exclusionary" approach addresses the ability of courts to rule on the existence or validity of an arbitration agreement, as the "exclusionary" approach endorses a doctrine often referred to as the "negative" effect of competence-competence.

That is, on the "exclusionary" view, allowing State courts to rule on the existence or validity of an arbitration agreement is an undue interference of the State in the private dispute resolution mechanism of arbitration. Consequently, in order to preserve the autonomy of arbitration from courts, arbitral tribunals are granted an almost-exclusive competence to rule on the existence or validity of an arbitration agreement. Prior to an arbitral tribunal being constituted, a court may rule on the existence or validity of an arbitration agreement only if it finds that the agreement is manifestly void or inapplicable – that is, if there is simply no reasonable argument that there is a valid arbitration agreement between the parties that covers the parties' present dispute. If there is even a weak argument that a valid and applicable arbitration agreement exists, even if the court does not accept that argument, the parties must be referred to arbitration, where the existence, validity or applicability of the arbitration agreement will be decided by an arbitral tribunal. Moreover, this single avenue of court review only exists prior to the constitution of an arbitral tribunal. As under the "compatibility" approach, once a tribunal has been constituted even this power is removed from courts, and every question of the existence, validity or applicability of an arbitration agreement must be referred to the arbitral tribunal.

Clearly this approach has fundamental consequences for the relationship between courts and arbitral tribunals. While the "compatibility" approach attempts to construct a system in which both courts and tribunals are able to exercise their functions, the "exclusionary" approach gives an initial priority to arbitral tribunals. While such a prioritising of arbitral tribunals can make sense where parties have indeed agreed to arbitrate their disputes, it is far more problematic when the existence of that agreement is precisely what is in question – this approach, that is, knowingly and unavoidably strips some parties of their right of access to court, even though they have never consented to arbitration, and even though arguments in favour of the independence of arbitration from judicial control invariably emphasise that arbitration is based on party consent. There is, then, good reason to argue that the "exclusionary" approach simply goes too far in its support of arbitration. It guarantees that parties cannot use court proceedings as a way of avoiding an arbitration to which they have indeed consented, but does so in a way that also undermines the very consensual nature of arbitration that justifies courts referring parties to arbitration in the first place.

However, this point being made, it should be emphasised that this prioritising of arbitration under the "exclusionary" approach is only temporary, as once a final award has been delivered courts are then free to rule on the existence or validity of the arbitration agreement in any subsequent annulment or enforcement proceeding. Indeed, under the standard version of the "exclusionary" approach, a court examining the existence or validity of an arbitration agreement after an award has been delivered will do so *de novo*, giving no deference at all to the prior determination by the arbitral tribunal. The "exclusionary" approach does not, then, require the courts to abdicate their responsibility to enforce the law. Nonetheless, while this does give some protection to parties from being bound by the results of an arbitration to which they never consented, by the time this protection arises a party that never agreed to arbitrate its dispute has already been forced to spend sometimes significant amounts of time and money taking part in an arbitral process. As a result, it is far from clear that even this final level of protection truly respects the importance of the consensual foundation of arbitration.

6. Parties may agree the law to be applied to their arbitration agreement

No-one familiar with international dispute resolution would be surprised that parties in international commercial arbitration have the ability to select the substantive law to be applied to their dispute. After all, this is also a power that is usually given to parties in litigation. More notable, however, is that parties in international commercial arbitration are also generally acknowledged as having the power to select the law to be applied to their arbitration agreement. That is, parties can enter into an arbitration agreement that itself specifies which law should be applied in deciding whether the arbitration agreement is valid.

There is an unquestionable circularity in this, since it is only if an arbitration agreement is valid that its provisions have legal effect – which means that only if the arbitration agreement is valid does the agreement's choice of law regarding its own validity have effect; but you can't determine if it is valid until you know which law to apply to the question of its validity; but the law to be applied is determined by the arbitration agreement; but only if the arbitration agreement is valid; which you can't know until you determine the law to be applied to the question of its validity; which is determined by the arbitration agreement . . .

Nonetheless, jurisdictions around the world have agreed that as a practical matter questions of circularity will just be ignored, as respecting the ability of parties to an arbitration agreement to design their own dispute resolution procedure would be significantly hampered by not respecting their choice of law regarding their arbitration agreement. Parties often choose arbitration in order to escape specific national laws or national court systems, after all, and refusing to recognise their choice of law governing their arbitration agreement would frustrate this goal. As a result, as a matter of practical desirability, this principle was incorporated into Article V(1)(a) of the New York Convention, which states that recognition and enforcement of an arbitral award can be denied if the arbitration agreement "is not valid under the law to which the parties have subjected it or, failing any indication thereon, under the law of the country where the award was made". This rule implicitly embraces the idea that parties to an arbitration agreement have the power to subject that agreement to whichever law they prefer, and this principle is now a standard feature of arbitration law around the world.

In practice, however, it is uncommon for parties to specify which law governs their arbitration agreement. After all, many commercial contracts do not even specify which law governs the substantive obligations being entered into by the parties, and far fewer parties are sophisticated enough in their understanding of arbitration law that they realise that the "separability" of an arbitration agreement means that selection of the substantive law for a contract does not also qualify as selection of the law applicable to an arbitration agreement in that contract.

Not all jurisdictions address this problem in the same way. According to some courts, when the parties have chosen a substantive law to be applied to a contract, that same law should be held to apply to an arbitration agreement in that contract: after all, this is the only clear indication that has been given by the parties of which law they wish to govern their relationship. On the other hand, other courts have rejected this view, embracing separability completely, and instead applying to the arbitration agreement either the law of the seat of the arbitration chosen by the parties, or even a different law determined by the conflict of laws rules of the court's jurisdiction. Such an approach can be seen in Article V(1)(a) of the New York Convention itself, which requires that the law of the seat of arbitration be applied when the parties have not agreed on a law to be applied to the arbitration agreement. Finally, some jurisdictions adopt as an overwhelming goal protecting the effectiveness of arbitration agreements, providing that arbitration agreements should be enforced as long as they are valid under either the law chosen by the parties, the law applicable to the main contract or the local law of the jurisdiction in question.[15]

Understanding arbitration through case-law

Choice of law clauses and arbitration agreements

Case details: *Sulamerica v Enesa Engenharia* [2012] EWCA Civ 638

Authority deciding the case: Court of Appeal of England and Wales

Facts of the case: The parties entered into an insurance agreement. They agreed that the contract would be governed by Brazilian law and included an arbitration clause, selecting England as the seat. A dispute arose between the parties and Enesa started litigation before Brazilian courts, disregarding the arbitration agreement. Sul América then asked the English courts to issue an anti-suit injunction against Enesa, ordering it to stop the litigation.

However, a further complication arose. In order to issue an anti-suit injunction, the English court had to be persuaded that a valid arbitration agreement existed. In the case at hand, however, the agreement was valid under English law, but not valid under Brazilian law, as the latter contained additional formal requirements of validity that had not been complied with. The question, then, was whether the choice-of-law clause included in the contract, providing for Brazilian law, would extend its effects to the agreement to arbitrate as well. If it did, then the English court would not be able to issue an anti-suit

> injunction, as no valid arbitration agreement bound the parties. On the other hand, if the law of the seat of arbitration (England) governed the agreement, then the arbitration clause was valid, and an anti-suit injunction could be issued.
>
> **Decision:** The Court held that the common law rules for the ascertainment of the proper law of an arbitration agreement are not different from the rules determining the law applicable to any other contract. More specifically, those rules prescribe a three-step analysis. In the first step, the Court must recognise and give effect to the parties' express choice of law, if any. In the second step, failing any express choice, the Court must give effect to the parties' implied choice, if any. In cases where no implied choice has been made, the Court must proceed to the third stage, and identify the legal system with which the contract has "the closest and most real connection".
>
> In this case, the parties had not expressly indicated the law applicable to the agreement to arbitrate, as there was no choice of law clause in the arbitration agreement itself, but they had nonetheless specified the law governing the main contract. The question, then, was whether such a general choice-of-law clause can constitute an implied choice of law with respect to the arbitration clause.
>
> The court held that the existence of a choice of law clause applicable to the main contract generated a rebuttable presumption that the parties implicitly intended to subject the arbitration clause to the same law. In this case, however, the presumption was rebutted by the circumstance that, were Brazilian law to apply, the arbitration agreement would be invalid. It would not be logical for the parties to enter into an agreement to arbitrate, and at the same time subject it to a law that would make that agreement invalid. For this reason, the Court concluded that the parties had made no implied choice of the law applicable to the arbitration clause and proceeded to the third stage of the analysis, concluding that the law most closely connected to the arbitration agreement was the law of the seat, i.e. English law.

The better solution to this issue is unquestionably to apply the law of the seat of the arbitration to the question of the validity of the arbitration agreement, where this has been specified by the parties, even if this differs from the law chosen by the parties to govern the substantive legal obligations in their contract. In such a case the parties have given a clear indication of which law should apply to their arbitration, and applying this law to the question of the validity of their arbitration agreement gives maximum respect to that choice. Indeed, even where the parties have not selected a seat, the law of the seat as determined at a later stage by an arbitral tribunal or institution should be regarded as applicable to all questions focused on the arbitration itself, including the validity of the arbitration agreement. While the third approach discussed above, which enforces an arbitration agreement if it is valid under any of the potentially applicable laws, might on its face seem to support the autonomy of the parties, in reality it deprives parties of the power to limit the effectiveness of their arbitration agreement, and in an overly strong attempt to support arbitration, it overrules the autonomy of the parties on which arbitration is supposed to be based.

74   *The agreement to arbitrate*

7. The standards to be used in determining the existence and validity of an arbitration agreement will be decided by the applicable law, and can vary from one jurisdiction to another

7.1 Importance of the requirements of existence and validity

Of course, the reason it matters that parties be able to select the law to be applied to questions of the existence or validity of their arbitration agreement is that the legal requirements for a valid arbitration agreement differ between jurisdictions. Moreover, the consequences of a finding that an arbitration agreement is invalid or otherwise not binding can be significant. Firstly, any arbitral award delivered by a tribunal operating under that agreement will likely be annulled by the courts of the seat of the arbitration.[16] In turn, any attempt to have such an award recognised and enforced outside the seat of the arbitration will likely be refused in accordance with Article V(1)(a) of the New York Convention. Consequently, the question of what limitations jurisdictions place on the existence and validity of arbitration agreements has a fundamental importance for the effectiveness of an entire arbitration.

7.2 Existence of an agreement to arbitrate

It may initially seem that the question of the existence of an arbitration agreement will very rarely arise in practice. After all, the parties either have or have not agreed to arbitrate, and as most jurisdictions require that an arbitration agreement be in writing to be enforced, a party can either show the written arbitration agreement or cannot. In reality, though, questions about the existence of an arbitration agreement arise quite regularly, because an arbitration agreement incorporates not only the parties' agreement to arbitrate, but to arbitrate in a particular way. That is, not only are parties only obligated to arbitrate if they have agreed to do so, but they are only obligated to arbitrate in accordance with their agreement. Because of this, questions of the existence of an arbitration agreement include not only questions as to whether there is an arbitration agreement between the parties at all, but also questions as to whether there is an agreement between the parties to arbitrate in the specific way that the arbitration is being performed.

Traditionally courts were often strict in their determinations regarding the existence of an arbitration agreement, on the ground that arbitration precludes litigation, and opting out of court litigation involves the waiver of a fundamental right, i.e. access to courts. However, contemporary jurisdictions are more varied. Some will enforce an arbitration agreement so long as it evidences the agreement of the parties to resort to arbitration, even if the details of that consent are unclear,[17] while others retain a heightened standard of review, requiring a clear choice by the parties to resort to arbitration.[18]

Even if it is clear that the parties have agreed to some kind of arbitration, questions can still arise regarding the existence of the parties' consent to arbitrate at a particular time or in a particular way. For example, the parties may have entered into what is called a "multi-tiered" dispute resolution clause, requiring that disputes initially be addressed through meetings between senior representatives of both parties, followed by formal mediation if necessary, and arbitration if mediation is unsuccessful.[19] In such a case, unless the clause has been written very precisely, stating deadlines or triggering events for the conclusion of each phase, questions may arise once arbitration has commenced as to whether it has been commenced too early. That is, the parties have only agreed to arbitrate if negotiation and mediation have both proven unsuccessful. However, if one party still insists that negotiation/mediation can succeed, while the other regards them as failed, can the first party be forced to arbitrate the dispute? Certainly that first party will argue that it only agreed to arbitrate after both negotiation and mediation failed, and it does not believe that they have failed yet. In this situation, the objecting party is arguing that there is no agreement between the parties for the specific arbitration that has been commenced, even though it acknowledges that there is agreement for arbitration of another type. How such questions will be resolved will be a function of the degree to which agreements to negotiation/mediation are regarded as contractually enforceable under the law applicable to the interpretation of the arbitration agreement.

Similarly, an arbitration agreement may refer to an arbitral institution that no longer exists, or which has never existed, or may specify that a particular individual will serve as arbitrator, but she has recently died or is no longer willing to serve as arbitrator. In such cases it is clear that the parties have indeed agreed to arbitrate their dispute, but it is literally impossible for them to do so in accordance with their arbitration agreement. The question this gives rise to is whether the parties should be held to their overarching agreement to arbitrate their dispute, or if they should be released from that obligation on the ground that the only consent to arbitration that exists is to a form of arbitration that is impossible. Courts remain divided on how such a situation should be addressed, but the increasingly dominant approach around the world is for courts to attempt to preserve the fundamental consent to arbitration, irrespective of whether certain aspects of the arbitration agreement are incapable of being performed. That is, unless the party resisting arbitration can demonstrate that a particular feature of the arbitration agreement that is now impossible to perform was so central to the parties' agreement that there would have been no agreement to arbitrate unless that element was included, then the arbitration agreement will be enforced despite the impossibility of that element. For example, if an arbitration agreement merely misspells the name of an existing arbitral institution, or misidentifies the city in which that institution is located, the court will "correct" the drafting of the agreement, and hold that the parties are obligated to arbitrate under the auspices of the institution that the court believes they were intending to reference. Alternatively, if the agreement specifies an arbitral institution that no longer exists, the court may refer the parties to an existing similar institution, or even just refer them to *ad hoc* arbitration, allowing them to agree between themselves on a replacement institution if that is their preference. So long as such "corrections" are undertaken in a genuine effort to enforce the essence of the parties' agreement, rather than from a policy-based insistence that arbitration agreements should as a matter of principle be enforced, there is little to criticise in an approach to the interpretation of arbitration agreements that emphasises the substance of an agreement over the dispensable technicalities of form in which the parties' consent to arbitration was expressed.

7.3 *Validity of the agreement to arbitrate*

Even if it is clear that an arbitration agreement actually exists between the parties to a dispute, all States place restrictions on the standards arbitration agreements must meet in order to be valid and enforceable. Parties can still arbitrate disputes even if the law of the seat says that their arbitration agreement is invalid, but they cannot expect the courts to assist their arbitration, or to enforce any award delivered. The specific rules applied to the validity of arbitration agreements vary from one jurisdiction to another, but certain rules consistently found in arbitration laws are worth noting.

Firstly, it is generally regarded as essential that an arbitration agreement refer to a defined legal relationship. In other words, parties may not simply agree to arbitrate any dispute that may arise between them. Such an agreement will generally be held to be invalid.[20] This does not mean that arbitration agreements need to be narrow, but only that they must clearly indicate the legal relationship, whether a contract, transaction or other relationship, with respect to which the parties are agreeing to arbitrate their disputes.

Many arbitration laws also identify specific formal requirements arbitration agreements must meet if they are to be valid. This tendency arises from traditional concerns that arbitration may be used to deprive parties of their right of access to court and of the proper application of the substantive law. Nonetheless, while historically such concerns were often overstated, the procedural freedom given to parties involved in arbitration and the extremely limited review of arbitration awards is consistently defended on the ground that parties should be allowed to use the dispute resolution procedure they agreed to use – and so ensuring that parties have indeed agreed to use arbitration is a legitimate justification for legal constraints on the validity of arbitration agreements.

The New York Convention has had a fundamental influence over this question of the formal validity of arbitration agreements, through the requirement in Article II(1) of the Convention that Contracting States must recognise an arbitration agreement "in writing". While this does not prevent Contracting States also recognising oral agreements to arbitrate, States have overwhelmingly endorsed the Convention's preference for written arbitration agreements, with only a minority of States enforcing purely oral arbitration agreements.[21] Notably, when the UNCITRAL Model Law was revised in 2006, 21 years after it was first adopted, substantial efforts were made by many in the arbitration community to incorporate the enforceability of oral arbitration agreements into it. Nonetheless, despite the unquestioned importance of arbitration in contemporary cross-border dispute resolution, and the efforts many States make to emphasise their "arbitration friendly" credentials, this proposal met with strong resistance. As a result, an approach was adopted that is unique within the Model Law, with two versions of Article 7 being included, leaving enacting States to choose between them: Option One requires that arbitration agreements be in writing to be enforced, while Option Two recognises the validity of oral agreements to arbitrate as well.

Nonetheless, it is important to recognise that even in jurisdictions requiring that arbitration agreements be in writing, that requirement is generally interpreted very liberally. For example, while the expression "in writing" may naturally suggest words written on paper, it is standardly accepted that agreements sent electronically, such as via e-mail, also count as "in writing". This is particularly important with respect to international commercial arbitration, as international commercial relations increasingly rely on electronic and other long-distance communication systems. Importantly, while the New York Convention obviously did not anticipate the specific means of communication we use today when it was adopted in 1958, the idea that what constitutes an arbitration agreement "in writing" should be interpreted broadly was already understood when the New York Convention was drafted: under

Article II(2) of the Convention, the term "agreement in writing" is explicitly stated to include "an arbitration agreement, signed by the parties or contained in an exchange of letters or telegrams" – a telegram being the closest 1958 came to email or instant messaging. Given the Convention's recognition of the need to take into account technological development, there is little ground to argue that an arbitration agreement formed via telegram should be valid, while an arbitration agreement formed via email, instant messaging, or fax should not be. Reflecting this, some national arbitration laws expressly state that an arbitration agreement shall be treated as in writing so long as it is included in an electronic communication that makes the information it contains accessible for future reference.[22] However, even where the applicable law does not make such an express statement, there is little justification for restricting the formal mechanisms through which parties can enter into arbitration agreements based solely on a traditional interpretation of the word "writing".

In many jurisdictions arbitration agreements may even be incorporated by reference: in other words, the parties never actually expressly agree to arbitrate, but include in their contract an agreement to follow the terms of a separate document, which itself includes an arbitration agreement. That separate document need not be drafted or signed by the parties: it can be a standard terms and conditions form, for example, or any other document that includes an agreement to arbitrate. So long as the reference to the separate document is worded in a way that makes clear the parties intended to make it part of their contract, courts will usually treat that document as incorporated into the main agreement, including any arbitration agreement it contains.[23] However, while this rule is in principle common, courts vary significantly with respect to the factual conditions under which they will find that an arbitration agreement included in a separate document has been incorporated into a contract. For example, according to some courts, that one of the parties did not have a copy of the document containing the arbitration agreement is irrelevant to whether it has been incorporated into the parties' contract, while other courts have required that all the parties be aware of the contents of the separate document if it is to be incorporated into the parties' contract. So long as such constraints on incorporation by reference operate generally as a matter of the applicable contract law, rather than constituting arbitration-specific rules intended to limit the ability of parties to enter into arbitration agreements, there is little to object to in them.

Understanding arbitration through case-law

General terms and conditions containing an arbitration clause

Case details: *Kastrup Trae-Aluvinduet A/S (Denmark) v Aluwood Concepts Ltd (Ireland)*, case no 129 MCA, 13 November 2009

Authority deciding the case: High Court of Ireland

Facts of the case: Kastrup and Aluwood engaged in a commercial relationship, in which Kastrup supplied doors and windows to Aluwood, which would then use them in its construction projects. This relationship was initiated with a quotation letter, sent by

Kastrup to Aluwood. After that first letter, Aluwood placed an order, and Kastrup sent a confirmation of order. Both the initial quotation letter and the confirmation of order specified that the transaction was governed by Kastrup's Common Terms and Conditions of Sale (CTCS). The CTCS contained a clause providing for arbitration at the Danish Court of Arbitration for the Building and Construction Industry.

Kastrup delivered some windows to Aluwood and requested payment for them. Aluwood, however, replied that the windows were defective, and therefore the price had to be reduced. Kastrup disagreed and commenced arbitration proceedings in accordance with the CTCS. Kastrup objected to the jurisdiction of the arbitral tribunal, arguing that no valid agreement to arbitrate existed. It was argued, in particular, that Kastrup had failed to draw Aluwood's attention to the specific fact that the CTCS contained an arbitration clause. The arbitral tribunal dismissed the objection and rendered an award in favour of Kastrup. At this point, Kastrup sought recognition and enforcement of the award in Ireland. The High Court of Ireland, as a result, had to determine whether the arbitration agreement was valid and binding between Kastrup and Aluwood.

Decision: The Court held that the arbitration agreement had been validly incorporated by simple reference to the CTCS, without any need to draw Aluwood's attention to the specific fact that the CTCS contained an arbitration clause. The Court also added that, in fact, it was irrelevant whether Aluwood even had a copy of the CTCS. To corroborate this conclusion, the Court observed that Aluwood had acted for eighteen months in accordance with the CTCS before raising the issue of the invalidity of the arbitration agreement.

Further expanding the meaning of "in writing", in many jurisdictions an arbitration agreement will be held to be "in writing" even if it was actually concluded orally, so long as the contents of the agreement are recorded in some written form.[24] So, for example, if Beverley and Gwion agree over coffee to arbitrate any disputes that arise from their upcoming business venture, that will in many jurisdictions be held to be an unenforceable oral agreement to arbitrate. However, if at some point after the agreement was reached, Beverley were to send Gwion an email saying "I'm glad we agreed to arbitrate any disputes", and Gwion were to respond by email "Yes, that will definitely be better than going to court", Beverley and Gwion will usually be held to have an arbitration agreement "in writing" – even though the agreement itself was purely oral. The arbitration agreement was oral, but there is written evidence that it was voluntarily entered into by the parties.

This example tells us something very important about rules that arbitration agreements must be "in writing". The concerns about oral arbitration agreements do not focus on anything "magical" about the written word, but on evidentiary concerns that unavoidably arise when two parties argue about what was said in a purely oral conversation. However, such concerns vanish when there is written evidence of the oral agreement, and the underlying rationale for the policy opposing enforcement of oral arbitration agreements no longer applies.

An interesting question that is less clear is whether an arbitration agreement will be treated as "in writing" if it is recorded in some form other than a written form. For example, what if Beverley recorded her meeting with Gwion on her mobile phone, including a clear audio or audiovisual recording of the two agreeing to arbitrate? There is no sense in which such a recording can literally be said to be "in writing", and yet such a recording would clearly satisfy the evidentiary concerns that motivate the policy opposing the enforcement of oral arbitration agreements. Indeed, it has been argued that such an agreement would be held to satisfy the "in writing" requirement of the English Arbitration Act 1996,[25] and this must be the correct approach. Insisting on a literal "writing" evidencing an arbitration agreement, when equally authoritative non-"written" evidence of the agreement is available, is to prioritise form over purpose, and ignore the reality of technological advances.

Nonetheless, as has already been noted, there are some jurisdictions in which purely oral agreements to arbitrate are indeed enforceable.[26] In contrast to the dominant approach, which argues that a written arbitration agreement should be required because agreeing to arbitration entails giving up the fundamental right of access to court, the policy in these jurisdictions emphasises the reality that contract law in most jurisdictions allows oral contracts to be enforced, and arbitration agreements are merely a form of contract. In turn, it is argued, arbitration has now developed to a level of professionalism that there is no justification for disfavouring arbitration agreements compared with any other contractual term, as there is no reason to presume that a party compelled to arbitrate its dispute will not receive just as fair a dispute resolution procedure as it would receive in court.

In principle, this view is surely correct. However, the drive to create "arbitration friendly" rules can result in the true complexities of the issue being ignored. After all, it is certainly not the case that arbitration agreements are the only form of contractual arrangement for which a heightened standard of proof is required. In many common law jurisdictions, for example, a "statute of frauds" exists requiring that contracts relating to such matters as transfer of property in land, third-party guarantees, and long-term service agreements, be in writing. The requirement of a written contract, that is, is a standard mechanism for the protection of parties when a contract relates to a particularly serious issue. There is no question, however, that arbitration does indeed raise important questions of access to justice: an effective arbitration is at least as good at ensuring justice as an effective court litigation, but whereas publicity and the protections inherent in a tiered national court system provide some level of certainty regarding the fairness of litigation procedures, the procedural freedom granted to parties in arbitration combined with the very minimal review of arbitration awards undertaken by most courts means that similar assurances simply do not exist for arbitration. As a result, while enforcement of oral agreements to arbitrate will clearly help facilitate arbitration, better protection of the legitimate interest of parties in securing access to justice is ensured by retaining a requirement that arbitration agreements be "in writing" while expanding the definition of "in writing" to allow even non-"written" evidence of an arbitration agreement so long as it is sufficiently reliable in form.

Nonetheless, whatever view one takes of the virtues or otherwise of enforcing purely oral arbitration agreements, it is also necessary to consider the complications that such a rule can produce given the international legal framework that currently exists. Firstly, Article II(3) of the New York Convention, which imposes on courts an obligation to refer parties to arbitration when a litigation is commenced that is covered by a valid arbitration agreement, does not cover purely oral arbitration agreements. As a result, even if the courts of the seat of the arbitration will enforce an oral arbitration agreement, courts of another jurisdiction may refuse to do so, resulting in the parties having to simultaneously arbitrate their dispute at the seat of the arbitration and litigate their dispute abroad. Similarly, as the policy against the enforcement of purely oral agreements to arbitrate rests on concerns about the use of arbitration to deprive parties of their fundamental right of access to court, courts may refuse enforcement of an arbitral award arising out of an arbitration based on a purely oral arbitration agreement under Article V(2)(b) of the New York Convention. The consequence of this is that even if the agreed seat of an arbitration allows the enforcement of purely oral arbitration agreements, parties would be well advised nonetheless to place their agreement to arbitrate in writing.

Finally, consideration should be given to a mechanism by which parties can be found to have agreed to arbitrate their dispute, even though they have never knowingly entered into an agreement to arbitrate: conduct-based estoppel. In general terms, conduct-based estoppel is a rule of law according to which a party should not be allowed to adopt a particular position in a dispute resolution process when that position is inconsistent with actions the party has previously taken and on which the other party has relied. In the context of agreements to arbitrate, issues relating to estoppel will arise when a claimant commences arbitration proceedings and the respondent substantively participates in those proceedings without objecting that there is no binding arbitration agreement between the parties. In short, say Levison and Xuefeng have a contract that includes an arbitration clause, but one that does not cover the particular dispute that has arisen between them. Levison nonetheless commences arbitration against Xuefeng, and Xuefeng participates in the arbitration. Both courts and arbitral tribunals will standardly hold that by participating in the arbitration without objection, Xuefeng implicitly accepted the jurisdiction of the arbitral tribunal over the dispute, and so waived his right to contest that jurisdiction – even though there was indeed no binding arbitration agreement between the parties.[27]

Understanding arbitration through case-law

Time limits to object to the jurisdiction of the tribunal

Case details: *A v B [2017] EWHC 3417 (Comm)*

Authority deciding the case: English Commercial Court

Facts of the case: A and B entered into two separate contracts, whereby B would sell two consignments of crude oil to A. The contracts were governed by English law and provided for arbitration in London, under the auspices of the LCIA.

A dispute arose between the parties. In September 2016 B filed a single request for arbitration, claiming payment of the prices due under both the first and the second contract. A filed a response in which it denied liability and specified that its defence on the merits should not be construed as a submission to the jurisdiction of the arbitral tribunal. The parties then exchanged further correspondence with the LCIA and with the arbitrators, in which A repeated similar reservations.

> On 24 May 2017 A objected to the jurisdiction of the tribunal, arguing that B was bringing two separate claims under two contracts, and therefore could not commence a single arbitration. On 7 July of the same year, the arbitral tribunal dismissed the objection, arguing that it had been put forth too late in the arbitration. The tribunal referred in particular to Article 23.3 of the 2014 LCIA Rules, according to which jurisdictional objections must be raised "as soon as possible but not later than the time for its Statement of Defence". A's statement of defence was due on 2 June 2017, just a few days after the date A raised its objection. Nonetheless, the arbitrators held that A's objection was untimely, as it had not been raised "as soon as possible", and that A was therefore estopped from challenging the jurisdiction of the tribunal.
>
> A challenged the arbitral award under Section 67 of the English Arbitration Act, asking the English Commercial Court to set it aside on the ground that, among other things, the tribunal had mistakenly held that the objection to the tribunal's jurisdiction was time-barred.
>
> **Decision:** The Commercial Court upheld the challenge and annulled the award. The Court reasoned that the words "as soon as possible" in the LCIA Rules are not meant to impose stricter requirements than those generally imposed by the English Arbitration Act, but simply to avoid untimely objections. Under Sections 31 and 73 of the English Arbitration Act, A would have until the submission of its statement of defence to raise the objection. Therefore, since the objection was raised a few days earlier than the submission of A's statement of defence, the arbitral tribunal should have regarded the objection as timely.

This is not to say, of course, that parties denying the existence or validity of an arbitration agreement should refuse to participate in an arbitration, out of concern that they will be held to have submitted to the tribunal's jurisdiction through their participation. After all, if a party does not participate in an arbitration, the tribunal can nonetheless continue with the proceedings and even deliver an award, which will then be binding on the party, despite that party's non-participation (and since only its opponent presented evidence and legal arguments to the tribunal, it is highly likely that the non-participating party will not be happy with the content of that award). However, while parties disputing the existence or validity of an arbitration agreement are well-advised to nonetheless participate in any arbitral proceedings brought against them, they must ensure that they raise their objection to the jurisdiction of the arbitral tribunal before taking any other action in the proceeding, and that they repeat that objection clearly and consistently throughout the proceedings – lest a subsequent reviewing court decide that at a certain point in the proceedings the objection was dropped: once it is dropped, it can never be recovered.

7.4 Applicability of contract law defences to the arbitration agreement

The discussion up to this point has concentrated on issues arising specifically from an arbitration agreement's connection with arbitration, such as consent and the question of precluding access to court. However, an agreement to arbitrate is fundamentally a contract, and so can also be attacked on grounds applicable to any contract. This principle is included in Article II(3) of the New York Convention, which provides that national courts can refuse to enforce an arbitration agreement if it is "null and void, inoperative or incapable or being performed", and similar provisions are standardly included in national arbitration laws. The consequence of such provisions is that a party may challenge the validity of an arbitration agreement on grounds such as unconscionability, fraud, incapacity, or any other standard contract law principle. Of course, the specific grounds available will depend on the law applicable to the arbitration agreement, as this is also the jurisdiction whose contract law should be applied to its interpretation.

Nonetheless, it is important to re-emphasise a point that was made earlier when discussing the separability of an arbitration clause from the contract in which it is contained: as the arbitration clause constitutes a separate contract from the contract in which it is contained, flaws of the main contract do not necessarily also affect the arbitration agreement. By way of example, if Tashan and Katey have entered into a sales contract containing an arbitration agreement, and Tashan knowingly provides false information concerning the quality of the goods to be sold, this may constitute fraud that invalidates the sales contract – however, the fraud alleged had no connection to the arbitration agreement, and so under the dominant interpretation of the doctrine of separability will not also invalidate the agreement to arbitrate. By contrast, Katey was under a legal incapacity when entering into the contract, this will usually invalidate both the main contract and the arbitration agreement it contains, as she was not able to express valid consent to either of those agreements.

In short, while contract law defences are applicable to arbitration agreements, a separate examination must be undertaken to determine if a contract law defence affects the arbitration agreement – the mere fact that the defence is effective against the contract containing the arbitration agreement does not mean that the arbitration agreement is also affected.

8. Even if an arbitration agreement is valid, its scope may be unclear

8.1 Disputes as to the scope of an arbitration agreement

Even when parties acknowledge that a valid arbitration agreement exists between them, disputes can nonetheless arise regarding the exact scope of that arbitration agreement, and whether it covers the precise dispute that has arisen between them. After all, an agreement to arbitrate is not a universally applicable consent by the parties to that agreement to opt out of national courts and arbitrate every dispute that may ever arise between them. Arbitration agreements are by their nature limited in scope: they cover only a certain category or categories of disputes, as specified in the language of the arbitration agreement itself. Any dispute that arises between the parties that is not covered by the arbitration agreement can still be taken to court.

Disputes regarding the scope of an arbitration agreement can occur with respect to both pre-dispute and post-dispute arbitration agreements, but are particularly characteristic of pre-dispute arbitration agreements – that is, arbitration agreements entered into by the parties before any dispute has arisen between them, in which they agree to arbitrate any future disputes that fall into a certain category or categories. While post-dispute arbitration agreements can be worded quite precisely, as the parties know exactly the dispute they wish to arbitrate, it is inherent in the nature of a pre-dispute arbitration agreement that its wording will be vague and expansive: the parties have no idea what disputes might arise between them, and so in order for the arbitration agreement to be effective they must adopt language likely to capture even disputes they cannot currently envision. Of course, this broad and vague language then also provides an opportunity for a party wishing to avoid arbitration to argue that the arbitration agreement does not cover the dispute that has actually arisen between the parties – after all, the language of the arbitration agreement is vague, so does not specifically refer to this type of dispute.

The reality this underlines is that the drafting of arbitration agreements is enormously important: not only may a poorly worded agreement be invalid, but even if it is valid it may be held not to cover the dispute that has actually arisen between the parties. Unfortunately, drafting of arbitration agreements is too often done by people unfamiliar with arbitration, or even unfamiliar with legal drafting, and as a result far too many arbitration agreements do not actually achieve the effect the parties intended them to have.

One effective solution that has been developed for this problem is "model" arbitration clauses, such as those provided by many arbitral institutions. These provide language that parties can incorporate into their contract, which the institution knows from experience will provide an enforceable and broad arbitration agreement. By way of example, the International Chamber of Commerce model arbitration clause reads as follows:

> "All disputes arising out of or in connection with the present contract shall be finally settled under the Rules of Arbitration of the International Chamber of Commerce by one or more arbitrators appointed in accordance with the said Rules."

Similarly, the Vienna International Arbitral Centre (VIAC) proposes the following model arbitration clause:

> "All disputes or claims arising out of or in connection with this contract including disputes relating to its validity, breach, termination or nullity shall be finally settled under the Rules of Arbitration of the International Arbitral Centre of the Austrian Federal Economic Chamber in Vienna (Vienna Rules) by one or three arbitrators appointed in accordance with the said Rules."

Both the ICC and VIAC then suggest potential additions to the agreement, VIAC suggesting the following:

> "(1) The provisions on expedited proceedings are applicable; (2) The number of arbitrators shall be . . . . (one or three); (3) The substantive law of . . . . shall be applicable; (4) The language to be used in the arbitral proceedings shall be . . . ."

The expression "arising out or in connection with" that is used in both of these model clauses is a consequence of legal decisions in certain jurisdictions that treated these two expressions differently, often holding that an arbitration clause covering disputes "arising out of" a contract covered a narrower range of disputes than a clause covering disputes "in connection with" a contract.[28] The model clauses above attempt to avoid this issue by simply incorporating both expressions into the agreement.

84 *The agreement to arbitrate*

Of course, model arbitration clauses suggested by arbitral institutions invariably incorporate an agreement to arbitrate under the auspices of that institution. This can be desirable, as such a clause also incorporates the arbitration rules of the institution into the agreement between the parties, resolving in advance many further disputes that may arise about the procedures to be used in the arbitration. However, *ad hoc* arbitration (arbitration without using an arbitral institution) is also legitimate, and in some jurisdictions is quite common. The need for a model arbitration agreement for *ad hoc* arbitration has been addressed by the United Nations Commission on International Trade Law (UNCITRAL), which provides the following clause in an appendix to its Arbitration Rules:

> "Any dispute, controversy or claim arising out of or relating to this contract, or the breach, termination or invalidity thereof, shall be settled by arbitration in accordance with the UNCITRAL Arbitration Rules."

UNCITRAL then suggests as potential additions to this agreement:

> "(a) The appointing authority shall be . . . [name of institution or person]; (b) The number of arbitrators shall be . . . [one or three]; (c) The place of arbitration shall be . . . [town and country]; (d) The language to be used in the arbitral proceedings shall be. . . . "

The reference to an "appointing authority" is particularly important for *ad hoc* arbitration, as it addresses the situation in which one of the parties to the arbitration agreement refuses to participate in selecting the arbitral tribunal. In an institutional arbitration, the institution's rules will include a mechanism for an arbitrator to be appointed on the defaulting party's behalf. In an *ad hoc* arbitration, on the other hand, the parties must agree on an individual or institution to perform this role, i.e. the appointing authority, unless such a mechanism is provided by the applicable law.

This divergence between the UNCITRAL model clause and the institutional clauses that preceded it underlines why it is usually best to use a model arbitration clause specifically designed for its intended purpose, rather than merely taking an arbitral institution's suggested clause and deleting the reference to the institution, or changing the institution's name.

8.2 Interpretation of the scope of an arbitration agreement

Whether arguments relating to the scope of an arbitration agreement are brought before an arbitral tribunal or a court, the question will arise as to the approach the tribunal should take in interpreting the agreement.[29] Some courts and arbitral tribunals adopt a "pro-arbitration" approach, construing the argument broadly to cover all disputes potentially covered by the language of the agreement.[30] This approach is often motivated by the rationale that the parties have clearly agreed to arbitrate some types of dispute, and it is unlikely that parties would voluntarily create an arbitration agreement that only covered a limited range of disputes, thereby potentially requiring them to both arbitrate and litigate at the same time. Other courts and arbitral tribunals, by contrast, are more restrictive and will only hold an arbitration agreement to be applicable to a dispute if it clearly falls under the language of the arbitration agreement.[31] This approach is motivated by traditional concerns, discussed above, regarding the impact of an arbitration agreement on the fundamental right of access to court.

Ultimately there is good reason to question the "pro-arbitration" approach taken by a growing number of courts and arbitral tribunals. Such an approach is certainly preferable to the restrictive approach still taken by many courts in less "arbitration-friendly" jurisdictions, which will often deprive parties of the benefits of the arbitration agreement they negotiated.[32] However, an approach that simply presumes that parties would want all their disputes to be arbitrated, for the sole reason that they have agreed that some of them should be, similarly deprives parties of the ability to choose their forum for a particular type of dispute – in this case, choosing litigation. Courts and arbitral tribunals that take seriously the idea that arbitration is about party consent and autonomy should also take seriously the idea that sometimes parties don't want to arbitrate, and that choice should not be overridden just to facilitate a "pro-arbitration" policy that the parties themselves may not share.

9. An agreement to arbitrate can be viewed as both a procedural agreement and as a substantive contract

9.1 Nature of the agreement to arbitrate

One particularly complex issue relating to the nature of an arbitration agreement centres on whether an arbitration agreement is properly understood as only a procedural agreement between the parties regarding how to resolve their substantive dispute, or as itself a substantive contract between the parties. This may seem like an oddly technical and inconsequential question, but it can have important consequences for parties who take actions subsequently found to have breached a valid arbitration agreement.

From the first point of view, an arbitration agreement does not involve any substantive rights of the parties, but instead merely reflects an agreement between the parties as to the forum in which disputes relating to their substantive obligations should be resolved. The consequence of this view is that where a party breaches an arbitration agreement by, for example, commencing litigation, the other party is only entitled to have the dispute referred to arbitration. If the litigation has resulted in a judgement, then that judgement can be refused enforcement, as it arose from a proceeding inconsistent with the agreement between the parties.

From the second point of view, an arbitration agreement is a standard contract between the parties, giving rise to substantive rights and obligations. As a result, if a party breaches the arbitration agreement, such as by commencing litigation, the other party is entitled to any of the standard remedies for breach of contract, including damages.[33] Under English law, for example, these damages have been held to include not only any expenses the non-breaching party incurred defending the litigation (e.g. attorney's fees and expenses, witness expenses, etc.), but even the value of any judgement given by the court against the non-breaching party.[34]

Perhaps unsurprisingly, the second point of view has particular support amongst arbitration professionals, as it provides the strongest support to arbitration. However, in cases in which the party now claiming damages for breach of the arbitration agreement had the opportunity to argue before the court that a binding arbitration agreement existed, whether

86 *The agreement to arbitrate*

it chose to take advantage of this opportunity or not, and where there is no fundamental objection to the fairness of the court proceeding, an award of damages is problematic, as it prioritises support for arbitration over respect for a legitimate decision by a court of a foreign jurisdiction.

9.2 Anti-suit injunctions in support of arbitration

While the preceding section has focused on the consequences that should follow when a party breaches an arbitration agreement, some jurisdictions also make available a mechanism designed to prevent such a breach happening in the first place, namely the anti-suit injunction. While anti-suit injunctions are available in some jurisdictions (e.g. England and Wales, the United States of America),[35] they are not available in others (e.g. the European Union if the injunction is directed against proceedings in another European Union court).[36] In general terms, an anti-suit injunction is a measure through which a court orders a party to refrain from commencing or continuing litigation before a foreign court, or arbitration before an arbitral tribunal. In the context of arbitration, this can happen in two forms, as illustrated by the following examples.

Firstly, say Julia and Nafisa have entered into a contract, and a dispute arises between them. Julia insists that the dispute is covered by an arbitration agreement, and so commences an arbitration seated in Moldova. Nafisa denies that there is a binding arbitration agreement between them that covers the dispute, and so commences litigation of the dispute in the courts of England and Wales. Nafisa convinces the English court that there is no binding arbitration agreement, and so the court issues an anti-suit injunction ordering Julia to terminate the arbitration. An injunction that is directed against an arbitration, rather than court litigation, is also sometimes called an "anti-arbitration injunction".

Secondly, imagine alternatively that Zoe has commenced litigation of her dispute with Montana in the courts of Mexico, even though Montana argues that there is a binding arbitration agreement between them which covers their dispute. Montana then goes to the courts of Australia, selected as the seat of the arbitration in the disputed arbitration agreement, and convinces a court that there is indeed a binding arbitration agreement which covers the dispute between her and Zoe. As a result, the Australian court issues an anti-suit injunction ordering Zoe to terminate her litigation in Mexico.

In the context of arbitration, then, an anti-suit injunction can be both a means of ensuring that parties adhere to arbitration agreements into which they have entered, and a means of ensuring that parties are not forced to arbitrate disputes they have not agreed to arbitrate.

It is, however, important to note against whom an anti-suit injunction is ordered, as this can differ significantly when the purpose of the injunction is to prevent an arbitration, compared with when the goal is to prevent a foreign litigation. That is, when a court is issuing an anti-suit injunction in order to prevent a litigation in a foreign court, the court does not actually tell the foreign court it cannot hear the case. Not only do courts in unconnected jurisdictions lack the power to force one another to refuse to hear a case, but judicial "comity" entails that it would be inappropriate for the courts of any State to order those of another State to take or not take any particular action.[37] As a result, an anti-suit injunction intended to terminate a foreign litigation is actually directed at the party that commenced the litigation, rather than at the court in which the litigation was commenced. It does not, that is, say to the court "you cannot hear this case", but says to the party "you must stop litigating in that other court".

An arbitral tribunal, however, is not part of any State court system, and so does not receive the same deference and respect as is received by foreign courts because of judicial "comity". As a result, courts can and do issue anti-suit injunctions specifically directed to an arbitral tribunal, ordering it not to continue with an arbitration. Because arbitrators are merely private individuals, there is nothing inappropriate in a court making such an order.

The question remains, of course, if the recipient of an anti-suit injunction, whether a party or an arbitral tribunal, must actually do what the court has ordered it to do. After all, while the intuition of most people is that we must do what a court has told us to do, this is less obviously true if the court is in a foreign jurisdiction with which we have no connection. For many people the natural response in such a situation would not be "I need to do what the court says", but "What right does this court have to tell me what to do?".

For a party in an arbitration or litigation ordered to refrain from that proceeding, then, this question is fundamentally a practical one. If the party will at any point require the assistance of the court issuing the anti-suit injunction, such as to enforce the award or judgement arising out of the proceeding he is being ordered not to continue, then there is little benefit in ignoring the anti-suit injunction, as the court has told him by issuing the injunction that he will not get that assistance.

In addition, however, some courts, particularly those in common law jurisdictions, can also enforce an anti-suit injunction by imposing "contempt" sanctions against a party that continues to arbitrate or litigate despite being ordered not to do so. Such sanctions could result in a fine far greater in value than the amount the party hopes to recover through the arbitration/litigation.[38] As a result, if the party receiving the anti-suit injunction has assets in any jurisdiction in which an order of the court issuing the injunction will be enforced, or plans future activities in any such jurisdiction, the anti-suit injunction needs to be obeyed.

Arbitrators receiving an anti-suit injunction, however, also have additional considerations that must be taken into account. While practical considerations such as those just mentioned are certainly relevant to arbitrators, and can justify arbitrators resigning their position on a tribunal, by agreeing to serve on a tribunal arbitrators have voluntarily incurred an obligation to assist the parties in arbitrating in accordance with their arbitration agreement. As a result, while some arbitrators see themselves as operating independently of State control, and so as not bound by an anti-suit injunction by a State court, the better view is that the tribunal is indeed bound when the court issuing the injunction is from the seat of the arbitration. The seat is the jurisdiction that the parties have selected to provide the law governing their arbitration, and so is the jurisdiction that provides the source of the tribunal's legal authority. As a result, valid orders of the courts of the seat should be respected and obeyed. On the other hand, however, where the court issuing the injunction is not from the seat of the arbitration, the tribunal has an obligation to continue with the arbitration, subject only to the practical considerations discussed above.

10. An arbitration agreement is technically only binding between the parties to the agreement, but non-parties can be bound under limited circumstances

10.1 The exceptional nature of non-parties being bound by an arbitration agreement

Because arbitration is based on consent, an arbitration agreement is only binding on those individuals or entities that have voluntarily agreed to be parties to the agreement. This is one of the significant limitations of arbitration: by way of example, if three companies are involved in a dispute, and two of them have agreed to arbitrate that dispute, the third company can effectively ignore any arbitration the other two parties commence; it can not only commence litigation in court regarding precisely the dispute covered by the arbitration agreement between the other two parties, but it is also not bound by any award delivered in that arbitration.

Courts have, however, held that in certain circumstances individuals or entities that are not formally parties to an arbitration agreement should nonetheless be held to be bound by that agreement. Such cases are exceptional, and do not undermine the general rule that an arbitration agreement only binds those individuals or entitles that have agreed to be bound by it. Rather, these cases are best understood as reflecting situations in which either a non-party to the agreement is so closely connected to one of the parties to the agreement that they should be treated as effectively the same as that party, or in which a non-party has led one or more of the parties to the arbitration agreement to believe that it will be bound by the arbitration agreement even though it is not formally a party to it.

This section will provide a brief overview of the primary grounds on which it has been found to be appropriate to bind a non-party to an arbitration agreement.

10.2 Agency

The use of agents is a standard part of commercial activity, and it is commonly accepted in legal systems around the world that if a party (the "principal") uses another party (the "agent") to conduct its business, then the agent will have the power to enter into agreements on the part of the principal in certain circumstances. The principal will then be bound by those agreements, even though it was not directly involved in their conclusion, and usually even if it did not know those agreements existed.[39]

Fundamentally an arbitration agreement is a type of contract, and so it should be unsurprising that it is generally accepted that an agent also has the ability to bind a principal to an arbitration agreement. Given that an arbitration agreement deprives a party of its fundamental right of access to court, it might seem that legitimate questions can be raised about the application of this doctrine in the context of arbitration. However, ultimately the principal has voluntarily decided to conduct its activities through the use of an agent, and there is no reason that the standard principles of agency law should not be applied to an arbitration agreement in the same way that they are applied to any other contract – the consequences of which, after all, might be significantly more harmful to the principal than a simple obligation to arbitrate.

10.3 Succession

Another context in which questions have been raised about whether a party is bound by an arbitration agreement despite not having agreed to arbitrate, is when one party succeeds another as a party to an arbitration agreement. This can happen both to individuals, whose obligations and rights may be transferred to another person upon their death, and to corporations and other entities, such as when two corporations merge.

While the laws relating to succession vary from one jurisdiction to another, it is now widely accepted that arbitration agreements are indeed binding on a successor, even though the successor has not itself agreed to arbitrate.[40] This must be the correct conclusion. After all, the other party to the arbitration agreement potentially relied upon the existence of the arbitration agreement when deciding to enter into the contract or transaction from which the successor is now drawing benefits. It would, as a result, be fundamentally unfair to that party to deprive it of its contractual right to arbitrate.

10.4 Assignment

Related to succession, assignment involves one of the original parties to a contract transferring its rights and obligations under the contract to a different party. For example, Shivam enters into a contract containing an arbitration agreement with Rhona. Rhona then enters into an agreement with Haaris under which Haaris takes on all of Rhona's obligations under the contract, and also gains all of the contractual benefits that Rhona would otherwise have gained. Is Haaris obligated to arbitrate any disputes that are covered by the arbitration agreement, even though there is no arbitration agreement directly between Shivam and Haaris?

While some authorities hold that assignment of an arbitration agreement is not automatic, but rather requires a specific agreement between the assignee and the original counterparty to the contract (i.e. between Haaris and Shivam),[41] the prevailing view is that the obligation to arbitrate is indeed transferred to the assignee.[42] The assignee has, after all, voluntarily agreed to take on the assignor's role in the transaction, and the arbitration agreement was an essential component of that transaction. As a result, holding that the assignee is not bound to arbitrate with the counterparty deprives the counterparty of an important component of the transaction to which it agreed.

There is, however, a generally acknowledged exception to the possibility of assigning or transferring an arbitration agreement that should be noted given the centrality of the doctrine of separability to arbitration. That is, an assignee will usually not be bound by an arbitration agreement in a contract if that contract excludes the possibility of assignment or transfer of its obligations. In such a situation, the assignment of the main contract will usually be held to be null and void, and the arbitration clause will similarly be held to not bind the assignee – even though the arbitration clause is regarded as a separate contract from the contract in which it is contained, and itself includes no provision forbidding assignment.

10.5 Piercing the corporate veil

One of the realities of contemporary business is that it is often conducted by companies with complex internal structures, involving a plurality of legally distinct entities that are ultimately part of a broader overarching structure. While such structures can create significant benefits for the companies that use them, they can also create difficulties for individuals and entities that enter into transactions with entities within that structure.

By way of example, presume that Tempest Acoustics is negotiating a commercial contract with the multinational corporation Sprite Productions, for a transaction to be performed in Mozambique. The contract, which includes an arbitration agreement, is entered into by Tempest Acoustics and by "Sprite Productions Mozambique", an entity incorporated in Mozambique but legally distinct from Sprite Productions itself. "Sprite Productions Mozambique", however, is what is sometimes called a "mailbox" company: it has a formal legal existence, so can enter into contracts, but it has no assets and performs no actual commercial activity. Instead, all the obligations under the contract between Tempest Acoustics and Sprite Productions Mozambique are actually performed by Sprite Productions. In such a situation, if a dispute arises Tempest Acoustics will have little interest in arbitrating with Sprite Productions Mozambique – it has no assets, and so could not pay an award even if Tempest Acoustics were to be successful. Instead, Tempest Acoustics will want to commence arbitration proceedings against Sprite Productions, even though only Sprite Productions Mozambique, not Sprite Productions itself, entered into the arbitration agreement.

In some legal systems it is possible for Tempest Acoustics to "lift" or "pierce" the "corporate veil", i.e. to argue that Sprite Productions and Sprite Productions Mozambique should be treated as effectively the same entity, thereby giving Tempest Acoustics the right to arbitrate with Sprite Productions based on the agreement to arbitrate between Tempest Acoustics and Sprite Productions Mozambique.[43] While the expression "piercing the corporate veil" is sometimes used quite broadly to refer to any attempt to hold one member of a corporate group responsible for the actions of another, it is used here in its more specific meaning, referring to the narrower question of when a parent company or shareholder should be held to be effectively the same as a formally separate entity, and thus responsible for that entity's actions and liabilities.

Standards vary significantly between jurisdictions as to when such "piercing" will be allowed, and in some jurisdictions (e.g. England and Wales) attempts to pierce the corporate veil are rarely successful. However, in other jurisdictions Tempest Acoustics may be successful in its attempt to force Sprite Productions to arbitrate, particularly if Sprite Productions is found to have been using Sprite Productions Mozambique as nothing more than an "alter ago", such as if Sprite Productions and Sprite Productions Mozambique were in reality actually run as a single company despite their formal separation, with the same corporate officers controlling both entities, money being transferred between the two entities at will, etc. In such a case, courts in some jurisdictions will disregard the formal separateness of Sprite Productions and Sprite Productions Mozambique, concentrating instead on the substantive identity of the two companies, and as a result will hold Sprite Productions to be bound by the same obligations that bind Sprite Productions Mozambique, including the obligation to arbitrate with Tempest Acoustics.

10.6 The group of companies doctrine

An alternative approach to the issue of corporate structures exists in some jurisdictions under the name of the "group of companies" doctrine.[44] Under this doctrine, a group of formally separate companies that are nonetheless part of the same corporate "group" can be treated as a single economic reality, thereby binding all the members of the group to an arbitration agreement concluded by only one of them, so long as (i) the role played by each of them in the conclusion, performance or termination of the contract that includes the arbitration agreement indicates that their participation in the contract was actually as a single entity, despite their formal separateness, and (ii) it is established that it was the common intention of the parties to the arbitration agreement that the non-signatory parties also be bound.

In other words, while piercing the corporate veil will usually only occur when a tribunal has determined that two or more related corporate entities should be treated as effectively the same entity, the group of companies doctrine requires merely that in terms of the substance of the transaction to which the arbitration agreement relates, those entities acted as a single economic whole, and the parties to the arbitration agreement mutually intended that it would also bind those other entities. As a result, while the specific circumstances in which the group of companies doctrine will be applied can vary from one jurisdiction to another, where the doctrine is accepted it provides an alternative and often more generous approach to obligating non-parties to arbitrate than will be found in jurisdictions that rely instead on principles relating to piercing the corporate veil.

Understanding arbitration through case-law

Group of companies: endorsement

Case details: *Dow Chemical France, The Dow Chemical Company and others v ISOVER Saint Gobain*, Interim Award, ICC Case No. 4131, 23 September 1982

Authority deciding the case: ICC arbitral tribunal

Facts of the case: The French company ISOVER Saint Gobain was a party to two distribution contracts with the Dow Chemical Group, a multinational group of companies. A first contract, concluded in 1965, was entered into between ISOVER Saint Gobain and Dow Chemical (Venezuela), the latter later assigning it to Dow Chemical A.G., a subsidiary of the Dow Chemical Company. A second contract, concluded in 1968, was entered into between ISOVER Saint Gobain and Dow Chemical Europe, a subsidiary of Dow Chemical A.G.

According to the contracts, ISOVER Saint Gobain would distribute on the French market thermal isolation equipment produced by the Dow Chemical Group. Both contracts included an ICC arbitration clause and specified that deliveries of materials could be made by Dow Chemical France, or any other subsidiary of the Dow Chemical Company.

A complex dispute arose between the parties, and several companies belonging to the Dow Chemical group commenced ICC arbitration against ISOVER Saint Gobain. More specifically, the claimants in the arbitration were Dow Chemical A.G., Dow Chemical Europe, Dow Chemical France and the Dow Chemical Company. While the first two claimants had signed an arbitration agreement (respectively in the 1965 and in the 1968 contracts), the other two claimants had not signed the contract containing the ICC arbitration clause. For this reason, ISOVER Saint Gobain objected to the jurisdiction of the arbitral tribunal, arguing that the effects of the agreement to arbitrate did not extend to those members of the Dow Chemical Group (Dow Chemical France and the Dow Chemical Company) that had not signed it.

Decision: The tribunal dismissed the objection and held that it had jurisdiction over all of the parties in the arbitration. To reach this conclusion, the tribunal adopted a pragmatic approach, considering the practical reality of the commercial relationship between the parties rather than the formal corporate structure of the Dow Chemical group.

First of all, the tribunal noted that during the negotiations of the contract, neither of the parties attached importance to which of the companies forming the Dow Chemical group would sign the contract. That is, ISOVER effectively negotiated with the "aggregate" of those companies, rather than with one of them in particular. Furthermore, both contracts specified that deliveries could be made by Dow Chemical France or any other subsidiary, and in fact Dow Chemical France did perform the obligations arising out of the contracts. Dow Chemical France, hence, played an important role in the performance of the contract, as did the "mother" Dow Chemical Company. Namely, the Dow Chemical Company owned the trademarks and had absolute control over the subsidiaries engaging in a commercial relationship with ISOVER Saint Gobain.

On these grounds, the tribunal concluded that the companies forming the Dow Chemical group constituted "a single economic reality". The arbitration agreement, hence, should bind the members of the group which, in light of their role in the conclusion, performance or termination of the contract and in accordance with the parties' intention, have *de facto* been parties to the contract, although without directly signing it. The tribunal further noted that this pragmatic approach is consistent with the needs of international commerce.

Group of companies: rejection

Case details: *Peterson Farms Inc. v C&M Farming Ltd* [2004] EWHC 121 (Comm)

Authority deciding the case: English Commercial Court

Facts of the case: C&M and Peterson entered into a sales contract. The contract was governed by Arkansas law and included an arbitration clause, providing for ICC arbitration with seat in London.

> A dispute arose and C&M commenced arbitration against Peterson, alleging that Peterson had caused losses not only for C&M, but also for other companies belonging to the C&M group, which were not parties to the arbitration agreement. The arbitral tribunal awarded damages to C&M and to the other entities of the C&M group. In order to justify its decision, the arbitrators relied (among other arguments) on the authority of the *Dow Chemical* award (see p. 000) and held that the group of companies doctrine justified the extension of arbitral jurisdiction over claims of non-parties *de facto* belonging to the same economic entity. Specifically, the tribunal argued that the doctrine of separability entailed that the arbitration clause did not have to be interpreted in accordance with the law of Arkansas, which governed the main contract, and held that instead it would be interpreted "in accordance with the common intent of the parties".
>
> Interestingly, the tribunal did not merely refer to the "group of companies" doctrine, but specifically stated that it was "following" the *Dow Chemical* and two other awards, just as a court will describe itself as "following" non-binding decisions by another court within the same legal system. In effect, that is, the tribunal treated these awards as sources of a form of transnational arbitrator-made law.
>
> Peterson challenged the award before the English Commercial Court, which was competent to hear the case because London had been set as seat of arbitration.
>
> **Decision:** The Commercial Court rejected the tribunal's reliance on a generalised notion of the "common intent of the parties", holding instead that the issue of which entities were and were not party to the arbitration agreement had to be resolved in accordance with Arkansas law, as the law applicable to the main contract. The parties had agreed that Arkansas law was the same as English law, and so the principles of English law were applied. The Court held that the group of companies doctrine "forms no part of English law" and therefore annulled the part of the award that ordered Peterson to pay damages to other members of the C&M group.

Notes

1. Some authors have argued that arbitration should become the fall-back dispute resolution mechanism for international commercial relationships, to be automatically used whenever the parties have not included a different provision in their contract: see, e.g., Gary B Born, "BITs, BATs and Buts: Reflections on International Dispute Resolution", ESIL Lecture, Nottingham School of Law, 25 March 2015; Gilles Cuniberti, *Rethinking International Commercial Arbitration: Towards Default Arbitration* (Elgar 2017). These proposals, however, have not yet been implemented, and there are strong reasons to doubt the desirability of such an approach.
2. See e.g. Japanese Arbitration Law, Article 13(1).
3. See e.g. French Civil Code, Article 2059, Article 2 of the Spanish Arbitration Act, or Article 1 of the Brazilian Arbitration Act.

94 *The agreement to arbitrate*

4   *Mitsubishi Motors Corp. v Soler Chrysler-Plymouth, Inc.*, 473 US 614 (1985). For a detailed explanation, see the box in the main text.
5   Case C-126/97, *Eco Swiss China Time Ltd v Benetton International NV*, ECLI:EU:C:1999:269. For a detailed explanation, see the box in the main text.
6   The World Intellectual Property Organization (WIPO) offers administrative services for arbitrations concerning intellectual property rights. The prominence of WIPO as an administering institution demonstrates that intellectual property disputes are routinely submitted to arbitration.
7   See e.g. Article 7(2) of the Indian Arbitration and Conciliation Act, based on the UNCITRAL Model Law.
8   See, e.g., Section 63 of the 2007 Guernsey Trusts Law; Article 41 of the 1984 Panama Trust Law.
9   See, e.g., Article 3 of the 1992 Finish Arbitration Act; Article 1163 of the Polish Code of Civil Procedure; Article 11(bis)(3) of the Spanish Arbitration Act; Articles 34–35 of Italian Legislative Decree 5 of 17 January 2003.
10 There are, however, some legal systems that recognise the validity of arbitration clauses in testamentary wills: see Article 3 of the 1992 Finnish Arbitration Act and Article 10 of the 2003 Spanish Arbitration Act.
11 There are, however, exceptional cases in which an arbitral tribunal is seised of the question concerning the existence of a valid arbitration agreement as a main subject matter of the arbitration: an example in this respect is the *Gazprom* case, that was eventually referred to the Court of Justice of the European Union: see Case C-536/13, *"Gazprom" OAO v Lietuvos Respublika*, ECLI:EU:C:2015:316. For a detailed overview of the complex procedural development of the case see the opinion of the Advocate General, ECLI:EU:C:2014:2414.
12 Given its German origins, this approach to the doctrine is sometimes referred to with its German name: "Kompetenz-Kompetenz".
13 Along similar lines, the courts of a State other than the seat of an arbitration may also not be bound to respect the judgment rendered by the courts of the seat concerning the existence and validity of the agreement to arbitrate. In the European Union, in particular, Regulation 1215/2012 (the Brussels I *bis* Regulation) clarifies, at Recital 12(2), that "a ruling given by a court of a Member State as to whether or not an arbitration agreement is null and void, inoperative or incapable of being performed should not be subject to the rules of recognition and enforcement laid down in [the Brussels I *bis*] Regulation, regardless of whether the court decided on this as a principal issue or as an incidental question".
14 In *Republic of Kazakhstan v Istil Group Inc*. [2006] EWHC 448 (Comm), the English Commercial Court set a London Court of International Arbitration award aside on the grounds of lack of substantive jurisdiction, as the arbitrators had ignored a previous French court judgment holding that the arbitration agreement in question did not cover the dispute between the parties. In *Fomento de Construcciones y Contratas SA v Colon Container Terminal S.A.* (2001) 19 ASA Bull 555, the Swiss Federal Tribunal set an award aside, as the arbitrators had claimed jurisdiction and failed to apply *lis pendens* in favour of Panamanian courts, which eventually ruled that the arbitration agreement was inoperative due to one party's failure to raise the issue of the agreement's existence in a timely fashion.
15 See Article 178(2) of the Swiss Private International Law Statute.
16 See Article 34(2)(a)(i) of the UNCITRAL Model Law.
17 *Camimalaga, S.A.U. v DAF Vehiculos Industriales S.A.U.*, Madrid Audiencia Provincial Civil, Decision No. 147/2013; *Rampton v Eyre*, Ontario Court of Appeal [2007] ONCA 331; *P. T. Tri-M.G. Intra Asia Airlines v Norse Air Charter Limited*, Singapore High Court [2009] SGHC 13; German Bundesgerichtshof, VII ZR 105/06; *Librati v Barka Co. Ltd*, Superior Court of Quebec [2007] QCCS 5724.

The agreement to arbitrate 95

18 *Kenon Engineering Ltd v Nippon Kokan Koji Kabushiki Kaisha*, Hong Kong Court of Appeal [2004] HKCA 101; *Grandeur Electrical Co. Ltd v Cheung Kee Fung Cheung Construction Co. Ltd*, Hong Kong Court of Appeal [2006] HKCA 305; *WSG Nimbus Pte. Ltd v Board of Control for Cricket in Sri Lanka*, Singapore High Court [2002] SGHC 104.

19 Isabelle Hautot and Georges Flécheux, "La clause de règlement des différends dans les Conditions F.I.D.I.C. génie civil de 1987" (1989) 4 *Revue de l'Arbitrage* 609.

20 See e.g. Article II(1) of the New York Convention and Article 7(1) of the UNCITRAL Model Law.

21 UNCITRAL Working Group II (Arbitration), Compilation of Comments by Governments, Note by the Secretariat, UN Doc A/CN.9/661 (6 May 2008).

22 UNCITRAL Model Law, Option 1, Article 7(4). Along similar lines, see e.g. Article 1162 of the Polish Code of Civil Procedure or Article 13 of the Japanese Arbitration Law.

23 UNCITRAL Model Law, Option 1, Article 7(6).

24 UNCITRAL Model Law, Option 1, Article 7(3).

25 Neil Andrews, *Arbitration and Contract Law* (Springer 2016) 24.

26 See, e.g., Article 1507 of the French Code of Civil Procedure.

27 UNCITRAL Model Law, Option 1, Article 7(5); English Arbitration Act, Sections 31 and 73; Polish Code of Civil Procedure, Article 1180. Many sets of arbitration rules follow the same approach: see, e.g., Article 23.3 of the 2014 LCIA Arbitration Rules, providing that if the respondent wishes to object that the tribunal does not have jurisdiction, it must generally do so as soon as possible but not later than the time for its statement of defence.

28 *Ashville Investments Ltd v Elmer Contractors Ltd*, Court of Appeal (England and Wales) [1989] Q.B. 488.

29 In some cases, the law applicable to the clause provides guidance, by clarifying that the agreement should in principle be interpreted as encompassing all disputes arising out of the contract or the relationship to which the agreement refers. See, for example, Article 808 *quater* of the Italian Code of Civil Procedure; Article 15(2) of the 1996 Maltese Arbitration Act; Art 550(3) of the Romanian Civil Procedure Code.

30 See, e.g. German Bundesgerichtshof, judgment of 27 February 1970 (1990) 6 *Arbitration International* 79; *Premium Nafta Products Limited and others v Fili Shipping Company Ltd*, House of Lords [2007] 4 All ER 951; *Fiona Trust & Holding Corp v Privalov*, Court of Appeal (England and Wales) [2007] EWCA Civ 20.

31 See, e.g., *Shuffman v Rudd Plastic Fabrics Corp.*, 407 N.Y.S.2d 565, 566 (N.Y. App. Div. 1978).

32 See, e.g., *Guangdong v Conagra*, Hong Kong Court of First Instance 1992, 247, drawing an unusual distinction between "disputes" and "controversies".

33 Julio César Betancourt, "Damages for breach of an international arbitration agreement under English arbitration law" (2018) 34(4) *Arbitration International* 511.

34 Adrian Briggs, *Agreements on Jurisdiction and Choice of Law* (OUP 2008) 499–504.

35 Robert Merkin and Louis Flannery, *Arbitration Act 1996* (5th edn, Informa 2014) 187–188.

36 Regulation (EU) No 1215/2012 of the European Parliament and of the Council of 12 December 2012 on jurisdiction and the recognition and enforcement of judgments in civil and commercial matters; Case C-185/07, *Allianz SpA and Generali Assicurazioni Generali SpA v West Tankers Inc.*, ECLI:EU:C:2009:69; Case C-536/13 (n 11).

37 *British Airways Board v Laker Airways Ltd*, House of Lords [1985] A.C. 58, 95. Adrian Briggs, *Private International Law in English Courts* (Oxford 2014) 390; Neil Andrews, *Andrews on Civil Process* (Intersentia 2013) vol. 2, 229.

38 Criminal punishment for contempt of court is also possible, but far more rarely imposed.

39 *FR German buyer v Thai seller, Award*, WVHB Case No. 23/1982, 12 March 1984, in Albert Jan van den Berg (ed.), *ICCA Yearbook Commercial Arbitration*, XVI (ICCA 1991) 11.

40 Swiss Federal Tribunal, Judgment of 19 May 2003 (2004) 22 ASA Bull. 344.
41 Italian Court of Cassation, Judgment no. 12616 of 17 December 1998.
42 *HT of Highlands Ranch, Inc. v Hollywood Tanning Sys., Inc.*, 590 F.Supp.2d 677, 684 (D.N.J. 2008).
43 See, e.g., award in ICC Case No. 8385, in Jean-Jacques Arnaldez, Yves Derains and Dominique Hascher (eds), *Collection of ICC Arbitral Awards 1996–2000* (Kluwer 2003) 474; *Cape Pac. Ltd v. Lubner Controlling Inv. Pty Ltd*, South Africa Supreme Court of Appeal [1995] (4) SA 790 (AD).
44 See, e.g. *Dow Chemical France, The Dow Chemical Company and others v ISOVER Saint Gobain*, Interim Award, ICC Case No. 4131, 23 September 1982 in Pieter Sanders (ed.), *Yearbook Commercial Arbitration IX (ICCA 1984)*) 131–137. Note, however, that the doctrine has been rejected by some national courts. See, e.g. *Peterson Farms Inc. v C&M Farming Ltd* [2004] 1 *Lloyd's Rep* 603 (Q.B.).

4 The arbitral tribunal

Rules

1. Selecting your arbitrators is selecting your arbitration

Selecting an arbitral tribunal is not just a matter of selecting the people who will decide your dispute. No decision you make in the course of entering into your arbitration agreement or during the arbitration will have as great an impact on the arbitral process, and on the content of the final award, as the decision on who the arbitrator(s) should be.

2. Parties' choice of arbitrator is virtually unrestricted

Since the identity of arbitrators can have such a major impact on an arbitration, it is important that parties control this decision. As a result, in the most developed arbitration jurisdictions, parties are largely free to select any individual they wish to be their arbitrator.

3. Parties can state in their arbitration agreement how arbitrators are to be selected

If an arbitration agreement specifies a method for selecting arbitrators, then this method must be used unless the parties agree to change it. The most common method in international arbitration allows each party to select one arbitrator, with a third being selected either by agreement between the parties or by agreement of the party-appointed arbitrators. Parties can also agree to delegate selection of arbitrators to an independent third party.

4. Arbitration rules and laws often include a "back-up" method for selecting arbitrators

If parties haven't agreed on how to select their arbitrators, but have agreed to use a set of arbitration rules, they have thereby agreed to use whatever arbitrator selection mechanism those rules contain. If parties have not even agreed on a set of arbitration rules, the arbitration statute of the seat of the arbitration will usually include a mechanism for selecting arbitrators, which will then be applicable.

5. A tribunal can include any number of arbitrators

While most tribunals include either one or three arbitrators, few laws or arbitration rules limit the number of arbitrators that can be on a tribunal. As a result, parties are usually free to agree on any number of arbitrators they think is appropriate for their dispute.

6. The failure of a method of selecting arbitrators is rarely terminal for an arbitration

The parties' agreed mechanism for selecting a tribunal may be inconsistent with the law of the seat of the arbitration, or may simply not result in a tribunal being selected. In most jurisdictions, this does not invalidate the arbitration agreement, and the failed mechanism is simply replaced with another, provided either by the applicable arbitration rules or by the *lex arbitri* itself.

7. An arbitrator can be appointed on behalf of a party

If an arbitrator appointment mechanism grants a party the right to appoint an arbitrator, but the party doesn't do so, this does not stop the arbitration. Instead, arbitration rules and laws standardly allow an independent third party to appoint an arbitrator on that party's behalf.

8. Almost anyone can be an arbitrator

While there are still some jurisdictions that require arbitrators to have particular qualifications or characteristics, most jurisdictions do not. As a result, almost anyone can be an arbitrator, so long as parties are willing to appoint them.

9. Arbitral institutions often compile lists of potential arbitrators

Many arbitral institutions compile lists of potential arbitrators. While standards used in compiling such lists vary enormously, that an individual appears on one or more lists of prominent arbitral institutions can provide parties with some level of assurance that the individual has a reasonable understanding of arbitration.

10. Arbitrators must be both independent and impartial

Arbitrators can be prevented from joining a tribunal, or can be removed from a tribunal, if they do not meet applicable standards of independence and impartiality. "Independence" refers to the objective relationship between an arbitrator and either the parties or other important individuals in the arbitration. "Impartiality" focuses on the subjective mindset of an arbitrator with respect to the case or to the individuals involved in that case.

11. Interviews of prospective arbitrators have become more common

Interviewing an arbitrator before deciding whether or not to appoint her provides a valuable opportunity for one or both parties to get a clearer idea of an arbitrator's approach to her role, and to her views on matters of importance to them in selecting an arbitrator. However, it also creates significant risks for both parties and arbitrators, as a poorly conducted interview can subsequently give rise to a claim that an arbitrator lacks impartiality.

12. Arbitrators can be "challenged" by parties for lacking independence or impartiality

Arbitration laws and rules almost universally include mechanisms allowing any party in an arbitration to bring a "challenge" against an arbitrator, arguing either that the arbitrator should not be appointed to the tribunal, or that she should be removed. If the challenge is successful, a replacement arbitrator will have to be nominated, subject again to the same standards of independence and impartiality, and to the right of any party to bring a challenge against her.

13. In some circumstances arbitrators may be removed despite not being challenged by a party

Some arbitration rules and laws allow an arbitral institution or a court to remove an arbitrator who is not performing or is not able to perform the role of arbitrator, even when facts do not exist that would allow the arbitrator to be challenged.

14. Arbitrators who leave a tribunal are usually replaced, but in some circumstances will not be

If an arbitrator is removed from a tribunal, resigns, or becomes unable to perform her function, she will usually be replaced through a mechanism agreed by the parties, or alternatively through a mechanism derived from the applicable arbitration rules or from the law of the seat. However, in a limited number of situations, the tribunal may be allowed to complete the arbitration as a "truncated tribunal", with the missing arbitrator not being replaced.

15. Arbitrators work under a contract with the parties

Arbitrators are private individuals who have been hired by the parties to decide their dispute, and the rights and obligations of an arbitrator are defined in what is known as the "arbitrator's contract". This is a separate agreement from the arbitration agreement, and is an agreement between all the parties in the arbitration and the arbitrator.

16. Arbitrators are rarely legally liable for acts taken in performance of their function

Many arbitration laws grant arbitrators immunity for acts taken in their role as arbitrator, although the extent of arbitral immunity varies from one jurisdiction to another. Arbitral immunity is intended to ensure arbitrators can perform their role without being improperly influenced by the parties.

Analysis

1. Selecting your arbitrators is selecting your arbitration

Arguably the single thing most commonly identified as being a benefit of arbitration is its flexibility. Parties in an arbitration can agree where to hold any hearings, what procedural rules should be applied, how long the process should take, and even who decides their dispute. Indeed, this latter choice is probably the most important decision parties take when arbitrating, although it is often not appreciated just how important that decision can be.

By way of illustration, imagine you entered into an international sales contract for the shipment of chickens. You have already shipped the chickens to the other party, but they are now insisting that they only have to pay you half the amount you were expecting to receive, as half the chickens had black feathers. You check your contract, and realise that the language in the contract does seem to require that you ship white chickens – even though at the time of negotiating the contract you specifically agreed with the other party that some of the chickens would have black feathers. As a result, whether you get paid in full will depend on whether the arbitrator deciding your dispute emphasises the language included in the contract, or is willing to look at additional evidence regarding what you and the other party actually agreed – even if this contradicts the language of the contract.

The law applicable to the contract is that of State X, and there is an ongoing argument amongst legal scholars in State X as to whether contractual language is all that matters, or if the intentions of the contracting parties matters more.

The other party suggests to you that the fairest solution is to appoint as arbitrator Judge A, who recently retired from the commercial court in State X. They argue that as a former judge he can be trusted to be fair and unbiased, and will know the law in State X, including the subtleties of its contract law. Moreover, while he has no experience of being an arbitrator, he has dealt with arbitration agreements and awards while a judge, and so is familiar with arbitration. That proposal sounds reasonable to you, so you agree.

Unfortunately, what you didn't realise, was that just before retiring, Judge A delivered a judgement in which he held that contracts governed by the law of State X should always be interpreted in accordance with their clear language – even if this language contradicts the intentions of the parties.

Unless you can convince Judge A that his previous view was wrong, you have now lost your arbitration – simply because you picked the "wrong" arbitrator.

Of course, in real life disputes are rarely this simple, and will almost never turn on a single question of law. The point, however, is to emphasise just how significant an impact the selection of an arbitrator can have.

Moreover, the question is not just one of the substance of the law. Let's change the example, and assume that Judge A has actually never decided a case on whether contract language should be interpreted literally – so it is unclear what his view on this issue is. You agree to use him as your arbitrator, for precisely the reasons mentioned above.

However, as is usually the case, your arbitration agreement includes no details regarding the procedure for your arbitration. You and the opposing party discuss how you would like the arbitration to function, but you just can't reach agreement on a range of important issues. As a result, Judge A, as your arbitrator, ends up making the procedural decisions.

Judge A, though, has spent his entire life running proceedings in the courts of State X, and is worried that if he starts adopting new procedures, he might make a mistake. After all, he doesn't want his award to be unenforceable, or for the parties to complain about how he ran the arbitration. So he sticks with what he knows.

You now have an arbitration that is run exactly like a court, thereby losing you one of the major benefits of arbitration over litigation: its procedural flexibility. Of course, again, real life can be different, and there are certainly former judges and even current judges who are excellent arbitrators. However, there are also parties who have selected a judge as an arbitrator, only to find themselves effectively in a court room – although in some cases this is precisely what they wanted.

Selecting your arbitrators, that is, is not just a matter of selecting the people who will decide your dispute, by interpreting and applying the applicable substantive law. It is, in effect, selecting your arbitration, as no decision you make in the course of entering into your arbitration agreement or during the arbitration, will have as great an impact on the arbitral process, and on the content of the final award, as the decision on who the arbitrator(s) should be.

2. Parties' choice of arbitrator is often unrestricted

While there are risks in selecting an arbitrator, there are also clear benefits, and the ability to select the members of an arbitral tribunal is one of the key advantages of arbitration over litigation. Precisely because the identity of arbitrators can have such a major impact on an arbitration, it is important that parties have the ability to control this decision. The repeated assertions of the importance of "party autonomy" in arbitration would mean little if parties were simply told who their arbitrators were going to be.

Indeed, the importance of parties having the freedom to select their own arbitrators is so broadly recognised that few jurisdictions now place significant limits on who can serve as an arbitrator. Indeed, in the most developed arbitration jurisdictions, parties are free to select any individual they wish to be their arbitrator, so long as she is legally competent and thereby able to render an enforceable award.

One consequence of this freedom is, of course, that parties may choose badly, and end up with an arbitrator who doesn't understand the applicable law, or fails to run the arbitration in a competent manner. The parties may, in short, end up wishing they had gone to court. However, the benefits are potentially enormous, as parties involved in a dispute regarding complex technical matters can select a tribunal that understands those matters; parties from different cultural backgrounds can ensure that they both have someone on the tribunal who understands their perspective; parties whose dispute involves a relatively small amount of money can choose to use less prestigious arbitrators who will cost less, while those whose dispute involves a large amount can pay significantly more for a more experienced and high-profile tribunal, and so on. The ability to select arbitrators is a core component of the central role of the principle of party autonomy in arbitration, as it allows parties to tailor their arbitration to their specific needs and wishes.[1]

Consistent with this, the mechanism used for selecting arbitrators varies from case to case, in accordance with the arbitration agreement between the parties. Sometimes the parties' arbitration agreement expressly specifies a certain mechanism of appointment, and unless the parties mutually agree to change that mechanism, that is now how the arbitrators must be appointed. In other cases, and more commonly, the parties will have entered into an arbitration agreement but will not have specified how the arbitrators are to be selected. In this situation, the arbitration agreement remains valid, but the mechanism for appointing the arbitrators must be found elsewhere. These two different scenarios will be examined separately in the following pages.

3. Parties can state in their arbitration agreement how arbitrators are to be selected

Consistent with the role of party autonomy in international commercial arbitration, *lex arbitri* standardly grant parties significant discretion in choosing their mechanism for the selection of arbitrators. As a result, when parties have included a mechanism for selecting arbitrators in their arbitration agreement, this method will usually be applied. There are several common techniques used for the selection of arbitrators, but they can be understood under two broad headings, as follows.

3.1 Parties can appoint the arbitrators directly in their arbitration agreement

The most straight-forward method by which parties can select their arbitrators is simply to specify in the arbitration agreement who the arbitrator(s) will be. This often happens when an arbitration agreement is entered into by the parties after a dispute has arisen, but is much rarer in pre-dispute arbitration agreements. This is because in the case of post-dispute arbitration agreements, the parties are aware of the nature of their dispute when entering into the agreement, and so can make an informed choice as to who would be an appropriate arbitrator.

In pre-dispute arbitration agreements, however, which form the vast majority of arbitration agreements, specifying arbitrators by name can be far more problematic. Firstly, the choice will have been made before the parties are aware of the details of their dispute – as a result, they may end up with an arbitrator who does not have the expertise required to resolve their dispute well. Even more problematically, by the time a dispute arises, the arbitrator may no longer be available to serve, or one of the parties may no longer wish her to be the arbitrator.

For example, Blythe and Ava-May agree that Professor Streckland will be an ideal arbitrator, and so they specify in their arbitration agreement that Professor Streckland will be their arbitrator. However, if a dispute requiring arbitration does arise between Blythe and Ava-May, it may not do so for several years. What if Professor Streckland dies in the meantime? Do the Blythe and Ava-May still have an enforceable arbitration agreement? One of them may insist, after all, that they only agreed to arbitration because Professor Streckland was going to be the arbitrator, and that without that restriction, they would never have agreed to arbitrate.

Alternatively, what if Professor Streckland is still alive, but just no longer wishes to be the arbitrator, or there is some obstacle making it difficult for her to perform the role? Perhaps she has retired, and no longer serves as an arbitrator.

Alternatively, maybe she is willing to be arbitrator, but now has a very active arbitration practice, and so would not be able to commence the arbitration for at least another 18 months, significantly delaying the process.

Again, what if Professor Streckland is happy to commence the arbitration immediately, but has left her university position and now works for Blythe? Or, more colourfully, what if Ava-May recently had an affair with Professor Streckland's husband?

Jurisdictions differ on how such cases should be resolved, and those jurisdictions most supportive of arbitration will attempt to determine whether Professor Streckland serving as the arbitrator was indeed essential to the arbitration agreement, or just something the parties saw as desirable. If the former, then the arbitration agreement won't be enforced, while in the latter scenario it will. However, in other jurisdictions courts will simply refuse to enforce an arbitration agreement that specifies an individual as arbitrator if that individual cannot perform the role.

Specifying the identify of an arbitrator at the time of entering in an arbitration can seem appealing, as it allows the parties to agree on an arbitrator while they are happy to cooperate, before any dispute has arisen. However, for the reasons just given, it is rarely a good idea.

3.2 Parties can select a method of appointment in their arbitration agreement

The more common approach to addressing the selection of arbitrators in an arbitration agreement is by specifying the method through which the members of the arbitral tribunal must be appointed, rather than by naming particular arbitrators. The principle of party autonomy means that parties are usually free to use almost any mechanism for selecting their arbitrators, although obviously some methods are more common than others.

By far the most commonly used method in international commercial arbitration, sometimes referred to as the "binary clause", results in the selection of a tribunal of three arbitrators. Under this method, each of the parties has the right to unilaterally appoint one arbitrator, these two arbitrators often being referred to as "party-appointed" arbitrators, or less commonly "wing" arbitrators. Usually, the claimant will appoint its preferred arbitrator when it files the Request for Arbitration, commencing the proceedings. The respondent will then appoint its own preferred arbitrator when it files its Answer, responding to the Request. The third arbitrator, usually referred to as the "Chair" or the "presiding" arbitrator, is either appointed by agreement between the parties, or more commonly by agreement between the party-appointed arbitrators. This latter alternative avoids the need to secure agreement between the parties at a time when they are in dispute, and agreement over important issues is often difficult to reach.

Another commonly used mechanism of appointment is for the parties to agree on an "appointing authority". In this case, the parties agree to delegate the appointment of arbitrators to a third-party. This may be done with respect to all the arbitrators on the tribunal, or in some cases only with respect to the Chair. The role of appointing authority is usually performed by an arbitral institution (such as, by way of example, the ICC International Court of Arbitration, or the London Court of International Arbitration), however it can also be performed by individuals, companies, or even courts.

The significant benefit of using an arbitral institution as appointing authority is that the institution, if selected well, will both understand arbitration and know many local arbitrators. A good institution is, therefore, well positioned to identify an appropriate arbitrator for a particular dispute. However, it should be emphasised that use of an arbitral institution as an appointing authority does not itself transform an arbitration from *ad hoc* to institutional, as the institution is only performing a single, discrete role in the arbitration, in exchange for a fee. The institution does not then necessarily administer the arbitration, and the parties have no obligation to involve the institution further in their arbitration.

As already noted, one prominent alternative to using an arbitral institution as appointing authority is to have a court at the seat of arbitration perform the role. Of course, a court may only do this if the applicable law permits it to do so, but most modern arbitration laws explicitly authorise local courts to act as appointing authorities. However, while this method generally ensures that the appointment will be made by a neutral and reliable third party, many judges have limited knowledge of arbitration, and even more limited knowledge of available arbitrators. As a result, rather than resulting in the appointment of an arbitrator well-suited to the parties' arbitration, use of a court as appointing authority can result in the appointment of an arbitrator whose primary qualification is that they are known to the judge making the appointment.

A more appealing method may seem to be the use of an individual as appointing authority, as the parties can agree on a person they both trust, and that they know has knowledge of arbitration and of available arbitrators. However, while this method can potentially work well, it suffers from the difficulties discussed above with respect to the specification of an individual as arbitrator (e.g. the individual may be unavailable when needed), and so is generally best avoided.

4. Arbitration rules and laws often include a "back-up" method for selecting arbitrators

While addressing the mechanism of appointment of arbitrators in the arbitration agreement is ideal, the practical reality is that arbitration agreements are often drafted by business people with little knowledge of arbitration. As a result, many arbitration agreements say nothing at all about how the arbitrators are to be selected. This does not, however, invalidate the arbitration agreement, or mean that arbitrators cannot be appointed, as certain default rules have been developed to address this situation. Such rules are usually found either in the arbitration rules the parties have agreed to use, or in the *lex arbitri*.

4.1 Arbitration rules

Arbitration rules will often include provisions specifying how arbitrators are to be appointed, absent any alternative mechanism of appointment agreed between the parties. As a result, if the parties have specified in their arbitration agreement that they will arbitrate in accordance with a specific set of arbitration rules, they have often thereby also agreed on the mechanism to be used for appointing arbitrators.

This situation usually arises in the context of institutional arbitration, as by agreeing to arbitrate under the auspices of a particular arbitral institution, the parties also agree to use that institution's rules. However, even in the case of *ad hoc* arbitration, it is possible for parties to agree to use a pre-designed set of arbitration rules. The most common rules used in this context are the UNCITRAL Arbitration Rules, developed by the United Nations Commission on International Trade Law (UNCITRAL), and consciously designed to provide an effective basis for *ad hoc* arbitrations.[2]

Of course, not all arbitration rules adopt the same default mechanism for appointment of arbitrators, and so parties need to be clear on the contents of any rules they are considering adopting. For example, under some rules, such as those of the ICC and the LCIA, if the parties have not agreed on the number of arbitrators, the dispute will usually be resolved by a sole arbitrator;[3] by contrast, other rules, such as the UNCITRAL Arbitration Rules, adopt a default rule of a panel of three arbitrators.[4] In addition, who has the power to nominate arbitrators can also vary: under the UNCITRAL Arbitration Rules, for example, each party may select one arbitrator, and the two party-appointed arbitrators will then select the Chair.[5] By contrast, under the LCIA Arbitration Rules, all arbitrator appointments are made by the LCIA, albeit "taking into account any written agreement or joint nomination by the parties", and "[n]o party or third person may appoint any arbitrator".[6]

4.2 Arbitration laws

If parties have not agreed to use a particular set of arbitration rules, a default mechanism for selecting arbitrators can usually be found in the *lex arbitri*.[7] Again, however, the specific mechanism varies, and parties need to be aware of these variations when considering where to seat their arbitration. Under the UNCITRAL Model Law, the relevant provisions of which are included in many arbitration laws around the world, if the parties have failed to agree on a mechanism for the appointment of the arbitrators, the tribunal will consist of three arbitrators, with each party selecting one arbitrator, and the Chair being agreed between the two party-nominated arbitrators.[8] By contrast, under the Federal Arbitration Act of the United States of America,[9] if the parties have failed to agree on a mechanism for the appointment of the arbitrators, the tribunal will consist of a sole arbitrator, appointed by a court at the seat of the arbitration.

5. *A tribunal can include any number of arbitrators*

Parties are generally unrestricted on the number of arbitrators they can use to resolve their dispute.[10] After all, it is the parties' arbitration, and they are in the best position to decide how large a tribunal should be to deliver the type of dispute resolution process they wish to have. Where the parties have failed to specify the number of arbitrators and the mechanism of arbitrator appointment, this issue will be resolved by any arbitration rules to which the parties have agreed, or if they have not agreed to any arbitration rules, by the *lex arbitri*. Nonetheless, while parties are technically free to agree on any number of arbitrators, by far most common alternatives are a sole arbitrator or a panel of three arbitrators.[11]

It should be noted, though, that there are a limited number of jurisdictions that require that a tribunal must consist of an odd number of arbitrators.[12] The *lex arbitri* in these jurisdictions usually specifies that if parties have agreed to use an even number of arbitrators, an additional arbitrator must nonetheless be appointed, and sometimes also specifies a mechanism through which the appointment must be made. The rationale behind restrictions of this type is that a tribunal consisting of an even number of arbitrators may become "deadlocked" – that is, unable to deliver a decision because half the arbitrators believe the dispute should be resolved one way, while the other half believe it should be resolved another way. As there is an even number of arbitrators, no "majority award" can be delivered, and the arbitration has therefore failed to result in an enforceable award.

Nonetheless, while this is a legitimate concern, a tribunal containing an even number of arbitrators can provide benefits when used in certain contexts. Most prominently, when two parties expect to have an ongoing relationship, even after the conclusion of the arbitration, a tribunal composed of two arbitrators, with each party appointing one arbitrator, maximises the likelihood that the dispute will be resolved in a way that is acceptable to both parties – as any award must result from the agreement of both arbitrators. As a result, while the use of tribunals with an even number of arbitrators is not a move to be taken lightly, since it involves a significant risk that no enforceable award will be delivered, it is doubtful that such tribunals should be prohibited, as there are contexts in which an informed decision to use a tribunal with an even number of arbitrators can make sense.

In practice, however, even when the *lex arbitri* does not require an odd number of arbitrators, parties overwhelmingly opt for either a sole arbitrator or a panel of three arbitrators, thereby avoiding the risk of a deadlock. The reasons parties pick one or the other of these options will always be tied to the specific facts of their dispute, but there are some general principles that can be identified.

Firstly, a sole arbitrator is generally preferable where the amount in dispute in an arbitration is comparatively small. While a tribunal of three arbitrators may not cost three times as much as a sole arbitrator, it will unavoidably cost more, both in terms of arbitrator fees and in terms of expenses incurred by the arbitrators that must be reimbursed by the parties.

Secondly, a sole arbitrator is likely to deliver a faster proceeding than will a tribunal of three arbitrators. While this is not necessarily true, scheduling is unavoidably more complex with three arbitrators than with one, the arbitrators will need to consult with one another on important issues rather than simply making a decision, and an award will need to be drafted that is acceptable to at least two of the arbitrators.

In addition, a sole arbitrator is likely to deliver a more intellectually coherent award than a tribunal of three arbitrators. The award may or may not be of higher quality than if it had been delivered by a tribunal of three arbitrators, but a sole arbitrator does not need to compromise in the drafting of an award in order to secure the agreement of other tribunal members. As a result, an award by a sole arbitrator is more likely to reflect a coherent and consistent line of legal reasoning, rather than a set of compromises or a patchwork of not-entirely-consistent arguments.

On the other hand, while a tribunal of three arbitrators will be more expensive than a sole arbitrator, that expense can be justified when a larger amount is at stake in the arbitration. One of the significant risks of using a sole arbitrator is that the award will result from just one individual's deliberations. It might, as a result, include a misunderstanding of the facts that would have been corrected by another tribunal member, or even a misunderstanding of the law. A tribunal of three arbitrators, then, serves as a defensive measure to reduce the risks of a poor decision. The award the tribunal delivers may lack intellectual coherence to some degree, but it is less likely to be significantly wrong or to reflect a highly unconventional interpretation of the applicable law.

Similarly, a tribunal of three arbitrators can make sense when a range of different expertises are relevant to the dispute. Rather than, for example, trying to find a single individual who understands Turkish contract law, shipping law, and the technicalities of livestock care during transportation, which might be a challenge, a tribunal could be composed of individuals who each contribute a particular type of expertise. As a result, the dispute is decided on the basis of expert understanding of the relevant issues, even though no single individual possesses that expertise in all the relevant areas.

Finally, of course, use of a tribunal of three arbitrators avoids the need to secure agreement of the parties on a sole arbitrator, or to delegate the selection of the arbitrator to a third party. Instead, each party can be confident that at least one individual on the tribunal understands its perspective on the dispute, and/or its cultural background. It can, as a result, be a way of enhancing the parties' faith in the arbitral process.

6. *The failure of a method of selecting arbitrators is rarely terminal for an arbitration*

One issue that obviously arises from allowing parties to decide their preferred mechanism for appointing a tribunal is the risk that they will select an unworkable mechanism, either because it violates the applicable law or because it simply does not result in the selection of a tribunal. While in some jurisdictions the failure of a mechanism for appointing arbitrators may be seen as invalidating the agreement to arbitrate (since the parties had only agreed to arbitrate under a tribunal selected through the mechanism specified),[13] most jurisdictions simply allow the parties' preferred mechanism of appointment to be replaced with another, provided either by the applicable arbitration rules or by the *lex arbitri*.

6.1 Incompatibility with mandatory provisions of the lex arbitri

While overwhelmingly modern *lex arbitri* provide "fallback" rules, designed to facilitate the parties' arbitration rather than restrict them in their choices, even the most pro-arbitration jurisdictions accept they have a responsibility to ensure the fundamental fairness of arbitrations. As a result, while parties are largely permitted to use any mechanism they prefer to select their tribunal, the parties' preferred mechanism may be held to be invalid if it will undermine the fairness of the resulting arbitration, or is inconsistent with any other mandatory rule of the *lex arbitri*. The classic example of such a restriction would be if the parties' arbitration agreement provided that one of the parties could unilaterally appoint the arbitrator, with no involvement of the other party. Under some national laws such a procedure, even if agreed to in advance by the parties, is invalid, as it does not ensure due process by protecting the equal rights of all parties.[14] Nonetheless, such rules vary between jurisdictions, and so

108   *The arbitral tribunal*

no general rules can be stated regarding what arbitrator selection mechanisms are inherently unacceptable.

As already noted, however, even if the parties' preferred arbitrator selection mechanism is invalid under the *lex arbitri*, this will not usually mean that the parties no longer have a valid agreement to arbitrate. Rather, the parties' chosen method will simply be replaced by the method specified by the *lex arbitri* itself.[15]

6.2 Inoperativeness for factual reasons

Even when the parties' agreed arbitrator selection mechanism is valid under the *lex arbitri*, it might nonetheless not result in the selection of an arbitrator. In the most straightforward case, the parties may have agreed to have a specified individual act as sole arbitrator, but that individual is now dead or otherwise unable to serve as arbitrator. Alternatively, the parties may have selected as an appointing authority an arbitral institution that either never existed (e.g. the arbitration agreement refers to the Vienna Chamber of Arbitration, rather than correctly to the Vienna International Arbitral Centre), or has ceased existing since the parties entered into their arbitration agreement. In such cases, the mechanism for arbitrator appointment is formally valid, but it simply cannot select an arbitrator in practice.

While there are again jurisdictions in which it will be held that such failures invalidate the parties' arbitration agreement, in most jurisdictions the parties' preferred mechanism will simply be replaced by a mechanism specified in the *lex arbitri*.[16]

7. An arbitrator can be appointed on behalf of a party

While the ability of parties to select their arbitrators is one of the primary attractions of arbitration, it also potentially creates a significant problem: what happens if the parties fail to do what they are supposed to do according to the arbitration agreement? For instance, what happens if the arbitration agreement states that the parties have a right to appoint one arbitrator each, but one of the parties refuses to make its appointment, in an attempt to disrupt the proceedings? Alternatively, what if the parties are required to agree on a sole arbitrator, and simply cannot agree?

After all, one of the parties may no longer wish to arbitrate. Yet if the rules or laws applicable to the parties' arbitration require that both parties participate in the selection of the arbitral tribunal, whether by agreeing on a sole arbitrator or by each appointing a party-nominated arbitrator, this provides an ideal opportunity for a party wishing to avoid arbitration. That party, in short, can simply refuse to participate in the selection of the tribunal. Alternatively, both parties may be willing to arbitrate, but are required to agree on a sole arbitrator, and simply cannot agree.

While this might seem to identify a significant problem with arbitration, it actually happens relatively rarely. This is not, however, because parties are always happy to arbitrate, but because arbitration rules and arbitration laws have been designed to support parties that are unable to agree on an arbitrator, and simultaneously to prevent parties frustrating an arbitration agreement by simply refusing to participate in the selection of the arbitral tribunal.

Most arbitration rules, for example, set a time limit within which parties must appoint an arbitrator. If that time limit expires before the appointment has been made, the institution itself can make the appointment.[17] Similarly, most *lex arbitri* allow a party to an arbitration agreement to request a court of the seat to appoint an arbitrator if another party has failed to make a required appointment, or if the parties have been unable to agree on an appointment.[18]

Because of such provisions, while parties can still delay arbitral proceedings by refusing to participate in the appointment of a tribunal, they cannot completely frustrate the agreement to arbitrate. As a result, such attempts are only made in a small proportion of arbitrations.

8. Almost anyone can be an arbitrator

If asked to imagine an arbitral tribunal, few people would summon up an image of a perpetually distracted 18 year-old surfer, a circus performer who never finished high school, and a murderer who has only just been released from prison. Yet one of the consequences of the centrality of party autonomy to arbitration, is that if these three individuals are indeed the tribunal that the parties want to resolve their dispute, then any award that tribunal delivers should be just as enforceable as an award delivered by a trio of leading arbitration experts.

Reflecting this idea, while there remain some jurisdictions that require arbitrators to meet certain standards if their awards are to be enforceable, most contemporary *lex arbitri* do not contain any such limitation,[19] or at most only require that arbitrators have full legal capacity.[20] As a result, in most jurisdictions, anyone can be an arbitrator. All that is required is that someone is willing to appoint them, and that they are willing to serve.

Of course, parties themselves can place restrictions on who can arbitrate their dispute by specifying in their arbitration agreement what qualifications individuals must have to serve on a tribunal constituted under their agreement.[21] In addition, some arbitration rules include restrictions on who can serve as an arbitrator in proceedings operating under those rules, and by agreeing to arbitrate in accordance with such rules, the parties also thereby agree on the restrictions those rules contain. Indeed, any restrictions agreed between the parties are usually not binding only on the parties themselves, but also on any court, arbitral institution or appointing authority that makes an appointment of an arbitrator.[22]

Understanding arbitration through case-law

Religious affiliation as a requirement for an arbitrator

Case details: *Jivraj v Hashwani* [2011] UKSC 40

Authority deciding the case: Supreme Court of the United Kingdom

Facts of the case: Jivraj and Hashwani entered into a joint venture contract containing an arbitration clause. The clause provided that all disputes would be resolved by a panel of three arbitrators, and specified that all arbitrators had to be "respected members of the Ismaili community" (a branch of Islam) and "holders of high office within the community".

A dispute arose and Hashwani commenced arbitration against Jivraj. According to the clause, both parties had the power to appoint one arbitrator. Hashwani appointed an arbitrator who did not belong to the Ismaili community, arguing that the requirement included in the arbitration clause was not binding, as it amounted to religious discrimination and so was incompatible with the Human Rights Act 1998 and European regulations prohibiting discrimination in regards to employment.

Jivraj commenced proceedings at the Commercial Court in London, seeking a declaration that Hashwani's appointment was invalid because the arbitrator was not a member of the Ismaili community. The case ended up before the Supreme Court of the United Kingdom, which was asked to determine whether the parties' freedom to set out specific arbitrator requirements is limited by anti-discrimination legislation aimed at ensuring equality of treatment in the context of employment.

Decision: The Supreme Court held that arbitrators are not employees of the parties, but rather "independent providers of services who are not in a relationship of subordination with the person who receives the services". To stress this difference, the Court highlighted that an arbitrator is "in effect a quasi-judicial adjudicator". As a result, when agreeing on the requirements that an arbitrator must possess, parties are not bound by the same restrictions that bind an employer when selecting an employee. The requirement included in the arbitration clause concluded by Jivraj and Hashwani was, therefore, valid and binding.

In sum, unless the parties themselves have imposed restrictions on who may arbitrate their dispute, they will usually be free to select anyone they think will perform the role in the way they want it performed. As has already been emphasised in this chapter, selection of an arbitrator is arguably the most important thing any party does in an arbitration, and so it is a choice that should be taken extremely seriously. Indeed, too often parties appoint arbitrators simply because they have a good reputation, or an impressive CV, without giving serious consideration to the appropriateness of that arbitrator for their particular arbitration.

9. Arbitral institutions often compile lists of potential arbitrators

An obvious difficulty inherent in the ability of parties to select their own arbitrators is that most parties won't actually know any arbitrators. As a result, even a party that recognises the importance of selecting a good arbitrator may simply not know how to go about doing it.

While parties often attempt to resolve this difficulty just by asking for recommendations from anyone they know who has ever had experience with arbitration, an important assistance is available to parties in the form of lists maintained by many arbitral institutions of potential arbitrators, i.e. names of individuals who can be appointed as arbitrator. In some cases these lists are kept confidential, and are only used when an institution needs to appoint an arbitrator in an arbitration it is administering, but in other cases the lists are public, allowing even parties involved in an *ad hoc* arbitration to benefit from them.

Moreover, the fact that an arbitral institution maintains a list of prospective arbitrators does not usually mean that the parties arbitrating under the auspices of that institution must pick their arbitrators from the list. Rather, the list is a resource for parties to use when attempting to identify a potential arbitrator, and a tool for the institution to use when required to appoint an arbitrator itself.

Institutions take varying approaches to the compilation of such lists, with some listing anyone interested in serving as an arbitrator, while others place significant restrictions in terms of experience. Similarly, for some institutions the list plays an important role as a source of arbitrator appointees, while for others it is little more than a mechanism for arbitrators to promote their own services, while the institution itself makes appointments without regard to whether individuals are on their list or not.

Ultimately, however, in a field in which the primary qualification for being an arbitrator is a willingness to say "I am an arbitrator", the fact that an individual appears on one or more lists of prominent arbitral institutions can provide parties with some level of assurance that the individual has a reasonable understanding of arbitration.

10. Arbitrators must be both independent and impartial

10.1 The concepts of independence and impartiality

Identifying an arbitrator to appoint is not the only complication that parties face when attempting to form an arbitral tribunal. After all, the decision delivered by that tribunal will be enforceable through national courts, with very little review, and in most jurisdictions no review at all as to whether the award is substantively correct or not. It is not, therefore, enough that the parties have identified a potential arbitrator who has the knowledge and expertise to deliver a high quality decision, it is also important that she will make any decision on the basis of the merits of the case. After all, it provides little solace to a losing party in an arbitration to know that their arbitrator was an experienced arbitration specialist if they lost not because the other side had a stronger case, but because the arbitrator dislikes people from their country, or because the arbitrator is regularly appointed as arbitrator by the other party and won't rule against them out of fear that she will lose a valuable source of income.

This need to ensure that arbitrators perform their role in a way that is fair to both parties has come to be addressed under the separate but closely related concepts of "independence" and "impartiality", and one or both of these concepts is found in most contemporary arbitration statutes,[23] as well as in the major arbitration rules.[24] Notably, however, "independence" and "impartiality", as the terms are used in arbitration, are so closely related that even when a statute or rule only refers to one of them, that term is standardly interpreted as actually constituting a reference to both concepts. This said, they are nonetheless separate concepts, with importantly different focuses, often characterised in terms of "objective" and "subjective".

"Independence" refers to the objective relationship between an arbitrator and either the parties or other important individuals in the arbitration (primarily counsel for one of the parties). It addresses the concern that an arbitrator may be influenced in her decision-making by certain relationships or connections. For example, if an arbitrator is a shareholder in one of the parties, then she has a financial interest in that party succeeding in the arbitration, as losing the arbitration may affect the company's profitability, and thus the value of her shares. Similarly, if one of the parties is a family member of the arbitrator, she may be unwilling to rule against them out of concern that doing so will harm her relationship with them. In such cases, even if the arbitrator insists she will perform her role fairly and professionally, she may be regarded as lacking the "independence" that a neutral adjudicator requires.

"Impartiality", on the other hand, focuses on the subjective mindset of an arbitrator with respect to the case or to the individuals involved in that case. It reflects a recognition that even if an arbitrator lacks the type of connections that might create an incentive for her to make a decision on a basis other than the merits of the case she is deciding, nonetheless that arbitrator's views on certain issues relevant to the case may themselves deprive one of the parties of a fair dispute resolution process. She may, for example, believe that individuals from the country of one of the parties are particularly willing to lie, and so will be less willing to believe the testimony of that party simply because of his nationality. Alternatively, she may have heard details about the case prior to being appointed, and thereby have formed a view on how it should be resolved before the parties have made their arguments. In both cases, the arbitrator may see herself as acting with perfect integrity, and willing to decide the case on the basis of the law and the facts presented to her, but the reality is that certain views that she holds simply make this impossible.

The requirements of "independence" and "impartiality", then, are ultimately complementary means of ensuring that an arbitrator appointed by parties to resolve their dispute does so on the basis of the merits of the case, and in a way that is fair to both parties.

It is worth emphasising that while in some jurisdictions local traditions have lower expectations of independence and impartiality for party-appointed arbitrators than for sole arbitrators or chairs of a tribunal, this difference is not accepted in international commercial arbitration. All arbitrators on an international commercial arbitration tribunal are expected to be both independent and impartial, no matter who appointed them.

Of course, this idea of the independent and impartial arbitrator is a nice one, but it raises an obvious question: How can the parties know whether an arbitrator meets these standards or not? The mechanism that has been developed to address this problem is what is known as "disclosure".

Under this principle, which is a standard feature of arbitration laws[25] and institutional rules,[26] if an arbitrator is aware of any circumstance that might give rise to justifiable doubts as to her impartiality or independence, she is obligated to tell the parties and provide them with the information necessary to make a judgement on whether they believe it affects her independence or impartiality. Arbitrators are usually required to make such disclosures prior to accepting any appointment, or as soon as they learn the information themselves, if this happens after the appointment has been accepted. Importantly, an arbitrator making such a disclosure does not need to resign from the tribunal if she herself believes that the circumstance in question does not affect her independence or impartiality. However, the disclosure of the information gives the parties the ability to "challenge" her role on the tribunal if they disagree, and potentially have her removed.[27]

Of course, in practice it is usually very difficult to demonstrate that an arbitrator lacks sufficient independence or impartiality to serve on a tribunal. If the problem is obvious, parties will usually refrain from nominating that arbitrator, or the arbitrator will decline to serve. It is, after all, a significant professional embarrassment for an arbitrator to be removed from a tribunal for lack of independence or impartiality, so arbitrators will rarely see this as a risk worth taking.

Yet if the problem is not obvious, how do you prove that it exists? The existence of a connection between an arbitrator and a party may be easy to establish, but how do you establish that the connection is something that will stop the arbitrator acting fairly between the parties when the arbitrator herself downplays its importance to her? Perhaps ten years ago the arbitrator was fired from a law firm now representing one of the parties in the case – but time has passed, the specific lawyers in this case are not the ones who fired her, and she has gone on to become successful as an arbitrator. How do you establish that she still bears a grudge against the firm, and would love to see it lose the high profile arbitration she is now hearing?

Because of these difficulties, the accepted requirement in such situations is not that the complaining party must prove, on the balance of the evidence, that the arbitrator actually is not independent or impartial. Rather, it must only establish that there are "justifiable doubts" as to the arbitrator's independence or impartiality. That is, that it may well be that the arbitrator is, as matter of fact, independent and impartial, but the circumstances the arbitrator has disclosed are sufficiently concerning that a reasonable party would be justified in doubting her independence or impartiality. Actual proof of a lack of independence or impartiality is unnecessary.[28]

Understanding arbitration through case-law

LCIA challenge: publications expressing opinions about a party's parent company

Case details: LCIA Reference No. UN152998, Decision rendered on 22 June 2015

Authority deciding the case: Former Vice President of the LCIA Court

Facts of the case: The parties entered into a contract containing a binary clause, under which each party had the right to appoint one arbitrator. The claimant commenced arbitration and appointed an arbitrator. The respondent submitted a response, challenging the appointment made by the claimant.

The challenge was based on the contents of three publications authored by the arbitrator. In these publications, the arbitrator made critical remarks about the respondent's parent company, and in particular with respect to "how it is managed, the way it conducts its business and how experts in arbitration view that company", including alleged "frivolous acts of mismanagement".

The LCIA appointed one of its former Vice Presidents to determine the challenge and decide whether the contents of the publications gave rise to justifiable doubts as to the arbitrator's impartiality and independence.

> **Decision:** The Vice President noted that the arbitrator was a Professor of commercial law and an attorney with over 45 years of professional experience: as such, no doubts in principle existed as to his qualifications. Nonetheless, this did not change the fact that the arbitrator had made critical remarks aimed specifically at the respondent's parent company, describing its management in negative terms. The Vice President found that, while these remarks did not directly relate to the case submitted to arbitration, they did justify doubts as to whether the arbitrator was able to hear the case "in an unbiased manner with an open mind". As a result, the challenge succeeded.

10.2 IBA Rules of Ethics for International Arbitrators and IBA Guidelines on Conflicts of Interest in International Arbitration

Arguably the most important developments on the topic of the independence and impartiality of arbitrators have come through the efforts of an organisation not directly focused on arbitration, the International Bar Association (IBA), in the form of the 1987 IBA Rules of Ethics for International Arbitrators and the 2004 IBA Guidelines on Conflicts of Interest in International Arbitration. Importantly, the IBA does not license or otherwise authorise individuals to act as arbitrators, and so neither the Rules nor the Guidelines are directly binding on arbitrators. However, the Guidelines in particular have come to play a central role in how arbitrators involved in international commercial arbitration understand their own obligations, as well as being regularly relied upon by courts and other bodies or individuals asked to decide on the challenge of an arbitrator.[29] Moreover, parties involved in an arbitration or entering into an arbitration agreement have the ability to agree that the Rules or Guidelines will be applicable in their arbitration – as a result of that agreement they then become directly binding on all arbitrators involved in the arbitration. While both the Rules and the Guidelines remain in effect, the Guidelines are expressly stated to supersede the Rules in any topic addressed in the Guidelines.[30]

While both the Rules and the Guidelines were developed by the IBA, they adopt significantly different approaches. The Rules, as the name suggests, lays out a broad set of general rules focused on how arbitrators should fulfill their responsibilities, taking into account both an arbitrator's obligation to be fair and neutral, and the desirability of an efficient arbitral process. While Rule 2.4, for example, states that "It is inappropriate to contact parties in order to solicit appointment as arbitrator", Rule 7 requires, in part, that arbitrators "shall do their best to conduct the arbitration in such a manner that costs do not rise to an unreasonable proportion of the interests at stake".

The Guidelines, on the other hand, are exclusively focused on the question of conflicts of interest, and attempt to create a detailed and practical approach to this question. They are divided in two parts: Part One lays out certain basic principles to which arbitrators should adhere with respect to impartiality, independence and disclosure, much as do the Rules with respect to an arbitrator's broader obligations; Part Two, which has arguably been the most influential and effective element of the Guidelines, elaborates how the general standards in Part One should be applied in practice, in the form of a non-exhaustive list of possible "conflicts of interests", classified into three lists: the red list, the orange list and the green list.

The red list incorporates situations that in the view of the drafters of the Guidelines give rise to justifiable doubts as to an arbitrator's independence or impartiality. That is, these are situations in which an arbitrator should not accept an appointment, or in which an arbitrator should be removed from a tribunal. Unlike the other two lists (orange and green), the red list contains an internal division, between the "non-waivable" red list and the "waivable" red list.

The Non-Waivable Red List addresses those situations that create such a severe conflict of interest that parties should, for example, be allowed to rely on them to resist enforcement of any award resulting from the arbitration, even if at the time of the arbitration they knew about the situation but failed to object, or even stated that they saw it as unproblematic. These situations, in other words, are regarded by the drafters of the Guidelines as fundamentally inconsistent with the very nature of arbitration as a fair dispute resolution process. By way of example, situation 1.1 of the Non-Waivable Red List addresses cases in which "There is an identity between a party and the arbitrator, or the arbitrator is a legal representative or employee of an entity that is a party in the arbitration" – that is, where the arbitrator is actually one of the parties to the dispute, or is otherwise under the direction and control of one of the parties.

The Waivable Red List, on the other hand, includes situations in which the drafters of the Guidelines believed there would clearly be justifiable doubts as to an arbitrator's independence or impartiality – but which are not so extreme as to be fundamentally inconsistent with arbitration as a fair dispute resolution process. As a result, parties should be given the right to decide for themselves whether they wish to have the arbitrator serve on the tribunal, so long as they are accurately informed of all relevant information, and able to make an informed decision. The Waivable Red List, then, includes situations such as an arbitrator serving as a lawyer in the same law firm as the counsel to one of the parties, the arbitrator holding shares in one of the parties, and the arbitrator having a close family relationship with one of the parties. Each party in the arbitration has the right to unilaterally decide whether an arbitrator in such a situation should be allowed on a tribunal – and if either party objects, then the arbitrator should not serve, no matter how much support she may have from the other party.

The Orange List, in turn, covers situations which are regarded as less serious than those in the Red List but that may, depending on the particular context in which they occur, give rise to justifiable doubts about an arbitrator's independence or impartiality. As a result, an arbitrator is obligated to disclose the existence of situations included in the Orange List, but need not refuse to serve on a tribunal even if one of the parties objects that the situation disclosed undermines her independence or impartiality. Rather, the objecting party has the additional obligation of establishing, on the balance of the evidence, that justifiable doubts do indeed exist. Examples of situations included on the Orange List include when an arbitrator has been appointed as arbitrator by one of the parties on two or more occasions within the past three years, or when a close personal friendship exists between an arbitrator and counsel for one of the parties.

Finally, the Green List includes situations that were judged by the drafters of the Guidelines to be unproblematic. As a result, they do not need to be disclosed by arbitrators, and should not serve as the basis for removing an arbitrator from a tribunal. Examples include situations such as when an arbitrator is a member of the same professional association as counsel for one of the parties, or when the arbitrator is "connected" to one of the parties through social media, such as LinkedIn or Facebook.

It is, however, important to reiterate that while the Guidelines have been enormously influential, and are regularly relied upon when deciding challenges to arbitrators, they are not universally accepted. This is most prominently illustrated by fact that the Green List includes situations that have occasionally resulted in successful challenges to arbitrators, most notably when an arbitrator has written a book or article on a legal issue arising in the arbitration.

The Rules and the Guidelines are, therefore, important sources for guidance on how arbitrators should perform their role – but they are just guidance, and can be rejected for the simple reason that an arbitrator or an individual deciding on a challenge to an arbitrator believes that they are wrong.

11. Interviews of prospective arbitrators have become more common

An increasingly important mechanism adopted by parties to assist them in identifying an appropriate arbitrator is the use of interviews of prospective arbitrators. Interviewing an arbitrator before deciding whether or not to appoint her provides a valuable opportunity for one or both parties to get a clearer idea of an arbitrator's approach to her role, and to her views on matters of importance to them in selecting an arbitrator. As a result, it is a useful way for parties to take control of their arbitration, and reduce the risk that they will end up with an arbitrator that they subsequently regret appointing.

This said, interviews also create significant risks for both parties and arbitrators, as a poorly conducted interview can subsequently give rise to a claim that an arbitrator lacks impartiality. Interviews should not, for example, be seen as an opportunity to present a potential arbitrator with the facts of the case and get an early indication of how they will likely decide. Similarly, they should not be used as an opportunity to comment on the actions or character of the other party in the dispute, thereby potentially biasing the arbitrator against that other party. Evidence that actions such as these were taken in an interview could subsequently be used by the other party to have the arbitrator removed from the tribunal.

As a result, while interviews of prospective arbitrators are becoming increasingly common, and when used properly are a desirable feature of arbitration, some arbitrators refuse to participate in them, while others approach them "defensively", agreeing to be interviewed only if certain precautions are taken. This might include, for example, the presence of a representative of both parties at the interview, the recording of the interview, or an agreement that all questions must be submitted to the arbitrator in writing in advance of the interview. These measures are designed to counteract a party's natural desire to find out as much as possible about how an arbitrator is likely to decide a case, and protect both the arbitrator's professional integrity and her position on the tribunal.

12. Arbitrators can be "challenged" by parties for lacking independence or impartiality

12.1 What is a challenge?

Because of the importance of ensuring that any arbitration is decided by an independent and impartial tribunal, arbitration laws and rules almost universally include mechanisms allowing any party in an arbitration to bring a "challenge" against an arbitrator, arguing either that the arbitrator should not be appointed to the tribunal, or that she should be removed.[31] If the challenge is successful, a replacement arbitrator will have to be nominated, subject again to the same standards of independence and impartiality, and to the right of any party to bring a challenge against her. Depending on the applicable law and on the agreement of the parties, challenges may be brought before a local court or under the rules of the arbitral institution administering the arbitration. In the former case the challenge will be decided by a judge who may or may not understand arbitration and the role of an arbitrator, while in the latter case the decision will likely be made by one or more arbitration professionals. While there is no empirical evidence available on whether a challenge is more likely to be successful when decided by a judge or by arbitration professionals, anecdotal reports might be taken to suggest that arbitration professionals often have a great deal of sympathy with arbitrators, and can be very reluctant to potentially damage an arbitrator's career by suggesting that she had not met the professional standards required of her.

12.2 Challenges under arbitration rules

As already noted, arbitration rules will usually include a mechanism through which parties can bring a challenge against an arbitrator. This possibility, however, is usually subject to a strict time limit, requiring that the challenge be brought within a few days of the arbitrator being nominated, or of the time at which the party became aware of the information that is alleged to justify the arbitrator's removal from the tribunal. That is, a party may not receive information that they believe creates justifiable doubts about an arbitrator's independence or impartiality, but then simply hold onto that information until they can decide whether the arbitrator is likely to rule in their favour or not. If a challenge is not brought against an arbitrator within the period allowed by the applicable rules, then the objection is taken to have been waived, and the party cannot later use that information either as a ground for challenging the arbitrator, or as basis for seeking annulment or resisting enforcement of an award. By way of example, the UNCITRAL Arbitration Rules set a time limit of 15 days for bringing of any challenge,[32] while the ICC Rules allow 30 days.[33]

The aim of such strict time limits is clear, as they stop parties trying to manipulate the arbitral proceedings, creating a "heads I win, tails you lose" situation in which they reveal the information they have discovered about an arbitrator if they think they will lose the case, but keep it concealed if they think they will win. That said, there is some ground for questioning the very short time limits many arbitration rules contain, as they are arguably based on an inaccurate conception of how rapidly most arbitrations will proceed. Most international commercial arbitrations, for example, take between one and two years to conclude, so it is difficult to see the justification for requiring challenges to be brought within only 15 days. If a time limit is too short it can actually harm the fairness of an arbitration, by eliminating the incentive for parties to properly investigate information they receive about an arbitrator, out of concern that if they don't rapidly bring a challenge they may be held to have waived their right to do so.

In contrast with the detailed examples of potentially problematic situations included in the IBA Guidelines on Conflicts of Interest in International Arbitration, arbitration rules generally do not specify the grounds on which arbitrators can be successfully challenged, instead merely including a general right of parties to challenge an arbitrator for any alleged lack of independence or impartiality.[34] The burden is then on the challenging party to describe the circumstances they believe justify the challenge, and to persuade the decision-maker specified under the arbitration rules that the arbitrator in question should not serve on the tribunal.

When the challenge has been made, the challenged arbitrator and any non-challenging parties will be informed that a challenge has been brought. In some cases, an arbitrator may voluntarily withdraw at this stage, although this is relatively rare in practice unless information is presented of which the arbitrator herself was unaware. After all, if the arbitrator believed there were good grounds for challenging her appointment to the tribunal, she would be unlikely to have accepted the appointment in the first place. However, an arbitrator may decide to withdraw not because she accepts the challenge is correct, or even because she thinks it will succeed, but merely because the challenge highlights a deterioration of the relationship of trust and confidence that must exist between parties and an arbitrator if an arbitration is to be successful.[35] This is, though, particularly rare, as withdrawing when only challenged by one party risks unfairness to the other party, who is content to have the arbitrator on the tribunal.

If the arbitrator refuses to withdraw, the challenge proceedings will continue. While such proceedings are generally conducted swiftly, to ensure that the challenge of an arbitrator cannot be used to slow or otherwise derail an arbitration, all parties and individuals with a legitimate interest in the outcome of the challenge must be given the right to present their views. As a result, the challenge will not be decided based only on the information provided by the challenging party, but also on the basis of any response to the challenge from the challenged arbitrator, and from any other parties to the dispute. Once these additional views have been received, a decision will be made in accordance with the rules of the institution. If the decision is to reject the challenge, as is most common, the challenged arbitrator will continue performing her role, and the occurrence of a challenge will have no further impact on the arbitration. On the other hand, if the challenge is successful, the arbitrator will be removed from the tribunal and must usually be replaced in accordance with the same mechanism through which the challenged arbitrator herself was appointed (e.g. nomination by a party, agreement of the parties, appointment by the institution, etc.).

One problematic feature of decisions on arbitrator challenges at most arbitral institutions is that while a decision will usually be given in writing, no reasons for the decision will be given. That is, a party who has expressed a concern that an arbitrator lacks independence or impartiality will only be told "Your challenge does not succeed", but will not be told why it didn't succeed. The problematic nature of this approach is obvious, as it undermines the confidence parties have in both the tribunal and the institution. Ironically, the same institutions that refuse to provide reasons for their decisions on arbitrator challenges will often require that arbitrators provide reasons for their decisions in cases, precisely on the rationale that providing reasons both enhances the quality of decision-making and gives parties confidence in the arbitral process. There is, however, a slow movement towards the provision of reasons for decisions on arbitrator challenges, with the LCIA doing so since 2006, the ICC since 2015, and the SCC since 2018.[36] It is, however, a practice that should be adopted by all institutions.

12.3 Institutional confirmation of an appointment

In addition to allowing challenges to be brought by parties against arbitrators, some institutional rules also require that any arbitrator must be confirmed by the institution if she is to serve on a tribunal.[37] This provides the institution with an opportunity to evaluate the independence and impartiality of a nominated arbitrator even if she has not been challenged by a party.

Confirmation decisions are made on the basis of information provided by the arbitrator, and so cannot serve as a replacement for challenges by parties, as in the latter instance the disclosures by an arbitrator will be supplemented by any information the challenging party is itself able to generate. However, the confirmation process provides an important protection for parties unfamiliar with arbitration, who may not have the experience necessary to recognise that an arbitrator has a conflict of interest. It also provides an important protection for the institution, the reputation of which will be damaged if it regularly administers arbitrations involving arbitrators who are not independent and impartial.

12.4 Challenge under national statutes

Not all arbitrations take place under the auspices of an arbitral institution, however, and so *lex arbitri* standardly provide a mechanism through which the appointment of an arbitrator can be challenged in court. As with challenge procedures at arbitral institutions, such laws also usually specify a short time limit within which any challenge must be made, to avoid the challenge being used to undermine the arbitration.

The substantive grounds on which arbitration statutes allow challenges against arbitrators to be brought can vary. In some jurisdictions, the law simply makes a general reference to independence and impartiality, similar to the approach usually taken by institutional rules, without describing specific situations in which challenges can successfully be brought.[38] In other jurisdictions, however, the arbitration statute specifically lists those situations that can serve as the basis of a successful challenge, with situations that do not fall within the scope described, either directly or by analogy, not serving as grounds for a challenge.[39]

A further approach is found in the United States of America, as the 1925 Federal Arbitration Act is almost universally understood as precluding challenges to arbitrators.[40] Rather, parties must wait until the final award has been delivered by the tribunal, and then attempt to have the award annulled on the basis of the "evident partiality" of the tribunal.[41] This approach is seen as minimising the ability of parties in an arbitration to delay or derail the proceedings by bringing a challenge in the courts, however it also imposes a significant cost on the parties, who must spend time and incur expenses pursuing an arbitration that does not result in an enforceable award.

While it may seem obvious that a challenge procedure in the *lex arbitri* will be available in any arbitration, whether *ad hoc* or institutional, the relationship between court challenge procedures and challenge procedures in arbitration rules is actually quite controversial. After all, a court may decide that by agreeing to arbitrate under a particular set of arbitration rules, whether institutional rules or the UNCITRAL arbitration rules, the parties have agreed to abide by the challenge procedures in those rules, to the exclusion of those in the *lex arbitri*. Alternatively, the two challenge procedures may be viewed as complementary.

Under the Model Law, for example, parties retain the right to challenge arbitrators before state courts even if they have agreed to arbitrate under rules that include their own challenge procedure. Under Article 13 of the Model Law, parties must first bring their challenge through the procedure they have agreed to use, and only once this procedure has completed may they then bring a challenge in national courts.[42] By contrast, under some arbitration statutes, such as Switzerland's Federal Statute on Private International Law, parties who have agreed to use a certain challenge procedure may only use that procedure, and may not bring a challenge against the arbitrator in court.[43]

13. In some circumstances arbitrators may be removed despite not being challenged by a party

Of course, even if an arbitrator is both independent and impartial, circumstances may exist that mean she is nonetheless unable to properly perform her role. For this reason, many arbitration rules and national statutes also allow arbitrators to be removed from a tribunal for reasons other than a lack of independence or impartiality.

Under Article 15(2) of the 2017 ICC Rules, for example, an arbitrator can be removed by the institution if she is "prevented *de jure* or *de facto* from fulfilling the arbitrator's functions, or . . . is not fulfilling those functions in accordance with the Rules or within the prescribed time limits". Similarly, under Article 10(1) of the 2014 LCIA Rules, the institution can remove an arbitrator if she "falls seriously ill, refuses or becomes unable or unfit to act", and Article 10(2) specifies that an arbitrator can be considered "unfit to act" when he or she "does not conduct or participate in the arbitration with reasonable efficiency, diligence and industry". In essence, rules such as these allow an institution to remove an arbitrator who is not performing or is not able to perform the role of arbitrator, even when facts do not exist that would allow the arbitrator to be challenged. They serve, that is, as a method of "quality control", allowing the institution to ensure that the arbitrations it administers meet minimum standards of quality and efficiency. Importantly, these rules standardly allow the institution to remove an arbitrator on its own initiative, rather than waiting for a request to be made by one of the parties, in recognition of the institution's legitimate interest in its own reputation for effectively administering arbitrations.

Similarly, most *lex arbitri* also include a mechanism for the removal of arbitrators under similar circumstances. Article 14 of the 2006 UNCITRAL Model Law, for example, provides that if an arbitrator "becomes de jure or de facto unable to perform his functions or for other reasons fails to act without undue delay", all parties involved in the arbitration may collectively agree to remove the arbitrator, or alternatively any party may request the appropriate court at the seat of the arbitration to remove the arbitrator. Importantly, while institutional rules standardly allow the institution to remove an arbitrator on its own motion in such situations, arbitration laws will usually only allow a court to do so if a request is made by a party. The court, after all, does not need to worry about its reputation for the effective administration of arbitrations. On the other hand, allowing a court to remove an arbitrator against the wishes of all the parties in an arbitration would undermine the independence of arbitration from national courts, eliminating one of the primary attractions of international commercial arbitration.

14. Arbitrators who leave a tribunal are usually replaced, but in some circumstances will not be

Given the possibility that arbitrators can be removed from a tribunal, may resign, or may become unable to perform their function, there must be a mechanism through which a replacement arbitrator can be appointed. After all, the parties have agreed to arbitrate under a tribunal composed in accordance with certain procedures. If a successful challenge, resignation or removal results in the tribunal no longer meeting the requirements of the arbitration agreement, then any award delivered by that tribunal may be unenforceable, as well as simply being the decision of a tribunal substantively different than the one the parties agreed could decide their dispute.

Unsurprisingly, the fundamental rule in this situation is that of party autonomy: if the parties have agreed a specific procedure for the appointment of replacement arbitrators, then that procedure must be followed – even if it differs from the procedure used to appoint the original tribunal. In reality, of course, parties rarely include such a provision in their arbitration agreement, and so the procedure through which a replacement arbitrator is to be appointed will be decided by the applicable arbitration rules or by the *lex arbitri*. In both cases, the standard approach is simply to require that any replacement arbitrator be appointed through the same mechanism as was used to appoint the arbitrator she is replacing,[44] although in some cases institutional arbitration rules will allow the institution the discretion to decide whether or not the original procedure should be followed.[45] This latter flexibility is an important benefit available from arbitration at those institutions, as it allows the institution to ensure that an arbitrator is appointed in an efficient and effective manner, when use of the original appointing procedure would be unnecessarily slow or otherwise difficult.

In addition, some institutional rules also allow a "truncated" tribunal – that is, for the arbitration to be completed without a replacement arbitrator being appointed. At first glance this may seem inconsistent with any arbitration agreement which specifies that a certain number of arbitrators will be on the tribunal. However, by agreeing to arbitrate at an institution, parties have agreed to arbitrate in accordance with that institution's rules. As a result, while the institution's rules may not be directly written into the parties' arbitration agreement, they do constitute part of the parties' arbitration agreement.

By way of example, the ICC Rules[46] allow a truncated tribunal to complete an arbitration if an arbitrator dies or is removed after the proceedings have closed, and the tribunal's sole remaining function is to render its final decision – if the institution decides this is appropriate. On the other hand, the rules of some institutions allow truncated tribunals in a wider range of situations. For example, under Article 12.1 of the 2014 LCIA Rules, if an arbitrator has refused or persistently failed to participate in the deliberations of the tribunal, the remaining arbitrators may jointly decide to continue the arbitration as a truncated tribunal, if this is approved by the LCIA.[47]

Rules allowing a truncated tribunal are certainly not unproblematic, as the award that will be delivered by the remaining two arbitrators may be substantively different than the award that would have been delivered if all three arbitrators had been involved in deliberations and in the drafting of the award. However, this risk must be counterbalanced against the significant problems that might be caused if a long and expensive arbitration must be completely re-run, doubling both the amount that the parties end up paying in legal and other costs, and the time taken before their dispute is resolved.

Unavoidably, the possibility of a truncated tribunal is far more problematic in *ad hoc* arbitration, if the parties have not agreed that an award may be delivered by a truncated tribunal or to the use of arbitration rules that include such a rule. Ultimately, if the parties have agreed that an award must be delivered by a tribunal of three arbitrators appointed in accordance with a certain procedure, then an award delivered by a truncated tribunal will not accord with the parties' agreement, and should not be enforced. The parties may, of course, agree at any time to alter their arbitration agreement, and allow the truncated tribunal to deliver an award, and in that case the award will be enforceable. However, unless permission to do so is given by all parties involved in an arbitration, a tribunal should not unilaterally decide to proceed as a truncated tribunal, no matter what the consequences, in terms of time and cost, of not doing so.

15. Arbitrators work under a contract with the parties

Because judges are employed by a government and exercise State power, the limits of their power and the terms of their employment are not decided by the parties involved in the cases they are hearing. The judge's salary, and the powers she can exercise, are instead set by the government and are consistent across cases.

Arbitrators, on the other hand, are private individuals who have been hired by the parties in a dispute to decide their dispute. Their powers and obligations depend on what the parties have agreed that their arbitrator can and cannot do, and their income will be determined contractually. As a result, both the remuneration and what an arbitrator must, can and cannot do varies significantly from one arbitration to another. An arbitrator is in effect, although not necessarily in law, an employee of the parties – hired to do a certain job in a particular way, and promised a specified income if the work is done.

Because of this, just as an employee's rights and obligations will be defined in a contract of employment, so the rights and obligations of an arbitrator are defined in what is known as the "arbitrator's contract". Importantly, this is a separate agreement from the arbitration agreement, and while the arbitration agreement is an agreement between the parties in the dispute, the arbitrator's contract is an agreement between all the parties in the arbitration and the arbitrator. Moreover, because each arbitrator is able to negotiate the terms on which she is willing to serve on a tribunal, every arbitrator on a tribunal will standardly have her own contract, with those contracts sometimes varying significantly from one arbitrator to the next.

However, while in some respects thinking of arbitrators as employees of the parties is helpful, it is also important to keep in mind that arbitrators differ from regular employees. Indeed, an arbitrator's contract is best understood as being what is referred to in some jurisdictions as a "mandate", rather than a contract of employment: it identifies the role that the arbitrator must perform, and the essential terms under which the arbitrator must act, but does not give the parties the right to direct the arbitrator in the details of her performance of that role. The parties cannot, for example, direct the arbitrator to reach a certain conclusion in the award, or require the arbitrator to undertake her role in a way that she regards as inconsistent with her professional obligations as an arbitrator. An arbitrator is hired to be an independent decision-maker, and if that independence is ever removed, then the arbitrator is no longer acting as an arbitrator, and any award delivered cannot be enforced as an arbitral award.

16. *Arbitrators are rarely legally liable for acts taken in performance of their function*

Since arbitrators perform in accordance with the terms of a contract, it might seem obvious that arbitrators could also be held liable for breaching the terms of that contract. After all, the purpose of a contract is to ensure that the parties to it act in certain ways, and laws around the world enforce contractual obligations by the imposition of liability on parties who breach their contracts, usually in the form of the payment of damages to the non-breaching party.

It is significant, then, that many *lex arbitri* expressly limit the liability of arbitrators for actions taken in the performance of their role. This is what is known as "arbitral immunity". While the specific details and extent of arbitral immunity vary from one jurisdiction to another, its underlying rationale is to ensure that arbitrators are able to properly perform the role they were hired to perform.

That is, an arbitrator's role is to resolve a dispute between two or more disputing parties, delivering a decision that will be binding on those parties even though at least one of them is almost certain to be unhappy with the result. While the limitations on appeal of arbitral awards ensure that an arbitrator's decision, once delivered, will almost always be final, if an arbitrator could be sued by a party for the actions she took while serving as arbitrator, parties would have a powerful means of preventing tribunals delivering decisions unfavourable to them.

By way of example, Weronika may know that a certain document in her possession will prove she has been lying, and so does not want Duane, the opposing party in an arbitration, to get access to the document. As a result, when Duane submits a disclosure request, arguing that he should be given the document, Weronika insists that the arbitrator has no legitimate power to force her to disclose the document, and threatens to sue the arbitrator if she orders that it be disclosed to Duane. While we might all think that if we were the arbitrator in such a situation, we would not be intimated and would do our job anyway, the reality is that arbitrators are human. They have families, they have homes, they have professional reputations that can be damaged. There is, therefore, a real risk that an arbitrator faced with such a threat will give in to the pressure, and not order the document disclosed, even though Duane has legitimate grounds for requesting it.

Arbitral immunity is designed to address this problem by protecting arbitrators while they perform their role. It will sometimes result in parties being deprived of legal recourse against an arbitrator who has taken wrongful actions that have harmed them, but without arbitral immunity of some form arbitration as a dispute resolution procedure simply could not function.

The important question, of course, is how extensive an arbitrator's immunity should be, and not all *lex arbitri* adopt the same approach. Indeed, the UNCITRAL Model Law deliberately avoids addressing the immunity of arbitrators precisely because it varies so significantly around the world. In the United States of America, for example, arbitral immunity is almost absolute,[48] while in England and Wales Section 29 of the Arbitration Act 1996 grants arbitrators immunity for "anything done or omitted in the discharge or purported discharge of his functions as arbitrator unless the act or omission is shown to have been in bad faith." On the other hand, in Spain arbitrators are liable not only when they act in bad faith, but also if they have acted recklessly in the performance of their obligations, while in the Czech Republic arbitrators have no immunity at all, except in so far as that immunity is granted through the arbitrator's contract or because they have acted in an arbitration administered by an institution.[49]

Arbitral immunity is unquestionably a difficult subject, as granting arbitrators too much immunity allows arbitrators to perform their role poorly, with no immediate consequences. Moreover, the confidentiality of most arbitration means that information on an arbitrator's poor performance will rarely be made public. Nonetheless, granting arbitrators too little immunity undermines the ability of arbitrators to perform their role fairly and objectively, and so undermines the entire arbitral process. Ultimately, however, while it is clear that arbitral immunity needs to be extensive, there is little justification for granting arbitrators immunity for acts taken in bad faith. An arbitrator who has acted in bad faith has not been acting as an arbitrator, and does not deserve to receive the benefit of an immunity granted to ensure that arbitrators are free to perform their role honestly and with professionalism.

Notes

1 The principle of party autonomy is clearly enshrined in Article V(1)(d) of the New York Convention, whereby the recognition of an arbitral award may be denied if the composition of the arbitral tribunal was not in accordance with the agreement of the parties. National statutes and rules of arbitration generally concur in attributing a prevailing role to party autonomy: the mechanisms of appointment set forth in such instruments generally operate only in the absence of any diverging agreement between the parties.
2 Articles 8–10 of the 2010 UNCITRAL Arbitration Rules set forth a mechanism of arbitrator appointment whereby, in the silence of the parties, the dispute will be resolved by a tribunal composed of three arbitrators. Pursuant to Article 9, "each party shall appoint one arbitrator. The two arbitrators thus appointed shall choose the third arbitrator who will act as the presiding arbitrator of the arbitral tribunal".
3 2017 ICC Rules, Article 12(2); 2014 LCIA Rules, Article 5(8). However, the institution often has the possibility to adapt the rule to the specificity of the case at hand, for example appointing a sole arbitrator when the case is simple (even if the fall-back rule provides for a tribunal with three arbitrators) or, vice versa, nominating a three arbitrators panel if the dispute is complex (although the rules in principle provide for a sole arbitrator). The discretional power of the arbitral institution in this regard varies, depending on the wording of the rules.
4 2010 UNCITRAL Rules, Article 7.
5 2010 UNCITRAL Rules, Article 9.
6 2014 LCIA Arbitration Rules, Article 5(7).
7 It is important to emphasise that the appointment procedure set forth in the *lex arbitri* is standardly a residual, fall-back mechanism: as such, it only applies in the absence of any alternative mechanism agreed between the parties.
8 2006 UNCITRAL Model Law, Articles 10(2) and 11(3)(a).

9   US Federal Arbitration Act, Section 5.
10 According to Article 10(10) of the UNCITRAL Model Law, "the parties are free to determine the number of arbitrators".
11 In commercial practice, tribunals with more than three members are extremely rare. By contrast, tribunals with more than three members are sometimes appointed for the resolution of disputes concerning matters of public international law: for example, the Iran – US Claims Tribunal is composed of nine members.
12 See, e.g. Belgian Judicial Code, Article 1684(1)-(2); Italian Code of Civil Procedure, Article 809. The UNCITRAL Model Law does not include any mandatory provision on the number of arbitrators, thereby allowing tribunals with an even number of arbitrators.
13 See, e.g. 23 Cdo 1098/2016 (Czech Supreme Court).
14 § 1034(2) ZPO; Code of Civil Procedure of the Netherlands, Article 1028(1); 23 Cdo 1098/2016 (Czech Supreme Court)
15 It should be noted that, in this context, the limitation of party autonomy is in the interest of the parties themselves, since it aims at avoiding a nullity of the award: an award could be annulled when the parties have not been given an equal opportunity to present the case (UNCITRAL Model Law, Articles 34(2)(a)(ii) and 34(2)(b)(ii)).
16 UNCITRAL Model Law, Article 11(4)(c). The failure of the appointing authority can depend on several factors: in some cases, the parties might have selected an arbitral institution which no longer exists by the time the dispute eventually arises. In such cases, the arbitration agreement generally continues to be valid (unless the identification of the administering institution is clearly construed in the agreement as the decisive reason why the parties have decided to submit to arbitration) and the appointment mechanism selected by the parties is substituted by the *lex arbitri*. In this sense, see the case-law in the US (*In re HZI Research Center v Sun Instrument Japan*, (1995) WL 562181 (S.D.N.Y. 1995); *Warnes SA v Harvic Int'l Ltd*, 1993 WL 228028 (S.D.N.Y. 1993); *Rosgoscirc v Circus Show Corp.*, 1993 U.S. Dist. LEXIS 9797 (S.D.N.Y. 1993); *Tennessee Imp., Inc. v Filippi*, 745 F.Supp. 1314 (M.D. Tenn. 1990); *Astra Footwear Indus. v Harwyn Int'l, Inc.*, 442 F.Supp. 907 (S.D.N.Y. 1978)), France (Court of Appeal of Paris, 7 February 2002, *SA Alfac c/ Société Irmac Importacão, comércia e industria LTDa* (2002) *Revue de l'arbitrage* 413; Court of Appeal of Paris, 24 March 1994, *Deko c/Dingler* (1994) *Revue de l'arbitrage* 515; Court of Appeal of Paris, 14 February 1985, *Tovomon c/ Amatex* (1987) *Revue de l'arbitrage* 325; French Court of Cassation, 14 December 1983, *Epoux Convert c/ Droga* (1984) *Revue de l'arbitrage* 483), Hong Kong (*Lucky-Goldstar Int'l (HK) Ltd v Ng Moo Kee Eng'g Ltd* (1994) *Arbitration and Dispute Resolution Law Journal* 49), Switzerland (Swiss Federal Tribunal, 21 November 2003, DFT 130 III 66; 8 July 2003, DFT 129 III 675; 7 February 1991 (1991) 9 ASA Bulletin 269) and Germany (27 September 2005, Oberlandesgericht Hamm, in Albert Jan van den Berg (ed), *Yearbook Commercial Arbitration XXXI* (ICCA 2006) 685, 693; 15 October 1999, Kaammergericht Berlin, in Albert Jan van den Berg (ed), *Yearbook Commercial Arbitration XXVI* (ICCA 2001) 328; 5 December 1994, Oberlandesgericht Dresden, in Albert Jan van den Berg, *Yearbook Commercial Arbitration XXII* (ICCA 1997) 266).
17 2017 ICC Arbitration Rules, Articles 12(3) – (4); 2014 LCIA Arbitration Rules, Article 7(2).
18 UNCITRAL Model Law, Articles 11(3) – (4).
19 In Austria, Belgium, Bulgaria, Croatia, Cyprus, Denmark, England and Wales, Finland, France, Germany, Greece, Ireland, Lithuania, Luxembourg, Malta, the Netherlands, Poland, Portugal, Romania, Slovenia and Switzerland, the local arbitration law does not set forth any specific requirement for arbitrators.
20 This is the case in the Czech Republic, Italy, Scotland, Spain and Sweden.
21 In *Jivrai v Hashwani* [2011] UKSC 40, the UK Supreme Court stated that parties are free to specify any kind of requirement for the arbitrators, including their religion. According to the Court,

126 *The arbitral tribunal*

arbitrators are quasi-judicial adjudicators and, as such, the parties can set forth any requirement of their preference in the agreement, even if in contrast with labour anti-discrimination legislation. For a longer discussion of the case, see the main text.

22 E.g. pursuant to Section 19 of the English Arbitration Act 1996, when acting as appointing authority, the court at the seat must have due regard to any agreement of the parties as to the qualifications required of the arbitrators.
23 UNCITRAL Model Law, Article 12(2).
24 2017 ICC Rules, Article 11(1); 2014 LCIA Rules, Article 5(3); 2010 UNCITRAL Arbitration Rules, Article 12(1); Article 20 of the Arbitration Rules of the Milan Chamber of Arbitration; Article 11(2) of the Netherlands Arbitration Institute Arbitration Rules; Article 11 of the 2018 HKIAC Administered Arbitration Rules; Section 8 of the Rules of the Lewiatan Court of Arbitration.
25 UNCITRAL Model Law, Article 12(1).
26 See, e.g. 2017 ICC Rules, Article 11(3); 2014 LCIA Rules, Articles 5(4) – 5(5).
27 See p. 116–120 for a discussion of arbitrator challenge procedures.
28 The problem of independence and impartiality arises with respect not only to arbitrators, but also to State judges. For this reason, it is interesting to analyse whether the same standards of independence and impartiality apply to both. According to a line of case-law, arbitrators are not bound to the same standards of impartiality as State judges. This idea has been expressed in US Courts' interpretation of the "evident partiality" standard set forth in Section 10(a) of the Federal Arbitration Act: according to the leading decisions, arbitrators have the duty to disclose possible conflicts of interest at the outset of the proceedings, but they are not bound to the same impartiality standards applicable to State judges (*Commonwealth Coatings Corp. v Continental Casualty Co.*, 393 US 145, 89 S.Ct. 337, 21 L.Ed.2d 301 (1968); *Applied Indus. Materials Corp. v Ovalar*, 492 F.3d 132 (2d Cir. 2007); *Ometto v Asa Bioenergy Holding A.G.*, 12–4022(L) (2d Cir. 2014)). In particular, a judge could be disqualified whenever "his impartiality might reasonably be questioned" (*Apple v Jewish Hosp. & Med. Ctr.*, 829 F.2d 326, 332–333 (1987)), whilst an arbitrator could be disqualified only when a reasonable person "would have to conclude" that there was a partiality to one of the sides (*Morelite Construction Corp. v New York City District Council Carpenters Benefit Funds*, 748 F.2d 79, 84 (2d Cir. 1984)). However, it would be wrong to draw universally-valid conclusions from the above case law. The London Court of International Arbitration (LCIA), for example, shows a tendency to apply to its arbitrators the same standards of independence and impartiality that would be applicable to State judges. In a 2009 decision (Parties Not Indicated, LCIA Court Decision on Challenge to Arbitrator, LCIA Reference No. 81160, 28 August 2009 (2011) 3 *Arbitration International* 442, 447), a Division of the LCIA relied on a series of judicial decisions stating that, by virtue of the Human Rights Act 1998, the UK legislative standard of independence and impartiality had been further defined in accordance with the European Convention of Human Rights (*Director General of Fair Trading v Proprietary Association of Great Britain* [2001] EWCA Civ. 1217; *Porter v Magill* [2001] UKHL 67; *Lawal v Northern Spirit Ltd* [2003] UKHL 35). Therefore, according to the Division, the "justifiable doubts" standard set forth in section 33(1)(a) of the Arbitration Act also must be interpreted in a manner compatible with the Convention. In conclusion, the LCIA Division argues that the structural difference between arbitrators and State judges is not enough ground to differentiate the applicable standards of independence and impartiality.
29 See, e.g. *New Regency Productions Inc. v Nippon Herald Films Inc.* C.A.(CAL.), 2007; Cour d'Appel de Bruxelles, 17ème Chambre, *République de Pologne c. Eureko B.V. et Schwebel Stefen M*, R.G.No 2007/AR/70; Swedish Supreme Court, Judgment of 19 November 2007, *Anders Jilken v Ericsson AB* Case No. T 2448–06.
30 2004 IBA Guidelines on Conflicts of International in International Arbitration, paragraph 8 of the Introduction.

31 The US Federal Arbitration Act (FAA) is an important exception to this almost universal rule, as it does not allow arbitrators to be challenged before courts, requiring instead that parties wait until an award is delivered, and then seek to have the award annulled because of the "evident partiality" of the arbitrator. Of course, parties may still agree on the use of a non-judicial mechanism for challenging arbitrators, such as through the decision of an arbitral institution.
32 2006 UNCITRAL Arbitration Rules, Article 13(1).
33 2017 ICC Rules, Article 14(2).
34 2017 ICC Rules, Article 14(1); 2014 LCIA Rules, Article 10; 2010 UNCITRAL Rules, Article 12(1).
35 The 2010 UNCITRAL Rules (Article 13(3)) also regulate the case where the non-challenging party agrees with the challenging party: in this case, similarly to the hypothesis of the arbitrator voluntarily resigning, the arbitrator is excluded from the tribunal, but the challenge is not to be considered as accepted. Rather, in this case, the challenge has been prevented and made superfluous by the agreement between all parties.
36 A collection of LCIA challenge decisions has been published in (2011) 3 *Arbitration International*.
37 2017 ICC Rules, Article 13; 2014 LCIA Rules, Articles 5 and 7; 2016 SIAC Rules, Article 9(3).
38 2006 UNCITRAL Model Law, Article 12(2). Many jurisdictions follow the Model Law, such as Spain, Ireland, Belgium, Germany, Austria, Croatia, Hungary, Bulgaria, Poland and Lithuania.
39 This is the case in Romania, Italy and Sweden.
40 But see *Third Nat. Bank In Nashville v WEDGE Group, Inc.*, 749 F.Supp. 851 (M.D.Tenn., 1990).
41 *Gulf Guar. Life Ins. Co. v Connecticut Gen. Life Ins. Co.*, 304 F.3d 476 (5th Cir. 2002); *Larry's United Super, Inc. v Werries*, 253 F.3d 1083 (8th Cir. 2001); *Aviall, Inc. v Ryder Sys.*, 110 F.3d 892 (2d Cir. 1997).
42 If the arbitration is *ad hoc*, the challenging party first needs to apply for the disqualification of the challenged arbitrator before the arbitral tribunal, pursuant to Article 13(2). If the arbitrator does not withdraw voluntarily and the other party does not agree to the challenge, the arbitral tribunal decides on it. If the tribunal rejects the challenge, the party can activate the procedure set forth in Article 13(3).
43 Swiss Law on Private International Law, Articles 179–180.
44 See, e.g. 2006 UNCITRAL Model Law, Article 15; Article 14(1) of the UNCITRAL Rules.
45 See, e.g. Article 15(4) of the 2017 ICC Rules; Article 11(1) of the 2014 LCIA Rules.
46 2017 ICC Rules, Article 15(5).
47 Under Article 12.2, "(i)n deciding whether to continue the arbitration, the remaining arbitrators shall take into account the stage of the arbitration, any explanation made by or on behalf of the absent arbitrator for his or her refusal or non-participation, the likely effect upon the legal recognition or enforceability of any award at the seat of the arbitration and such other matters as they consider appropriate in the circumstances. The reasons for such decision shall be stated in any award made by the remaining arbitrators without the participation of the absent arbitrator".
48 *Hoosac Tunnel Dock & Elevator Co. v O'Brien*, 137 Mass. 424 (Mass. 1884). See also David J. Branson and Richard E. Wallace Jr., Immunity of Arbitrators under United States Law, in Julian D M Lew (ed.), *The Immunity of Arbitrators* (Informa 1990) 85.
49 In which case it is the institution that is civilly liable, not the arbitrator.

5 Arbitral proceedings

Rules

1. Parties are free to choose their own arbitral procedure, although there are limits

Arbitration statutes now almost universally adopt a "hands off" approach to arbitral procedure: rather than specifying in detail how an arbitration must function for any resulting award to be enforceable, they recognise that questions of procedure are for the parties to agree on, so long as the fundamental fairness of the proceedings is maintained. Governments ultimately have every right to tell parties how they must arbitrate if they want their award to be enforceable, but the justification for allowing parties to agree on their preferred procedure is a practical one: the arbitral process will work better that way.

2. Parties are free to select the seat of the arbitration

Selection of the seat of an arbitration is a matter for the parties. That choice can be made in the arbitration agreement or at any time prior to delivery of an award. If the parties don't agree on a seat, the choice will be made by the tribunal or in accordance with any applicable institutional rules. If no choice has been made by the time a party wishes to enforce the award or have it annulled, the reviewing court will make the choice.

3. Whether an arbitration is confidential depends on the law of the seat

Many people think that arbitration is inherently confidential, but this is not true. Rather, whether an arbitration is confidential varies significantly from one jurisdiction to another. However, even if the law of the seat does not state that arbitration is confidential, parties can usually make their arbitration confidential by entering into a confidentiality agreement or by agreeing to use arbitration rules that include a confidentiality obligation.

4. There is a typical procedural development of an arbitration

While the procedural flexibility of arbitration makes it impossible to provide any sort of standardised account of arbitral procedure, there is a general form that many international commercial arbitrations take: the parties normally submit written claims and defences, exchange documents and similar evidence, put forth their arguments at one or more oral hearings, cross-examine witnesses, and then wait for the tribunal to deliver its decision. In effect, arbitration procedure is often just a more flexible version of conventional litigation procedure.

5. *Approaches to evidence in international commercial arbitration usually attempt to strike a balance between different legal traditions*

Strict rules of evidence are rarely used in arbitration. While parties can agree to use any set of evidence rules they wish, allowing the tribunal flexibility on questions of evidence lets it tailor an approach that takes into consideration the different legal traditions and expectations of all parties. Non-binding sets of rules, such as the IBA Rules on the Taking of Evidence in International Arbitration and the Prague Rules on the Efficient Conduct of Proceedings in International Arbitration, have been developed to encourage consistency and predictability.

6. *The proceedings may involve more than two parties*

While arbitration is usually thought of as involving two parties, a Claimant and a Respondent, a "multi-party" arbitration can involve any number of parties. Those parties may fall naturally into two groups, again forming a Claimant and a Respondent, but they may instead raise a diversity of cross-cutting claims and conflicting interests. Multi-party arbitrations raise particularly difficult issues with respect to the right of parties to appoint an arbitrator to the tribunal, and whether every party in a multi-party arbitration has that right.

7. *Arbitration can be quick but it can also be "expedited"*

While arbitration is often thought of as a faster alternative to litigation, in some cases a standard arbitration will still take too long. It is in response to this concern that "expedited" arbitration has been developed, which aims to complete a full arbitral process in a much-reduced period of time. Expedited arbitration is now offered by many arbitral institutions, although it is also possible in *ad hoc* arbitration if all parties agree. However, the prioritising of speed over other considerations such as thoroughness and fairness raises risks, and while expedited arbitration is a valuable option it must be used carefully if serious injustice is to be avoided.

Analysis

1. *Parties are free to choose their own arbitral procedure, although there are limits*

One of the ideas that was introduced at the very beginning of this book is that there really is no such "thing" as arbitration, but rather just many things that are <u>not</u> arbitration. That is, that it is part of the essence of arbitration that parties are free to arbitrate in almost any way they wish to do so. Parties who choose to take their dispute to a court will be obligated to follow that court's rules and procedures, but as an arbitration is a private dispute resolution procedure, controlled by the parties, it is now almost universally recognised that parties should have the freedom to choose how they wish to arbitrate. Do you want to have a hearing in Paris but require that everyone speaks Russian at all times? That's fine. Do you want to require that all witnesses be connected to a lie detector while testifying? Sure, you can do that. Do you want to require that everyone in the hearing room must dress in red, call one another Bob, and can only speak if they are hopping up and down on one leg while two other people stand behind them humming the Marseillaise? Absolutely, that's not a problem.

Party autonomy, you will have recognised by now, infuses every aspect of arbitration, and that is no more true than when it comes to questions of arbitral procedure. As a result, arbitration statutes now almost universally adopt a "hands off" approach to the topic: rather than specifying in detail how an arbitration must function for any resulting award to be enforceable, they instead specifically recognise that questions of procedure are for the parties to agree on, so long as the fundamental fairness of the proceedings is maintained. The classic statement of this approach is contained in Article 19(1) of the UNCITRAL Model Law: "Subject to the provisions of this Law, the parties are free to agree on the procedure to be followed by the arbitral tribunal in conducting the proceedings." Similar provisions are included in arbitration statutes around the word.[1]

On the one hand, it may seem unsurprising that parties are left free to choose how they wish to arbitrate. After all, the parties, not the government, are paying for the arbitration, and the parties have consciously chosen to arbitrate rather than go to court. If arbitrations were required to operate in accordance with the same procedural rules as State courts, the parties would lose one of the primary benefits of choosing to resolve their dispute through a private proceeding. Even more strongly, one might argue that as an arbitration is a private proceeding, organised by and paid for by the parties, it is ultimately none of the government's business how the parties choose to arbitrate, any more than the government can legitimately tell you how to dress or where to go on holiday.

You will quite often find views along these lines expressed by arbitration practitioners, combined with passionate disapproval of any governmental attempt to control arbitral procedure. Essentially, "it's the parties' arbitration, so it's their business how they do it."

There is, of course, a clear truth to this idea. Arbitration is a private procedure, so the parties who are paying for that procedure should be allowed to use whatever procedure they wish to use. However, adopting this view too strongly ignores a fundamental reality of arbitration: parties don't want a truly private procedure – they want a private procedure that will result in an award that will be enforced by State courts. It is standardly said, for example, that an arbitrator's fundamental obligation is to deliver an "enforceable" award. What parties want, that is, is not a private dispute resolution process, but a dispute resolution process that is solidly enmeshed in the conventional government-controlled legal system, but over which they personally maintain control.

Once this is recognised, it becomes clear that States have every right to tell parties how they must arbitrate if they want their award to be enforceable. Parties want to be able to rely on government assistance if they need it, and governments have every right to say "Sure, we will assist you, but only if you obey these rules". The parties, in turn, can reject those rules and still arbitrate however they want, but they just can't then expect to have their award recognised or enforced through State courts.

So, does this mean that the modern trend of arbitration statutes to simply state that it is up to the parties to decide how to arbitrate is wrong? Should arbitration statutes include detailed procedural rules that arbitrations must follow if any resulting award is to be enforced?

No. What it means is that the justification for parties having the freedom to arbitrate however they want does not come from the "private" nature of arbitration. It is not that parties have some inherent "right" to arbitrate however they want, and that governments are wrong if they ever interfere with that right. The freedom to choose your arbitral procedure is not a human right.

Rather, the justification for allowing parties to agree on their preferred procedural rules is a practical one. It's simply a good idea.

State courts have to use a standardised procedure because they are open to anyone, and the costs of the process are paid by the government. In any given case, the procedures being used may not be the perfect ones for the resolution of that dispute, but if the court's procedural rules are well designed then they are a good balance between an effective procedure and an affordable one.

The procedure used in an arbitration, however, does not have to be suitable for a wide range of disputes. It only needs to be suitable for the particular dispute that is being heard between the particular parties involved. As a result, it is possible to adopt a procedure in one arbitration that would be inefficient, impractical, or even unjust in the vast majority of arbitrations. In this way, allowing each individual arbitration to function in accordance with the specific procedures that are most appropriate for that arbitration results in a system that is actually more effective and efficient than could ever be the case if arbitral procedure were dictated by governments. Arbitration can never replace State courts, as State courts provide an essential guarantee that a fundamentally fair dispute resolution process is available to everyone. But arbitration provides an important alternative, able to provide a more "tailored" process for those able to afford it and with adequate understanding of how it needs to be pursued.

Of course, by the time an arbitration is commencing, the parties are involved in a dispute, and will often be quite hostile to one another. In addition, even when the parties have no ill-feeling towards one another, the enforceability and finality of an arbitration award means that they will approach the arbitration as a procedure to be "won", with every tactical advantage worth considering. For this reason, it is rarely the case that parties will directly agree on the procedures to be used in their arbitration. Instead, this agreement will normally be indirect, such as by the parties having specified in their arbitration agreement that they will arbitrate in accordance with a specific set of institutional rules (e.g. the ICC Rules of Arbitration, the SIAC Rules or the Cairo Regional Center For International Commercial Arbitration (CRCICA) Arbitration Rules) or, if they do not want to involve an arbitral institution, the UNCITRAL Arbitration Rules.

When even that indirect agreement does not exist, however, arbitration statutes normally provide a back-up, often in the form of a delegation to the arbitrators of all questions of procedure. Article 19(2) of the Model Law, for example, provides that if the parties have not agreed on the applicable procedural rules, "the tribunal may (. . .) conduct the arbitration in such manner as it considers appropriate." Such a rule does not only ensure that there is clarity on how questions of procedure will be resolved, it ensures that procedural decisions will be made by individuals aware of the subtleties of a case, rather than by legislators unable to take individual case needs into account.

2. Parties are free to select the seat of the arbitration

While perhaps not immediately obviously a "procedural" decision, one of the most important procedural decisions that will be taken in any arbitration is the selection of the arbitral seat. This may, and usually should, have been specified in the arbitration agreement itself. However, since every international commercial arbitration must have a seat, where it has not been specified in the arbitration agreement one must be determined. While the choice of the seat is not, as such, the choice of a "procedure", the arbitral law of the seat sets the framework within which the procedures of the arbitration must stay if any resulting award is to be legally valid in that jurisdiction. As a result, it is essential to be clear on the seat of the arbitration prior to important procedural decisions being taken.

Overwhelmingly, arbitration statutes give parties the freedom to agree on the seat of their arbitration, rather than mandating a procedure that must be used to determine the seat.[2] In turn, courts in modern arbitration jurisdictions are generally quite liberal in the interpretation of agreements selecting the seat of arbitration, accepting even barebones designation of an arbitral seat (e.g. "Arbitration: Hamburg") as sufficient.[3] Nonetheless, parties must be careful to avoid ambiguity in their specification of the arbitral seat, or they risk subsequently being told by a court that their award is unenforceable because their arbitration violated the mandatory rules of State A, even though they thought they had agreed that their arbitration was seated in State B.[4]

As already noted, the choice of the arbitral seat will usually be found in the arbitration agreement itself, but even when this is not the case, parties retain the right to agree on the seat of their arbitration prior to the final award being delivered. In addition, even if the parties themselves cannot agree on the seat, the arbitral tribunal is often recognised as having the right to make this determination in an order or even in the final award. Indeed, specification of the seat is one of the fundamental components of a properly drafted award. It does nonetheless happen that a tribunal does not perform this fundamental obligation, and in such a case the applicable arbitration rules and arbitration statutes will provide a fall-back mechanism for the determination of the seat.[5]

There is, however, diversity in how arbitral institutions and arbitration statutes approach this issue. While the UNCITRAL Arbitration Rules,[6] some institutional arbitration rules[7] and most arbitration statutes[8] entrust the task of choosing the seat to the arbitral tribunal, other institutional arbitration rules instead allocate that decision to the institution itself.[9] Such an approach allows the institution to determine the seat of arbitration, when necessary, even if no arbitral tribunal has yet been constituted. In turn, other institutions specify a fall-back seat that will be applicable when the parties have not agreed on a seat: under the LCIA Rules, for example, in the absence of agreement by the parties, the seat of arbitration is London, unless and until the tribunal determines that another seat is more appropriate.[10] In turn, other institutional rules, such as the International Centre for Dispute Resolution (ICDR) Arbitration Rules, may combine the preceding approaches, allowing the institution itself to initially select the seat of the arbitration, but subject to any subsequent determination by the arbitral tribunal.[11]

This does not, however, mean that identification of an arbitral seat is never a problem. Situations can arise, after all, in which the parties have not agreed on a seat, and the arbitration is *ad hoc* or the applicable institutional rules do not specify how a seat should be chosen. In this situation, the decision on how the seat should be determined will be left to a court – with the court being tasked with this job not because it possesses a particularly good understanding of arbitration, or a good knowledge of the parties' dispute, but simply because one of the parties has chosen to bring a case in that court, either in an attempt to avoid the arbitration agreement or, in some jurisdictions, in order to receive a declaratory judgement specifying the seat of the arbitration.

While some arbitration statutes, such as the English Arbitration Act 1996, instruct courts to take a flexible approach to this question, and determine the seat with "regard to the parties' agreement and all the relevant circumstances", other legal systems are far less flexible. Some courts, for example, have held that an arbitration agreement that does not specify a seat is invalid due to its vagueness.[12] Other arbitration laws will resolve that vagueness for the parties, but will do so in accordance with a rule, rather than through an exercise of the court's judgement. Under Italian law, for example, the seat of the arbitration will be held to be the place where the agreement to arbitrate was concluded.[13] On the other hand, under Swedish law, an arbitration can be seated in Sweden simply because the respondent is domiciled in Sweden.[14] As a result, parties who have not specified the seat of their arbitration, or a means of selecting that seat, can end up being told that they don't actually have a valid arbitration agreement, or that the seat of their arbitration is one that the parties would not have agreed upon at the time of entering into their arbitration agreement.

There is, however, one further difficulty that must be emphasised, which arises from the diversity between arbitration statutes regarding how the seat of an arbitration should be determined: courts may disagree. That is, say that Faizaan and Phy are involved in an arbitration. The final award has been given by the arbitral tribunal, which negligently fails to specify the seat of the arbitration. Faizaan takes the award to a court in Bosnia and Herzegovina, seeking to have the award annulled. The courts of Bosnia and Herzegovina only have jurisdiction to hear annulment applications if the arbitration was seated in Bosnia and Herzegovina, and the court decides that Bosnia and Herzegovina is indeed the seat and annuls the award. However, Phy takes the award to a court in Algeria, which in turn determines that Algeria is the seat of the arbitration and that the award is valid and enforceable.

The simple solution to all these problems, of course, is for the parties to agree on the seat of the arbitration, either in their arbitration agreement or upon commencing the arbitration. However, if the parties cannot agree it is incumbent on the arbitral tribunal, as a matter of professional competence, to address the question and resolve it, preferably in the initial stages of the arbitration.

There is one final point that must be made about the choice of the seat of an arbitration, and that is that it can change. The parties may, for example, have agreed to arbitrate in State X, but subsequently decide that it was a bad choice, perhaps because of certain features of the arbitration law of State X, or of the hostile view of arbitration held by the courts of State X, which neither of the parties was aware of when they selected State X as the seat. So long as the parties agree to do so, they retain the right to change the seat at any time. However, that decision must be clear and explicit, and simply taking actions such as holding the hearings in State Y will not usually be found to constitute an agreement to make State Y the new seat of the arbitration.

3. Whether an arbitration is confidential depends on the law of the seat

A further foundational issue that should be resolved before any other important procedural decisions are taken, is that of whether or not the arbitration will be confidential. It is surprising to most people not intimately familiar with arbitration that this is even an issue, as the confidentiality of arbitration is often referenced as one of arbitration's distinctive and attractive features. Yet, as already noted in Chapter 1, the reality is far more complex than is widely appreciated, with the question of arbitration's confidentiality being resolved in different ways in different jurisdictions. Indeed, the level of international disagreement regarding the confidentiality of arbitration is so high that the Model Law, which was consciously designed to help bring consistency to arbitration laws around the world, simply avoids the issue entirely.[15]

Arbitration is unquestionably a "private" procedure. It is a process based on the agreement of the parties, and controlled by the parties. As a result, while many legal systems give the general public a right to attend court proceedings, parties involved in an arbitration may exclude all third parties from their proceeding. Strangers have no more right to come to your arbitration than they do to come to your birthday party – it's your party, so you get to decide who can and cannot be there.

"Privacy", though, is different to "confidentiality", and while you may be able to stop people coming to your birthday party, you cannot stop people who did come telling everyone else about it. This latter question is what the "confidentiality" of arbitration is about. It addresses when and in what ways information about the arbitration may be communicated to non-parties.

As noted above, while many people associate arbitration with confidentiality, the reality is that the law on the confidentiality of arbitration varies significantly between jurisdictions. For example, the Spanish Arbitration Act expressly imposes an obligation of confidentiality.[16] The English Arbitration Act 1996, on the other hand, follows the Model Law's example in not addressing confidentiality – but English courts have held that the private nature of arbitration results in an implied obligation of confidentiality for every arbitration, subject to certain exceptions.[17] By contrast, while the US Federal Arbitration Act similarly does not address the topic of confidentiality, US courts have held that no implied obligation of confidentiality exists in arbitration.[18] In turn, the French arbitration statute expressly states that domestic arbitrations are confidential unless the parties agree otherwise,[19] but doesn't impose such an obligation in international arbitrations other than with respect to the tribunal's deliberations, which are confidential.[20]

> **Understanding arbitration through case-law**
>
> *Confidentiality under English Law*
>
> **Case details:** *Emmott v Wilson & Partners Limited* [2008] EWCA Civ 184
>
> **Authority deciding the case:** Court of Appeal (England and Wales)
>
> **Facts of the case:** A solicitor joined a legal services company. The agreement between the solicitor and the company contained an arbitration clause providing for arbitration in England. A dispute arose and arbitral proceedings were commenced against the solicitor. In the arbitration, the company initially made allegations of fraud, but later amended its claims and withdrew those allegations.
>
> The company also initiated proceedings in court against two colleagues of the solicitor, largely based on the same facts as in the arbitration involving the solicitor. The question arose whether the documents submitted in the arbitration could be disclosed in the court proceedings.
>
> **Decision:** The Court of Appeal recognised that the parties to an arbitration have an implied obligation to keep documents submitted in an arbitration confidential. However, the Court observed that there are some exceptions to the implied obligation of confidentiality under English law. The parties may, of course, mutually consent to the disclosure of the documents. In addition, the obligation of confidentiality does not apply when disclosure is necessary to protect the legitimate interests of a party to the arbitration, or when it is necessary in the interests of justice.
>
> Notably, the Court also expressed the view that because the confidentiality obligation derives from the agreement to arbitrate, disputes concerning the applicability and scope of this obligation should in principle be resolved by the arbitral tribunal, rather than by a court. In the case at hand, however, none of the parties objected to the Court ruling on the issue.

Nonetheless, while confidentiality is not an inherent feature of arbitration, even those jurisdictions in which no obligation of confidentiality exists usually allow parties to create such an obligation. For example, parties who wish their arbitration to remain confidential can enter into a confidentiality agreement at the beginning of their arbitration. Once this has been done, the arbitration is now covered by a legally enforceable confidentiality obligation, even though one created by contract, rather than by statute. To return to the examples just given, both the US courts and French courts have recognised the enforceability of confidentiality agreements relating to arbitration, despite there being no express confidentiality obligation in their arbitration statutes.[21]

Of course, the enforceability of confidentiality agreements in jurisdictions that do not impose an obligation of confidentiality in arbitration does not create as strong a protection for those desiring confidentiality. After all, a confidentiality agreement can only be entered into if both sides want the arbitration to be confidential, and unless such a provision has been included in the arbitration agreement (which is usually not the case), it must be agreed when the parties are already in dispute. However, at this point one of the parties may see an advantage in making some or all of the dispute public, and refuse to enter into a confidentiality agreement.

On the other hand, though, the imposition of an express or implied obligation of confidentiality creates problems of its own, as many parties will not have seriously considered the question of confidentiality when agreeing to arbitrate. They will likely have considered the "privacy" of arbitration, and the fact that it means they will be able to control their own procedure and keep third parties away from their hearings. But unless the subject matter of the underlying transaction expressly raises questions of confidentiality (e.g. trade secrets), many parties will not have considered their own inability to discuss publicly the wrongs they now believe the other party has done to them.

It is this reality that ultimately argues in favour of making the confidentiality of arbitration "opt in", rather than "opt out". In other words, as a policy matter, it is better to require the parties to expressly choose confidentiality, rather than providing that all arbitrations are confidential unless the parties expressly agree otherwise. Where the nature of the dispute is such that the public release of any information regarding it will unfairly harm one of the parties, such as where trade secrets are at stake, this will usually (although not always) have been predictable to the parties from the outset, giving them the ability to ensure the confidentiality of their arbitration by including a confidentiality provision in their arbitration agreement. As a result, those parties most likely to be harmed by an "opt in" approach to confidentiality are well placed to protect themselves from that harm.

Where an "opt out" approach is taken, however, parties who have never even considered the question of confidentiality will find themselves unable to publicly discuss a wrong they believe they have suffered, and other parties will be unable to learn about potential repeated wrongs committed by a party, because each wrong was resolved through mandatorily confidential arbitration. When arbitration was a niche choice as a mechanism of dispute resolution, restricted in its use to large companies involved in international transactions, this situation may not have been problematic. The growth of international commercial arbitration, however, means it now plays a far more central role in dispute resolution in many States around the world, involving parties of all sizes, from large corporations to individuals. In this new context, a presumption of confidentiality stands to cause injury to parties who would not have voluntarily chosen confidentiality, far more often than it will provide protection to parties who would have chosen it but failed to do so.

4. There is a typical procedural development of an arbitration

Given the inherent procedural flexibility of arbitration, it is impossible to provide any sort of standardised account of arbitral procedure. That said, there is a general form that many international commercial arbitrations take, serving in many respects as merely a more flexible version of conventional litigation procedure. This section, then, will focus on this approach, laying out the steps usually found in an international commercial arbitration, and what role each of them has in the overall process. It must be remembered, though, that as parties retain

4.1 Initial submissions

An arbitration will be commenced by a party, standardly called the "Claimant", stating that it wishes to arbitrate a dispute currently existing between it and the other party to the arbitration agreement, standardly called the "Respondent". Precisely how this is done will depend on the arbitration agreement between the parties, and if the arbitration agreement specifies steps that a Claimant must take to commence an arbitration, those steps much be followed. Importantly, this can include waiting for a certain period of time (often referred to as a "cooling off period"), or even undertaking a separate dispute resolution procedure (e.g. mediation) before commencing arbitration.

For example, the parties' arbitration agreement may specify that either party must wait until six months have passed since they initially raised their complaint to the other party, before they can commence arbitration. If a party attempts to commence an arbitration before the applicable six months period has expired, their attempt to commence arbitration may be found to be invalid, and they will be required to commence arbitration again once the six months is over.[22]

Alternatively, a particularly common feature of arbitration agreements is a requirement to attempt to resolve the dispute by negotiation or mediation prior to commencement of arbitration, creating what is often called a "multi-tier dispute resolution clause".[23] However, agreements of this type need to be approached with caution, as while some jurisdictions will enforce them,[24] in others their enforceability is much less certain, often depending on whether the parties have expressly stated that failure to follow the listed steps should prevent commencement of arbitration,[25] or if the parties have provided sufficient detail in the clause, such as by specifying how long the obligation to mediate lasts.[26]

Assuming there are no such obstacles to the commencement of the arbitration, the Claimant will usually initiate proceedings by filing what is standardly referred to as a "Request for Arbitration"[27] or "Notice of Arbitration".[28] Precisely what needs to be included in this document will vary depending on the arbitration agreement, any applicable arbitration rules, and the *lex arbitri*. Claimants will usually only provide basic information on the claim they are bringing against the Respondent, rather than providing a detailed statement of their claim. However, parties drafting a Request for Arbitration should be guided by the fundamental need to provide adequate notice to the Respondent of the subject matter of the arbitration. A central feature of arbitration, after all, is the ability of parties to nominate their preferred arbitrator, and a Respondent cannot do this properly if it does not know what the arbitration will be about. As a result, failing to provide adequate information in the Request for Arbitration of the nature of the claim risks depriving the other party of a fundamental procedural right.[29]

A useful example of the kinds of information usually included in a Request for Arbitration can be found in Article 4(3) of the ICC Rules of Arbitration:

- the name and details of each of the parties;
- the name and details of the representatives of the claimant in the arbitration;

- a description of the nature and circumstances of the dispute and of the basis upon which the claims are made;
- a statement of the relief sought, together with the amounts of any quantified claims and, to the extent possible, an estimate of the monetary value of any other claims;
- any relevant agreements and, in particular, the arbitration agreement;
- observations or proposals concerning the number of arbitrators and their choice (if necessary, depending on the applicable mechanism for the constitution of the arbitral tribunal: see *supra*, Chapter 4);
- observations or proposals as to the seat of the arbitration, the applicable rules of law and the language of the arbitration.

How a Request for Arbitration must be served will, of course, vary from one arbitration to another. In *ad hoc* arbitration, as well as under some institutional arbitration rules, the Request for Arbitration must be served by the claimant directly on the defendant.[30] However, other institutional rules require instead that the Request for Arbitration be served on the arbitral institution itself, which will then notify the Respondent that a Request for Arbitration has been served.[31]

Upon receipt of the Request for Arbitration, the Respondent will usually be required to submit an "Answer" within a time limit specified by any applicable arbitration rules. An Answer largely parallels the Request for Arbitration in both form and content, with the Respondent usually required to provide similar factual information as was required in the Request for Arbitration, as well as a brief response to the claim being brought against it.[32]

Importantly, however, the Answer also provides the Respondent with an opportunity to bring its own claims against the Claimant (usually referred to as "counterclaims"), so long as they fall within the limits of the arbitration agreement.[33] Indeed, more than one Claimant has brought a relatively modest claim against a Respondent, only to receive a much larger counterclaim in response.

If the Respondent does file a counterclaim, that part of the Answer functions, in effect, as its own Request for Arbitration, thereby allowing the Claimant to file its own Answer, responding to the Respondent's counterclaim. This is an early example of the kind of "back and forth" that characterises much arbitration practice. While court litigation often focuses on ensuring that parties adhere to preset procedural rules, arbitration focuses instead on the overall fairness of the process, and in particular on the necessity for both parties to have the opportunity to comment on anything that may substantively impact on the tribunal's decision.

4.2 Constitution of the arbitral tribunal and the "emergency arbitrator"

As part of the Request for Arbitration and the Answer, the Claimant and Respondent will usually both have been required to address the constitution of the arbitral tribunal – that is, who the arbitrator(s) should be. The specific mechanism that must be used to create the tribunal can vary, depending on what is required by the arbitration agreement, any applicable arbitration rules, and the *lex arbitri*. However, since no procedural decisions can be taken in an arbitration without arbitrators, the tribunal must be constituted as rapidly as possible. A detailed discussion of arbitral tribunals is included in Chapter 4.

One recent development worth acknowledging is the increasing availability under the rules of arbitral institutions of an "emergency arbitrator".[34] This innovation is designed to address the need of parties to obtain a ruling from an arbitrator before the tribunal has actually been constituted. For instance, there may be an urgent need for an order requiring a party to preserve certain evidence that will be useful at a later stage in the arbitration. While under some *lex arbitri* orders of this nature can be obtained from the courts of the seat, if the parties have agreed to the use of arbitration rules that provide for the appointment of an emergency arbitrator, either party may require that the institution appoint a temporary arbitrator, whose role is to make specific decisions pending the appointment of the actual tribunal.

While parties will normally have the right to participate in the selection of their arbitrator(s), an emergency arbitrator will usually be selected by the arbitral institution, often within one or two days, and often without consultation with the parties. In addition, while it is normally possible for the parties to challenge the appointment of an emergency arbitrator on the standard grounds of a lack of independence or impartiality, any such challenge must similarly be made within only a few days.[35] Once appointed, the emergency arbitrator will hear the arguments of the parties on the issue she was appointed to resolve, and deliver a decision. While this decision will be binding on the parties, it is usually not binding on the arbitral tribunal itself once it is constituted, and can be reversed.

This possibility of reversal, however, raises one complexity that should be noted about the use of emergency arbitrators, namely whether an emergency arbitrator's decision constitutes an "award" or merely an "order". If the former, it would be enforceable under the New York Convention, while if the latter it will not. It is, though, generally seen to be a defining character of an award that it finally resolves a substantive issue between the parties. The ability of the arbitral tribunal to review and reverse the emergency arbitrator's decision, therefore, raises serious questions about whether an emergency arbitrator's decision may only qualify as an order, and so not be enforceable under the New York Convention. This topic is addressed more fully in Chapter 6.

4.3 Before the final award is rendered, the parties may need provisional relief

The central motivation for the development of the role of "emergency arbitrator" was recognition of the difficulties and delays that can arise from the need of parties in an arbitration to secure immediate assistance once a dispute has arisen, even though it may take time for an arbitral tribunal to be appointed. For example, in a supply contract, if the supplier stops delivering the goods, the counterparty may be unable to continue its business activities. Alternatively, the need may centre around the preservation of assets or evidence located on a certain site in order to determine whether a given contractual obligation has been discharged; but it is impossible to maintain the *status quo* of the site for a long period of time. Alternatively, the financial situation of the Claimant may be so unstable that the Respondent is concerned that it will be unable to recover the costs of the arbitration if it prevails; as a result, the Respondent wants the Claimant to provide adequate "security", often in the form of a bank guarantee or deposit payment, upon which the Respondent can draw if the Claimant fails to meet its obligations.

If such situations occur, a party can request a measure designed to address the issue temporarily, rather than to finally resolve the matter, known as a "provisional measure" or "interim measure". In essence, "provisional" or "interim" measures are a means of ensuring the effectiveness of the arbitral process, rather than a means of resolving the party's dispute.

While historically it was often the case that arbitral tribunals were not permitted to issue interim measures, this being a power reserved to national courts, most modern arbitration statutes recognise the ability of arbitral tribunals to do this.[36] By way of example, pursuant to Article 17 of the UNCITRAL Model Law, the arbitral tribunal can grant interim measures at the request of a party, unless the parties have agreed otherwise. The same approach has been adopted by courts in the United States of America, where the Federal Arbitration Act is silent on the issue.[37]

Moreover, even where the arbitration law itself does not expressly allow arbitrators to issue interim measures, it is often accepted that a tribunal can do so as long as the parties have agreed to give it this power. This becomes an important route because many institutional arbitration rules now allow arbitral tribunals to issue interim measures,[38] and by agreeing to arbitrate under such a set of rules, parties will usually be taken to have agreed to the tribunal issuing interim measures.

However, an important "quirk" exists with respect to interim measures in arbitration, namely that even in jurisdictions in which arbitral tribunals are expressly permitted to issue interim measures, it is often also true that parties nonetheless retain the right to seek interim measures from the courts instead.[39] Importantly, it is widely accepted that an application to a court for an interim measure does not constitute a waiver or an infringement of the agreement to arbitrate.[40] As a result, even if one of the parties asks a court to grant interim relief, the court only has the power to grant or deny that specific temporary relief, and the arbitral tribunal maintains its exclusive jurisdiction over the merits of the case.

It might not be immediately obvious why a party might seek interim measures from a court when an arbitral tribunal is available, however the power of the arbitral tribunal to issue provisional measures is subject to some limitations. Perhaps most obviously, arbitral tribunals have no power over third parties who have not entered into the arbitration agreement. As a result, if a party requires an interim measure against a third party, that measure must be sought from a court.

Furthermore, in some cases, in order to ensure the effectiveness of provisional relief, it may be necessary to issue and enforce the interim measure without notice to any other party. In other words, it is sometimes crucial to "catch a party by surprise", so as to ensure that the practical effects of an interim measure are not nullified. By way of example, imagine a dispute between Karter and Imani concerning the ownership of a painting. The painting is currently held by Karter, but Imani claims to be the true owner. Imani has good reason to be concerned that Karter may hide the painting, or even destroy it, to prevent her obtaining it through success in the arbitration. In this case Imani may need a provisional measure, such as safe storage, aimed at preserving the painting pending the arbitration. However, if Imani discloses to Karter her intention to obtain an interim measure, there is a risk that Karter may hide the painting before the interim measure is executed, or even before it is granted.

This problem is resolved in many court systems by allowing the court to issue the interim measure *ex parte*, i.e. without the party against whom the measure will be issued being told that the measure has been requested. Equality of arms between the parties is then restored at a later stage: once the measure has been granted *ex parte* and executed, all of the parties in the dispute will be permitted to make arguments in favour of or against the measure. After having heard the parties, the court will decide whether to confirm the measure or repeal it.

However, unlike State courts, arbitral tribunals have limited ability to issue *ex parte* measures because of the importance to arbitral tribunals of avoiding any appearance of partiality (i.e. of favouring one party over the other). For this reason, arbitrators generally refrain from engaging in any type of *ex parte* communication with only one or some of the parties in an arbitration, requiring instead that all parties participate in all communications. Indeed, many arbitration statutes explicitly preclude arbitrators from engaging in *ex parte* communications, and many sets of arbitration rules follow the same approach (e.g. under Article 25.1 of the 2014 LCIA Rules, an arbitral tribunal has the power to issue interim measures "upon the application of any party, *after giving all other parties a reasonable opportunity to respond to such application*" (emphasis added)). This exclusion of *ex parte* communication, however, means that an arbitral tribunal usually has no ability to issue interim measures *ex parte*, as any application submitted to the tribunal by one of the parties must be communicated to all other parties as well.

The Model Law follows a different approach, with Article 17B enabling arbitral tribunals to issue *ex parte* measures, but through an unusual process. To return to the previous example, Imani can request an interim measure from the tribunal, while also requesting a "preliminary order" directing Karter not to "frustrate the purpose" of the interim measure. The tribunal then assesses whether prior disclosure of the request for an interim measure will frustrate the purpose of the measure, and if so it will issue the preliminary order.[41] However, it will also simultaneously give notice to Karter of the request for the interim measure and of any communications that occurred relating to the measure. The tribunal must also give Karter an opportunity to present his case against the measure "at the earliest practicable time".[42] Notably, a preliminary order cannot be enforced by a court[43] and will, no matter what, expire 20 days from the date on which it was issued by the tribunal. However, after the tribunal has heard all of the parties on the appropriateness of the measure, it will then decide whether or not to issue an interim measure that adopts or modifies the preliminary order.[44] Under this process, then, the tribunal only issues an interim measure once the parties have had a chance to present their arguments for and against the measure, but the preliminary order has prevented the purpose of the interim measure being frustrated before a decision could be made (e.g. it has stopped Karter hiding the painting). Albeit ambitious, this attempt to empower arbitrators to issue *ex parte* orders has not proven very successful, as many States that have based their arbitration statute on the Model Law have deleted this mechanism from their own law.

There is, though, also a third reason why parties may choose to request interim measures from a court, rather than an arbitral tribunal. Provisional measures are binding on the parties, but if one of the parties refuses to comply with a measure issued by the arbitral tribunal, the tribunal has very limited power to enforce that measure. As a result, if Karter decides to ignore the tribunal's interim measure and hides the painting, Imani may have to go to court to have the tribunal's interim measure enforced. That may lead her to conclude that she should have simply gone to court in the first place, rather than spending time asking the arbitral tribunal for a measure that it could not itself fully enforce.

142 *Arbitral proceedings*

In addition, it must also be acknowledged that in some jurisdictions there are substantive limitations on the types of interim measures that arbitral tribunals are allowed to issue.[45] As a result, any party seeking certain types of interim measures simply has no option but to turn to a court.

Finally, there are questions regarding the enforceability of arbitral tribunal-issued interim measures outside the seat of the arbitration. While some arbitration statutes expressly allow for the enforceability of interim measures awarded by arbitral tribunals, even if the tribunal is seated abroad,[46] where no such provision exists enforcement may depend on the New York Convention. However, as mentioned above, according to some State courts provisional or interim measures are not "awards", and so cannot be enforced through the New York Convention.[47]

4.4 Challenging the validity or scope of the arbitration agreement

Chapter 4 discussed the fact that parties have the right to challenge the appointment to the arbitral tribunal of any arbitrator they believe is not independent or impartial. Parties also have the power to argue that a claim being brought by the other party does not fall within the scope of the arbitration agreement, or even that the arbitration agreement is entirely invalid. Arbitration, after all, is based on consent, and this means not only that parties are only obligated to arbitrate if they have agreed to do so, but they are only obligated to arbitrate to the extent they have agreed to do so. Any claim brought to arbitration that does not fall within the scope of a valid arbitration agreement cannot be decided upon by the tribunal.

Challenges based on the scope or validity of the arbitration agreement have already been discussed in Chapter 3, but they need to be mentioned again here because any challenge of this type must be brought at the commencement of the arbitral process. Indeed, it is generally accepted that challenges of this type must be brought before or at the same time as the challenging party takes any substantive step in the arbitration, such as responding to the other party's claims. If this is not done, the party will be taken to have agreed to participate in the arbitration, and to have waived its right to object.[48] For this reason, as a matter of practice challenges to the arbitration agreement are often raised at the very first opportunity, such as in the Answer. Waiting any longer entails the risk that the tribunal or a court will subsequently decide that the objection was waived. This doesn't mean that the challenging party must present a fully detailed and fully argued version of the challenge at this early stage, but it must at least provide sufficient detail that both the tribunal and the other party are aware that the scope or validity of the arbitration agreement is being challenged, and what the nature of that challenge is.

4.5 The initial stages of the arbitration and the case management conference

Thus far this discussion has concentrated on what might be called the negative aspects of the early stages of an arbitration, such as securing interim measures, challenging arbitrators, and challenging the arbitration agreement. However, while such things are hardly rare, they are not found in every arbitration, and many arbitrations proceed in a constructive and collaborative fashion. Moreover, even when an arbitration is more antagonistic, featuring one or a number of challenges, the overwhelming majority of arbitrations proceed to some form of address of the merits. For example, in a 2014 survey of European arbitration practitioners, 90% of respondents reported that challenges to the validity of an arbitration agreement were successful in fewer than one quarter of the international arbitrations in which they had been raised in the past five years, with 55% reporting that no challenge raised had been successful.[49] Similar results were obtained in a 2016 survey of arbitration practitioners in the Americas, with 93% of respondents reporting that challenges to the validity of an arbitration agreement were successful in fewer than one quarter of the international arbitrations in which they had been involved in the past five years, and 71% reporting that no challenge raised had been successful.[50]

In short, then, arbitrations happen. A party may be able to use challenges to alter the composition of the arbitral tribunal, or to stop certain issues being addressed, but once an arbitration has been commenced, it is relatively rare for it to be completely avoided.

Parties in an arbitration, therefore, will nearly always be forced to turn to the question of how the arbitration can best be run, even if only because the attempt of one of the parties to avoid the arbitration has failed. As already noted, there is no procedural template an arbitration must follow, and so the parties are free to structure their procedure however seems best to them, so long as fundamental fairness is ensured for all parties. Nonetheless, it is possible to lay out certain considerations that all parties must address, even though different parties may choose to resolve them differently.

Some of the issues are purely procedural, such as whether a particular set of arbitration rules should be used (if this has not been specified in the arbitration agreement or otherwise agreed by the parties); how many submissions each party will be permitted to make; how documents should be submitted to the tribunal; what languages may be used in the arbitration without translation; how disputes regarding the disclosure of documents should be resolved; when any hearings will be held, etc. On the other hand, some will have a far more direct substantive impact, such as how the seat of the arbitration should be determined (if this has not been specified in the arbitration agreement or otherwise agreed by the parties); what matters are actually in dispute between the parties; whether any interim measures are required, etc.

These issues are standardly addressed in what is often referred to as a "case management conference" or "preliminary meeting". While such a meeting can take place online or even by phone, it is usually preferable for it to take place in person where practicable, as it provides an opportunity for the tribunal and the parties to meet and gain a sense of one another to a degree that is difficult to do other than through physical presence. Indeed, while as is always the case in arbitration, approaches to case management conferences can differ depending on the preferences of the tribunal members, of the parties, and even of the parties' counsel, a consistent overriding goal of any properly handled case management conference is to achieve agreement between the parties and the tribunal as to the procedure to be used.

The specific topics addressed in a case management conference will, of course, vary depending on the needs of the arbitration, but the purpose of the meeting is captured well in the "case management" label. It is to resolve any initial procedural obstacles to the success of the arbitration and lay out a "map" for the progress of the arbitration that will maximise the likelihood that the arbitration will be successful.

Typically, in this initial stage the tribunal and the parties will agree on a procedural timetable. The timetable is effectively a calendar of the proceedings, detailing the time-limits within which each of the activities relevant for the arbitration (e.g. the filing of written submissions) should be carried out. For the arbitration to be efficient, it is of course crucial that the timetable be both precise and reasonable in terms of how much time should be spent for each of the steps constituting the procedure.

Ultimately, however, parties in an arbitration are in dispute, and sometimes they will be unwilling or unable to agree on certain important procedural matters. In such cases the tribunal has the inherent power to impose procedures on the parties, in order to ensure that the arbitration can nonetheless proceed. This is, though, a decidedly less desirable situation than if agreement of the parties can be gained, as it entrenches an adversarial context into the arbitral process, almost guaranteeing that further disputes will arise in the future. This is, then, one of the contexts in which an arbitrator's skills as a mediator can be most important – not in helping the parties to settle a dispute they may be unwilling to settle, but just in helping the parties to recognise that the arbitral procedure into which they are now entering is a fair and effective one, and so should be supported rather than undermined.

4.6 Terms of reference

While the use of case management conferences is widespread in both institutional and *ad hoc* arbitration, as well as being fundamentally just an element of good arbitral practice, certain institutional arbitration rules, most famously those of the ICC, require that an additional step in case management be adopted. Specifically, under Article 23 of the 2017 ICC Rules of Arbitration, the tribunal and the parties must agree on what are called "terms of reference" for the arbitration.

Notably, the ICC Rules require that a case management conference be held in addition to the drawing up of the terms of reference (Article 24), although both can be done in the same meeting if agreed. This indicates the specific focus of the terms of reference, which is not primarily on the procedures through which the arbitration is to be conducted, but instead on clarifying the substantive scope of the arbitration. As specified in Article 23 of the 2017 ICC Arbitration Rules, then, the terms of reference must contain:

a) the names in full, description, address and other contact details of each of the parties and of any person(s) representing a party in the arbitration;
b) the addresses to which notifications and communications arising in the course of the arbitration may be made;
c) a summary of the parties' respective claims and of the relief sought by each party, together with the amounts of any quantified claims and, to the extent possible, an estimate of the monetary value of any other claims;
d) unless the arbitral tribunal considers it inappropriate, a list of issues to be determined;
e) the names in full, address and other contact details of each of the arbitrators;
f) the place of the arbitration; and
g) particulars of the applicable procedural rules and, if such is the case, reference to the power conferred upon the arbitral tribunal to act as *amiable compositeur* or to decide *ex aequo et bono*.

Importantly, because the terms of reference must be agreed to and signed by the arbitral tribunal, they can also serve as an arbitration agreement themselves, potentially eliminating problems that may exist regarding the enforceability of the original arbitration agreement. Indeed, they were reportedly developed by the ICC to serve precisely this role, ensuring that arbitrations would produce enforceable awards at a time at which French law restricted the enforceability of arbitration agreements entered into before a dispute had arisen.[51]

The ICC Rules specify that the terms of reference must be drafted by the arbitral tribunal, rather than by the parties, however in practice tribunals will sometimes request that the parties provide a description of their claims and relief sought. The parties must, after all, agree to and sign the terms of reference, so there is little to be gained by refusing their input during the drafting of the document. Then, once the document has been prepared, it will usually be sent to the parties, who will have an opportunity to comment and propose any amendments. It is important to remember, however, that ultimately it is the tribunal that is responsible for the drafting of the terms of reference, and so while the parties may suggest alterations, the tribunal retains the right to decide not to include any or all of the parties' suggestions. Finally, the parties and the tribunal will all sign the document, which is then submitted to the ICC.[52]

Once this has been done, the terms of reference are then binding on both the parties and the tribunal. Most importantly, parties may no longer make additional claims, or substantially alter their current claims, unless permission to do so is obtained from the tribunal. The terms of reference, then, actually serve as a limitation on party autonomy in the arbitration. They do so, however, with the goal of enhancing the quality and efficiency of the arbitral process, and after agreement has been secured from the parties regarding the claims they wished to bring.

The requirement that parties sign the terms of reference raises the question, of course, of what happens if one party refuses to sign. Perhaps that party simply does not want to participate in the arbitration at all, or perhaps they are happy to arbitrate but disagree with the substance of the terms of reference as written. Under Article 23(3) of the 2017 ICC Rules of Arbitration, if any party refuses to sign the terms of reference, they must be submitted to the ICC for approval. If the terms of reference are approved by the ICC, then the arbitration may proceed as normal. Refusing to sign the terms of reference is, therefore, not a method by which an arbitration can be avoided, although it is a means by which a party can protest against terms of reference that it believes are unacceptable in some way.

Views on the helpfulness of requiring terms of reference vary significantly amongst arbitration specialists. While some argue that they are just an unhelpful piece of additional bureaucracy that requires little more than repetition of information already in the case file,[53] others argue that they can help the tribunal and the parties clarify the content of the arbitration at its outset, and so result in a more efficient process.[54] Ultimately, however, as with many things, the usefulness of terms of reference will primarily depend on how they are approached. If arbitrators simply copy-and-paste the contents of the parties' initial written submissions, then completing the terms of reference provides no benefit. However, arbitrators who choose to engage with the terms of reference seriously, as a means of helping the parties clarify from the outset the subject-matter of the dispute and the procedural rules to be applied, can indeed generate significant benefits for the arbitration. By way of example, one or both of the parties may have intentionally formulated their initial claims and objections in a broad and vague fashion, in order to minimise the advance notice they provided to the other side. In such a case, discussions around the drafting of the terms of reference can provide a means of inducing the parties to clarify their respective positions at an early stage.

4.7 Bifurcation

Once the foundational elements of the arbitral procedure have been decided, the tribunal should then consider whether it would be appropriate to "bifurcate" the case at all. "Bifurcation" refers to a situation in which the tribunal has decided that rather than all disputed matters being addressed at the same time, the arbitration is best approached by certain issues being addressed first, and others left for a later stage if necessary.

The classic example of a matter that is often bifurcated is jurisdiction. If one of the parties objects to the jurisdiction of the tribunal (arguing, for example, that the claims raised by the Claimant do not fall within the scope of the arbitration agreement), the arbitrators may simply decide that it makes sense to resolve the question of jurisdiction first, and only turn to the substance of the parties' dispute once the tribunal has decided that it has jurisdiction over that dispute. After all, if the tribunal does not have jurisdiction over all or part of the dispute, then the time and money spent by the parties addressing those matters over which the tribunal has no jurisdiction has been wasted. Proceedings will not always be bifurcated when there is a challenge to the tribunal's jurisdiction, as a tribunal may decide that the issues relating to their jurisdiction overlap significantly with the issues relating to the merits of the dispute, meaning that it will actually be more efficient to address both jurisdiction and merits at the same time. However, while bifurcation of jurisdictional decisions may not always be appropriate, the question whether jurisdiction should be bifurcated is one that every tribunal should always explicitly address.

It must be emphasised, however, that while jurisdiction is the most prominent example of bifurcation, bifurcation is also possible with respect to different elements of the substance of the dispute. By way of example, the tribunal may decide to first examine whether the Respondent is liable for the claims brought by the Claimant (*an debeatur*), leaving the often complex question of the calculation of damages (*quantum debeatur*) to a later stage, if necessary.

The desirability of bifurcation will vary from one arbitration to another, as will the specific issues that can sensibly be bifurcated. Moreover, the decision whether or not to bifurcate proceedings is not purely a matter of efficiency, but also involves consideration of the possible benefits of focusing on specific complex issues independently. Yet arbitrators must be cautious when deciding whether or not to bifurcate: while it is often a desirable step, in some cases the Claimant's various claims or the Respondent's various defences may be so tightly connected that addressing them separately actually harms that party's ability to fully present its case.

4.8 Advance on costs

Arbitration, of course, is a private process, and one consequence of this is that it must be paid for by the parties. It will, however, be unsurprising to most people to hear that parties who lose an arbitration often feel less inclined to pay for that arbitration than do parties who win. The mechanism that has been developed to address this problem, as well as to address the simple fact that some bills will have to be paid long before the final award in an arbitration is delivered, is the "advance on costs", or the requirement to make a payment at or near the commencement of the arbitration, for costs that will be incurred during the proceedings. Most institutional arbitration rules provide for such advance payments[55] and national arbitration statutes often similarly allow arbitrators to request such a payment from the parties at the outset of the proceedings.

One obvious problem this gives rise to is that one party may not make the required payment. It might simply refuse to do so, or it might be unable to do so because of its current financial situation. The arbitration cannot proceed if there is no money to pay the bills that will arise, and neither the arbitral tribunal nor any selected arbitral institution can reasonably be expected to "carry the cost" for the parties. As a result, if the arbitration is to proceed then the other party must pay the entire advance on costs, rather than only its own portion. Nonetheless, a party placed in this position can take some comfort from the fact that at the end of the arbitration it will be able to recover this cost if it prevails, as part of the tribunal's final determination of the allocation of costs between the parties. How large the advance on costs will be varies significantly, of course, primarily depending on the amount in dispute in the arbitration, but most arbitration institutions publish tables or mathematical formulas that can assist the parties in predicting the size of the payment they will be required to make.

Understanding arbitration through case-law

Is the advance payment of costs a condition precedent to arbitration?

Case details: *BDMS Ltd v Rafael Advanced Defence Systems* [2014] EWHC 451 (Comm)

Authority deciding the case: High Court of Justice (England and Wales)

Facts of the case: Two parties entered into a contract containing an ICC arbitration clause. The Claimant initiated arbitration. The ICC fixed an advance on costs and asked the Respondent to pay half of it in accordance with the ICC Arbitration Rules.[56] The Respondent, however, refused to make the payment unless the Claimant provided security for costs.

The Claimant argued that payment of the advance constituted a condition precedent to the arbitration and that by failing to pay the Respondent had repudiated the agreement to arbitrate. Following this line of reasoning, the Claimant terminated the arbitration proceedings and brought the same claim before the High Court (Commercial Court) in London. The Respondent, however, objected to the jurisdiction of the High Court, arguing that the arbitration agreement was still valid and operative despite the Respondent's refusal to pay half of the advance on costs.

Decision: The Court observed that the payment of advance costs constitutes a contractual obligation between the parties to an arbitration. For this reason, if one of the

> parties (the Respondent in this case) fails to pay the advance, a breach of the arbitration agreement has occurred. According to the Court, however, this breach does not amount to a repudiation of the agreement to arbitrate, especially when the party that refuses to make the payment participates in the proceedings and does not try to hinder the arbitration in any other way. The Court further stated that for repudiation to take place, a party must be deprived of the entire benefit deriving from the contract. As a result, the Respondent's refusal to pay did not deprive the Claimant of its right to arbitrate, as it was possible for the Claimant to continue the arbitration by posting a guarantee for the half of the advance that should have been paid by the Respondent.

4.9 Statement of claim, statement of defense and other pre-hearing written submissions

With the arbitral tribunal in place and the preliminary arrangements made, it is finally time to turn to the parties' substantive submissions. No, arbitration is not the informal "We'll just walk into the room and make our case" that parties sometimes expect it to be. It is more procedurally flexible than litigation, but it is fundamentally an adversarial form of legal dispute resolution, and if the parties are to be assured of a fair procedure, a lot of preliminary work needs to be done.

By this point, of course, both parties will already have made an initial submission. However, that submission will often have been very basic, merely identifying the parties' claims and defences in general terms, without providing any of the detailed argumentation that is necessary to convince a tribunal. This new round of submissions, then, will be far more detailed, and in the most complex arbitrations each submission may extend to hundreds of pages, full of detailed factual discussion, intricate legal argument and extensive citation. If the thought of such a document does not fill your heart with excitement, then perhaps being an arbitrator is not the job for you.

While sometimes both the Claimant and the Respondent will submit their memoranda, as they are often called, at the same time, the more common approach is for the Claimant to make the first submission. Often referred to as the "Statement of Claim" or "Statement of Case", the purpose of this document is to lay out the Claimant's view of the facts underlying the dispute, as well as the legal arguments that the Claimant asserts justify the compensation or other remedy it is claiming. Approaches to drafting a legal memorandum can differ greatly, particularly between lawyers from different legal cultures. However, the fundamental goal of the Statement of Claim is to convince the arbitral tribunal that the Claimant has been wronged by the Respondent, and is entitled to some form of remedy. Because of this, it is important to avoid being both too neutral and too partisan. A Statement of Claim that is entirely neutral in its presentation of the facts and arguments it contains will do little to persuade the tribunal that the Claimant is the wronged party, while a Statement of Claim that is too openly partisan will simply convince the tribunal that the Claimant cannot be relied upon to present an accurate account of the facts or the law. Realistically, no competent tribunal will be persuaded by the Statement of Claim that the Claimant is in the right, as the arbitrators will be well aware that they have only heard one side of the dispute. However, while arbitrators may be professionals, they are also human, and humans can always be influenced by a persuasively presented argument, no matter how neutral they wish to be. As a result, if the tribunal finishes reading the Statement of Claim without thinking that the Claimant certainly seems to have a good reason for commencing the arbitration, the benefit of being the first party to make its case to the tribunal has been lost.

Once the Statement of Claim has been submitted, the Respondent will then be given an opportunity to submit its own document, often called the "Statement of Defence". The Statement of Defence is similar to the Statement of Claim, in that it is the Respondent's first real opportunity to present its case to the tribunal. As a result, it needs to be approached with a view to persuading the tribunal of the correctness of the Respondent's positions, rather than as an objective account of the facts and law. There is, though, an important difference between the Statement of Defence and the Statement of Claim, namely that the former occurs after the latter. Because of this, while the Claimant is generally free to decide how to make its claim, the Respondent is more restricted in the matters it should address. The purpose of the Statement of Defence, after all, is fundamentally to convince the tribunal that the Statement of Claim is not as persuasive as it may have seemed to be. As a result, the Statement of Defence is properly approached as a focused attack on the Statement of Claim, both in terms of the accuracy of its presentation of the facts, and the correctness of its legal arguments. Just as the goal of the Statement of Claim is to convince the tribunal that the Claimant was justified in commencing the arbitration, the goal of the Statement of Defence is to convince the tribunal that it is actually the Respondent that is the wronged party, by being subjected to a claim for which there simply is no legal foundation.

The psychological nature of the goal of both of these documents is worth emphasising. Fundamentally an arbitration will be won or lost because the tribunal decides that the facts and/or the law favour a particular party. A tribunal does not do its job properly if it lets emotion, rather than analysis, decide a case. Nonetheless, facts are never entirely clear, and legal arguments are never completely decisive. There is always "room for interpretation" of both facts and law in every case of any complexity. The Statement of Claim and Statement of Defence, then, need to achieve two purposes. Firstly, they need to lay out the facts and the relevant law clearly and in detail, as the arbitrators will rely on these documents when familiarising themselves with the details of the case, when preparing for the hearing, and even when drafting the award. But as well as fulfilling this "reference" function, an effective Statement of Claim and Statement of Defence will also "tell a story" that encourages the tribunal to see the case through the viewpoint of the party drafting the document. If this is done successfully, the tribunal will be more likely to interpret the facts and the law in a way consistent with the story they have found persuasive, and hence consistent with the interests of the party that told that story. A great story cannot make up for terrible facts or weak legal argument, but it can take supportive facts and strong arguments and make them truly compelling.

After the submission of the Statement of Defence, the Claimant will usually be allowed to make another submission, commonly called the "Reply". Much as the Statement of Defence responded to the Statement of Claim, the purpose of the Reply is to respond to the Statement of Defence. The same considerations apply to the drafting of the Reply as have been described above for the preceding two documents.

While in some cases pre-hearing written submissions will end with the Reply, in many international commercial arbitrations the Respondent will be permitted its own second submission, often referred to as the "Rejoinder". The Rejoinder responds to the Reply just as the Reply responded to the Statement of Defence. The underlying rationale for allowing a Rejoinder is to ensure that both parties have been allowed an equal number of submissions, preventing the Respondent objecting that it has not been treated equally by the tribunal. However, the Rejoinder also provides the Respondent with a similar persuasive opportunity as was provided to the Claimant with the Statement of Claim. While the Claimant received the first opportunity to present the case to the tribunal, and frame the tribunal's perception of the case to its own advantage, the Rejoinder gives the Respondent the last opportunity before the oral phase of the proceedings. It allows the Respondent to summarise the arguments that the parties have made, and present them in a way that is most favourable to it, and that is the last presentation of the case that the tribunal will receive before the hearings.

Technically it is possible for there to be further written submissions, and there are even titles for them, such as "Surrejoinder", "Rebuttal" and "Surrebuttal". But other than in particularly complex arbitrations further submissions are rarely permitted, and while they can sometimes be justified, they are most often a sign that a tribunal is failing to exercise proper discipline over the proceedings.

4.10 Oral hearings

While it is certainly possible to have an international commercial arbitration without any hearings, and this in itself will not affect the enforceability of the resulting award, it is relatively rare outside certain specialised fields, and international commercial arbitrations typically involve at least one oral hearing. This is because hearings present the best opportunity for the parties to present oral evidence and get direct feedback from the tribunal on the strengths and weakness of their case. This feedback may be explicit (e.g. an arbitrator states she needs more evidence that a certain statement was made if she is to be convinced that it was made), or it may be impressionistic (e.g. counsel can tell from the body language and comments of the tribunal that they are not being persuaded by what she thought was her strongest argument), but the unique opportunity a hearing presents to get immediate feedback on how a tribunal is viewing a case means hearings can be essential for parties to be able to fully and properly present their case. Indeed, for precisely this reason, hearings are mandatory under many sets of arbitration rules[57] and national arbitration statutes[58] whenever one of the parties requests them.

A major complication with hearings, of course, is that they require coordination. While communications will have been exchanged and memoranda submitted prior to hearings taking place, each party will largely have undertaken this work on its own, with only short coordinated interactions such as the procedural meeting. A hearing, on the other hand, often requires substantial organisation, including coordination between not only the parties and the tribunal, but other individuals as well. Firstly, the hearings will require a room large enough to accommodate the tribunal, the teams of party counsels, translators, stenographers, witnesses, and the equipment and documents each of these individuals brings. In addition, counsel for each of the parties will require their own "break-out" room where they can discuss matters confidentially, and an additional room will be needed for the tribunal.[59] In addition, the hearing room will not only need to be large enough to fit a significant number of people, but it will usually need to be equipped with adequate access to information technology and audio/visual resources, from the simplest level of a large number of power sockets (as almost everyone will have their own laptop) to reliable high-speed internet access, and potentially even teleconferencing facilities. Finally, the room must be located somewhere that provides easy access to the ability to print and copy documents, potentially basic secretarial services, and at the very least enough support to provide assistance if something goes wrong.

Happily, the growth of arbitration around the world means that many major cities now have dedicated "dispute resolution" centres that can provide rooms purpose-built for use in modern arbitrations, with administrative support available when needed. Similarly, many arbitral institutions will offer their own rooms for use by arbitrations they are administering, and large law firms will often also have rooms that can be used for arbitration hearings. Nonetheless, such options are not always available, and in this case finding an appropriate location for the hearings can be a challenge.[60]

Of course, the planning of a hearing does not end with locating a room in which it can be held. Hearings are enormously expensive, with counsel and arbitrators often billing by the hour for days at a time, expenses being incurred for travel, accommodation and subsistence, witnesses being forced to take time from their regular work, and many other expenses such as those already discussed above. As a result, it is desirable for a hearing to be as short as possible, ensuring that the parties are given the time they need to present their case properly. Detailed planning of a hearing is therefore essential. To achieve this, just as a case management conference will normally be held at the beginning of an arbitration, so a pre-hearing conference will normally be held prior to a hearing. Often conducted by teleconference, the purpose of this meeting is to get clarity on how much time the parties will require to present their case, what facilities might be needed, and how the time within the hearing should be divided up, e.g. how many hours for opening statements, when witnesses should be scheduled, etc.

Hearings can, of course, be structured however the parties and tribunal wish. That is the great advantage of arbitration's procedural flexibility. Nonetheless, there is a fairly standardised structure that most international commercial arbitration hearings follow. The hearing will normally start with both parties making what is usually called the "opening statement", with the Claimant presenting first, followed by the Respondent. While it is ultimately up to the parties' counsel to decide the format of their opening statement, based on what they believe will be most effective for their case, it is generally approached as a broad overview of the case, rather than a detailed discussion of the facts or law. In essence, it provides the parties with an opportunity to create a "narrative frame" through which they want the tribunal to view all the evidence and legal argument with which they will be presented over the course of the hearing. By way of parallel, before attempting to explain to your parents how you ended up in jail in a neighbouring town dressed as a chicken with the word "LEGEND" tattooed on your forehead, you might start with the "opening statement": "You've got to remember, Eddie and I have been best friends since we were kids, and he was leaving the country the next day and we might never see each other again." A case will never be won or lost solely because of an opening statement, but they play an essential role in effective case presentation, and their importance should never be underestimated. As the saying goes "First impressions last".

As a rule, parties will be allocated the same amount of time for their opening statement, which can vary from an hour or less to several hours. Indeed, in complex international cases, it is not uncommon for opening statements to last for two full days, with the first day being devoted to the Claimant's statement and the second one being reserved for the Respondent's statement. Parties do not, of course, have to use all of their allocated time, but it is essential that there be an equal allocation, to avoid concerns that the tribunal has acted partially towards either party.[61] However, while the time allocated for each party's opening statement is for that party's counsel to control, it is important that counsel remember that the tribunal may have questions they wish to ask, and some degree of back and forth between the tribunal and counsel is common in international commercial arbitration hearings. Counsel must, therefore, incorporate time for such discussion in their planning for their opening statement, and come prepared for any questions they think the tribunal may ask.

Once the opening statements have concluded, the hearing will turn to the taking of evidence through the examination of witnesses and experts. This process will occupy most of the time in the hearing. It will be addressed in Section 5 of this Chapter, which focuses on the complex issues that can arise in international commercial arbitration with respect to questions of evidence.

Finally, when the evidence-taking portion of the hearing is concluded, the hearing will close. This will be done in one of two ways. Firstly, parties may be given an opportunity to make a closing statement, similar to the opening statement made at the beginning of the hearing. Closing submissions tend to be significantly more detailed than opening submissions, because they occur after the tribunal has been exposed to the evidence in the case. As a result, the primary purpose of the closing statement is to address the evidence and argument that the tribunal has heard over the course of the hearing, and "re-frame" the case for the tribunal in a way that is most favourable for the party in question. Nonetheless, while it is important that closing statements include sufficient detail, it is also essential that counsel remember that a closing statement is an opportunity to be persuasive, not merely a summary of the party's case. Too much detail and a tribunal can easily feel lost; not enough and the tribunal may wonder why the party in question cannot summon more support for its position. A closing statement is, then, another opportunity to *persuade* the tribunal, and should not be wasted by counsel merely reciting the evidence the tribunal has heard.

Nonetheless, while closing statements provide an important opportunity to counsel to persuade the tribunal of the correctness of their party's case, some hearings will dispense with them entirely, with counsel making written post-hearing submissions. The primary rationale for such an approach is that an oral statement at the end of a hearing must be drafted very quickly, often in response to important new evidence that counsel was unaware of before the hearing began. A written post-hearing submission, on the other hand, can be drafted and re-drafted carefully, and so minimises the risk that a misstatement will be made, important evidence missed, or simply that counsel will be unconvincing in their oral performance. The risk inherent to skipping the oral closing statement to rely on written post-hearing submissions, of course, is that by the time the tribunal reads the party's submission they will already have had time to develop their own impressions of what happened at the hearing, and at that point their minds may be significantly more difficult to change than if their concerns had been addressed at the immediate end of the hearing.

4.11 Post-hearing submissions

Finally, particularly in larger and more complex arbitrations, the parties will also have the opportunity to submit post-hearing briefs. These will be significantly more detailed than a written post-hearing submission, as their purpose is not, as such, to persuade the tribunal, but rather to provide the tribunal with a detailed explanation of how the facts in the case and the law applicable to the case should be understood. Their purpose, in short, is to give the tribunal a detailed written account of the case upon which they will hopefully rely when drafting their award.

4.12 Closing of the proceedings

Once all the parties' agreed submissions have been made, and all other "live" issues resolved, the tribunal will "close" the proceedings. This does not mean that the arbitration is over, as the parties have not yet received the tribunal's award. However, from this moment on, the parties may no longer submit additional evidence or argument, unless given permission to do so by the tribunal. This latter qualifier is important, as it is a distinctive feature of the practical reality of arbitration practice.

The dominant approach in court litigation is that once a court has decided to close proceedings and prevent any new submissions, then the proceedings are indeed closed. In exceptional circumstances parties may be allowed to present new evidence or arguments after this time, such as if important evidence was knowingly concealed by the other party. However, the standard rule in litigation is that the parties have a time at which they are allowed to make submissions, and should come prepared at that time. Courts are publicly funded and have an obligation to all their users not to allow resources to be used inefficiently simply because a party did not present evidence or make arguments when they had the opportunity to do so.

The relationship between a tribunal and the parties is, however, different than that between a court and parties. The parties are paying for the arbitration, and the tribunal has a fundamental obligation to ensure that the parties receive an appropriate opportunity to present their case. Indeed, as will be discussed in Chapter 7, that a tribunal has not allowed a party to present its case is one of the very few grounds on which an award may be annulled, or recognition and enforcement successfully resisted.

Because of both the nature of the relationship between the parties and the tribunal, and the risk that an award may not be enforceable, arbitral tribunals are often far more flexible than courts when it comes to allowing parties to re-open a case after it has been closed. This does not mean that it can always be done, and a party will be expected to provide a good reason why the evidence or argument it now wishes to present was not presented when the opportunity was given. In addition, the party wishing to re-open the proceedings may be required by the tribunal to bear all the costs that arise from that re-opening (i.e. including the costs that would normally have been paid by the opposing party). However, a party wishing to make a new submission after closing of the proceedings should at least make its case to the tribunal, as such requests have been known to succeed.

154 *Arbitral proceedings*

4.13 Deliberation and drafting of the final award

Finally, once the proceedings have indeed been closed, the tribunal will "deliberate". It should be emphasised, however, that while tribunals are described as deliberating after the closing of proceedings, the reality is that they will have been considering the submissions of the parties and how they may rule in the final award throughout the process described above. Arbitrators could not, after all, provide useful guidance in the hearings on the issues they need addressed, could not ask intelligent questions, etc., if they had not already begun to consider the details of the case and how they might ultimately rule. However, arbitrators will attempt to avoid reaching final and resolved positions on important issues prior to the deliberations, in order to ensure that they enter the deliberations with an adequately open mind. The period of deliberation after the closing of proceedings, then, is the period in which the arbitrators finalise their positions on the issues in dispute between the parties, rather than the time at which they start to think about them.

Once the tribunal has deliberated sufficiently, it will then turn to drafting the award. It is often the Chair of the tribunal who takes the lead in drafting the award, although this will vary depending on the respective expertises of the arbitrators, the degree to which the tribunal is in complete agreement, and so forth.

Drafting an award is often a poorly understood part of an arbitrator's role, even by arbitrators themselves. To some arbitrators it is little more than putting down in writing the conclusions they have already reached during their preceding deliberations, and arguments have been made that as a result drafting can reasonably be delegated to more junior lawyers, with the arbitrators merely ensuring that the award as written is consistent with the conclusions they have reached during deliberation. This is a mistake, and reflects a failure to appreciate the importance of the drafting process.

Anyone who has seriously attempted to write a properly reasoned explanation of the facts in a case and how the law applies to those facts will be familiar with the experience of sitting down to write a decision that says one thing, only to realise in the course of writing that the analysis you have been using doesn't quite work. Indeed, an arbitrator may well sit down to write an award holding that Party A wins, only to end up concluding that Party B wins instead. This is not a sign that the arbitrator failed to deliberate properly prior to drafting the award, but is merely a consequence of the detailed attention that serious award writing requires. Sadly, in too many cases arbitral awards are poorly drafted, even at the highest levels of the field,[62] and some seem to have been drafted with the primary goal of including so little reasoning that it will be impossible for the award to be challenged. When properly approached, however, award writing is part of the deliberative process, and as a result should never be delegated to a non-tribunal member.[63]

5. Approaches to evidence in international commercial arbitration usually attempt to strike a balance between different legal traditions

One of the most important features of any dispute resolution system is the rules that will be applied to the admission and consideration of evidence. Any decision, after all, will be made not just based on the legal arguments offered by the parties, but also on the evidence they present to support their position. In itself this is a fairly obvious observation, and yet rules on the admission of evidence are a major source of difficulty in international commercial arbitration, for the simple reason that its "international" nature means that there is no obvious source for the rules of evidence that should be applied.

By way of example, consider a relatively standard arbitration in which one party is from Canada and the other from Germany. The Canadian party's lawyers are from the United States of America and the German party's lawyers are from Switzerland. One arbitrator is from Ireland, one from Russia and one from Italy. The arbitration is seated in France and the contract is governed by English law. This may sound like a relatively diverse range of nationalities, and there are certainly many arbitrations in which the diversity is smaller. However, diversity of nationalities is simply a practical reality of international commercial arbitration, and arbitrations of this nature are anything but rare.

The immediate question that arises, of course, is where the rules of evidence for the arbitration should be derived from. It is very rarely the case that any international commercial arbitration will use the evidence rules of any national court system without alteration, as the ability to adapt evidence rules to the specific needs of a case is one of the benefits that arbitration provides. Indeed, in many, if not most, international commercial arbitrations no formal rules of evidence are adopted at all – the tribunal simply makes decisions on questions of evidence as they arise.

Nonetheless, even if formal rules of evidence are not adopted, it is difficult for parties to make arguments about whether evidence should or should not be considered, and equally difficult for arbitrators to make reasoned decisions on such questions, without referencing evidence rules at all. However, in the arbitration just described the Canadian party would be uncomfortable with decisions based on a German or Swiss approach to evidence, the German party would be uncomfortable with decisions based on a Canadian or US approach to evidence, and while the three arbitrators may have some experience in the evidence rules of States other than their own, it is unlikely that all three will be highly knowledgeable about the rules of the same State.

The obvious approach, of course, is for the tribunal to adopt a uniquely "international" approach to questions of evidence that draws from the different legal traditions represented in the arbitration, so that both parties feel that they have been through a dispute resolution process that used fair and understandable evidence rules. It is, though, a lot to ask of any tribunal to craft a new set of evidence rules for every new arbitration, and the "pick and choose" nature of such an approach would create a serious risk that the parties would see the evidence rules adopted in the arbitration as lacking any real coherence. As a result, the parties' faith in the process would actually be undermined, rather than enhanced.

This problem has primarily been addressed by arbitration practitioners through a growing informal set of norms regarding proper evidentiary procedure. That is, rather than any binding set of rules being adopted, leading international commercial arbitrators gradually evolved, including through informal discussions in articles and conference presentations, what they believed to be principles of "good practice" regarding evidence in international commercial arbitration. The consequence of this was that while approaches to evidence in domestic commercial arbitrations and in many smaller international commercial arbitrations still varied significantly depending on where the arbitration was seated and on the identities of those involved, by the early 2000s counsel and parties involved in larger international commercial arbitrations would encounter an increasingly predictable set of evidentiary practices, regardless of where the arbitration was seated or who the arbitrators were.

A major step in this development of a harmonised set of evidentiary practices occurred in 2010 with the adoption of the International Bar Association's "IBA Rules on the Taking of Evidence in International Arbitration". While the Rules are not binding unless expressly agreed to by the parties, they have had a significant impact on international commercial arbitration practice, often being relied upon by tribunals as persuasive guidance, and often invoked by counsel when attempting to argue an evidentiary point.

Nonetheless, while the Rules have unquestionably been influential, they remain controversial and are disliked by a significant number of practitioners. Indeed, while a central goal of the Rules was to strike a balance between common law and civil law approaches to questions of evidence,[64] dissatisfaction with the nature of this balance has been significant enough that in 2018 an alternative set of rules was released, the "Rules on the Efficient Conduct of Proceedings in International Arbitration (Prague Rules)". Developed by a Working Group of leading arbitration practitioners from primarily civil law backgrounds, the goal of the Prague Rules is to provide an alternative to the IBA Rules that more strongly reflects civil law approaches to evidence.

It is beyond the scope of this chapter to undertake a detailed examination of all the intricacies of evidence in international commercial arbitration, or even of the two competing sets of rules just discussed. The following sections will, however, address certain discrete issues in evidence practice that have a particular importance in international commercial arbitration.

5.1 Production of documents

Documentary evidence is indisputably central to convincing legal argument, whether in arbitration or litigation. Evidence can, of course, be given verbally by witnesses, however witnesses can lie, can forget, or sometimes can just be unconvincing even when they are telling the truth. In particular, a witness's credibility will often be in question simply because his testimony is being offered in the middle of a legal dispute, when he may have an incentive to present that testimony in a way that supports one party's position over the other. Documents, of course, can also be misleading or inaccurate. However, a document created prior to the existence of any dispute between the parties, particularly when the accuracy and correctness of the document was required for the success of a business transaction, can have an enormously persuasive impact on a tribunal.

For this reason, one of the central considerations for any party involved in an arbitration is how to gain access to documents that are in the possession of the other party. That party will not, after all, want the tribunal to see documents it may have that undermine its case, or even demonstrate the truth of something the other party is claiming.

While this is a familiar situation in litigation, and court systems around the world have developed rules regarding what documents parties in a dispute must provide to the other party, the "international" nature of international commercial arbitration makes this a particularly difficult question, as parties, counsel and arbitrators may come from legal systems with very different approaches to this issue. In most civil law jurisdictions, for example, parties involved in litigation are viewed as free to produce only documents beneficial to their case, keeping to themselves those which might assist the other side.[65] On the other hand, no such rule generally exists in common law jurisdictions, and parties are often expected to produce to the other side all documents relevant to the case, with the United States of America adopting a particular strong rule in this respect. This process of parties exchanging documents is generally referred to by the terms "discovery" or "disclosure".

Unsurprisingly, "discovery" can be the source of major disagreements in international commercial arbitration, with many from civil law backgrounds arguing that the enhanced disclosure required by the common law approach encourages parties to undertake a "fishing expedition" – that is, to bring a claim without supporting evidence, in the hope that sufficient evidence will be found during discovery. On the other hand, many from common law backgrounds believe that the common law approach to discovery is essential to ensuring that the tribunal's decision is based on a full awareness of all the relevant facts, while the civil law approach allows parties to undermine justice by hiding unfavourable evidence. Further arguments are also sometimes made based on the significant costs that can be involved in extensive discovery, which it is claimed is inconsistent with the potential cost-savings that motivate some parties to choose arbitration over litigation – although the plausibility of such arguments obviously varies from one arbitration to another, as the arbitrations most likely to generate extensive discovery are usually already expensive for the reasons discussed in Chapter 1.

One uncontroversial principle in this area is that if a party wishes to rely on a document in its possession, it must produce that document to the arbitral tribunal and to all other parties. That is, you cannot say "I have an email proving he promised X", and then refuse to show the tribunal and the other parties that email. Of course, you could refuse to produce that email, but then the tribunal will simply disregard your description of what the email contains. While there will be situations in which the confidential nature of a document will justify limiting who has access to it once it is produced, all documents on which a party wishes to rely must be made available to the tribunal, and must also be made available to the opposing parties' counsel. Parties themselves may in some exceptional circumstances be justifiably prevented from accessing a document produced by another party, but withholding the document from that party's counsel will undermine the party's ability to present its case, and thereby the fairness of the arbitration.

The real issue of controversy in this area relates to documents that are in the possession of one party, on which another party wishes to rely. In short, you may believe that the other party has documents that will support your case, but you do not yourself have a copy of them. This puts you in the position described in the previous paragraph, as although you are not refusing to produce a document, you nonetheless cannot produce it and the tribunal will not presume a document exists just because you insist you think it does.

The question this situation raises is what degree of discovery the tribunal should order. It is generally accepted in international commercial arbitration that parties should not be permitted to refuse to disclose a document simply because it may be unfavourable to their case, even if this is the accepted rule in their home jurisdiction. Similarly, however, it is extremely rare that a tribunal will order the kind of extensive discovery common in US courts. Instead, a good representation of the dominant approach is that found in the IBA Rules, which allow requests to be made for a "narrow and specific . . . category of Documents that are reasonably believed to exist".[66] This is, however, by no means a universally endorsed standard, as reflected by the different standard included in the Prague Rules, which requires that parties must request production of "specific" documents, rather than a "category" of documents.

In many arbitrations, exchanges of requests for document production between the parties are streamlined through the use of a special document referred to as a "Redfern schedule". The schedule is essentially a spreadsheet, on which each of the parties can describe the documents or categories of documents that they want the other party to produce. The party towards which each request is directed will then be able to respond on the schedule, specifying whether there are objections to the request and, if so, on what grounds. Of course, where there are objections, the arbitrators ultimately have the power to decide whether a certain document or category of documents should be produced. Use of a Redfern schedule can help a tribunal develop a synthetic overview of document production requests.

Arguments about the proper scope of discovery in international commercial arbitration are unlikely to end any time soon given the wide variety of legal traditions in this area. Moreover, there is no particular reason why the adoption of a single, universally applied approach would be desirable. As is constantly argued, one of the great benefits of international commercial arbitration is the freedom it allows for procedures to be matched to the circumstances of each arbitration, and there is little reason why a tribunal should insist on the use of the approach endorsed in the IBA Rules, for example, when the parties come from jurisdictions in which a more restricted approach to discovery is practiced. Similarly, the approach adopted in the Prague Rules will be less appropriate in an arbitration involving parties from common law jurisdictions. Ultimately, the tribunal's responsibility is to balance the need to ensure that it has the information it requires to reach a justifiable decision with the legitimate expectations the parties possessed when they agreed to arbitrate as to what procedures would be followed and what expenses they would incur. This is an individualised question, and not one that can be captured in a universally applicable set of procedural rules.

5.2 Witness preparation

Just as in court litigation, testimony by witnesses plays a central role in many international commercial arbitrations, although unlike in some court systems witnesses in international commercial arbitration often file a written "witness statement" laying out their testimony, rather than presenting it orally at a hearing. These witness statements are normally filed with the tribunal by the parties, together with the Statements of Claim and Defence. While in many cases both parties will be satisfied if a witness merely produces a written statement, in others one or both parties will want the witness to be present at the hearing to offer testimony and be questioned on it. Sometimes this will be because the witness's testimony is central to the case of one of the parties and live testimony will allow the witness's credibility to be demonstrated or challenged, while in others it will be because a party has a number of questions to ask the witness and this can be done more efficiently in person than through written exchanges.

Few people have ever experienced being a witness in any form of legal proceeding, and the idea can be enormously intimidating. The witness may be concerned that they will misspeak, that they might not make themselves clear, that they will forget something important due to the pressure, or simply that they will be "tricked" by a clever attorney who has spent many years examining witnesses. Given these justifiable concerns, many witnesses are only too happy to receive assistance from counsel prior to offering their testimony. Such assistance, however, raises significant issues, as it is essential to the integrity of the evidence-gathering process that a witness's testimony be her own, rather than merely what she has been told to say by counsel or one of the parties.

For this reason, the ethics rules applicable to lawyers in many jurisdictions place limits on the kinds of assistance that counsel can offer to witnesses prior to a hearing. For example, English counsel are permitted to engage in "witness familiarisation", such as explaining how the hearing will work, and even undertaking a mock cross-examination based on hypothetical facts (i.e. not the facts in the actual case in which the witness will be testifying). On the other hand, counsel may not engage in "witness training", such as discussing with a witness what her testimony will be, and advising the witness on how to testify and on how to answer questions that may be asked. In Austria, by contrast, strong limitations are placed on the witness preparation and counsel limit their contact with witnesses in order to avoid any potential ethics charges. The United States of America, on the other hand, goes to the other extreme: while counsel may not tell a witness to change her testimony so that it is false or misleading, "witness coaching" that is designed to ensure that the witness gives the best presentation possible of her own testimony is regarded as acceptable, including suggesting to witnesses how they might best phrase their testimony (although this must be done carefully to avoid altering the substance of that testimony) and undertaking mock cross-examinations using the actual facts about which the witness will be testifying.

The clear difficulty this diversity in rules creates in international commercial arbitration is that a single arbitration may involve lawyers from more than one jurisdiction. To use the examples just given, one side might be represented by Austrian lawyers, who face strict restrictions on witness preparation, while the other might be represented by US lawyers, who are permitted to engage in extensive witness coaching. If both sets of counsel adhere to their applicable ethical obligations, the arbitration will be fundamentally unfair, as one party's witnesses will be substantially better prepared, and so likely more convincing, than the other party's witnesses. One simple solution to this problem, of course, would be if local or national ethics rules were not applied in international arbitrations, but few jurisdictions have adopted express exceptions of this nature.[67]

Nonetheless it is now broadly accepted that counsel in international commercial arbitrations may engage in some degree of witness preparation, even if it would not be permitted in court litigation in their jurisdiction. Indeed, in 2013 the International Bar Association released a non-binding set of "Guidelines on Party Representation in International Arbitration" that expressly permit counsel to "meet or interact with Witnesses and Experts in order to discuss and prepare their prospective testimony".

As a result, whatever the limitations that apply to engagement with witnesses in court proceedings in the jurisdiction in which counsel are registered, when acting in international commercial arbitrations they should regard themselves as obligated to ensure that any witnesses they present are sufficiently prepared to present their testimony accurately and effectively. Anything less should be seen as a failure by counsel to fulfill her professional duties to her client. If providing such preparation would potentially subject her to ethics charges in her home jurisdiction, then the only acceptable choice open to her is simply not to work in international commercial arbitration until her local ethics rules change.

5.3 Witnesses who refuse to appear voluntarily

As has been repeatedly stated, arbitration is fundamentally based upon consent. This fact has an important consequence, however, that is not always immediately appreciated by those new to arbitration. That is, while it follows from this principle that no-one can be forced to arbitrate without having consented in some acceptable form, it also follows that an arbitral tribunal cannot force anyone to cooperate with the arbitration if they are not willing to do so.

The problem this creates is that in many disputes a party may need evidence that is in the possession of a non-party to the arbitration agreement, or want testimony from a non-party. If this issue arises in litigation, the judge can simply compel the non-party to testify or provide the requested evidence. The judge, after all, is ultimately a manifestation of the State, and so can compel individuals to take actions in the same way that the government more generally can do. Arbitrators, however, are private individuals. They have no more legitimate right to order non-parties to assist an arbitration than you have to walk up to a complete stranger on the street and demand that they buy you dinner. They may be willing to cooperate, but if they won't, you're going to stay hungry.

Governments around the world, however, have decided that arbitration is a good thing, and should be supported. One way to provide this support would be to allow arbitrators to compel cooperation from non-parties. Giving power of this nature to arbitrators, though, would clearly be unacceptable. Most arbitrators are professional and reliable, and could be expected to use that power appropriately, however arbitrators are selected by the parties, and not every arbitrator is either good or honest. As a result, allowing arbitrators to compel cooperation from non-parties would create an opportunity for parties to secure information from non-parties that they know the relevant courts would not be willing to give, as well as simply causing inconvenience to non-parties from poorly considered orders issued by inexperienced or incompetent arbitrators.

Instead, the problem of securing evidence and testimony from non-parties has generally been resolved by allowing courts to decide when a non-party should or should not be compelled to cooperate with an arbitration. The specific procedure to be followed will vary between jurisdictions, but it will often involve the tribunal issuing an order for the production of evidence by a non-party; if the recipient of the order does not comply with the order voluntarily, the party who requested the order will then take it to the relevant court, and ask for it to be enforced. At this point the court has the ability to review the order and refuse enforcement if it thinks that the tribunal is overstepping its legitimate bounds. In most cases, however, enforcement will be ordered and the non-party will be required to cooperate.[68]

A procedure of this nature might seem to be inconsistent with the idea that arbitration is an alternative to national courts, and should be allowed to function without court interference. However, it provides a necessary oversight of arbitral power in so far as it affects individuals who have not consented to cooperate with the arbitration. As a result, it is not just consistent with the consensual nature of arbitration, but ultimately required by it.

6. *The proceedings may involve more than two parties*

The traditional picture of arbitration, that you will also have seen mirrored in the language used in this book, involves two parties who have agreed to let an arbitrator resolve their dispute. There is, though, nothing that requires that an arbitration involve only two parties. Indeed, there is no formal limit to the number of parties that can participate in a single arbitration. As long as all the parties have agreed to arbitrate with all the other parties, then the consensual foundation of arbitration has been satisfied. The most common term used for this type of arbitration, which admittedly is relatively uncommon, is "multi-party arbitration".

Multi-party arbitrations can occur for different reasons, but the following four examples provide a good illustration of the circumstances in which they can arise:

a. Leonard, Jess and Gina have all signed the same contract, which includes an arbitration agreement. Two of the parties may decide to jointly commence arbitration against the third party, acting as co-claimants. For example, Leonard and Gina may agree to jointly bring a claim against Jess. Alternatively, one of the parties may commence arbitration against the other two parties, e.g. Gina brings a claim against both Leonard and Jess. In cases such as these, the arbitration involves more than two parties from the very beginning.
b. Kelan and Anabella have entered into a contract, and Kelan files a request for arbitration against Anabella, alleging that she breached their contract. Anabella, however, argues that the breach was actually caused by Cohen, who is not a party to the contract, and wants Cohen to participate in the arbitration. This may be possible through a mechanism called "joinder", which is common in court litigation. However, reflecting the consensual nature of arbitration, joinder is only available in arbitration if all parties agree to the third party being joined (including the third party himself), although this consent may have been given by agreeing to arbitrate under institutional rules that permit joinder at the discretion of the tribunal.
c. Bronwen and Gracie-Mae are involved in an arbitration. Marius wishes to join the arbitration, arguing that a decision in the dispute between Bronwen and Gracie-Mae will also affect his own legal rights. This is possible though a mechanism called "intervention". However, again, because of the consensual foundation of arbitration, intervention is only possible if all parties agree.
d. Nathalie has commenced arbitration against Nela. At the same time, Nela has commenced arbitration against Tashard. Both arbitrations involve very similar issues, to an extent that it is impossible for an arbitral tribunal to resolve one of the disputes without delivering a decision that also resolves at least some issues in dispute in the other arbitration. In such cases, it may be possible to merge the arbitrations, thereby reducing costs and avoiding the risk that the awards from the two arbitrations will contradict one another. This is called "consolidation". As always, though, because of the consensual nature of arbitration, consolidation is only possible if all parties agree to it.

Alternatively, as an informal alternative to consolidation, the parties may agree to conduct the two arbitrations in parallel, appointing the same tribunal in both proceedings, adopting the same procedural time-table and having joint oral hearings. In this scenario, although the two arbitrations are not technically consolidated, they are in practice held together, so that costs can to a certain extent be reduced and the risk of inconsistent outcomes is minimised.

While there are also other ways that a multi-party arbitration might occur, these examples provide a good illustration of the variety of ways in which they can arise, as well as the central role of party consent in making such an arbitration possible. However a multi-party arbitration arises, though, the participation of more than two parties in an arbitration can have important consequences. Most obviously, an arbitral award is only binding on the parties involved in the arbitration; as a result, if more than two parties are involved in a dispute but only two participate in the arbitration, the remaining parties will not be bound by the tribunal's award. On the other hand, both parties that participated in the arbitration will be bound by the award, even though the award may have been substantially different if the other parties had been involved in the proceedings as well, made their own arguments, presented their own evidence, etc.

It is, therefore, essential when planning an arbitration to consider whether there are indeed only two parties who should be participating in the arbitration. Overwhelmingly this will indeed be the case, but where it is desirable that another party or parties be bound by the award, their participation should be secured – and if this is not possible it may be necessary to reconsider the use of arbitration.

6.1 Multi-party arbitration and appointment of arbitrators

One particularly complex issue that arises in the context of multi-party arbitrations is the appointment of arbitrators. After all, if an arbitration agreement requires the appointment of a single arbitrator mutually agreed between the parties, this can be difficult enough to achieve when only two parties are involved, let alone three, four or more. In addition, the primary solution used in international commercial arbitration to avoid requiring party agreement on a single arbitrator is the three-arbitrator tribunal, with each party appointing one member of the tribunal and the remaining member usually being agreed between the party-appointed arbitrators. But how should this mechanism work if there are more than two parties in the arbitration?

There is as yet no clear answer to this question, although the rules of some institutions now incorporate mechanisms to address the issue. As a result, if parties are arbitrating under the auspices of an institution whose rules address appointment of arbitrators in multi-party arbitrations, the mechanism adopted in those rules will be applicable. In any other situation, however, the correct approach is much less clear.

One potential approach would be to examine the parties' claims and defences in order to determine whether there are in reality more than two positions being advanced. It may be the case, for example, that while Elisabeth and Alexandra are both bringing a claim against Ophelia, their claims are fundamentally identical. It is sometimes argued that in such a situation, assuming the parties have agreed on a three-arbitrator tribunal, Elisabeth and Alexandra should be required to agree on a single arbitrator, while Ophelia appoints one on her own behalf.

The rationale for this approach is that if Elisabeth and Alexandra are both permitted to appoint their own arbitrator, then the resulting panel will actually include twice as many arbitrators selected by one side of the dispute than were selected by the other. This situation would be fundamentally unfair to Ophelia. The difficulty, however, is that while the claims being brought by Elisabeth and Alexandra may be substantively similar, they may have very different preferences regarding arbitrators. To give just one example, perhaps Elisabeth wants a non-lawyer appointed to the tribunal who understands the technical details of the transaction underlying the dispute, while Alexandra believes that this would be a mistake and strongly wants to appoint a lawyer. Requiring that Elisabeth and Alexandra agree on a single arbitrator would ensure that the two sides of the dispute were equally represented on the tribunal, but would also deprive Elisabeth and Alexandra of the right to appoint an arbitrator of whom they personally approved, even though Ophelia still retained this right.

Further complications arise if it is not possible to argue that there are only really two different sides to the dispute. Elisabeth and Alexandra, that is, may both be bringing a claim against Ophelia, but they may have very different claims, and may even have partially or entirely conflicting claims – that is, Elisabeth can only be successful if Alexandra is not. In such a situation requiring Elisabeth and Alexandra to agree on a single arbitrator is fundamentally unfair to both of them. This problem might be resolved by allowing each party to appoint its own arbitrator, and then requiring that those party-appointed arbitrators agree on the appointment of two further arbitrators, thereby ensuring that the tribunal still has an odd number of members. However, a tribunal with five members can raise significantly more complications than will a tribunal with three members: hearings and other meetings can only be scheduled when all five tribunal members are free; hearings may be longer because there are now more tribunal members examining the parties' evidence and arguments; costs will be substantially increased because not only must the parties now pay for five arbitrators, rather than three, but every document must now be supplied to two additional tribunal members, travel and accommodation must be paid for an additional two tribunal members, and so on. Moreover, what if there are more than three parties involved in the arbitration? With five parties involved, the tribunal would need to include at least seven members.

Understanding arbitration through case-law

Multiple parties and right to appoint an arbitrator

Case details: *Siemens v BKMI and Dutco*, 7 January 1992

Authority deciding the case: French Court of Cassation

Facts of the case: Siemens, BKMI and Dutco entered into a contract for the construction of a factory. The contract contained an arbitration clause, according to which each party had the right to appoint one arbitrator. A dispute arose and Dutco filed a request

164 *Arbitral proceedings*

> for arbitration against both BKMI and Siemens. While both claims arose out of the same contract, the claim against BKMI was partially different from the claim against Siemens. In its request for arbitration, Dutco appointed one arbitrator.
>
> BKMI and Siemens argued that each of them had the right to appoint one arbitrator, and refused to make a joint appointment. The ICC warned BKMI and Siemens that, if they failed to make an appointment, the ICC would choose an arbitrator for them. At that point BKMI and Siemens made a joint appointment under protest, but objected to the jurisdiction of the tribunal.
>
> The arbitral tribunal rejected the objection to its jurisdiction and rendered an award on the merits. Siemens applied to have the award annulled before French courts. The annulment application was rejected by the Court of Appeal of Paris. Siemens then filed a further appeal with the French Court of Cassation.
>
> **Decision:** The French Court of Cassation reversed the decision of the Court of Appeal of Paris. The Court's primary rationale was that the parties to an arbitration cannot be deprived of their right to appoint arbitrators if this right is established in the agreement to arbitrate. The Court stressed the importance of the fact that BKMI and Siemens did not share the same interests in the case, and in fact were facing significantly different claims. It was therefore considered unfair to force them to make a joint appointment while the claimant was able to appoint another member of the tribunal freely and without limitations.
>
> The outcome of the *Dutco* case prompted a revision of the ICC Rules, which now empower the ICC to appoint each member of the tribunal in cases in which a joint appointment by multiple parties proves impossible.[69]

There is unfortunately no ideal solution to this problem. The simplest approach is that adopted by the leading arbitral institutions, which allows the institution itself to appoint the members of the tribunal if the parties cannot agree on either the arbitrators or a mechanism for their appointment.[70] This approach is also taken by some national laws.[71] On the other hand, French law requires that unless the parties have agreed on an alternative mechanism for the appointment of arbitrators (including by agreeing to use institutional rules that incorporate such a mechanism), each party has a fundamental right to appoint its own arbitrator.[72]

Proponents of both views indisputably have strong arguments on their side. The approach preferred by arbitral institutions denies parties the right to select their own arbitrator, which is a fundamental benefit that arbitration provides over litigation. The French approach, on the other hand, compels parties to participate in a larger and more complex form of arbitration than they had agreed upon. Ultimately, however, the French approach is preferable, as most accurately reflecting the centrality to arbitration of party autonomy. If parties have agreed to arbitrate under institutional rules that allow the institution to appoint arbitrators itself, then they have agreed to give up their control over the tribunal in the interest of certainty regarding the number of arbitrators, and hence the size and complexity of the arbitration. However, where no such choice has been made, it is a fundamental unfairness to deprive a party of its right to participate in the constitution of the tribunal, and thereby of its power to ensure that its viewpoint on the dispute and its cultural or other preferences are properly taken into consideration by the tribunal when the dispute is decided. This may result in a larger and more complex arbitration than the parties expected when entering into the arbitration agreement, but this is a less fundamental violation of procedural fairness than is a change that directly impacts on the substantive resolution of the parties' dispute.

7. Arbitration can be quick but it can also be "expedited"

One of the benefits that arbitration is often argued to provide over litigation is speed, and while it is true that in many, if not most, States arbitrating an international commercial dispute will take less time than litigating it in court, that does not mean that the arbitration itself is necessarily fast – rather, it is often just that courts can be extremely slow. In reality, international commercial arbitration is not usually a very rapid process, and parties agreeing to arbitration with the expectation that any dispute will be resolved in a matter of months will often find themselves still arbitrating after one or even two years.

It is important to emphasise that this is not, as such, a flaw in arbitration, but a nearly unavoidable consequence of the need to ensure that the arbitral process is fair. Time must be allowed for the parties to select their arbitrators, and to resolve any challenges; time must be allowed for the production of documents and for those documents to be examined; time must be allowed for the parties to prepare their arguments and draft their memoranda; delays will be incurred even for a short hearing because a time must be found at which arbitrators, counsel and witnesses can all be present; then time must be allowed for any post-hearing written submissions; and finally time must be allowed for the arbitrators to reach a decision and draft their award. This is not to suggest that there are not ways in which current arbitration practice could be improved, and one well-recognised problem is that leading arbitrators often take on more cases than they can efficiently handle, resulting both in delays relating to scheduling of hearings and other meetings, and delays in the delivery of the final award. However, if arbitration is going to be fair, it will take time.

These observations point to the real conflict at issue in this context, namely the need for a trade-off between the parties receiving a decision quickly and receiving a decision that is thorough and correct. To many people the idea that the correctness of a decision should be traded away for speed is initially nearly heretical – the fundamental point of any dispute resolution procedure is surely to deliver a just and justified resolution of the dispute. A simple example, though, will illustrate that this idea is not as obvious as it may seem. Imagine your mother arrives home one evening and announces that she has been given two tickets to see a concert by the world's greatest living singer: Rick Astley. However, she has to leave within five minutes or she will miss the show, and she asks who would like to go with her. Both you and your brother are, of course, enormous Rick Astley fans and both desperately want to go with her, and you each launch into a series of arguments as to why you should be the one to go. The only way your mother can fairly decide which of you should come is to sit down and listen to your arguments and discuss them with you. But that will take much longer than five minutes, so you will all miss the show and neither you nor your brother will get to see Rick Astley. In this situation, speed matters more than fairness or correctness, and the only reasonable solution is for your mother to hear the best case you can make in a limited amount of time and then make the best decision she can.

The same sort of situation arises in international commercial arbitration, although rarely involving Rick Astley. Yes, everyone always wants a fair arbitration leading to a justified and correct decision, but sometimes the consequences of waiting for such a process to complete will eliminate or seriously undermine the value of the decision.

It is precisely in a context such as this, however, that arbitration can truly shine. After all, one of the major benefits of arbitration, as has been repeatedly emphasised in this Chapter, is its procedural flexibility. While parties who take their dispute to a court will have to accept whatever speed the court is able to deliver, if the parties to an arbitration agreement all want their dispute to be resolved quickly, then procedures can be adopted that will allow this to happen.

In some cases the possibility of an accelerated arbitral process will be available to the parties because they have agreed to institutional arbitration and the rules of the institution in question expressly include provisions for an expedited or simplified form of arbitration.[73] Such provisions may include alterations to the arbitral process such as:

– the use of a sole arbitrator, rather than a panel of three arbitrators;
– an express limitation on the number of written submissions;
– the conduct of only a single hearing, or perhaps the complete exclusion of hearings;
– a specific and short time-limit within which the arbitrators must deliver the final award;
– permission for the arbitrators to deliver an award that only summarises their reasoning, or even an award that simply announces the decision without providing any reasons at all.

Expedited arbitration, however, is not only available through the use of an arbitral institution, and in *ad hoc* arbitration the tribunal can simply adopt an accelerated process, so long as the parties have consented to this.

As with every benefit, though, accelerating the arbitral process comes at a cost, and "cost" is a key word in this context, because an accelerated arbitration may end up actually being more expensive than would be a regular arbitration resolving the same dispute. Some savings will be made, of course, as fewer documents will need to be produced, hearings will be shorter, etc., but completing an arbitration in a reduced time-frame requires that both arbitrators and counsel be willing to lay aside other work obligations in order to concentrate on this single arbitration. They will rarely do this unless they are paid additional amounts as compensation for the other work they will lose.

Moreover, while arbitrators can certainly understand the willingness of parties to compromise on the quality of the tribunal's decision in exchange for a speedier process, they will be unwilling to take on a case that does not allow them time to do their job to an acceptable level of professionalism. There are, as a result, limitations on how little time a good tribunal will be willing to spend resolving a complex dispute, no matter how willing the parties are to compromise on quality in exchange for speed.

It will, of course, always be possible to find someone willing to make that compromise, so a tribunal will always be available. However, a poorly handled accelerated process will not just result in a compromise between justice and speed, but can easily lead to a fundamental violation of a party's procedural rights. This may mean not only that the parties receive less justice than they were expecting for the amount of speed they received, but even that courts refuse to enforce the resulting award, thereby rendering the entire arbitral process a waste of time – precisely the "time" that the parties were attempting to save.

The possibility of accelerating the arbitral process is, therefore, an important feature of arbitration, and one of the primary advantages that arbitration can have over litigation. It is, however, not something to be undertaken lightly, and never to be undertaken without a high quality tribunal that takes its professional obligations seriously and will ensure that the parties receive the trade-off they have decided to accept, while still receiving a fundamentally fair arbitral procedure.

Notes

1   See e.g. Section 34 of the English Arbitration Act 1996 and Article 182(1) of the Swiss Private International Law Statute.
2   Article 20(1) of the UNCITRAL Model Law, for example, the parties can agree on the seat of arbitration; most other national arbitration statutes follow a similar approach, granting the parties a wide margin of discretion in the selection of the seat.
3   Hanseatisches Oberlandesgericht, Hamburg, 24 January 2003 in Albert Jan van den Berg (ed.), *Yearbook Commercial Arbitration XXX* (ICCA 2005) 509.
4   Oberlandesgericht München, 3 February 2010 (2010) *SchiedsVZ* 336.
5   See e.g. Article 20(1) of the Model Law.
6   Article 18(1).
7   See e.g. Article 21(1) of the 2016 SIAC Rules.
8   Article 20(1).
9   See Article 18(1) of the 2017 ICC Rules.
10 Article 16(2) of the 2014 LCIA Rules.
11 Article 17(1) of the 2014 ICDR Rules.
12 *Lea Tai Textile Co. v Manning Fabrics, Inc.*, 411 F.Supp. 1404, 1407 (S.D.N.Y. 1975).
13 Article 816(2) of the Italian Code of Civil Procedure.
14 Section 47 of the Swedish Arbitration Act.
15 "Report of the United Nations Commission on International Trade Law on the work of its thirty-second session" UN Doc A/54/17 (17 May – 4 June 1999) paras 358–359.
16 Article 24(2) of the Spanish Arbitration Act.
17 For a discussion of the confidentiality presumption and its exceptions under English law, *see Emmott v Wilson & Partners Limited* [2008] EWCA Civ 184.
18 *United States v Panhandle Eastern Corp.*, 119 F.R.D. 346 (D.Del.1988).
19 Article 1464(4) of the French Code of Civil Procedure.
20 Article 1479 of the French Code of Civil Procedure.
21 *ITT Educational Services v Arce*, 533 F.3d 342 (5th Cir. 2008).
22 Practitioners and scholars debate whether the imposition of this type of requirement concerning the commencement of the arbitration gives rise to an issue of jurisdiction, or rather of admissibility. In other words, if the Claimant does not comply with the conditions set forth in the agreement, does this entail that the tribunal has no jurisdiction to hear the case, or is it merely a procedural issue that can be disregarded if the tribunal finds that the Claimant was justified in its decision not to wait? The question is not merely theoretical, as this qualification entails crucial consequences, especially concerning the degree to which the tribunal's ruling may be subject to judicial review at the seat of arbitration. For an analysis of this problem see Jan Paulsson, "Jurisdiction and Admissibility" in

168 *Arbitral proceedings*

Gerald Aksen, Karl-Heinz Böckstiegel, Paolo Michele Patocchi and Anne Marie Whitesell (eds), *Global Reflections on International Law, Commerce and Dispute Resolution, Liber Amicorum in Honour of Robert Briner* (ICC 2005) 601.

23 See generally IBA Litigation Committee, "Multi-Tiered Dispute Resolution Clauses", 1 October 2015.
24 See e.g. French Court of Cassation, *Poiré v Tripier*, 14 February 2003 (2003) 19 *Arbitration International* 368.
25 See e.g. the US Court in *HIM Portland, LLC v DeVito Builders, Inc.*, 317 F.3d 41, 42 (1st Cir. 2003).
26 See for instance, in Ireland, *Esso Ireland Limited & Anor v Nine One One Retail Limited* [2013] IEHC 514.
27 Article 4 of the 2017 ICC Rules; Article 1 of the 2014 LCIA Rules.
28 Article 2 of the 2014 ICDR Rules.
29 See, e.g. Supreme Court of Austria, 6 February 2018, OGH 18 ONc 4 / 17h.
30 Article 2(1) of the 2014 ICDR Rules; Article 1(1)(vii) of the 2014 LCIA Rules.
31 Article 4(5) of the 2017 ICC Rules; Article 9(1) of the 2017 SCC Rules.
32 Pursuant to Article 5(1) of the ICC Rules, for example, the answer must be submitted within 30 days from the receipt of the request. Similarly, a time-limit of 30 days is set by Article 8(1) of the 2018 VIAC Rules.
33 Article 5(5) of the 2017 ICC Rules.
34 Article 9B of the 2014 LCIA Rules; Article 29 of the 2017 ICC Rules; Article 6 of the 2014 ICDR Rules; Article 30 of the 2016 SIAC Rules.
35 Three days, pursuant to Article 3 of Appendix V to the 2017 ICC Rules; 24 hours, pursuant to Article 4(3) of Appendix II to the 2017 SCC Rules.
36 There still are, however, some exceptions to this general trend: see e.g. Article 818 of the Italian Code of Civil Procedure.
37 *Arrowhead Global Solutions, Inc. v Datapath, Inc.*, 166 F.Appx. 39, 44 (4th Cir. 2006).
38 Article 28(1) of the 2017 ICC Rules; Article 23 of the HKIAC Rules; Article 33 of the VIAC Rules; Article 30 of the SIAC Rules; Article 8 of the Asian International Arbitration Centre (AIAC) Rules; Article 26 of the Milan Chamber of Arbitration Rules (for proceedings seated outside of Italy)
39 Article 17J of the UNCITRAL Model Law.
40 Article 28(2) of the 2017 ICC Rules.
41 Article 17B(2) of the UNCITRAL Model Law.
42 Article 17C of the UNCITRAL Model Law.
43 Article 23(5) of the UNCITRAL Model Law.
44 Article 17C(4) of the UNCITRAL Model Law.
45 See Article 17 of the UNCITRAL Model Law, detailing the types of interim measures that a tribunal may issue. It is noteworthy that the measures listed in the provision are conservatory in nature; this makes it doubtful that the Model Law enables arbitrators to issue provisional measures that effectively anticipate the effects of the final award, rather than simply protecting the *status quo*.
46 Article 17H of the UNCITRAL Model Law.
47 *Resort Condominiums International Inc. v Bolwell*, 29 October 1993 (1994) 10(2) *Arbitration International* 385.
48 For instance, according to Article 7(5) [Option 1] of the Model Law, an "exchange of statements of claim and defence in which the existence of an agreement is alleged by one party and not denied by the other" will constituted a valid arbitration agreement in writing.
49 Tony Cole, Pietro Ortolani, et al., "Legal Instruments and Practice of Arbitration in the EU" (European Parliament 2015), available at www.europarl.europa.eu/thinktank/en/document.html?reference=IPOL_STU(2015)509988.

50 Tony Cole, Pietro Ortolani, et al., "Arbitration in the Americas", available at https://www2.le.ac.uk/departments/law/research/arbitration.
51 Eric A Schwartz and Yves Derains, *Guide to the ICC Rules of Arbitration* (2nd edn, Kluwer 2005) 246–250.
52 Article 23(2) of the 2017 ICC Rules.
53 J Gillis Wetter, "The Present Status of the International Court of Arbitration of the ICC: An Appraisal" (1990) 1 *Am Rev Int Arb* 91.
54 Gary B Born, *International Commercial Arbitration* (2nd edn, Kluwer 2014) 2247.
55 Article 37 of the 2017 ICC Rules.
56 See Article 37(2) of the 2017 ICC Rules.
57 Article 25(6) of the 2017 ICC Rules; Article 19(1) of the 2014 LCIA Rules.
58 Article 24 of the UNCITRAL Model Law.
59 While it might be thought that the tribunal could simply use the hearing room once it had been emptied of other individuals, the range of ways in which it is now possible to make audio recordings means that a separate room for the tribunal should be regarded as essential.
60 In one arbitration in which one of the authors was involved many years ago, the administering arbitral institution (which did not have rooms of its own to offer) proposed a location in which only one party would have a break-out room, the other party being expected to use a publicly accessible reception room for its confidential discussions. Ultimately the arbitration was held in the offices of a law firm at which one of the arbitrators was a partner.
61 In some cases the time that each of the parties uses will be controlled through a "chess clock" system, in order to ensure that by the end of the hearing each of the parties has been given an equal amount of time to speak and to examine witnesses.
62 Investment arbitration awards, for example, are often criticised for their drafting, despite investment arbitrators being leading figures in the field and despite investment arbitrations paying enormously well.
63 This is all the more true in cases in which the arbitrators are, for practical reasons, unable to meet in person for long periods of time to discuss the award. In such cases, tribunals will often deliberate shortly after the closing of the proceedings, discussing only the most important elements of the case, and will then refine the details of the award by exchanging drafts. It is, thus, fundamental that those drafts be actually written by the arbitrators, rather than by their assistants.
64 While the distinction between civil and common law is necessarily simplistic and to a certain extent even misleading, the former category broadly refers to that family of legal system originating from continental Europe, while the latter alludes to Anglo-American systems and, more generally, to legal orders formally conceiving of precedent as a source of law. For a general introduction to these notions and their relevance from a comparative perspective see Mathias Reimann and Reinhard Zimmermann (eds), *The Oxford Handbook of Comparative Law* (OUP 2006).
65 This rule traces back to the traditional principle in Roman law *nemo tenetur edere instrumenta contra se*, or no-one is bound to produce writings against himself, or more casually to accuse himself.
66 Article 3(3)(a)(ii) of the IBA Rules.
67 *Resolution du Conseil du l'Ordre des Avocats*, 26 February 2008 (France); Article 7 of the *Code suisse de déontologie* (Switzerland).
68 Article 27 of the UNCITRAL Model Law.
69 See Article 12 of the 2017 ICC Rules.
70 See, e.g. the arbitration rules of the ICC, HKIAC, the Belgian Centre for Arbitration and Mediation (CEPANI), SCC and LCIA.
71 See, e.g. Finland. In Italy a special regime exists for arbitration in corporate matters. Since corporate disputes are often multi-party, the law requires the parties to specify the number and the

170 *Arbitral proceedings*

    method of appointment of arbitrators, requiring that all arbitrators be nominated by an external appointing authority: see Article 34 of legislative decree no. 5 of 2003.
72 As mentioned on p. 00, this was the main problem arising in the *Dutco* case, which prompted the revision of the ICC Rules.
73 See e.g. the 2017 Rules for Expedited Arbitrations of the SCC, Article 30 of the 2017 ICC Rules or Article 5 of the 2016 SIAC Rules.

6 The arbitral award

Rules

1. An arbitral award is a private decision with public consequences

Fundamentally, an arbitral award is just a statement by one or more private individuals on how a dispute between two or more other private individuals should be resolved. In itself it has no more importance than a statement of opinion by any other private individual. What gives an arbitral award its legal importance is that governments around the world have decided that arbitration should be encouraged and supported, and that one effective way to do this is to let arbitral awards be enforced through the State's legal system, just as happens with court judgments.

2. There is more than one type of award

While people often refer to "the award" from an arbitration, a tribunal may issue a number of awards in a single arbitration. The award delivered at the end of an arbitration, finally resolving the entire dispute, is called the "final award". A tribunal may, however decide to resolve some elements of the parties' dispute earlier than the rest, by delivering what is best referred to as a "partial award". A tribunal may also issue a "default award" if one of the parties refuses to participate in the arbitration.

3. An award can incorporate a settlement agreement

While arbitrations normally take place after attempts to settle a dispute have failed, sometimes parties will reach agreement on how best to settle their dispute after the arbitration has commenced. In such a case, the tribunal may issue a "consent award", incorporating the substance of the parties' agreement into an arbitral award. This allows the parties to take advantage of the enforceability of arbitral awards to ensure both sides fulfill their agreement.

4. There are formal rules to which arbitral awards must conform

While technically arbitrators can draft an award in any form acceptable to the parties, in reality parties want to be able to have their award enforced in court if this turns out to be necessary. This means that an award should obey the formal rules set out by any relevant arbitration law, by the applicable arbitration rules, and by the parties' arbitration agreement.

5. *There may also be rules specifying how or when an award must be delivered*

Ongoing concerns about the efficiency of international commercial arbitration have resulted in an increasing number of rules designed to ensure that arbitral proceedings do not last too long. These rules often involve time limits within which the tribunal must deliver the award, and can derive from either the applicable arbitration rules or from the law of the arbitral seat.

6. *A wide range of remedies can be awarded by arbitral tribunals*

While a payment of money is by far the most common remedy in international commercial arbitration, other remedies are available. A tribunal may, for example, grant declaratory relief, which clarifies the rights and obligations of the parties but doesn't require that any party actually do anything, or specific performance, which requires a party to take a specified action rather than to pay money. The tribunal may also be able to rectify or adapt a contract, changing the terms of the party's written contract to reflect either the parties' actual original intentions or that a fundamental change in circumstances has occurred.

7. *An award may also say who pays for how much of the arbitration*

An arbitral award will often specify how the parties are to split the costs of the arbitration, including the fees of the parties' lawyers, or even state that one party must pay everything. There is no single rule used in allocating costs in arbitration, and tribunals are generally free to use the approach they believe most appropriate in each individual case.

8. *An award has* res judicata *effect*

Although an arbitral award is a decision by private individuals, it cannot just be ignored by the parties. Once an award has been issued, a losing party cannot just re-start the dispute in another forum, whether in court or in another arbitration. However, the exact rules that apply in this situation vary significantly around the world.

9. *Arbitrators can issue separate opinions in addition to the award*

While international commercial arbitrations almost always end with the issuance of a final award agreed by all the members of the tribunal, sometimes one arbitrator will disagree so strongly with the rest of the tribunal that she insists on drafting her own decision, known as a "dissent", or "dissenting opinion". Even more rarely, an arbitrator may issue a "concurring opinion", laying out her own reasoning for the conclusion reached by all members of the tribunal. Dissenting and concurring opinions have no legal impact on the award, but can be seen by the arbitrator as a professional obligation.

Analysis

1. An arbitral award is a private decision with public consequences

1.1 The idea of an arbitral award

Fundamentally, arbitration is a private process: two parties get into a dispute and instead of taking their dispute to court they pay one or more private individuals to decide it for them. This book has discussed a number of reasons why parties might choose to spend money on arbitration even though courts are normally less expensive. However, it is important to note a fundamental consequence of the decision to use a private decision-maker to resolve your dispute: in and of itself, what a private individual (including an arbitrator) says about how your dispute should be resolved is largely irrelevant.

That is, when a tribunal delivers its decision, referred to as an "award", that decision is just the personal opinion of the members of the tribunal on how the dispute should be resolved. It has no more importance, in and of itself, than if the disputing parties had stopped a passing stranger in the street and said "We're having a disagreement. These are the facts. Who is right?" It might be interesting to hear someone else's opinion on how your dispute should be resolved, but ultimately it's just their opinion, and if you think they are wrong you can just ignore them.

So what, then, is it that makes an arbitrator's award so much more important than just a random stranger's opinion? As already said, it is nothing at all about the award itself. No matter how wise, how well drafted, how brilliantly reasoned the award is, it's still just "someone's opinion".

The only reason that arbitration awards are more important than the views of a random stranger is that governments have decided that they should be. That is, that governments have decided to stand behind and enforce arbitral awards just as they do court judgements. This doesn't mean that an arbitral award is a direct expression of the views of the State in the way that a court judgement is, of course. An arbitral award is still just the opinion of one or more private individuals. But an arbitral award is part of an exclusive subset of private opinions that the legal system says should be obeyed.

An arbitral award, then, is a private opinion with public consequences.

1.2 The difference between awards and orders

Given that an arbitral award has public consequences, it can matter greatly whether a particular decision by a tribunal qualifies as an award or not. After all, during the course of an arbitration, a tribunal will typically issue a number of decisions, covering matters ranging from mundane points of procedure, to decisions on the admissibility of pieces of evidence, to the final decision on the outcome of the dispute. Indeed, the central role of the tribunal in ensuring the effectiveness of the arbitral process means that an arbitral tribunal usually does far more than just listen to presentations by the parties before delivering a decision. In many arbitrations, it is crucial that the tribunal actively manages the process of the arbitration, making a series of decisions that are binding on the parties, or the arbitration will never progress to the point that a final award can be delivered.

Yet not every decision by a tribunal qualifies as an "award". For purely pragmatic reasons this must be true, as the public consequences of an award bring with them legal protections. That is, an award may be enforceable, but it can also be challenged in court to ensure its fundamental fairness. Yet if every decision by an arbitral tribunal qualified as an award, parties in an arbitration could potentially end up spending more time in court, fighting about the tribunal's decisions, than they spent in the arbitration itself.

For this practical reason, then, a distinction has been developed between "awards", which have public consequences, and "orders", which may not. That is, if a decision by a tribunal qualifies as an award, then the legal framework of the New York Convention and national arbitration laws can be used to enforce or challenge that decision. If the decision is merely an "order", then the Convention and national arbitration laws won't apply in the same way, and the parties will normally have to rely on the tribunal itself taking action to ensure the effectiveness of its orders.

Given the importance of this difference between awards and orders, you might think that there would be a clear and widely agreed definition of what is and is not an award. As with many things in arbitration, however, the reality is much vaguer and unclear. There are certain things that are uniformly accepted as being awards, most obviously the final award in an arbitration in which the tribunal issues its decision on the substantive dispute between the parties. Similarly, there are certain things that are uniformly accepted as being orders, such as procedural orders that specify the scheduling of the stages of a hearing. However, where the line is drawn between an award and an order is much less clear and the subject of considerable disagreement.

Moreover, this is not a matter that can be decided by the tribunal itself. That is, that the tribunal labels one of its decisions as an "award" does not mean it is an award; similarly, that the tribunal labels the decision as an "order" does not mean it is not an award. "Award" is a legal designation, and so whether a decision is an "award" or an "order" will ultimately be decided by a court.[1]

Ultimately, the best approach to distinguishing between awards and orders focuses on what the tribunal has been hired by the parties to do, and what the legal framework for the enforcement of awards has been designed to accomplish. That is, the tribunal has been hired to decide the dispute between the parties, and the purpose of an award is to embody that resolution. If a decision by the tribunal finally resolves all or part of the parties' dispute, then it is properly treated as an award. If it merely facilitates the arbitral process, or does anything other than finally resolve all or part of the parties' dispute, then it is properly treated as an order.[2]

2. There is more than one type of award

2.1 The difference between final and partial awards

Often when arbitration is discussed you will hear reference to "the" award, as though each arbitration only produces a single award, delivered at the end of the proceedings and including the tribunal's final decision on the issues in dispute. This is indeed accurate for many arbitrations, which result in the delivery of only a single award.

However, it is important to remember what it is that an award does: it finally resolves all or part of the parties' dispute. This reference to "part of" the dispute is key, because a tribunal may decide that one element of the parties' dispute can be decided without resolving the rest, and that it would be beneficial to deliver a decision on that element immediately, rather than waiting until the entire dispute can be resolved. If the tribunal delivers a decision on that element of the parties' dispute, then it has "finally resolved" that element, and the decision constitutes an "award".

The award delivered at the end of an arbitration, then, is properly called the "final award", even if it is the only award the tribunal has issued. With the final award the tribunal usually completes its function and gives up any remaining authority it has over the parties. In technical terms, the tribunal becomes *functus officio*. The tribunal was hired by the parties to perform a particular job: to deliver a binding decision on their dispute. It has now performed that job, and so the arbitrators now have no more authority over the parties than does any other private individual.[3]

As just emphasised, however, final awards are not the only possible type of award: a tribunal may decide to finally resolve some elements of the parties' dispute earlier than the rest. The terminology used to describe such an award can vary, with both "partial award" and "interim award" being common. However, the expression "partial award" is preferable as it accurately identifies that the tribunal is only ruling on part of the parties' dispute. By contrast, the expression "interim award" may be misunderstood as suggesting that such an award is not truly final, and that the tribunal remains free to revisit the issues in an interim award in the final award, potentially reaching different conclusions. As already emphasised, however, to be an award at all a decision by a tribunal must "finally resolve" all or part of the parties' dispute, and it is now accepted that when a tribunal issues a partial award the tribunal becomes *functus officio* with respect to the issues resolved in that award, and may not revisit them in the final award.

A couple of examples might be useful to clarify why a tribunal could decide to issue a partial award, rather than reserving all its decisions for the final award. The most common situation in which a partial award will be issued involves a decision on jurisdiction. Let's say Cristian commences arbitration against Vijay, claiming compensation for an alleged breach of contract. Vijay responds by objecting that there is no valid arbitration agreement between them, as well as denying that he breached their contract. If Vijay is correct that there is no valid arbitration agreement, then there is a clear unfairness to Vijay in requiring him to go through an entire arbitration only to be told in the final award "Actually, you never had to come to arbitration." To avoid this situation, it is relatively common for a tribunal to issue a partial award that solely addresses its own jurisdiction. Doing this allows the arbitration to be terminated quickly where the tribunal does not have jurisdiction, but also allows the partial award on jurisdiction to be immediately challenged in court. In either case, the efficiency of the arbitral process is enhanced.

This does not mean arbitral tribunals always issue partial awards on jurisdiction, of course, and there are cases in which the tribunal will properly conclude that efficiency is best served by delivering the decision on jurisdiction in the final award, such as because the facts and arguments the tribunal needs to consider to determine if it has jurisdiction are the same as those it must consider to resolve the parties' substantive dispute. However, although a partial award on jurisdiction will not always be appropriate, it is an option that a tribunal should always consider when an objection to the tribunal's decision has been raised.

While a partial award on jurisdiction is the most common type of partial award, tribunals can also issue partial awards resolving one or more elements of the parties' substantive dispute. For example, the tribunal may resolve a dispute between the parties regarding ownership of a certain item of property, thereby allowing the proper owner to immediately receive the benefits of ownership, while reserving questions regarding a claimed contractual breach to be determined in the final award. In order for a partial award to make sense, however, it must be possible for the issue resolved in the partial award to be detached from the issues remaining to be resolved in the final award. In short, a tribunal needs to avoid delivering a partial award resolving one element of the parties' dispute, only to have additional evidence or legal argument presented later in the arbitration that would have justified a different partial award.

2.2 The source of the tribunal's power to make a partial award

Some contemporary arbitration statutes expressly grant arbitrators the power to issue partial awards whether or not they have been requested by the parties, although this is usually subject to the right of the parties to agree that no partial awards may be made.[4] Similarly, the rules of many arbitral institutions expressly give this power to tribunals, relying on the fact that the parties have agreed to arbitrate under those rules and so have impliedly agreed that the tribunal may issue partial awards.[5] Alternatively, although more rarely, the parties may have expressly contemplated in the arbitration agreement that the tribunal would issue partial awards.

Nonetheless, even if neither the *lex arbitri*, the applicable arbitration rules, nor the parties themselves expressly grants the tribunal the power to issue partial awards, so long as none of them expressly prevents the tribunal doing so, the ability to issue partial awards should be seen as a standard feature of a tribunal's case management powers.

2.3 Challenges against a partial award

As already mentioned, one of the consequences of a partial award being an award is that it can usually be challenged in court under the procedures applicable to the challenge of awards. Challenging an award will be discussed in more detail in Chapter 7, so the only point that needs to be emphasised here is that when a tribunal issues a partial award, it thereby creates an opportunity for the involvement in the arbitration of courts. In jurisdictions that are supportive of arbitration this won't be a source of concern, as challenges to awards are rarely successful. However, where a tribunal is seated in a jurisdiction in which the courts are less friendly to arbitration, or perhaps might even be biased towards one of the parties, the risk of court interference in the arbitration while the proceedings are still in progress is something that should be taken into account by a tribunal considering issuing a partial award.

While in many cases the law applicable to the challenge of a partial award will be the same as that applicable to the challenge of a final award, some arbitration statutes treat awards on jurisdiction differently to other (partial or final) awards. For example, under Article 16(3) of the UNCITRAL Model Law, a challenge to a tribunal's decision that it has jurisdiction must be brought within 30 days of the decision being notified to the parties, while under Article 34(3) challenges to almost all other awards must be brought within three months. This approach derives from that fact that the Model Law also allows an arbitration to continue even though the tribunal's decision that it has jurisdiction is being challenged in court. As a result, requiring that the tribunal's decision be challenged rapidly brings certainty to the arbitral process, minimising the risk that a party will incur significant costs in an arbitration only to be told that the tribunal never actually had jurisdiction.[6]

2.4 Default awards

The expression "default award" derives from the "default judgement" that is available in court litigation in many jurisdictions. In essence, if someone sues you in court and you do not respond (i.e. in technical language, you do not "appear"), you haven't just found a remarkably clever way to avoid being sued. The court proceedings will take place anyway, and the court will be able to issue a judgment that binds you, even though you didn't participate.[7] Indeed, in some legal systems a defaulting party will automatically lose the case; in other words, if the respondent fails to appear in the proceedings, the court will simply award the claimant whatever remedy she is seeking.[8]

To give an example, your neighbor Fergus sues you for £5,000.00 because he claims you broke into his house and destroyed a painting. You can prove you were out of the country on the date Fergus says the painting was destroyed, so you just don't bother responding, because you know you will win. Because you have "defaulted", by not participating in the litigation, the court will issue a judgement stating that you have to pay £5,000.00 to Fergus. Moreover, there are very few situations in which a default judgement will be reversed, such as if you can show that you did not receive notice of the litigation or were otherwise prevented from taking part for reasons beyond your control. "I can prove I would have won" is not enough. You now owe Fergus £5,000.00.

However, while a "default award" receives its name from the "default judgement" and is similar to a default judgement in many ways, it is nonetheless different in one very important way: it is not truly "default".

Firstly, even if one of the parties is defaulting, while a court can simply issue a judgement awarding the participating party the remedy it has sought, an arbitral tribunal cannot do this. Instead, the tribunal is obligated to establish that it has jurisdiction over the dispute before a default award can be issued. Arbitration, after all, is based on the consent of the parties, and so the tribunal must first satisfy itself that the parties consented to arbitrate the dispute before it. If the non-participating party did not consent to arbitration, then it does not matter that it is not participating; the tribunal must announce that is has no jurisdiction and reject the claim. It should be emphasised that if the defaulting party argues, as it likely will, that the tribunal does not have jurisdiction over the dispute, it may nonetheless appear in the arbitral proceedings for the purpose of challenging the tribunal's jurisdiction without being found to have thereby consented to the tribunal's jurisdiction.[9]

Moreover, even if the tribunal finds that it does have jurisdiction, it still cannot simply award the participating party the remedy it has requested, because it only has jurisdiction to arbitrate the dispute in accordance with the consent given by the parties. It is certainly possible for the parties to have included in their arbitration agreement that if a party didn't participate then the tribunal could immediately grant the participating party whatever remedy it was seeking, but such a clause is obviously extremely rare.[10]

Instead, a tribunal faced with a defaulting party must nonetheless proceed with a full arbitration, undertaken in accordance with the details of the parties' arbitration agreement. Only one party will be participating, but all the formalities must nonetheless be followed. Moreover, a tribunal wishing to ensure the enforceability of its final award should avoid ignoring the defaulting party, and should instead continue to invite that party to make submissions, participate in hearings, and so forth. This must be done in a way that does not prejudice the rights of the participating party, but the tribunal will want to make clear that the defaulting party has received every opportunity to participate in the arbitration and has willfully decided not to.

Indeed, while the tribunal should certainly not argue the defaulting party's case on its behalf, it must approach the arguments and evidence of the participating party in a way that tests the accuracy of the facts presented and the persuasiveness of the legal arguments. It cannot simply accept everything presented to it on the ground that it has not been challenged by the other party. Of course, since there is no contradictory evidence or argument the participating party's evidence and arguments will likely be more persuasive than they would have been in a fully contested arbitration. But nonetheless, if the participating party does not adequately substantiate its case on any point, then the tribunal must rule against it on that point, despite the absence of the defaulting party.

A default award then, as originally noted, is not identical to a default judgement. Depending on the applicable rules of civil procedure, a default judgement may effectively say: "You didn't take part, so no matter what the truth of this dispute, you lose." The simple fact of non-participation determines the outcome. A default award, on the other hand, is a properly drafted, properly reasoned decision that is delivered after a complete arbitration. It is obviously rare that a participating party will lose a default arbitration, since it is the only party presenting evidence and legal argument, but it is possible.

Because of the background against which they are delivered, default awards often involve a far more detailed discussion of the procedural development of the arbitration than is the case in most awards, as well as a clear account of the attempts that were made to involve the defaulting party in the arbitration, thereby ensuring the defaulting party of an equal opportunity to present its case.[11] In other words, default awards are generally drafted less for the parties themselves than for a potential reviewing court that may in the future be asked by the defaulting party to annul the award or refuse its enforcement. The focus of the award is on illustrating how due process and both parties' procedural rights were respected, even though one of the parties did not take part in the arbitration.

3. An award can incorporate a settlement agreement

One of the things that is essential to an arbitration is that it be based on a dispute. Yet an obvious consequence of parties being in a dispute is that the dispute may settle. Importantly, this may happen even after the arbitration has commenced, as the parties have now had an opportunity to see how good one another's cases are. As a result, the optimism parties often initially have that "Of course I'll win, I'm right" can give way to recognition that the other side is at least partially right as well, or even just that being right is not always enough to win a legal dispute.

Now the obvious result of the parties settling their dispute is that they will terminate the arbitration. After all, there is no longer anything to arbitrate about.

This, though, comes with a risk. What if the settlement falls apart and the parties start fighting again? What if one of the parties does not do what she promised she would do? If that happens then the parties are yet again in dispute, but they cannot simply pick up the arbitration where they left off, as the tribunal will have been dismissed.

The parties could potentially reassemble the same tribunal, but only if all the arbitrators are both available and willing, and also only if both parties want the same tribunal. Indeed, one of the parties may oppose reforming the tribunal simply to create an additional obstacle to the other party collecting on a potentially valid claim.

Alternatively, the parties could have agreed when they reached their settlement that they would simply put the arbitration on hiatus, most likely paying the tribunal an additional fee to remain available should the settlement fall apart. This is quite common when parties are in negotiations and believe that a settlement may be reached, but it is much more unusual post-settlement. After all, it would require agreement by both parties that the likelihood of the settlement falling apart is high enough that it is worth paying extra money to keep the tribunal empaneled just in case. But that will usually only be true if one or both parties cannot be trusted to keep to the terms of the settlement, and if the parties believed that was true then it is unlikely they would have agreed to the settlement in the first place.

The mechanism that has been developed to deal with this situation is what is known as a "consent award", an "award on agreed terms" or an "award by consent". In a nutshell, the parties reach an agreement on the terms of a settlement of their dispute and then bring that settlement to the tribunal to be issued in the form of an award. A consent award, then, is one of which the substantive contents have been agreed by the parties themselves, rather than decided upon by the tribunal. The power of a tribunal to issue a consent award is included in many arbitration statutes[12] and arbitration rules.[13]

It is easy to see why this mechanism is attractive to parties. After all, arbitral awards benefit from greatly enhanced support from courts around the world. As a result, an arbitral award that incorporates the terms of a settlement can be enforced against a defaulting party much more easily than the settlement agreement itself, and may be enforceable even when the court would not enforce the settlement agreement itself.[14]

Yet the conceptual difficulty with a consent award is obvious: an award is supposed to reflect the tribunal's decision on the dispute, but in a consent award the tribunal is merely issuing an award that repeats the terms of a settlement agreed by the parties. That award does not, therefore, reflect the decision-making of the tribunal. How, then, is it actually an arbitral award?[15]

The explanation lies in the fact that an arbitral tribunal approached by the parties with a request that a consent award be issued retains the power to say "No". Article 30(1) of the UNCITRAL Model Law, for instance, states that the parties' settlement can be recorded in the form of an arbitral award "if requested by the parties and not objected to by the arbitral tribunal". That is, while a consent award does not reflect the tribunal's decision on the details of the dispute, it does reflect the tribunal's decision that the terms of the proposed settlement are a fair and appropriate resolution of that dispute.

Of course, there will rarely be reason for a tribunal to reject the parties' proposed settlement. However, such reasons can arise, and will most commonly involve a decision by the tribunal that the requested award would violate the public policy of the seat of the arbitration or of a jurisdiction in which the award is expected to be enforced.[16] The tribunal cannot, of course, compel the parties to continue to arbitrate, and if a tribunal will not issue the consent award requested by the parties, the parties can simply terminate the arbitration, without any decision on the merits being issued.

Understanding arbitration through case-law

Enforcement of a consent award in the United States of America

Case details: *Albtelecom SH.A v UNIFI Communications, Inc.*, 16 Civ. 9001 (PAE), 30 May 2017

Authority deciding the case: United States District Court, Southern District of New York

Facts of the case: Albtelecom and UNIFI concluded a contract for the provision of telecommunication services. The contract contained an ICC arbitration clause. A dispute arose, and Albtelecom initiated ICC arbitration proceedings against UNIFI.

After the appointment of a sole arbitrator, the parties reached a settlement agreement and asked the arbitrator to incorporate their agreement into a consent award. The arbitrator issued the consent award. Pursuant to the settlement agreement, Albtelecom was entitled to receive €1,088,000, to be paid by UNIFI in 39 instalments. Furthermore, in case of UNIFI's failure to pay these instalments in accordance with the schedule agreed by the parties, Albtelecom would be entitled to claim an additional sum of money.

Albtelecom submitted that UNIFI failed to pay some of the instalments and, for this reason, sought to obtain the recognition and enforcement of the consent award in the United States of America. UNIFI, however, claimed that the 1958 New York Convention does not apply to a consent award, which should not be considered as a genuine award as it is not based on an arbitrator's resolution of the factual and legal disputes, but rather on the agreement of the parties themselves.

Decision: The United States District Court for the Southern District of New York recognised the consent award. The Court noted that the consent award had been expressly requested by the parties, who even proposed small amendments to the draft award. The court found no reason to treat a consent award differently than any other type of award.

4. There are formal rules to which arbitral awards must conform

4.1 Implicit requirement of written form in the New York Convention

Given that arbitration is a private process, it is possible for an award to be delivered by a tribunal in any form at all. Perhaps as a sonnet, orally in a phone call, or even in person through an interpretative dance. As long as neither party wishes to challenge or enforce the award, then there are no formal requirements applicable to an arbitral award other than those agreed to by the parties.

Parties, though, do challenge arbitral awards, and do seek the assistance of courts in having awards enforced. The unavoidable consequence of this fact is that formal requirements can be imposed by the law, which an award must meet if a court is to give its assistance. In short, if you have opted for a private dispute resolution process, then the State's dispute resolution system (i.e. courts) has no obligation to help you if things go wrong, except on the terms that the State chooses to lay down.

The most famous and arguably the most important formal requirement for an arbitral award is the requirement in Article IV(1)(a) of the New York Convention that any party applying for recognition and enforcement of an arbitral award must supply "a duly authenticated original award or a duly certified copy thereof". This provision significantly limits the forms an arbitral award can take, and arguably implicitly requires that the award be in writing. Parties can, of course, ignore this requirement and agree that their award should be delivered orally, or in some other form that does not meet the requirements of the New York Convention, but then they will not be able to take advantage of the Convention if they want to have the award recognised or enforced.

4.2 Requirements of formal validity in the lex arbitri: written form and signature

The *lex arbitri* will also normally set forth requirements for the validity of an arbitral award, although these vary from one jurisdiction to another. If the award does not meet these requirements, it may be annulled by the local courts.[17] In most jurisdictions, however, the requirements imposed by local law are minimal, and are designed to avoid surprising tribunals and parties with unusual requirements that may result in the invalidation of an otherwise unimpeachable award. There are, though, jurisdictions in which unusual requirements apply, and arbitrators who do not make the effort to familiarise themselves with what the *lex arbitri* requires fail to fulfill their professional obligations to the parties.

Reflecting the influence of the New York Convention, most legal systems require that awards be in writing. There are some exceptions to this rule,[18] but there is no question that a written award is the standard practice worldwide in both domestic and international arbitration.

In addition, arbitration statutes generally require that an award be signed by the arbitrators, or at least by a majority of them. It may happen, after all, that one arbitrator is so unhappy with the content of the award that she refuses to sign it. If this were enough to invalidate an arbitral award, an arbitrator who is in the minority would have enormous power: she would

182 *The arbitral award*

be able to insist on changes to the award, or else she would refuse to sign it, thus rendering the award invalid. To avoid this problem, arbitration statutes typically affirm that an award is valid as long as it has been signed by a majority of the tribunal,[19] with Swiss law affirming that the signature of the chairperson alone will suffice.[20]

However, while the requirement that an arbitration award be signed is standard, most arbitration statutes do not impose formal requirements on how it must be signed, e.g. with all members of the tribunal present in the same geographical location. As a result, awards in international commercial arbitration are often signed in sequence, with the first tribunal member signing the award and then sending it by mail or courier to the second, then the second signing it and sending it to the third. Ultimately, the formalities of how an award is signed are largely irrelevant, as long as it is signed.

4.3 Requirements of formal validity in the lex arbitri: reasons

An additional requirement in many arbitration laws[21] is that an award must include a statement by the arbitrators of the reasons they concluded as they did.[22] That is, it is not enough that an award states "Kirsten must pay Liyah £500,000." The award must discuss the facts and the law in so far as they played a role in the tribunal deciding that this outcome was correct. Indeed, while in some jurisdictions parties may agree that the tribunal does not have to draft a reasoned award,[23] in others this is an absolute obligation: the tribunal must include its reasons in the award even if the parties don't want them to do so.[24]

It might not be immediately clear why parties would choose not to receive a reasoned award. After all, if you lose any dispute surely you want to know why. The standard explanation, though, is quite simple and reasonable: money. In many arbitrations, arbitrators are paid by the hour, and drafting a reasoned award can take a significant amount of time. As a result, eliminating the requirement for a reasoned award can save a significant amount of money. Moreover, even when arbitrators are paid a set amount for the arbitration, regardless of how much time they spend working on it, arbitrators will accept a lower amount for a case that does not require them to draft a reasoned award.

Yet despite the cost savings that come from not having a reasoned award, awards in international commercial arbitration are nearly always reasoned. One explanation for this is the one already given: if you lose, you want to know why. A second one is a broader consideration that applies to both parties, whoever wins: requiring a reasoned award may cost more, but it is a way to ensure that the tribunal fulfills its mandate properly. Parties, after all, pay arbitrators substantial amounts of money, and requiring the tribunal to deliver a reasoned award can be seen as a way of ensuring that they "earn their money" by reasoning through the case properly, rather than simply deciding on an outcome.

There is, though, an important third explanation for the desirability of reasoned awards that is often not fully appreciated: drafting a reasoned award is an essential part of thinking through the details of the case. Anyone who drafts awards regularly can confirm that there are times when you sit down to write an award, confident that you have examined the case properly and reached a justifiable conclusion, only to change your mind while you are writing. The writing process, that is, slows down your mind and makes you pay attention to small details of both the facts and the argument that might not have initially occurred to you. As a result, the analysis that you were so confident was correct, now seems clearly flawed. The third and best reason for requiring that arbitrators draft a reasoned award, then, is simply that doing so results in better decisions.

Yet not all international commercial arbitration awards are well drafted and well reasoned. Indeed, complaint about the quality of many arbitral awards is common. It is, then, important to acknowledge a countervailing pressure that actually undermines the arguments in favour of reasoned awards: the more explicitly an award is reasoned, the easier it is for a party to challenge it. That is, the first step for many parties when they lose an arbitration is to examine the award in detail to see if there is any ground on which it can be challenged. The more detailed the arbitrators' reasoning, the more likely counsel of the losing party will be able to construct an argument as to why the award should be annulled or refused enforcement. All arbitrators want to avoid having their awards annulled, and so this creates an incentive for arbitrators to limit the detail of the reasoning in their awards. The best arbitrators, of course, don't indulge in such practices, and rely instead on their ability to do their job well. But for some arbitrators, the temptation is a real one.

As already noted, the obligation to provide a reasoned award is often imposed by the *lex arbitri*, and it might be thought that this requirement would ensure that arbitrators provide clear and explanatory reasons in their award. It has to be remembered, though, that contemporary arbitration laws are (rightly) constructed around the idea that arbitration benefits from limiting the reviewing powers of courts. The consequence of this with regard to reasoned awards is that as long as some part of the award discusses why the tribunal reached the conclusion it did, at least referring to the law the tribunal applied, then this will in most cases meet the obligation imposed by the *lex arbitri*. A reviewing court, that is, will not evaluate the quality of the tribunal's reasoning, but will only ensure that some sort of reasoning is present. The court may think that the tribunal's reasoning is poor, but as long as it is present, the legal requirement to provide a reasoned award will have been met.

The legal obligation to provide reasons, then, is a purely formal one: there must be something in the award that can be described as "reasons", but as long as this is the case, a court will usually find the requirement to have been met.[25] The professional obligation to provide reasons, on the other hand, is a very different matter. The parties may choose to dispense with a reasoned award, where this is permitted by the *lex arbitri*, but as long as a reasoned award is required, arbitrators have a professional obligation to explain to the parties in clear and comprehensible language how the applicable law and the facts of the case led them to reach decision they reached.

4.4 Requirements of formal validity in the lex arbitri: date and place

A further requirement imposed by some arbitration statutes is that an arbitral award should state the date on which it was made and identify the place that it was made. While these are purely formal requirements, each has an important rationale in the context of the enforceability of arbitral awards.

The date is important because in many jurisdictions there are express limitations on how long a party may wait before seeking to have an arbitration award annulled or before enforcing the award.[26] If a party has not applied for annulment within the specified time period, then the award can no longer be annulled, even if an annulment application would have been successful.[27] Alternatively, if a party waits too long before enforcing an award, then they will find that it can no longer be enforced. Establishing clearly the date on which an award was made can, then, in some situations, be of critical importance.

The place the award was made is similarly important because it can determine the legal regime that will apply to any application to recognise or enforce the award. As will be discussed in the following chapter, the New York Convention doesn't only apply to awards from international arbitrations, but also more broadly to foreign arbitral awards, even if they were delivered in a completely domestic arbitration. Knowing where an award was made is, therefore, necessary to determine whether the Convention applies. In addition, some arbitration statutes adopt a different approach to the enforcement of domestic awards than they do for foreign awards. As a result, establishing clearly in an award where it was made can play an important role in clarifying the parties' legal rights and responsibilities.

Because of their potential importance, tribunals should ensure that both the date and the place of the award are clearly specified in every arbitration award, whether this is required by the law of the seat or not. Yet in some cases these details will not be clarified, and courts will be faced with the need to determine these matters for themselves. In such cases, the best approach with respect to the date is to adopt the date the award was delivered to the parties as the date of the award, since the date on which the parties received the award is an appropriate time from which to commence time periods within which the parties must take action with respect to the award. In turn, the place of the award should be held to be the seat of the arbitration, even if there is evidence that the award was physically signed somewhere else. Such an approach most accurately reflects the fact that the seat of an arbitration is a legal construct, rather than a reference to the physical location in which the arbitration took place.

4.5 Requirements of validity imposed by the parties

While formal requirements of an arbitration award are most commonly imposed by the law, they can be imposed by parties as well. It is, after all, the parties' arbitration, and if the arbitration agreement specifies that an award must include certain things, then an award that does not include those things is not the award required by the arbitration to which the parties agreed. As a result, it may not be enforceable, or may be subject to being annulled.

In reality, it is rare that an arbitration agreement will include details on the form of an arbitration award, but formal requirements can also be agreed upon by the parties indirectly through their agreement to arbitrate using a certain set of arbitration rules. Arbitration rules rarely impose highly detailed formal requirements on awards, but it is standard for at least minimal requirements to be imposed. The Cairo Regional Center For International Commercial Arbitration (CRCICA) Arbitration Rules, for example, require that the award be made in writing, that reasons be included (unless the parties have agreed otherwise), that it be signed by the arbitrators and include the date and place of the award, and that an explanation be given in the award if any arbitrator fails to sign. While requirements such as these are commonly found in institutional rules, further variations can occur, and must be adhered to. The Belgian Centre for Arbitration and Mediation (CEPANI) Arbitration Rules, for example, include a requirement that the award be delivered within a specified time period, while the Commercial Arbitration

Rules of the Japan Commercial Arbitration Association (JCAA) require that the award state the full names and street addresses of both the parties and their counsel.

It is, therefore, essential that a tribunal consults both the arbitration agreement and the applicable arbitration rules before finalising an award, to ensure that it conforms to any requirements agreed by the parties. Otherwise, this failure to conform to the parties' agreement may be invoked by an unhappy party in annulment proceedings or when resisting recognition and enforcement of the award.

5. *There may also be rules specifying how or when an award must be delivered*

5.1 Time-limit for the making of the award

One of the arguments that is traditionally made for arbitration as an alternative to litigation is that it is faster. In reality, of course, that may not be the case. Nonetheless, efficiency and speed are constant topics of discussion in arbitration, and as a result arbitral institutions routinely try to find new ways to ensure that arbitral proceedings do not last too long. One method that is regularly adopted is to incorporate in arbitration rules deadlines within which a final award must be delivered by the tribunal.

Some jurisdictions have also embraced the idea that arbitration should be quick, and in order to ensure this happens, they have incorporated into their arbitration statute a time limit within which an arbitration award must be made. For example, Article 37 of the Spanish Arbitration Act requires that an award be delivered within six months of the submission of the Statement of Defence, subject to a single extension of no more than two months, unless the parties have agreed otherwise. On the other hand, the Belgian Arbitration Act does not specify a time limit but creates a mechanism through which a time limit can be imposed by a court if the award has not been delivered within six months of the final arbitrator being appointed to the tribunal.[28]

Moreover, while the Spanish Arbitration Act specifies that failure to meet the deadline it imposes does not affect the validity of the award, this is not the case with all arbitration statutes that incorporate a time limit for delivery of an award. The Belgian Arbitration Act, for example, states that "[t]he mission of the arbitrators ends" if they do not deliver the award by the expiry of the deadline imposed by the court.

In sum, the consequences of failing to meet a deadline for the delivery of an award differ from one jurisdiction to another. However, there are jurisdictions in which a tribunal's failure to meet a deadline for delivery of an award will result in the award potentially being annulled by local courts, and so tribunals must be aware of the requirements of the *lex arbitri* and ensure that any deadlines for delivery of an award are met.

5.2 Delivery of the award

Finally, once the award has been drafted and agreed by the tribunal, it must be delivered to the parties. While on one level this is a purely mechanical exercise of notifying the parties of a decision that has already been taken, the act of notifying the parties has important consequences in most legal systems: most notably, the time limit for initiating annulment proceedings normally commences on the date on which a party receives the award.[29]

The specific mechanism that must be used to transmit the award to the parties can vary depending on the *lex arbitri*. The New South Wales (Australia) Commercial Arbitration Act, for example, merely states that the award must be "delivered to each party", without imposing further requirements. The Arbitration Law of Saudi Arabia, on the other hand, requires not only that the award be delivered to the parties, but also that it be deposited with the competent court, accompanied by an Arabic translation of the award if it is not in Arabic. In turn, French law requires that, unless the parties have provided otherwise, an award must be delivered by a bailiff, according to a specific notification procedure.[30]

Similarly, if an arbitration is being administered by an institution, that institution's rules may also impose procedures that must be followed for the delivery of the award. Conventionally, this will involve the award being transmitted to the institution, rather than directly to the parties, with the institution often withholding delivery of the award until the parties have paid the fees of the arbitration.[31]

6. A wide range of remedies can be awarded by arbitral tribunals

6.1 Monetary compensation

In principle, the parties can agree to grant the tribunal the power to award an almost unlimited range of remedies. Indeed, it is standardly accepted that a tribunal can be empowered to grant remedies that even the courts of the seat are not permitted to grant. Nonetheless, in practice a single remedy dominates international commercial arbitration: an award of money.

To those from a common law background this might seem unsurprising, as international commercial arbitrations generally focus on a claimed breach of contract, and an award of money is the standard remedy for breach of contract in common law jurisdictions. It is, however, more surprising when one considers that much international commercial arbitration takes place in civil law States, or involves arbitrators from a civil law background, and non-monetary remedies for breach of contract are more widely used in civil law jurisdictions.

Nonetheless, while other remedies are sometimes sought, as will be discussed below overwhelmingly it is an award of monetary compensation that is requested in the Statement of Claim. As a result, if the Claimant is successful in the arbitration, it is monetary compensation that will be awarded. The predominance of monetary awards in international commercial arbitration, that is, arises not from any legal or institutional obstacle to non-monetary awards, or from a resistance on the part of arbitrators to making non-monetary awards, but simply from the fact that it is primarily monetary awards that parties seek.

Given that international commercial arbitration typically concerns cross-border legal relationships, a natural question arises regarding the currency in which an award of monetary compensation should be made? Should it be in the currency of the award debtor, as the party required to make the payment? Or in the currency of the award creditor, as the party entitled to receive the payment? In some cases the *lex arbitri* will expressly state that the tribunal can order payments in any currency;[32] however, even when the law of the seat is silent on this question, the tribunal should see itself as free to award monetary compensation in any currency it deems appropriate, so long as it does not violate an express restriction imposed by the parties, the *lex arbitri* or the applicable arbitration rules.

6.2 Punitive damages

Although it is beyond dispute that arbitral tribunals have the power to include monetary compensation in their award, the award of punitive damages is more controversial. Punitive damages are, of course, themselves a form of monetary remedy, but rather than compensating a wronged party for the harm it has suffered, the goal of a punitive damages award is fundamentally to punish the party that committed the wrong. It is for this reason that an award of punitive damages by an arbitral tribunal is sometimes seen as controversial, even in jurisdictions in which such awards are regularly made by courts:[33] it involves private individuals (i.e. the arbitrators) wielding a power that is usually restricted to the State (i.e. the power to punish wrongdoing).

The relationship between arbitration and punitive damages is a complex one, and the ability of arbitral tribunals to award punitive damages varies substantially between legal systems. In the United States of America, for example, it is almost universally accepted that punitive damages can be awarded by tribunals as long as this power has not been excluded by the parties.[34] In many civil law jurisdictions, by contrast, such an award is considered contrary to public policy and unenforceable.[35]

The complexity of this issue is, however, not restricted solely to the power of the tribunal under the law of the seat to make an award of punitive damages. Because awards of punitive damages are seen in some jurisdictions as raising questions of public policy, a court asked to enforce an award of punitive damages may refuse to do so even when the law of the seat permits such an award to be made.[36]

As a result, even if the parties have expressly agreed that punitive damages can be awarded, and such an award is permitted by the *lex arbitri*, a tribunal should draft its award carefully to completely separate the compensatory and punitive elements of the award. Such an approach will help ensure that the compensatory portion of the award can still be enforced even if the award of punitive damages is rejected as against the public policy of the enforcing jurisdiction.

6.3 Interest

Judgements by State courts awarding monetary compensation often also include an award of interest on that compensation, in recognition of the fact that the wronged party has been deprived for a period of time of compensation it was owed. Arbitral tribunals routinely include interest in their awards as well, for precisely the same reason.

The interesting question about interest in the context of arbitral awards, then, concerns not whether interest can be awarded, but why it can be awarded. That is, not all legal systems explain arbitrators' authority to award interest in the same way. In some jurisdictions, interest is considered to be a matter of substantive law, and so a successful party in an arbitration has a right to an award of interest in so far as such a right exists in the law applicable to the merits of the dispute.[37] In others, the power of an arbitral tribunal to award interest is seen as a matter of procedural law, and so interest is available in so far as it is included under the *lex arbitri*.[38]

Further and more difficult issues arise with respect to how an award of interest should be calculated. In principle, the parties have the power to agree on how this question should be resolved, and if they have reached an agreement the tribunal should comply with it. If there is no agreement, the tribunal should next examine the law from which its power to award interest derives, as just discussed, and if this law requires that interest be calculated in a particular way, then it should be followed by the tribunal. In many cases, however, even if the relevant law expressly confirms that the tribunal can award interest, it will fail to specify how that interest should be calculated. In such cases, arbitral tribunals will normally request submissions from the parties on this question before deciding on the approach to be adopted.

A final consideration relates to post-award interest, which seeks to compensate the successful party for the time it will take the other party to pay the amount awarded, rather than for the time that has already been taken. Post-award interest is again common in arbitral awards, and is consistent with the purpose of an award of interest, namely to compensate the wronged party for the period of time for which it is being deprived of compensation to which it is entitled.

6.4 Declaratory relief

While monetary compensation is the most commonly requested form of relief in international commercial arbitration, parties can also request what is called declaratory relief, either in combination with monetary compensation or as the only relief requested. When a party requests declaratory relief, it is simply asking the tribunal to make a binding statement on the legal rights and obligations of the parties in a particular respect. By way of example, Bradley and Eileen may both claim that they own H.R. Pufnstuf II, a luxury yacht. Eileen is living on the yacht, and Bradley is happy for her to do so and has no damages that he can claim to have suffered. However, he would like the question of ownership to be settled, just in case it becomes a problem in the future. Both parties agree to arbitrate the issue, asking only that the tribunal determine which of them owns the yacht, with no compensation or other remedy to be awarded.

While purely declaratory awards are relatively rare in international commercial arbitration, declaratory relief is often requested alongside monetary compensation or other relief. Indeed, a tribunal may be requested to provide declaratory relief specifying that, for example, the Respondent breached its contract with the Claimant, while also awarding the Claimant compensation for the breach. An award of declaratory relief may seem superfluous in such a case, as the award of compensation necessarily requires a determination by the tribunal that the Respondent breached the contract, but it is important to remember that the rules regarding *res judicata* can vary significantly between jurisdictions.[39] As a result, the Claimant may receive an additional benefit from an express declaration of the parties' legal rights that it would not receive if the tribunal only awarded him compensatory damages.

Questions have at times been raised as to whether a purely declaratory arbitration award can be enforced by a court, as an award containing a simple declaration does not require that any action be taken.[40] However, it is now widely accepted that the clarification of legal rights that is given by a declaratory award constitutes a sufficiently clear and valuable remedy that recognition and enforcement is appropriate, and some arbitration laws expressly acknowledge that arbitral tribunals may issue declaratory awards.[41]

Yet even where no express statutory provision grants a tribunal the power to issue declaratory awards, arbitrators should understand themselves as having this power, unless it is expressly excluded by the arbitration agreement, the applicable rules or the law of the seat. In some jurisdictions, State courts will only grant a declaratory judgement if the requesting party can demonstrate that it has a legal interest in having that particular question resolved immediately, rather than leaving it to be resolved when a claim for payment of compensation or other action arises. However, such rules are best understood as reflecting a desire to avoid the use of public resources to resolve issues that may never lead to an actual dispute. An arbitration, on the other hand, is paid for by the parties, and so there is no parallel rationale for arbitrators to refuse to provide the parties with clarity as to their legal rights and obligations. There may be instances in which one party seeks such a declaratory award merely as a means of causing problems and expenses to the other party, by making them take part in an expensive arbitration, but such cases are best addressed through the tribunal's power to award the costs of the arbitration, rather than through refusing to hear the dispute at all. In short, if Bradley commences arbitration with Eileen not because he wants the question of ownership of H.R. Pufnstuf II settled, but because he is angry at Eileen for turning down his marriage proposal, this is not a reason for the arbitral tribunal to refuse to issue an award, whoever it declares to be the owner. It may, however, be a reason for the tribunal to require that Bradley reimburse Eileen for all or part of her expenses incurred during the arbitration.

6.5 Specific performance

A further type of non-monetary relief is that of specific performance: that is, where the Claimant requests that the Respondent be ordered to perform a certain action, rather than pay a certain amount of money. To give an example, say Kamal and Baxter entered into an agreement to buy a holiday home together, with each of them having the right to use it for half the year. The house is situated in a location in which the weather is beautiful for six months of the year, while there is constant torrential rain for the other six months. Kamal expected that they would both use for the house for three months each during the "good" part of the year, but this was never expressly discussed and is not specified in the contract. Baxter moves into the home immediately and refuses to move out for six months, despite requests from Kamal, even though this is the only six months in which there will be good weather. When he finally moves out, as the rains begin, he announces that he is going to move back into the house again in six months (when the weather will again be good), to take "his" six months. Kamal commences arbitration, requesting that the tribunal order Baxter to let him have the house for three months during the "good" part of the year, as he had expected would be the case when he entered into the contract with Baxter. This is an order for specific performance.

Views on specific performance vary significantly around the world, with States courts in common law jurisdictions very rarely ordering specific performance, and only when monetary compensation would not suffice, while in civil law jurisdictions parties alleging a breach of contract are usually seen as free to choose between monetary compensation and specific performance. Nonetheless, despite such differences in legal culture, the ability of arbitrators to award specific performance is generally accepted around the world. Individual arbitrators may differ in their willingness to make such an order, but this is a reflection of their legal background and training, rather than of their powers as arbitrators.

However, while as a matter of principle specific performance is an accepted remedy in international commercial arbitration, an order of specific performance raises practical difficulties that any tribunal must seriously consider, no matter the arbitrators' backgrounds and personal inclinations. To put it simply, the tribunal must be able to draft an award that the successful party can actually get enforced, if enforcement is needed. When the award is of monetary compensation that is relatively easy: an award that says "Baxter must pay Kamal £10 million" can be enforced by a State court simply requiring Baxter to pay Kamal £10 million. But when what Kamal wants is not money, but time in the house, how should that award be drafted? Remember, the award will be enforced by a court, not by the tribunal that actually wrote it. The tribunal may describe the actions required only vaguely (e.g. "Baxter must let Kamal use the house for three months in the good part of the year, and three months in the bad part"), but then the court must try to decide what the tribunal meant – and it may reach a completely different conclusion than the one intended by the tribunal, or even decide that the order is so vague that it cannot be enforced. On the other hand, the tribunal could include substantial detail in its award, setting out precisely what the parties must do (e.g. "Kamal has use of the house from 1 May to 31 July and from 1 November to 31 January each year. Baxter may not be on the premises at any point in this period, and must have removed his personal items from the premises prior to Kamal's arrival") – this makes enforcement easier for a court, but gives the court no flexibility to adapt enforcement to meet the actual intention of the award, if that turns out to be necessary.

Ultimately, while orders for specific performance can often be problematic for a tribunal to draft, there are times when specific performance is the most appropriate remedy. On such occasions, a more detailed order must be preferred, as the best way to ensure that the required performance is undertaken. However, once it has been decided that an order for specific performance will be made, it is good practice for a tribunal to consult closely with both parties on what the award should and should not contain, including presenting them with drafts of the order prior to the award being finalised. The parties, after all, are best placed to recognise problems that an order may create, as they have a far more intimate knowledge of the facts of their situation than even the most dedicated tribunal can ever attain.

6.6 Rectification and adaptation

While other remedies are also available, two in particular are worth noting in this section, namely rectification and adaptation. Neither is commonly requested or awarded, but both play an important role in ensuring that disputes are resolved justly.

Rectification (or "reformation") involves a request by one party to a contract to have the tribunal correct the contract on the ground that, as written, it does not reflect the actual content of the parties' agreement due to a mistake in the drafting. Importantly, the argument underlying the request for rectification is not that the contract as written is unfair, or that the requesting party did not realise what the contract said, but rather that the contract as written simply does not say what both parties believed it said. In some jurisdictions the arbitration law specifically acknowledges that arbitrators may order the rectification of a contract,[42] but even when it does not do so, a tribunal should see itself as being able to rectify a contract as long as such a power falls within the boundaries of the arbitration agreement and is not excluded by the applicable contract law.

While rectification focuses on an error made when a contract was entered into, adaptation focuses on changes to the factual situation underlying performance of a contract over time. It is, after all, a risk in any long-term commercial agreement that external circumstances will change, substantially altering the benefits and burdens the parties experience under the contract. Adaptation involves the tribunal varying the terms of the parties' contract to take into account the new situation in which the contract is being performed. In this way, the tribunal is able to restore the original balance of benefits and burdens between the parties, on which both parties relied when deciding to enter into the contract. It should be noted, however, that adaptation is a more controversial remedy than rectification, and is strongly disfavoured in some jurisdictions in which risk allocation is viewed as central to a contract. In these jurisdictions, parties are overwhelmingly held to the terms of their contracts no matter how difficult performance becomes, as they are viewed as having taken on the risk of more difficult performance when they entered into the contract without incorporating a clause addressing this risk.[43] Tribunals should, therefore, examine carefully the basis of any power they wish to claim to adapt the parties' contract, only doing so when it is expressly allowed under the arbitration law of the seat, or is justifiable under the terms of the arbitration agreement or the applicable contract law.

7. An award may also say who pays for how much of the arbitration

International commercial arbitration is often not a cheap procedure. Moreover, unlike in litigation, where the State usually covers many of the costs, in arbitration the parties must cover all the costs of the process. As a result, the question of "who pays what" has a particular importance in arbitration. These costs include not only the arbitrators' fees and expenses, but fees owed to any administering institution, costs of renting a hearing room and related expenses arising from the hearing, and even the fees of the parties' lawyers and expert witnesses.

It is possible that the parties' arbitration agreement specifies how costs will be allocated between the parties if an arbitration occurs, although this is very rare. But if this is the case, then the rule specified in the arbitration agreement must be followed unless the parties agree to change it. It is also possible that the rules used in the arbitration or even the arbitration law of the seat will specify how costs are to be allocated. Again, if either of these is the case, then this rule is to be followed.[44] However, it is common for arbitration rules and statutes merely to confirm that the tribunal may make a decision allocating costs, rather than to require that a certain approach be used.[45]

Ultimately, then, the most common source of any decision regarding the allocation of the costs of the arbitration between the parties will be the arbitral tribunal, in the form of a decision either included in the final award or in a separate award on costs. There are two dominant approaches to the allocation of costs, often referred to as the "American rule" and "outcome-based recovery".[46]

192 *The arbitral award*

Under the American rule, derived from US litigation, each party is expected to pay its own costs for the arbitration, primarily attorneys' fees, usually splitting those costs that are not directly incurred by either party, such as arbitrators' and institutional fees, hearing room rental, etc. The rationale for this approach is that it maximises access to justice, as parties will not avoid commencing arbitration out of fear that if they lose they will face substantial costs reimbursing the other party the expenses it incurred. In essence, the American rule enhances the predictability of costs in arbitration: arbitrator and institutional fees can usually be predicted in advance, or are subject to agreement, and as each party will have to pay its own legal fees, both parties can decide for themselves how much they are willing to spend.

Outcome-based recovery, on the other hand, is based on the idea that if a party has been successful in an arbitration, whether as Claimant or Respondent, then this means they should never have been forced to arbitrate the issue. The other party should simply have acted appropriately and all the costs of the arbitration would have been avoided. As a result, it is argued, it is appropriate that the unsuccessful party in an arbitration pay the other party's costs as well as its own.

In practice, of course, even when a tribunal adopts outcome-based recovery it is rare that one party is forced to pay 100% of the costs of the arbitration. After all, in most arbitrations there will be more than one claim made, sometimes including counterclaims by the Respondent. As a result, it is usual for a party to be successful on some claims while unsuccessful on others. Moreover, a party may be successful on a claim but receive substantially less compensation than was being claimed, raising questions about whether they should really be regarded as entirely successful on that claim. Consequently, even when a tribunal applies outcome-based recovery it will usually end up allocating costs between the parties to some degree, rather than awarding all the costs of the arbitration to a single party.

It is difficult to be sure how cost allocation is "usually" approached in international commercial arbitration, because so few arbitration awards are publicly available. However, one notable recent study of 53 international commercial arbitration awards, primarily from the ICC, found a distinction in approach with respect to costs of the arbitration itself (arbitrators' and institutional fees, etc.) and the fees of the party's attorneys. With respect to the costs of the arbitration, nearly 2/3 of awards followed an outcome-based recovery approach, reflecting the idea that the successful party should not have been forced to incur arbitration-related costs. On the other hand, when tribunals were allocating the cost of parties' legal representation this proportion dropped to approximately half.[47]

There is, then, no evidence that any single rule regarding the allocation of costs exists in international commercial arbitration, and that is appropriate. One of the primary benefits of arbitration, after all, is its procedural flexibility and the freedom that gives to parties and tribunals to fashion an approach that is appropriate to the particular dispute and the parties involved. There is no reason why the allocation of costs should not be part of that process of designing an appropriate arbitration.

8. *An award has* **res judicata** *effect*

One of the most important consequences of a court judgement is that it resolves as a matter of law the issues it addresses. That is, if Robyn brings a claim against Enrique for £10,000,000 and the court rejects her claim, that is not just one individual judge's view on the dispute. Robyn cannot just keep bringing her claim back to court until she finally finds a judge who is willing to find in her favour. Rather, except to the extent that the court system allows appeals of judgements, a court judgement constitutes the legal system's final position on the dispute between the parties. If Robyn attempts to bring her claim back to the same court system, it will simply be rejected, as it has already been decided that as a matter of law Robyn's claim is not valid.

This aspect of court judgements is referred to as *res judicata*, which is Latin for "thing decided". It is a doctrine that prevents courts within the same judicial system from contradicting one another, enhances legal certainty, and also avoids the waste of public money that would result from rehearing the same disputes over and over again. Once an issue has been decided, it is resolved and that court system will not revisit it no matter how unhappy a party may be at the decision that was reached.

When it comes to international commercial disputes, one important thing to know is that *res judicata* varies significantly in its effects from one jurisdiction to the next. As in many other areas of the law, this difference can be conveniently, if not always entirely accurately, described as being between common law and civil law jurisdictions.

In common law jurisdictions, the doctrine of *res judicata* is generally regarded as producing two types of effects, often referred to as "cause of action estoppel"[48] and "issue estoppel".[49] Cause of action estoppel is the principle that once a claim has been resolved by the court system, it may not be brought to the courts again involving the same parties.[50] Issue estoppel is a much broader principle, and is the idea that once a court has delivered its judgement on a dispute, the parties should not be allowed to dispute in any future court case between them any issue that the court decided as a means of reaching its final decision in the case.[51]

To give an example, say Robyn's claim against Enrique is that he received a shipment of antique guitars from her but never paid her for them. Enrique's defence is that he turned up to the dock to collect the guitars from the ship, but they were not on the ship. He presents testimony from the ship's captain that in a bad storm a shipping container fell overboard, and although he cannot prove what was in that container, as the paperwork was also lost, he is confident it did indeed contain the guitars. The court decides on the balance of the evidence that the lost shipping container was indeed the one containing the guitars, and under Robyn and Enrique's contract since Enrique did not receive the guitars he does not have to pay for them. Cause of action estoppel says that once Robyn has lost her case, she can never bring another claim against Enrique for the £10,000,000 she claims is owed. That claim has now been resolved as a matter of law.

But say that Robyn had also shipped to Enrique some antique violins, worth £5,000,000, and these had been packed into the same shipping container. There is no claim estoppel preventing Robyn bringing a new claim against Enrique about the violins, as the previous claim was about the guitars. However, in order to reach its conclusion that Enrique was not liable to Robyn for the cost of the guitars, the court had to decide that the shipping container containing the guitars fell overboard. The consequence of this is that in her new claim against Enrique, Robyn will not be permitted to deny that the shipping container containing the guitars fell overboard. That issue has been decided as a matter of law. As a result, as long as

Enrique can establish that the violins were in the same shipping container as the guitars, then he will win this case as well.

Moreover, in some common law jurisdictions there is also a further important doctrine in this area, usually referred to as "the rule in *Henderson v Henderson*" after the case in which it was adopted.[52] While *res judicata* focuses on preventing parties from re-litigating claims or issues that have already been decided by the courts, the rule in *Henderson v Henderson* prevents parties from raising in a later case any arguments, claims or defences that could and should have been raised in the earlier case. In essence, the rule in *Henderson v Henderson* requires that parties bring their "whole case" to court when they are involved in a dispute. If they have an argument, claim or defence available to them and choose not to raise it, they risk being prevented from raising it in any future case involving the same parties.

In civil law jurisdictions, on the other hand, *res judicata* is often a more limited doctrine than the one just described as existing in common law jurisdictions, although significant differences can exist between civil law systems. For example, German law recognises cause of action estoppel,[53] but rejects entirely any form of issue estoppel. By contrast, in some other civil law jurisdictions, such as Spain, at least some level of issue estoppel is recognised.[54] Similar variation exists regarding the rule in *Henderson v Henderson*. No such rule exists at all under German law, while under French law it was recognized for the first time in 2006,[55] although later French judgments have adopted a more cautious approach than is characteristic in common law jurisdictions in which the rule has effect.[56]

While it is now generally accepted that *res judicata* applies to arbitral awards as well as to court judgements, the diversity just discussed means that a single arbitral award may generate a range of different preclusive effects in jurisdictions around the world. That is, a court in England, for example, may hold that issue estoppel applies in a court case between two parties who have previously participated in an arbitration about a different but related claim, based on the issues decided in the resulting arbitral award. A court in Germany, on the other hand, may deny that the exact same arbitral award has any preclusive effect at all, and allow one of the parties to re-argue an issue already decided in the arbitration.

The cross-border nature of international commercial arbitration, then, means that while parties involved in an arbitration should expect that some level of *res judicata* will be applied to their award all around the world, their ability to prevent re-litigation of issues already addressed in the arbitration will depend on the rules in the jurisdiction in which the new claim has been brought. They may, therefore, find that even though the arbitral award prevents a losing party re-litigating the specific claim resolved in the arbitration, that party may nonetheless still be able to succeed on parallel claims by convincing a State court to reach different conclusions on important issues than the ones previously reached by the arbitral tribunal.

9. Arbitrators can issue separate opinions in addition to the award

9.1 The deliberations

An arbitrator's role is to take on the responsibility of deciding someone else's dispute, with substantial and even potentially catastrophic consequences for the losing party. It is not a job for anyone unwilling to stand up for her own reasoning and analysis when others disagree. Substantive disagreement, after all is a practical reality for any arbitrator serving on a three-member tribunal, as each arbitrator ultimately has responsibility for ensuring that she has performed her role properly. Simply letting others do the work and signing the award is not to do the job at all.

Nonetheless, a tribunal is also a collective, hired as a group to perform a single job. An arbitrator on a three-member tribunal, that is, must perform the job differently than when she is a sole arbitrator. She has, after all, been hired to work as part of a team, not just to give her own opinion on the parties' dispute.

This is where "deliberation" becomes an essential part of the arbitral decision-making process. The goal of any properly functioning arbitral tribunal must be to deliver a single opinion, which has the full support of all the members of the tribunal. This is a lofty goal, so it may not be achieved in practice, but it is the goal at which the tribunal should be aiming. The only way to achieve this goal, however, is for the tribunal to engage in substantive discussions about the case, each arbitrator advancing her own analysis of the facts and the applicable law, while considering and evaluating the analyses proposed by her colleagues.

Deliberation, then, is not a process in which each individual arbitrator sits down by herself to reach her own conclusion on how the dispute should be resolved (unless, of course, the case is being decided by a sole arbitrator). This sort of lone deliberation is an important part of the deliberative process, certainly, but it cannot suffice. A process in which three arbitrators reach their own decision and then simply select one of the three alternatives as the one to use in the award is not truly deliberative, and does not reflect a tribunal properly fulfilling its obligations to the parties.

Deliberation, rather, is necessarily a collaborative process, in which the arbitrators come together, each having considered the case independently, and then proceed to consider the case as a group, working together to identify the correct resolution of each issue and of the entire dispute. It is a means by which the views of three bright and talented individuals are further improved by allowing the final decision to be based on the best insights of all three members of the tribunal.

The reality, of course, is often very different. In practice, deliberation is often less a matter of three arbitrators coming together to benefit from one another's abilities and insights, as it is a matter of three strongly opinionated individuals coming together to craft a single decision that all three view as acceptable, even though none of them actually believes it is entirely right. An award, that is, often reflects compromise as much as it does consensus.

That is not, of course, to say that this reality somehow renders the deliberative process a sham, or the arbitral process dysfunctional. The exact same description can, after all, be given of groups of politicians, scientists, philosophers, and even, ironically enough, mediators. People disagree, and while it might be ideal if we could regularly resolve our disagreements by engaging in a dialectic that allowed us to move beyond our own preconceived positions to come together in agreement on a greater truth, it tends not to happen. It is, nonetheless, an important ideal, and one at which every tribunal should aim, even if it is an ideal not often achieved in full. Simply trying will ensure that the parties receive a higher quality award than they would have received if they had used only a sole arbitrator.

9.2 Dissenting opinions

One unavoidable consequence of the situation just described is that sometimes an arbitrator will simply not agree with the decision favoured by the other two members of the tribunal, and no compromise can be reached that is acceptable to all three arbitrators. It is now uniformly accepted that in such a situation the award can be issued reflecting the decision of only the two members of the tribunal who are in agreement, and this award will be just as binding on the parties as one issued by the entire tribunal.

The third arbitrator can, of course, refuse to sign the award.[57] In addition, however, she may then issue a "dissent", or "dissenting opinion", expressing her own view on how the dispute should have been resolved. Usually the dissent will be issued alongside the award and will acknowledge that the majority opinion constitutes the decision of tribunal. That is, the dissenting arbitrator accepts her place in the collaborative work of the tribunal, and endorses the outcome of that work even though it does not reflect her own views – however, as she feels that she cannot in good faith state to the parties that she feels the outcome is correct, she lays out her own reasoning as well.

It must be emphasised, however, that when a dissent is issued, the "award" in the arbitration consists solely of the majority opinion. The dissent will be issued to the parties for their consumption, but it will have no direct legal effect. This is the case even if the dissenting arbitrator disagrees so strongly with the majority opinion that she refuses to sign alongside her colleagues.

In practice, dissenting opinions are rare in international commercial arbitration, and the willingness of arbitrators to issue a dissent often varies based on the arbitrator's background and training. Arbitrators from a common law background have been trained in a legal system in which dissenting opinions by judges are common, and so they can be more comfortable with the idea of issuing a dissenting opinion than many arbitrators from civil law States, in whose jurisdictions dissenting opinions by judges are often much less common and in some jurisdictions are even formally prohibited.[58]

Ultimately, of course, a situation may arise in which a tribunal finds it impossible to adopt a majority opinion at all, with each arbitrator insisting on the correctness of her own approach. This represents a fundamental dysfunction of a tribunal, but can nonetheless occur. Under some institutional rules and arbitration laws, the award, which will be binding on the parties, will then be issued by the Chair of the tribunal, reflecting whatever the chair wishes to include in the decision.[59] However, if no such rule is applicable, the tribunal will either need to continue deliberating until a majority position can be found, or it must simply conclude the proceedings, acknowledging to the parties that it was impossible to make an award – and that the parties have, therefore, spent an awful lot of money to no real effect.

9.3 Concurring or separate opinions

One further possibility is that an arbitrator agrees with the other two arbitrators on the outcome of the dispute, but disagrees on the reason why this is the correct outcome. In such a situation, the arbitrator may decide to issue a "concurring" or "separate" opinion, laying out her own reasoning for the conclusion reached by all members of the tribunal. As with a dissent, a concurring opinion is properly understood as not constituting part of the award, and to be purely an explanation directed at the parties but without any legal effect.

In practice, concurring opinions are virtually unknown in international commercial arbitration, but there is no good reason why this should be the case. Parties are entitled to receive an explanation of the tribunal's reasoning, unless they have chosen to dispense with a reasoned decision, and if an arbitrator believes that the majority's reasoning is fundamentally incorrect, she fails in her responsibility to the parties if she does not explain her own reasoning.

Notes

1 This can happen, for instance, at the recognition and enforcement stage. In that context, the award debtor may try to resist recognition and enforcement not by invoking one of the grounds for refusal of Article V of the New York Convention, but simply by arguing that the document that the other party is seeking to enforce is not, in fact, an award in the sense of Article I(2) of the Convention at all.
2 By way of example, the decision to admit or not admit a piece of evidence can have a major impact on a party's case, but it does not itself resolve a portion of the parties' dispute. Such a decision merely has a significant impact on what that resolution will be; as a result, it is properly treated as an order. More controversially, some commentators have argued that interim decisions issued by tribunals should be treated as awards, as they "finally dispose of a request for relief by one of the parties through an application of legal rules to a factual record" (Gary Born, *International Arbitration: Law and Practice* (Kluwer 2012) 280. The interim nature of such decisions, however, necessarily leaves the tribunal free to revisit the matter and issue a final decision in conflict with the initial decision. They are, therefore, an important feature of case management, and so should be supported by courts for this reason, but they are not properly classified as awards.
3 Depending on the contents of the *lex arbitri*, however, there may be exceptions to the general rule that a tribunal immediately becomes *functus officio* after having delivered the final award. For instance, pursuant to Article 33 of the UNCITRAL Model Law, a party may within 30 days of receipt of the award ask the tribunal to correct the award, or to make an additional award. If this or similar rules are applicable, the tribunal maintains a certain power to rule on the dispute for a limited amount of time, after the issuance of the final award.
4 See, for instance, the English Arbitration Act, Section 47, or the Italian Code of Civil Procedure, Articles 820(4)(c) and 827(3).
5 See e.g. Article 2 of the 2017 ICC Rules; Article 32(1) of the 2012 Swiss Rules.
6 Notably, other arbitration statutes exclude the possibility of challenging a jurisdictional award altogether while the arbitration is still pending: see e.g. Article 827(3) of the Italian Code of Civil Procedure.
7 In the United States of America, see Rule 55 of the Federal Rules of Civil Procedure. For a comparative analysis of default judgments in the different Member States of the European Union see Paul Oberhammer, "Default Procedures and Judgments in Cross-Border Settings" in Hess and Ortolani (eds), *The Impact of National Procedural Laws and Practices on Mutual Trust and the Free Circulation of Judgments* (Hart Beck Nomos 2019) 87–130.
8 Ibid., 97–100.
9 This is acknowledged, *inter alia*, in Article 7(5) of the UNCITRAL Model Law.
10 After all, at the time of negotiating the arbitration agreement it will rarely be possible to determine which side will be the one defaulting, so it is not in the interest of either party to agree to a provision that could potentially be used against them.

198 *The arbitral award*

11 By deciding not to participate, the defaulting party obviously did not make use of this opportunity; nevertheless, it is important to show in the award that this opportunity has properly been given.
12 See e.g. Article 30 of the UNCITRAL Model Law.
13 See e.g. Article 33 of the 2017 ICC Rules, Article 26(9) of the 2014 LCIA Rules and Article 34(1) of the 2012 Swiss Rules.
14 In the future, settlement agreements may become more widely enforceable, depending on the success of the United Nations Convention on International Settlement Agreements Resulting from Mediation ("the Singapore Convention").
15 Some authorities indeed hold that a consent award, despite its name, is not really an award, and hence cannot be enforced as such. However, in most legal systems consent awards are indeed recognised as enforceable arbitral awards. See, e.g. English Arbitration Act, Section 51; *Société Dansk Eternit Fabrik 1994 c Société Copernit & C SpA*, 56 CA Angers, 16 September 2008, No 07/01636; *Transocean Offshore Gulf of Guinea VII Limited et al. v Erin Energy Corporation (f/k/a CAMAC Energy Inc.)*, United States District Court, Southern District of Texas, Houston Division, Civil Action No. H-17–2623, 12 March 2018 in Albert Jan van den Berg (ed.), *Yearbook Commercial Arbitration XLIII* (Kluwer 2018) 722; *Albtelecom SH.A v UNIFI Communications, Inc.*, United States District Court, Southern District of New York, 16 Civ. 9001 (PAE), 30 May 2017, ibid. 630 See generally the excellent discussion in Giacomo Marchisio, "A Comparative Analysis of Consent Awards: Accepting their Reality", (2016) 32(2) *Arbitration International* 331–348.
16 By way of example, if the settlement agreement states that the parties will form a cartel that is unlawful under European Union competition law, an arbitral tribunal seated in an EU Member State may refuse to issue a consent award on the ground that the award would violate the public policy of the European Union. See Court of Justice of the European Union, case C-126/97, *Eco Swiss China Time Ltd v Benetton International NV*, ECLI:EU:C:1999:97.
17 See e.g. Section 68(2)(h) of the English Arbitration Act.
18 Pursuant to Section 52(2) of the English Arbitration Act, for instance, the requirement that the award be in writing (Section 52(3)) only applies inasmuch as the parties have not reached an agreement on a different form (Section 52(1)).
19 Article 31(1) of the UNCITRAL Model Law.
20 Article 189(2) of the Swiss Private International Law Act. This derives from the fact that Swiss law allows the chairperson to deliver an award herself if there is no majority on the tribunal for any single resolution.
21 As well as in the 1961 European Convention on International Commercial Arbitration (Article VIII).
22 See e.g. Article 31(2) of the UNCITRAL Model Law. There are, however, also examples of statutes that do not contain such a requirement, including the Federal Arbitration Act of the United States of America.
23 Article 31(2) of the UNCITRAL Model Law.
24 See e.g. Article 1482 of the French Code of Civil Procedure.
25 See, e.g. *Bremer Handelsgesellschaft mbH v Westzucker GmbH (No.2)* [1981] 2 Lloyd's Rep. 130.
26 As far as annulment procedures are concerned, see e.g. Section 70(3) of the English Arbitration Act, according to which challenges against the award must be brought within 28 days of the date of the award. As for recognition and enforcement, see e.g. Section 207 of the US Federal Arbitration Act, indicating that confirmation of the award is possible within three years after the award is made.
27 In some legal systems it may be possible to resist the recognition and enforcement of the award on certain grounds, even if no annulment procedure has been commenced within the time-frame provided for by the *lex arbitri*. Notably, this is the case in the UNCITRAL Model Law. In other jurisdictions, by contrast, the award debtor who fails to commence timely annulment proceedings

28 Article 1713 of the Belgian judicial code.
29 Article 34(3) of the UNCITRAL Model Law.
30 Article 1484(3) of the French Code of Civil Procedure.
31 See e.g. Article 35 of the 2017 ICC Rules.
32 Section 48(4) of the English Arbitration Act.
33 See e.g. in New York law *Garrity v Lyle Stuart, Inc.*, 40 N.Y.2d 354; it must however be noted that such a prohibition does not exist in the Federal Arbitration Act, which will prevail over domestic New York when it is applicable. See *Mastrobuono v Shearson Lehman Hutton, Inc.*, 514 U.S. 52 (1995).
34 But see the previous note with respect to New York state law.
35 For a comparative overview see Markus A Petsche, "Punitive Damages in International Commercial Arbitration: Much Ado about Nothing?" (2013) 29(1) *Arbitration International* 89; Helmut Koziol, "Punitive Damages – A European Perspective" (2008) 68(3) *Louisiana Law Review* 741.
36 Article V(2)(b) of the New York Convention. Analogously, court judgments ordering the payment of punitive damages have been denied recognition and enforcement in EU Member States: see Benjamin West Janke and François-Xavier Licari, "Enforcing Punitive Damage Awards in France after *Fountaine Pajot*" (2012) 60 *American Journal of Comparative Law* 775; Lotte Meurkens and Emily Nordin (eds), *The Power of Punitive Damages – Is Europe Missing Out?* (Intersentia 2012); Jessica J Berch, "The Need for Enforcement of U.S. Punitive Damages Awards by the European Union" (2010) 19(1) *Minnesota Journal of International Law* 55.
37 This is the case in many civil law jurisdictions. It must be considered, however, that interest may be prohibited in certain legal systems. See Mahmoud A El-Gamal, "Interest" and the Paradox of Contemporary Islamic Law and Finance' (2003) 27(1) *Fordham International Law Journal* 108.
38 *National Housing Trust v YP Seaton & Associates Co Ltd* [2015] UKPC 43.
39 For a comparative overview see Frédérique Ferrand, "*Res Judicata*: From National Law to a Possible European Harmonisation?" in Jens Adolphsen, Joachim Goebel, Ulrich Haas, Burkhard Hess, Stephan Kolmann and Markus Würdinger, *Festschrift für Peter Gottwald zum 70. Geburtstag* (Beck 2014) 143.
40 See e.g. *Margulies Brothers Ltd v Dafris Thomiades and Co (UK) Ltd* [1958] 1 Lloyd's Rep (applying Section 26 of the English Arbitration Act 1950). But see *West Tankers Inc v Allianz SPA & Generali Assicurazioni SpA* [2012] EWCA Civ 27 (confirming that purely declaratory awards can be enforced under the English Arbitration Act 1996).
41 See, e.g. Section 48(3) of the English Arbitration Act 1996.
42 Section 48(5)(c) of the English Arbitration Act 1996.
43 See generally, Pietro Ferrario, *The Adaptation of Long-Term Gas Sale Agreements by Arbitrators* (Kluwer 2017) 71–194.
44 If both the *lex arbitri* and the applicable rules contain rules on cost allocation, and these rules are incompatible with each other, then the arbitration rules selected by the parties should prevail, as an expression of party autonomy, unless the relevant provision of the *lex arbitri* is mandatory in nature.
45 See e.g. Article 38(3–5) of the 2017 ICC Rules and Section 61 of the English Arbitration Act 1996.
46 "Outcome-based recovery" is also often referred to using the name of a specific prominent variant of this approach, "costs follow the event".
47 Christopher Koch, "Is There a Default Principle of Cost Allocation in International Arbitration?" (2014) 31(4) *Journal of International Arbitration*, 485–497.
48 Also known as "claim preclusion".

49 Also known as "issue preclusion".
50 See Yuval Sinai, "Reconsidering *Res Judicata*: A Comparative Perspective" (2011) 21 *Duke Journal of Comparative and International Law* 353, 357–366.
51 See, e.g. *Arnold v Nat'l Westminster Bank* [1991] 2 A.C. 93 (H.L.).
52 *Henderson v Henderson* (1843) 3 Hare 100, 115; 67 E.R. 313, 320. See also *Johnson v Gore Wood & Co* [2000] UKHL 65.
53 Section 322(1) ZPO.
54 Ferrand (n 39).
55 French Court of Cassation, 7 July 2006, No 03–10672 *(Cesareo)*. This rule is referred to as "obligation de concentration des moyens".
56 French Court of Cassation, 8 December 2011, No 10–27344.
57 Article 31(1) of the UNCITRAL Model Law.
58 European Parliament, Directorate General for Internal Policies, "Dissenting Opinions in the Supreme Courts of the Member States" www.europarl.europa.eu/document/activities/cont/201304/20130423ATT64963/20130423ATT64963EN.pdf.
59 See, e.g. Article 32(1) of the 2017 ICC Rules; Article 189(2) of the Swiss Private International Law Act.

7 Challenging and enforcing arbitral awards

Rules

1. Requests for annulment and enforcement of arbitral awards are increasingly decided using the same standards

While differences remain, arbitration laws around the world have increasingly converged on the same set of rules for the annulment of arbitration awards. These rules are also found in the New York Convention with respect to recognising and enforcing arbitration awards. As a result, while it is still essential to look at local rules, it is now possible to speak generally about common standards used when evaluating challenges to arbitration awards.

2. It is possible to challenge an arbitral award

One of the most common things said about arbitration is that there is no appeal to an arbitral award. In reality, while the possibility of challenging an arbitral award is, and has to be, very limited, challenging an arbitral award is possible.

3. Challenging an award is only possible within a certain time limit

Arbitration laws impose time limits within which any application for annulment or recognition/enforcement of an award must be brought. This prevents parties using the possibility of challenging or enforcing an award as an ongoing threat against the other party.

4. In a limited number of jurisdictions, parties can waive their right to seek annulment of an award

In some jurisdictions, parties can agree in advance of receiving their award that neither party should be allowed to request the courts of the seat to annul the award. This allows the parties to ensure that the arbitral process is final, and does not simply become a foundation for further court proceedings. However, it is usually still possible for recognition/enforcement of the award to be challenged, including at the seat of the arbitration.

5. Recognition and enforcement are different things

While it is common to refer to "recognition and enforcement" of arbitral awards, as though this is a single process, it is important to remember that "recognition" and "enforcement" are ultimately different things. In most cases parties will pursue both simultaneously, but there are cases in which "recognition" will be desired even though "enforcement" is not.

6. The procedures involved in recognising and enforcing an arbitral award are decided by local law

While discussions of cross-border recognition and enforcement of arbitral awards rightly focus on the New York Convention, the Convention itself includes very few details about the practicalities of recognition/enforcement, leaving the details of the procedure to be decided by each jurisdiction. As a result, the proceedings themselves and the actions a court will take in support of an award's enforcement can vary significantly depending on the jurisdiction.

7. The law applicable to the recognition and enforcement of an award may vary depending on whether the arbitration was domestic or international

The New York Convention applies not only to "foreign" awards, but also to "arbitral awards not considered as domestic in the State where their recognition and enforcement are sought". Some arbitration laws apply different substantive standards to the recognition and enforcement of domestic awards than are applicable under the New York Convention. As a result, even if an award is being recognised/enforced at the seat of the arbitration, the standards that will be applied by the court will depend on whether the court views the arbitration as domestic or international.

8. The New York Convention is the primary instrument regulating the recognition and enforcement of arbitral awards

The New York Convention is unquestionably the central legal instrument in international commercial arbitration, both in terms of its direct applicability and as a source of the substantive standards applied worldwide when reviewing arbitration awards. However, other international treaties addressing the enforcement of arbitration awards do exist and it is important to be aware of them, if only because Article VII(1) of the New York Convention specifically allows parties to rely upon other treaties or domestic laws that provide terms more favourable for the enforcement of arbitral awards than does the Convention itself.

9. Under the New York Convention, States are under a general obligation to recognise arbitral awards

The Convention has what is often described as a "pro-enforcement bias". The purpose of the Convention is not to identify a strict set of criteria that arbitration awards must meet, but to facilitate the recognition and enforcement of arbitral awards, almost no matter their quality or content. The Convention does include exceptions that allow courts to refuse recognition or enforcement of an award, but these exceptions are permissive: a court cannot refuse recognition or enforcement unless one of the exceptions applies, but the Convention allows a court to decide that an exception applies but to enforce the award anyway.

10. The New York Convention imposes some formal requirements if an award is to be recognised or enforced

Despite the unquestionable focus of the New York Convention on encouraging the enforcement of arbitration awards, there are nonetheless formal requirements that must be met for recognition or enforcement under the Convention to be possible. These requirements are, though, designed to ensure that what courts are being asked to recognise/enforce are indeed arbitral awards covered by the Convention, rather than to limit the recognition/enforcement of awards, and are minimal in nature.

11. The grounds for challenging an arbitral award are very limited

While the possibility of challenging an arbitral award is an important protection for parties, this must be balanced against the need to prevent an over-intrusive approach by courts to the examination of arbitral awards. In recognition of this, under both arbitration laws worldwide and the New York Convention, the grounds on which an arbitration award can be successfully challenged are very limited, whether the form of the challenge is a request for annulment or opposition to recognition and enforcement.

12. Challenges can be based on a tribunal's lack of power to adjudicate: "I never had to go to arbitration"

Arbitration requires consent. If there is no valid arbitration agreement between the parties, then the arbitral tribunal has no jurisdiction over any dispute between those parties, and any award the tribunal issues is invalid. Moreover, for an arbitration agreement to be legally binding, the parties must have had the legal capacity to enter into the agreement, not just the physical ability to do so.

13. An award can be challenged if it deals with matters not covered by the arbitration agreement or by the parties' submissions: "Okay, I agreed to arbitrate, but only that, not this"

The consent-based nature of arbitration means not only that no-one can be forced to arbitrate, but also that no-one can be forced to arbitrate any specific thing that they have not agreed to arbitrate. However, contemporary courts generally interpret arbitration agreements broadly, focusing on the intent of the parties to arbitrate rather than on the specific language used in their arbitration agreement. In addition, an arbitration agreement can be modified by conduct: if a party submits a claim that is not covered by the arbitration agreement and the other party defends against that claim, the parties will usually be found to have agreed to arbitrate that claim, despite the text of the original arbitration agreement.

14. The composition of the arbitral tribunal and the arbitral procedure must be in accordance with the parties' agreement or the lex arbitri: "Okay, I agreed to arbitrate, but not like this"

If the parties have agreed that a certain procedure must be used, then the arbitration will not have been performed in accordance with the arbitration agreement, and the resulting award can be challenged, if that procedure is not used. However, if an agreed procedure is not used, and neither party makes an objection, the parties will usually be found to have agreed to use whatever procedure was actually used, rather than the one specified in the arbitration agreement.

15. Challenges can be based on procedural aspects of the arbitration: "That wasn't fair"

All parties must receive proper notice of the arbitration, so that they can prepare for it adequately, including with respect to the appointment of arbitrators, and they must then be given an opportunity to actually present their case.

16. An award can be challenged if the dispute is not arbitrable: "Yes, I agreed to arbitration, but the law doesn't let us arbitrate this sort of thing"

In every jurisdiction there are certain types of disputes that cannot be taken to arbitration. An award addressing a matter that is not arbitrable in the reviewing jurisdiction can be challenged, even though the parties agreed to arbitrate the matter. This ground for challenge is of decreasing importance because limitations on arbitrability are becoming less common.

17. In a small number of jurisdictions challenges can be based on errors of law by the arbitrators: "The arbitrators were wrong"

As a rule, it is not possible to challenge an arbitral award because it was wrong on either the law or the facts. There are jurisdictions, most famously England and Wales, where it is sometimes possible to challenge an award on the ground that the tribunal was wrong in its understanding of the law.

18. Awards can be challenged on the ground of public policy: "This award is fundamentally unacceptable"

A challenge may succeed when the award is in some way irreconcilable with core values of the jurisdiction in which the challenge has been brought. This covers two broad categories: "procedural public policy", which focuses on the way the arbitral proceedings were conducted, and "substantive public policy", which focuses on the subject matter of the dispute or the contents of the award.

19. Annulment and recognition/enforcement can interact in important ways

It is widely accepted that recognition and enforcement of an arbitral award can be granted even though annulment is still possible at the seat of the arbitration, and indeed even though annulment proceedings have been commenced. However, the New York Convention expressly permits courts to suspend recognition/enforcement proceedings until an annulment application has been resolved, should they wish to do so. In addition, the Convention allows arbitral awards to be refused enforcement if they have been annulled at the seat of the arbitration, but also allows annulled awards to be enforced. Jurisdictions have approached this issue differently, some concluding that annulled awards should usually not be enforced, while others have concluded that annulment has no impact on the enforceability of an award.

20. There are alternatives to challenging an award in court

Many arbitration laws and rules allow an arbitral tribunal, after an award has been delivered, to make minor corrections of errors in the award, to issue an "interpretation" of an element of the award that a party finds unclear, or even to issue a supplementary award if the original award did not resolve all the issues submitted to the tribunal. The parties can also incorporate into their arbitration agreement the possibility of appeal of the award to a second arbitration tribunal.

Analysis

1. Requests for annulment and enforcement of arbitral awards are increasingly decided using the same standards

In most books on international arbitration, the annulment of arbitral awards is treated separately from recognition and enforcement. This book, however, takes a different approach, and will be treating both annulment and enforcement in this single chapter, largely at the same time.

The reason for this is simple. It is true that annulment and enforcement occur at different times and involve different considerations: a decision by a court on whether or not to annul an award requires the court to focus on its domestic arbitration laws to determine if the award adhered to those rules, while a decision by the same court on recognition/enforcement of an award will often require the court to look instead at the international obligations its State has entered into with respect to the cross-border recognition/enforcement of awards.

However, over the course of the second half of the 20th Century, this distinction became less and less substantive. Arbitration laws increasingly converged on the same set of rules for the annulment of arbitration awards, so that while differences still exist, there are broad similarities around the world in how courts will decide on an application for the annulment of an arbitral award. Just as importantly, the standards on which national arbitration laws have converged are those originally adopted in the Convention on the Recognition and Enforcement of Foreign Arbitral Awards ("the New York Convention"). Annulment and recognition/enforcement, that is, still require courts to look at different laws, but those laws now increasingly say very similar or the same things.

It would, of course, be a mistake to simply assume that the laws in any given jurisdiction on the annulment of arbitral awards reflect the same standards as are laid out in the New York Convention. Moreover, even when the same standards are adopted, there is always the possibility that courts from different jurisdictions will interpret those standards differently.

The purpose of this book, however, is to give readers a conceptual understanding of arbitration, rather than to provide them with a detailed discussion of national or international rules. For that reason, we decided that it was best to emphasise the convergence of these two topics, rather than to maintain the traditional insistence that they possess a distinctiveness that is often no longer entirely there.

2. It is possible to challenge an arbitral award

One of the most common things said about arbitration is that there is no appeal of an arbitral award. A moment's reflection, however, will make clear that no-one would want this to be entirely true. Imagine you were involved in an arbitration in which the sole arbitrator refused to allow you to present witnesses while allowing the other side to do so, repeatedly complained that people of your nationality are liars, and at the close of the hearing winked at the other party and said "Don't worry, they'll get what's coming to them." Unsurprisingly, when the award is delivered you have lost on every point. Would you really want there to be no possibility of challenging an arbitral award?

What is true, then, is that while the ability to challenge an arbitral award needs to be very limited, to ensure that the freedom of parties to arbitrate as they wish is not undermined by over-intrusive courts, the possibility of challenge must exist if parties are to be confident that the private dispute resolution process they are agreeing to use is going to be fair. Challenges to arbitral awards take two different forms: (1) requesting the "annulment" (or "setting aside") of an award and (2) resisting "recognition" and "enforcement" of an award.

In an annulment proceeding, the party challenging the award requests the courts of the seat of the arbitration to declare, in effect, that the award is invalid and has no legal effect. It involves convincing those courts that there was something so fundamentally wrong with the arbitration that it should not be regarded as an acceptable legal process. The usual consequence of a successful request for annulment is that the parties must restart their arbitration completely, usually with a new tribunal, as in the eyes of the courts of the seat they have not yet fulfilled the terms of their arbitration agreement. They spent time and possibly a lot of money doing something that looked a lot like arbitration, but ultimately that process didn't meet the legal standards required for something to qualify as arbitration, and so the "award" that was delivered has no more legal relevance than any other personal opinion of a private individual on which of the parties was right.

The most important thing to note about the annulment of arbitral awards, then, is that it can only be done by the courts of the arbitral seat. To give an example, if a Grenadian company and an Indonesian company have been involved in an arbitration that is seated in China, it is only Chinese courts that can annul the resulting award. The Grenadian company cannot return to Grenada and ask the courts there to annul the award, even if the award would indeed be annulled if the arbitration had been seated in Grenada. The application for annulment has to made to the courts of the seat.[1]

So what, then, do you do if you have received an arbitral award from what you believe was an unfair arbitral process, but the courts of the seat refuse to annul the award or perhaps you just lack the financial resources to pursue annulment in what is for you a very distant country? That is where the second possibility for challenge of an arbitral award comes in: resisting recognition and enforcement of the award.

An arbitral award, after all, as has been said many times in this book, is just a private individual's view on how a dispute should be resolved. If the other party refuses to do what the award says (e.g. pay you money) the simple fact that an arbitral tribunal has said they have to do it will have no greater effect than if you tried yelling at them "But my mum said you had to do it!" How, then, do you make a party obey an award? You ask a court to recognise and enforce the award. In effect, you ask the court to take the award and issue a decision, sometimes referred to with the latin word *exequatur*, that gives the award the same legal effect as a court judgement.[2] From that point on, if the other party continues to refuse to obey the terms of the award they are not just ignoring the views of an arbitrator, they are defying a court order. And courts can indeed enforce their orders.

But then the flipside is also true. What do you do if you believe that an award is unfair or resulted from an unfair arbitral process? You can, of course, simply refuse to obey the award, but as just pointed out, the other party can ask a court to recognise and enforce the award. The second possibility, then, involves resisting the recognition and enforcement of the award. That is, when the other party goes to the court to request recognition and enforcement of the award, you go to the court as well and try to convince the court that there is something so fundamentally wrong with either the award itself or the arbitral process that led to the award, that the court should refuse to use its powers to make you obey the award.

Annulment and resisting recognition/enforcement, then, both involve attempting to convince a court that there is something so wrong with either an award or its underlying arbitral process that the award should not be given legal effect. The most important difference between the two processes is where each takes place. As has already been said, annulment can only occur at the seat of the arbitration. Recognition and enforcement, however, can occur anywhere.

That is not to say, of course, that they will occur literally anywhere. After all, courts have limited jurisdiction. There is rarely any point in asking a court in Ethiopia to recognise and enforce an arbitral award against a French party that only has assets in France and has no other connection to Ethiopia. The Ethiopian court simply has no power to compel the French party to obey the award, even if it were to decide that it had the jurisdiction to do so. In reality, then, recognition and enforcement of an award will only be sought where a party has assets or in any other jurisdiction that can compel the party to obey the award. For smaller parties that may mean only their home State. For larger multinationals, however, that can mean a large number of possibilities, and a party attempting to resist recognition and enforcement of an arbitral award may find themselves having to do so repeatedly in one jurisdiction after another. Indeed, recognition and enforcement of an arbitral award can be requested simultaneously in multiple jurisdictions. After all, a decision by the courts of one jurisdiction not to enforce an arbitral award does not bind the courts of any other jurisdiction, and for some parties the process of resisting enforcement of an arbitral award has become a decades-long series of court battles. The arbitration may have ended quickly, but the after-effects did not.

3. Challenging an award is only possible within a certain time limit

As important as it is that there be at least some possibility to challenge an arbitral award, it is also important that an award be able to provide a final resolution of the parties' dispute. Arbitration laws provide this assurance by placing time limits on the period within which a request for annulment or for recognition/enforcement of an arbitral award can be made. This prevents a party waiting until it is tactically advantageous before seeking annulment of an award, as if they do not file for annulment within the applicable time limit they can never do so, no matter how fundamental the flaws in the award or the arbitral process may be. Similarly, a party that has been successful in an arbitration cannot keep an award in its "back pocket", as an ongoing threat against the other party, but must enforce the award within the specified period or lose the ability to do so.[3]

4. In a limited number of jurisdictions, parties can waive their right to seek annulment of an award

In some jurisdictions there can also be a further limitation on the right to seek annulment, although this depends on the parties agreeing to limit that right themselves. Arbitration, after all, as the saying goes, is based on the autonomy of the parties. It is a private dispute resolution process, and so absent fundamental unfairness, the parties should be allowed to arbitrate in any way they want. But what if what the parties want is to get rid of the "absent fundamental unfairness" restriction? The parties might, after all, value speed and certainty to such an extent that when they agree to arbitration they decide they want to completely exclude the possibility of appeal to the courts of the seat: they would rather accept the risk of an unfair process than the risk of a court appeal that may lead to them having to redo the entire arbitration.

In most jurisdictions it is not possible to completely exclude court review of the arbitral process. After all, an arbitration that is seated in Madagascar is benefiting from the legal framework put in place to support arbitrations in Madagascar, and will potentially benefit from international agreements into which Madagascar has entered that facilitate the cross-border enforcement of arbitral awards. As a result, it may be argued, Madagascar has a legitimate interest in ensuring that its legal system is not used to commit injustices in the form of fundamentally unfair arbitrations.

In a small number of jurisdictions, however, respect for the autonomy of the parties involved in an arbitration is regarded as a greater policy concern than avoiding that jurisdiction being the seat of an unfair arbitration. In these legal systems, parties can agree to exclude court review of their arbitration if that best suits their needs.

Most famously, pursuant to Article 192 of the Swiss Private International Law Act (PILA), the parties may, "by an express statement in the arbitration agreement or by a subsequent written agreement, waive fully the action for annulment". Alternatively, they may simply limit the grounds on which annulment can be granted, rather than excluding it altogether. Importantly, however, this is possible only "if none of the parties have their domicile, their habitual residence, or a business establishment in Switzerland'. Swiss nationals and other parties established or residing in Switzerland, that is, cannot waive their right to seek annulment of an arbitral award. This rule, that is, is aimed exclusively at entirely "international" arbitrations, in which neither party has a legitimate ground for expecting the protection of the Swiss legal system, except in so far as they agreed to arbitrate under Swiss arbitration law. This emphasis on the importance of the lack of any substantive connection between the parties and Switzerland is emphasised by the fact that under Article 192(2) PILA, even if the right to seek annulment has been waived, court review will still be available if one of the parties seeks to have the award recognised and enforced in Switzerland – with the standards of the New York Convention being applied by analogy, and the courts thereby having the ability to refuse recognition and enforcement on the grounds of fundamental unfairness.[4]

A similar approach has been adopted in France, as under Article 1522 of the French Code of Civil Procedure, parties are permitted to waive their right to seek annulment of an arbitral award. The French approach is more expansive than the Swiss one, as it is not restricted to arbitrations including only parties with no substantive connection to France, but is applicable in any international arbitration. However, again, the French courts do not lose all control, as if the award is to be enforced in France parties retain the right to resist enforcement on the same grounds that they could have used to seek annulment.[5]

On first consideration, then, the idea of a waiver of the right to seek annulment of an arbitral award is a problematic one. There is no question that arbitrations can result in significant injustices, and parties entering into arbitration agreements often have very limited understanding of arbitration and of the risks it can involve. As adopted in France and Switzerland, however, this possibility of the waiver of annulment is properly seen not as eliminating important protections against unfair arbitrations, but rather as merely embracing the alignment between annulment and enforcement of arbitral awards upon which this chapter is based. Waiver of annulment is possible, but only because review will be available at the place of enforcement, even if that place of enforcement is France/Switzerland itself. As long as this ultimate protection is retained, the ability of parties to agree to limit the review undertaken by the courts of the seat is largely unproblematic.

5. Recognition and enforcement are different things

As was discussed in Chapter 1, a primary benefit that arbitration provides over litigation is the relatively easy international enforcement of arbitral awards, primarily due to the New York Convention. Importantly, however, the Convention is not titled the "Convention on the Enforcement of Foreign Arbitral Awards", but the "Convention on the Recognition and Enforcement of Foreign Arbitral Awards". It is, therefore, important to understand what "recognition" of an arbitral award is, and how that differs from "enforcement".

Essentially, by "recognising" an arbitral award, the courts of a jurisdiction grant that award legal effect in their jurisdiction. An award may say that Cooper broke his contract with Shirley, but until that award has been recognised by the courts of Switzerland, then as a matter of Swiss law the question is still unsettled – the award is just the personal opinion of the arbitral tribunal. However, just as a Swiss court judgement saying that Cooper broke his contract with Shirley will settle that question as a matter of Swiss law, so the recognition by a Swiss court of an arbitral award saying this will also settle that question as a matter of Swiss law. Prior to recognition of the award, it was still possible for Cooper to argue in a Swiss court that he did not breach his contract with Shirley, even though there is an arbitral award saying that he did. Once the award has been recognised, he cannot: that question has now been resolved as a matter of Swiss law. As already mentioned, the decision whereby a State court recognises an arbitral award is sometimes referred to with the latin word *exequatur*.

"Recognition" of the award, however, does not get Shirley the compensation the tribunal said that Cooper had to pay her for his breach of contract. It resolves the question of breach of contract, but doesn't require Cooper to actually do anything. "Enforcement" is the process of compelling a party to take the actions required by the award.

As a practical matter recognition and enforcement are usually handled together by a court as part of a single process and in a single proceeding, but conceptually they are importantly different. Moreover, there are situations in which a party may wish to request recognition of an award even though they have no desire for its enforcement. Say, for example, that the arbitration between Shirley and Cooper resulted in an award rejecting Shirley's claim, and stating that Cooper did not breach his contract with her. Shirley can't enforce the award because she didn't win. Cooper can't enforce it because it doesn't actually require that Shirley do anything. However, Cooper may decide that he wants it to be legally established that he did not break his contract with Shirley. In such a case, he can request that a court recognise the award, even though he has no intention of enforcing it. Once this has been done, it is settled as a matter of law in the jurisdiction in question that Cooper did not breach his contract with Shirley in the way she claimed in the arbitration.[6]

6. The procedures involved in recognising and enforcing an arbitral award are decided by local law

Discussion of recognition and enforcement of international arbitration awards understandably focuses on the New York Convention, but it should be emphasised that, ultimately, recognition and enforcement are always subject to domestic court procedures. The Convention itself includes very few details about the practicalities of recognition/enforcement, leaving the details of the procedure to be decided by each jurisdiction. Typically, the civil procedure statute of the jurisdiction in which recognition/enforcement of an award is being sought will specify what the party seeking recognition/enforcement has to do to secure the court's assistance, as well as how and to what extent the State will take coercive actions to enforce the award. As a result, while the New York Convention largely harmonises the substantive standards courts will apply in deciding whether an award should be recognised or enforced, the proceedings themselves and the actions a court will take in support of the award's enforcement can vary significantly depending on the jurisdiction.

7. The law applicable to the recognition and enforcement of an award may vary depending on whether the arbitration was domestic or international

While the New York Convention is formally titled the "Convention on the Recognition and Enforcement of Foreign Arbitral Awards", this is misleading. Under Article 1(1) of the Convention, it applies not only to "foreign" awards (i.e. awards delivered in a State other than the State in which they are being enforced), but also to "arbitral awards not considered as domestic in the State where their recognition and enforcement are sought".

This is an important component of the Convention that is sometimes overlooked, because in some jurisdictions different laws are applied to the recognition and enforcement of domestic arbitral awards than are applied by the New York Convention. This is not always the case and the UNCITRAL Model Law, for example, applies the same standards to all arbitral awards, no matter where the arbitration was seated.[7] However, in France the Code of Civil Procedure sets forth two different procedures: one for the recognition of domestic awards rendered in France and a different one, implementing the New York Convention, for awards issued abroad or in international arbitrations.[8] The consequence of this situation is that, for example, two French parties engaged in an arbitration seated in France might both be expecting that French domestic arbitration law will be applied to the enforcement of their award. However, because a court decides that under French law their arbitration was "international", those provisions of French law dealing with the enforcement of international arbitration awards apply instead.

8. The New York Convention is the primary instrument regulating the recognition and enforcement of arbitral awards

Although certainly not the only treaty supporting the cross-border enforcement of arbitration awards, the New York Convention is unquestionably the central legal instrument in international commercial arbitration. Not only has it been adopted by the vast majority of States (160 as of July 2019), but as has been discussed above, the substantive standards relating to the review of arbitration awards that were incorporated into the New York Convention are now standard features of arbitration statutes around the world.

The Convention also incorporated a principle that was an essential foundation of the enormous growth in international commercial arbitration in the second half of the 20th Century, namely the independence of an arbitral award, once delivered, from the seat of the arbitration. That is, the New York Convention was actually a replacement for two previous international treaties on arbitration, The Geneva Protocol on Arbitration Clauses of 1923 and the Geneva Convention on the Execution of Foreign Arbitral Awards of 1927. The Geneva Convention, however, included a famous requirement that has come to be known as "double *exequatur*", under which arbitration awards could only be enforced through the Convention if they were "final" in the seat of the arbitration. That is, if it was no longer possible for the award to be challenged in the courts of the seat.

The problem this created was that, while not specifically required by the Geneva Convention, many courts required parties seeking enforcement of an arbitration award through the

Geneva Convention to first go to the courts of the seat and get a declaration that the award was no longer able to be challenged. As a result, any attempt at enforcement of an award required two separate court systems to rule on the award's validity: hence, "double" *exequatur*. The New York Convention, however, entirely eliminated this requirement, and as a result an award can be enforced through the New York Convention without the enforcing party having to interact with the courts of the seat of the arbitration at all. This separation of the arbitration award from the seat of the arbitration has played an important role in facilitating the smoothness of cross-border enforcement of arbitration awards, thereby increasing substantially the attractiveness of arbitration as a means of resolving international commercial disputes.[9]

As already noted, the New York Convention is not the only treaty addressing the enforcement of arbitration awards, other examples including the Riyadh Arab Agreement for Judicial Cooperation of 1983, the European Convention on International Commercial Arbitration of 1961 and the Inter-American Convention on International Commercial Arbitration of 1975. Importantly, Article VII(1) of the New York Convention specifically addresses how the New York Convention relates to other treaties, and does so in the manner most effectively designed to support the enforceability of arbitration awards. Article VII(1) provides not only that the Convention does not affect the validity of other treaties concerning the recognition and enforcement of arbitral awards, but specifically allows parties to rely upon other treaties or domestic laws that provide terms more favourable for the enforcement of arbitral awards than does the Convention. In this way, the Convention ensures, through its own provisions, a minimum standard for the enforcement of arbitration awards, but also expressly allows for the further development of arbitration law, as long as that development makes arbitration awards more enforceable, not less.

9. Under the New York Convention, States are under a general obligation to recognise arbitral awards

The New York Convention was not just designed to provide a formal legal framework that would support the cross-border enforcement of arbitration awards. It does this, of course, but the design of the Convention embraces a far more ambitious objective. The Convention, that is, has what is often described as a "pro-enforcement bias". Or, to put it another way, the New York Convention has rarely seen an arbitration award that it did not like.

Fundamentally, the purpose of the New York Convention is not to lay out a set of ground rules to which arbitration awards must conform if they are to be enforced, and then to provide a mechanism for the enforcement of those "good" awards. It is, rather, to enforce arbitration awards. Pure and simple. Good or bad, excellently or poorly drafted, if it is an arbitration award, the New York Convention wants to help enforce it.

There are, of course limits to this passion for enforcement, and Article V of the Convention, as will be discussed below, identifies certain types of awards that should perhaps not be enforced, primarily due to a fundamental procedural unfairness in the underlying arbitration, or because enforcement of the award would violate an important policy of the State whose courts are being asked for enforcement. The word "perhaps", though, is important, because there are simply no awards – none, no matter how horrible – that the New York Convention thinks should definitely not be enforced.

Rather, the Convention expressly places an obligation on all States that adopt it to "recognize arbitration awards as binding and enforce them".[10] In addition, not only must States recognise and enforce awards covered by the Convention, but they must do so in a way that is at least as favourable as the processes used for domestic arbitration awards.[11]

Moreover, even Article V, which lays out the limits of enforcement under the New York Convention, ultimately imposes no limits at all. It lists a series of grounds on which awards may be refused enforcement, but "may" is the word used, and it has an important effect. A court, that is, can look at an award and say, for example, "this falls clearly under Article V(1)(e) of the New York Convention, but I'm going to enforce it anyway". That is fully consistent with the New York Convention: the Convention gives courts *permission* to refuse enforcement in a limited number of circumstances, but does not *require* that enforcement be refused <u>ever</u>. By contrast, courts applying the Convention may <u>never</u> refuse enforcement of an arbitration award on any ground other than the seven grounds explicitly included in Article V.[12]

10. The New York Convention imposes some formal requirements if an award is to be recognised or enforced

Despite the unquestionable focus of the New York Convention on encouraging the recognition and enforcement of arbitration awards, there are nonetheless formal requirements that must be met for recognition/enforcement under the Convention to be possible. These requirements are, though, designed to ensure that what courts are being asked to recognise/enforce are indeed arbitral awards covered by the Convention, rather than to limit the recognition/enforcement of awards, and are minimal in nature.

10.1 The "award" requirement

It may seem obvious, but the New York Convention is about enforcement of "awards". As a result, if something is not an award, it is not enforceable under the New York Convention. As discussed in the previous chapter, however, this limitation can actually serve as a significant restriction, as not everything that may be labelled as an "award" by an arbitral tribunal actually qualifies as an "award" under the Convention. Instead, it may only be an "order", and so not enforceable under the Convention.

10.2 The "foreign" requirement

The formal name of the New York Convention is the "Convention on the Recognition and Enforcement of Foreign Arbitral Awards". What does "foreign" mean? According to Article I(1) of the Convention, arbitral awards are entitled to recognition and enforcement under the Convention if they were "made in the territory of a State other than the State where the recognition and enforcement of such awards are sought". In short, as long as the award has crossed a national border, it can be enforced under the New York Convention. Importantly, the word that is used here is "foreign", not "international". As a result, even if an award was delivered in an unquestionably domestic arbitration, so long as it is being enforced in a State other than the seat of the arbitration, it is enforceable under the New York Convention.

Notably, however, the notion of a "foreign" award as adopted in the Convention actually extends even more broadly to include some awards that have not even crossed a border. As discussed above, Article I(1) also allows for the enforcement under the Convention of awards "not considered as domestic awards in the State where their recognition and enforcement are sought". What qualifies as a "domestic" award varies from one jurisdiction to another, and is decided by local law. There is no "New York Convention definition" of a "domestic" arbitration award.

As might be expected from the pro-enforcement bias of the Convention, then, the "foreign" requirement is drafted deliberately broadly to capture any arbitration award that is at all plausibly international, whether because the arbitration from which it arose qualifies as an international arbitration under the relevant law, or just because it came from an arbitration seated in another State. The only awards clearly excluded from the Convention's reach are purely domestic awards that are being presented for enforcement to courts in the State in which the arbitration was seated.

10.3 The "documentation" requirement

The pro-enforcement bias of the Convention is also seen in the very limited documentary proof required for a party to have an award enforced under the Convention. The drafters of the Convention, that is, went out of their way to ensure that parties with a valid award would not find themselves unable to have their award enforced because they had not secured some piece of paperwork they could not reasonably have known would be required. The paperwork required by the Convention, then, is very basic, and entirely intuitive. Under Article IV(1) of the Convention, all that is required for an award to be recognised and enforced is:

1) The duly authenticated original award or a certified copy thereof;
2) The original agreement to arbitrate or a duly certified copy thereof.

In short, you need proof that the parties agreed to arbitrate (in the form of the arbitration agreement or a certified copy) and proof of what the award says (in the form of the award or a certified copy).

It should, of course, be unsurprising to anyone attempting to have an award enforced that they need to show what the award actually says, so that requirement will rarely cause difficulties. Problems will arise, however, if an arbitrator has been permitted to deliver an oral award, i.e. to simply announce her decision to the parties. Unsurprisingly, oral awards are extremely rare, precisely because parties prefer to have a clear statement of the contents of the decision in case there are disagreements. However, they are possible, and so parties considering permitting an oral award should be aware that it would not be enforceable through the New York Convention. That does not mean it would not be enforceable at all, but its enforceability would depend entirely on the law of the jurisdiction in which enforcement was being requested, rather than on the New York Convention.

The need for the arbitration agreement may be less intuitively obvious, as the party requesting enforcement may think that since they had the arbitration, and arbitration requires agreement, it must be self-evident that there was an arbitration agreement. However, it is important to remember that even if a party has participated in an arbitration, they may have done so after objecting to the jurisdiction of the tribunal. That objection may have been rejected by the tribunal, allowing the arbitration to proceed, but that party nonetheless retains the right to raise its objection again in opposition to any attempt to enforce the resulting award. It is, therefore, essential for the court considering enforcing an award to have access to the arbitration agreement on which the award was based, in order to be satisfied that there was indeed a valid agreement to arbitrate.

As will be discussed on p. 00, the invalidity of the arbitration agreement is one of the grounds listed in Article V of the Convention on the basis of which recognition and enforcement of an award can be refused. It could, therefore, have been left up to a party opposing recognition and enforcement to produce a copy of the agreement as part of its argument that the award should not be enforced. Indeed, such an approach might seem more consistent with the pro-enforcement bias of the Convention. Placing the burden on the party opposing enforcement, however, would ultimately be unworkable. If that party's argument was that the specific dispute resolved by the award was not covered by an otherwise valid arbitration agreement, then indeed they could produce that arbitration agreement to support their argument. But what are they to do if their argument is that there never was an arbitration agreement at all? By definition they cannot produce anything to prove that. Requiring the party seeking to enforce an award to also produce the underlying arbitration agreement is, therefore, the only practical way of ensuring that the enforcing court has access to the arbitration agreement that is claimed to be the basis for the award.

There is, however, a further complication raised by the requirement to produce a copy of the arbitration agreement, which mirrors an issue already discussed regarding the need to produce a copy of the arbitration award. In this context, however, the complication is more significant: what if the agreement to arbitrate was oral? That is, the parties verbally agreed to arbitrate, but never wrote that agreement down? There is then no agreement to be produced to the court, even though there was indeed an agreement.

In reality, oral agreements to arbitrate are very rare in international commercial arbitration. Moreover, almost every jurisdiction around the world mirrors the New York Convention's requirement that arbitration agreements be in writing, although those jurisdictions more supportive of arbitration take a very generous approach to what "in writing" means in the Convention (e.g. accepting that a written reference in an email to an oral arbitration agreement meets the Convention's requirement).[13] Nonetheless, there are jurisdictions in which oral arbitration agreements are valid and enforceable, most famously France.[14] Parties in such jurisdictions, then, need to be aware that while the flexibility of being able to rely on an oral arbitration agreement may initially be appealing, it will create problems with the international enforceability of their award under the New York Convention.

While at the beginning of this section it was said that only two forms of documentary support are required by the Convention, one additional requirement is worth noting. The New York Convention, after all, is designed to facilitate the international enforcement of arbitral awards, and many languages are spoken around the world. Yet it would be problematic if, for example, a court in Guinea-Bissau, where Portuguese is the official language, was presented with an arbitration award and an arbitration agreement in Kyrgyz. Article IV(2) of the Convention, therefore, requires that if the award and/or agreement is not in an official language of the State in which enforcement is being sought, then the party seeking recognition and enforcement is to produce a certified translation of the document(s) in question.

The New York Convention, in sum, adopts a very simple and straightforward approach to the recognition and enforcement of arbitration awards, requiring the minimum possible documentary support. Moreover, Article VII makes clear that even these minimal requirements can be waived if a State wishes to do so. The Convention, therefore, does not prevent the cross-border recognition and enforcement of awards where a party cannot meet the Convention's formal requirements (e.g. if the award or arbitration agreement is oral), and it is perfectly consistent with the Convention for another domestic or international legal instrument to facilitate recognition and enforcement of an award that does not meet the Convention's formal requirements.

11. The grounds for challenging an arbitral award are very limited

While the possibility of challenging an arbitral award is an important protection for parties, this must be balanced against the need to prevent an over-intrusive approach by courts to the examination of arbitral awards. In selecting arbitration, after all, the parties have agreed not to take their dispute to court. This choice would be undermined if, after the arbitral process was concluded, courts simply refused to enforce any award that reached a conclusion different from the one they would have reached themselves.

As a result, under both arbitration laws worldwide and the New York Convention, the grounds on which an arbitration award can be successfully challenged are very limited, whether the form of the challenge is a request for annulment or opposition to recognition and enforcement. Most importantly, it is uniformly accepted that review of an arbitration award cannot constitute a re-assessment of the case by the court. The question for the court, that is, is not "Was this dispute decided correctly?", but only "Was the arbitral process unfair?" and "Would enforcing this award violate an important policy of our jurisdiction?". If neither of these questions is answered "Yes", then the award should be enforced, even if the court believes that the award is seriously wrong on either the law or the facts.[15]

Of course, the specific grounds on which annulment may be granted or recognition/enforcement refused will vary from one jurisdiction to another, and even with respect to the New York Convention, courts in different jurisdictions may apply them in different ways. It is, therefore, essential for any arbitration practitioner considering or faced with a challenge to an arbitration award in the courts of any jurisdiction to examine the specific approach to review of awards in that legal system.

Nonetheless, the increased harmonisation of the law applicable to international arbitration around the world means that some general comments can be made about how courts in most jurisdictions approach an attempt to challenge an arbitration award. Moreover, as has already been noted, the widely accepted standards for such challenges are directly derived from those incorporated into the New York Convention for resisting recognition and enforcement of arbitral awards. The following sections of this chapter, therefore, will examine the grounds included in Article V of the Convention, as a way of explaining the principles generally used worldwide for any review of an arbitral award.

12. Challenges can be based on a tribunal's lack of power to adjudicate: "I never had to go to arbitration"

The most fundamental objection to any arbitration award, of course, is when one party argues that it simply never agreed to arbitrate with the other party at all. Arbitration, after all, requires the consent of the parties, and so if there is no valid arbitration agreement between the parties, then an arbitral tribunal has no jurisdiction over any dispute between them, and any award such a tribunal issues is invalid.

There are two standard ways in which this situation is reflected in arbitration laws, as seen in both the Model Law and the New York Convention. Under Article 34(2)(a)(i) of the Model Law and Article V(1)(a) of the New York Convention,[16] an award can be annulled or recognition and enforcement refused if the reviewing court concludes that either the arbitration agreement claimed to underlie the award was not valid, or if one or more of the parties to the agreement did not have the legal capacity to enter into that agreement. The distinction between the two possibilities is important, but ultimately both refer to a situation in which there simply was no binding arbitration agreement between the parties, and so the tribunal that issued the award had no jurisdiction to do so.

As discussed in Chapter 3, arguments about the validity of an arbitration agreement must first be raised to the arbitral tribunal, rather than saved for a reviewing court, and the doctrine of "competence-competence" allows the tribunal to decide for itself whether a valid arbitration agreement exists. If the objection was not properly raised to the tribunal, then a reviewing court will likely conclude that it has been waived, and cannot be raised at the annulment or recognition/enforcement stage. Nonetheless, it is important to remember that "competence-competence" merely entails that an arbitral tribunal makes the first decision on its jurisdiction; it does not preclude a reviewing court from subsequently re-examining whether the tribunal had jurisdiction or not. Indeed, the approach that a reviewing court will take to this re-examination is a matter of national law, and can vary from very deferential to the decision of the tribunal,[17] to a completely new decision with no deference at all to the tribunal's own determination.[18]

One important question that remains, however, is what law should be applied in determining whether a valid arbitration agreement exists. If you have an arbitration between an Angolan party and a party from Brunei, relating to a contract governed by Peruvian law and with the hearings held in Botswana, which law applies to determine if there was a valid arbitration agreement?

Both the Model Law and the New York Convention adopt the principle that in examining the validity of an arbitration agreement, the relevant law is "the law to which the parties have subjected it".[19] That is, regardless of the different States just listed in the example, and the different ways they relate to the arbitration, if the parties have included in their arbitration agreement a statement that it is to be governed by the law of the Russian Federation, then that is the law that any reviewing court must apply when determining if a valid arbitration agreement exists. Of course, in reality, parties rarely expressly state the law applicable to their arbitration agreement, and Chapter 3 discusses the different approaches jurisdictions take to determining in such cases what law the parties have subjected their arbitration agreement to. What is important to note in the present context, however, is that both the Model Law and the New York Convention give priority to the autonomy of the parties on the question. A reviewing court may

218 *Challenging and enforcing arbitral awards*

not simply apply its own law to determine the validity of the parties' arbitration agreement, but must instead respect any choice of applicable law the parties have made.

What if the court decides the parties have not chosen a specific law to be applied to their arbitration agreement, either explicitly or by implication? The Model Law and the New York Convention again both agree: the law that should be applied is that of the seat of the arbitration.[20]

A different situation, however, applies when the argument is not that there was no arbitration agreement as such, but rather that there was indeed an arbitration agreement, but one or more of the parties to that agreement did not have the legal capacity to enter into it. The legal consequence of this incapacity is still that no valid arbitration agreement exists, but both the Model Law and the New York Convention take a very different approach to the question of the law that should be applied in determining whether a party had the capacity to enter into the arbitration agreement. In short, even if the arbitration agreement specifies that questions of its validity should be determined in accordance with a particular law, under both the Model Law and the New York Convention the law that should be applied when examining the capacity of a party is the law applicable to that party. Thus, in the example above, while the law of the Russian Federation is applicable to questions of the validity of the arbitration agreement, the law of Angola determines if the Angolan party had the capacity to enter into the arbitration agreement, while the law of Brunei decides that question for the party from there.

This may seem surprising, given that ultimately the question is one of the validity of the arbitration agreement, and questions of validity are to be decided by the law agreed by the parties, namely that of the Russian Federation. However, the question of capacity is one that is prior to the question of what law the parties agreed should govern their arbitration agreement. That is, if one of the parties did not have the legal capacity to enter into an arbitration agreement, then it did not have the legal capacity to agree on the law applicable to that agreement. Any other approach would allow parties to contract out of the protections the law has given them, which is inconsistent with the entire purpose of those protections.

This first ground for challenging an arbitration award, then, is focused on the most fundamental question relating to the validity of an arbitration award: was there a valid arbitration agreement between the parties? As a result, while it provides a ground on which annulment or refusal of recognition and enforcement of an award can be granted, it is nonetheless essentially a means of respecting the autonomy of the parties – although in this case, not the autonomy of parties to an arbitration agreement, but of parties who were not parties to an arbitration agreement.

13. An award can be challenged if it deals with matters not covered by the arbitration agreement or by the parties' submissions: "Okay, I agreed to arbitrate, but only that, not this"

Once it has been established that the parties did indeed agree to arbitration, the next question is whether they agreed to arbitrate the specific claim that was actually brought before the tribunal. The consent-based nature of arbitration, after all, means not only that no-one can be forced to arbitrate, but also that no-one can be forced to arbitrate any specific thing that they have not agreed to arbitrate.

By way of example, Amy-Leigh and Keagan may have a contract that includes both a section in which Keagan agrees to rent a shop from Amy-Leigh, and a section in which Keagan agrees to sell Amy-Leigh's products in that shop. The arbitration clause in the contract specifies that any disputes relating to the sale of Amy-Leigh's products are to be taken to arbitration, while it says nothing about disputes relating to the rental of the shop. Keagan commences arbitration against Amy-Leigh over a dispute about rental of the shop, and the arbitrator issues an award in favour of Keagan.

The obvious problem that exists is that the tribunal has issued a decision on a matter that is not covered by the language of the arbitration agreement. Both the New York Convention and the Model Law address this situation by acknowledging as a valid ground for challenge of an arbitral award that "the award deals with a dispute not contemplated by or not falling within the terms of the submission to arbitration, or contains decisions on matters beyond the scope of the submission to arbitration".[21] As a result, a court may refuse to enforce the award on the ground that the decision given by the tribunal was on a matter that the parties never agreed to submit to arbitration.

The consequence of this rule is that arbitral tribunals must ensure that any claims presented to them by a party fall within the arbitration agreement. If the tribunal rules on matters not covered by the agreement, then there is a risk that the entire award may be annulled or declined recognition and enforcement, and at the very least that part of the award addressing these matters will be rejected.[22]

It is important to remember, however, that interpretation of an arbitration agreement is approached differently by different courts, some emphasising the explicit text of the agreement, while others focus on what they perceive to be the fundamental intent of the parties to arbitrate their disputes. English courts, for example, adopt a strongly purposive approach to the interpretation of arbitration agreements, to the extent that the House of Lords[23] in *Fiona Trust & Holding Corp v Privalov* [2007] UKHL 40 embraced a presumption that parties involved in a transaction would want all their disputes to be decided by the same tribunal. Therefore, if they have explicitly chosen to use arbitration to resolve disputes arising out of some parts of their transaction, they should be understood to have intended that arbitration agreement to cover all disputes arising out of that transaction, even when by its terms it doesn't do so. If they wish to exclude some elements of their transaction from arbitration, they need to do so clearly.[24] Similarly expansive approaches to the interpretation of arbitration agreements are adopted in other prominent arbitration jurisdictions.[25]

Understanding arbitration through case-law

One-stop shop presumption in the interpretation of arbitration agreements

Case details: *Fiona Trust & Holding Corp v Privalov* [2007] UKHL 40

Authority deciding the case: House of Lords

Facts of the case: The dispute concerned eight charterparties. The charterparties all contained arbitration clauses, referring to disputes "arising under the charter". The

> ship-owner argued that the charters were procured by bribery, and sought to rescind the charters on this ground. The issue in dispute, hence, was whether the owner was indeed entitled to rescind the charters because of the alleged bribery; however, the parties disagreed as to whether the issue should be determined by arbitration, or by a State court. The House of Lords was faced with the difficult question of whether a dispute concerning the circumstances under which a contract is concluded (in this case, the alleged bribery) may be considered as arising "under" a contract, and so as covered by the parties' agreement to arbitrate.
>
> **Decision:** The House of Lords held that the parties' purpose in entering into an arbitration agreement is presumed to be to have all disputes arising out a certain legal relationship decided by the tribunal they have chosen. Lord Hoffman drew an important inference from this observation: "if one accepts that this is the purpose of an arbitration clause, its construction must be influenced by whether the parties, as rational businessmen, were likely to have intended that only some of the questions arising out of their relationship were to be submitted to arbitration and others were to be decided by the national courts". According to the House of Lords, if the parties have not expressed their intention to carve out certain types of disputes from the scope of their agreement to arbitrate, there is a strong presumption that they intended to use arbitration as a "one-stop shop", to cover all disputes connected to their transaction. As a result, previous English caselaw that emphasised formalistic distinctions between arbitration agreements that referred to disputes "arising out of" the contract as opposed to those "in connection with" or "related to" the contract were inapt. In the view of Lord Hoffman, "the parties, as rational businessmen, are likely to have intended any dispute arising out of the relationship into which they have entered or purported to enter to be decided by the same tribunal".

In addition, it should also be remembered that consent to arbitration can be given by conduct, rather than just by written words. That is, to continue the above example, if Amy-Leigh takes part in the arbitration against Keagan without objecting that the arbitration agreement does not cover disputes relating to rental of the shop, then she will likely be held by any later reviewing court either to have agreed to modify the arbitration agreement to include disputes relating to rental of the shop (since she was indeed willing to arbitrate that dispute), or at the very least to have waived her right to make that objection to any later reviewing court.[26] This does not mean that Amy-Leigh needs to refuse to take part in the arbitration if she denies that the claim brought by Keagan is covered by the arbitration agreement, but she must be sure that she raises her objection to the tribunal. As discussed earlier in this chapter, even if the objection is rejected by the tribunal, she will nonetheless usually be allowed to raise the objection again when challenging the award. For a more in-depth discussion see Chapter 3.

A further variation of this principle addresses the situation in which all the matters dealt with in the award are covered by the arbitration agreement, but one or more of them were not covered by the parties' submissions. An arbitral tribunal may only rule on matters brought to it by the parties. There may be other disputes between the parties, and those disputes may be covered by the arbitration agreement, but unless they are included in a formal submission to the tribunal, the tribunal does not have jurisdiction to address them. When a tribunal ignores this principle and rules on matters that have not been formally submitted to it, it is referred to as "exceeding its authority", or as acting *ultra petita*. This can result in the award being successfully challenged, or at least a challenge being granted with respect to those portions of the award that dealt with matters not submitted to the tribunal.

A less clear situation exists when a tribunal acts *infra petita*, or fails to rule on matters that have indeed been submitted to it. Ideally, the applicable arbitration rules or law will expressly permit the tribunal to issue a supplementary award, addressing the issues omitted from the original award, thereby resolving the problem.[27] However, this will not always be the case, and as discussed in Chapter 6, the tribunal may be *functus officio* after issuing its final award, and so no longer have the power to issue a supplementary award. Some commentators argue that in this situation the award should be treated as invalid and unenforceable, as the tribunal has failed to perform the task that has been entrusted to it by the parties.[28] The stronger view, however, is that an *infra petita* award remains binding on the parties, as it constitutes a valid determination of at least part of their dispute, but that the parties remain free to recommence arbitration on the remaining, unresolved matters.[29]

14. *The composition of the arbitral tribunal and the arbitral procedure must be in accordance with the parties' agreement or the* **lex arbitri**: *"Okay, I agreed to arbitrate, but not like this"*

As repeatedly emphasised throughout this book, one of the greatest attractions and benefits of arbitration is the freedom it gives to the parties to construct a dispute resolution process that matches their dispute and their preferences. The centrality of this idea to arbitration is reflected in the inclusion in both Article 34(2)(a)(iv) of the Model Law and Article V(1)(d) of the New York Convention of the principle that an arbitration award can be challenged if the arbitration did not take place in the way required by the arbitration agreement.

In reality, in most cases the parties will not have specified in their arbitration agreement how any particular element of the arbitration must be performed. Moreover, while parties retain the right to agree on any element of the arbitral procedure until the arbitration is completed, by the time the arbitration has commenced they are in dispute, and so agreement on any point of real significance can be difficult to get. As a result, the practical reality in almost all arbitrations is that the tribunal, once appointed, will decide the procedures to be used.[30] Nonetheless, if the parties have agreed that a certain procedure must be used, then the arbitration will not have been performed in accordance with the arbitration agreement, and the resulting award can be challenged, if that procedure is not used.

Importantly, this rule applies to the constitution of the arbitral tribunal itself, and indeed it must do so given the central role of the tribunal in deciding the arbitral procedure. As a result, if the parties have agreed that the arbitrators must have certain qualifications, or must be appointed through a certain method, and that agreement is not followed, the award may be annulled or denied recognition/enforcement, as it did not arise from an arbitration of the form agreed to by the parties.

Nonetheless, while this ground for challenging an arbitral award lays out an important principle, it is rarely successful, because of the possibility of waiver/modification. That is, even if an arbitration agreement explicitly says that a certain procedure must be followed, the parties retain the right to agree to alter that procedure at any point. It is the parties' arbitration, so they are not bound by their own agreement – each of them is bound individually, but as long as both of them want the change, then they can agree to it.

However, agreement can be given through conduct, rather than only through words. That is, say Aneurin and Dewey have agreed to go to the movies to see *Hard Rock IV: Rick Astley Returns*, but when they get to the ticket counter Aneurin sees that a revival of *Hannah Montana: The Movie* is playing and instead purchases a ticket to that. Dewey says nothing, but also purchases a ticket to see *Hannah Montana*. By making that purchase without objecting, Dewey has agreed to change his agreement with Aneurin. He could have spoken up and said "Hang on, we agreed to see Rick", which would constitute asserting the validity of their original agreement. But by going to see *Hannah Montana* without making any objection, he agreed to change the terms of their original agreement.

The same principle holds in arbitration. If the tribunal announces that it is going to follow a particular procedure, which is inconsistent with the procedure specified in the arbitration agreement or otherwise agreed between the parties, and no objection is made, then neither party will be able to rely on this deviation from their agreement if they want to challenge the award. By remaining silent and following the tribunal's instructions, the parties agreed to change their arbitration agreement so that it no longer includes the original procedure.

As a result, if a party wishes to insist on an agreed procedure being retained, they must object to any attempt to deviate from that procedure. The tribunal may decide to make the change anyway, but the objecting party has now made clear that they do not agree to the change, and may challenge the tribunal's award on the ground that the arbitration was not conducted in the way required by the arbitration agreement. Importantly, however, they must also maintain their objection. That is, it may not suffice to simply object when the change is initially proposed, and then never raise the point again. A reviewing court may decide that although the objection was initially made, it was then dropped. It is, therefore, essential to keep objecting on a regular basis, and to explicitly object every time the non-agreed procedure is used. In this way it is put beyond doubt for any reviewing court that there was never any agreement to change the originally agreed procedure.

Consistent with this willingness to allow parties to waive objections, most jurisdictions take a very restrained approach to reviewing deviations from agreed procedures, only allowing a challenge if the deviation had a significant effect on the arbitration. So, for example, if the parties agreed that all documents were to be kept in blue folders, but the tribunal instead insisted that green folders be used, this in itself is not going to be the foundation for a successful challenge, no matter how clearly a party objects to the change. Absent some very unusual facts, such a change simply has no substantive impact on the arbitration, and a reviewing court will not throw out an otherwise valid award because of such a minor deviation from the parties' agreement.[31]

A more realistic example may help to illustrate this point. Parties sometimes agree that an arbitral award must be issued within a certain period of time, usually either from the date the notice of arbitration was filed or from the conclusion of hearings. In doing so, they hope to ensure that the arbitration is completed quickly. The question that arises is whether an award issued after the expiry of this time limit should be regarded as invalid. A strict reading of the parties' arbitration agreement would result in a conclusion that the award should be annulled or refused recognition/enforcement, as it was not delivered in accordance with the parties' agreement. However, many courts will instead approach the issue by examining how important this restriction was to the parties. That is, was it so important that they would rather have no award at all, rather than a late one, or was it just a way of emphasising that they wanted the process to be quick? If the parties have specified in their agreement that the tribunal will lose the power to issue a decision upon the expiry of the time limit, then that is clear, and the award should be found to be invalid. However, absent such an express statement, it is questionable that parties will generally prefer to have spent months of their time and large amounts of money only to be told that they have to start the process again, simply because an award was delivered several days or a couple of weeks late. Therefore, absent specific facts supporting a conclusion that a time limit included in an arbitration agreement was meant by the parties to result in the invalidity of the award, or if such a conclusion is required by the *lex arbitri*,[32] most courts will treat a late award as still binding and enforceable, and are correct to do so.

One further point about agreements between the parties on arbitral procedure should also be acknowledged: arbitration agreements, to put it simply, are not always fair. Sometimes they have been negotiated between parties of unequal power, and strongly favour one party over the other. Sometimes they were originally fair, but the specific facts of the dispute that has now occurred mean that the agreed procedure will be unfair. As will be discussed in the following section, arbitrators have a fundamental obligation to ensure that the arbitral process is fair to all parties, and this obligation must be seen as overriding the obligation to respect the parties' agreements on arbitral procedure. The fact that a party has agreed to a certain procedure may be a relevant consideration in deciding whether using that procedure is fair, but it cannot be entirely dispositive, and when a procedural agreement between the parties will result in a fundamentally unfair arbitral process, arbitrators are obliged to refuse to use the agreed procedures, and if necessary to resign.

Up to this point, the focus has been on procedures agreed between the parties, but it is important to acknowledge that procedures can also be mandated by the *lex arbitri*. This is rarely an issue, as while it was not unusual a hundred years ago for arbitration laws to specify how arbitrations needed to be conducted, modern arbitration laws rarely do so. They may provide a fall-back mechanism designed to support arbitrations by ensuring that necessary rules are available even if the parties have not thought to agree on them: such rules most commonly specify a method for the appointment of arbitrators, simply because once a tribunal has been constituted, that tribunal can make decisions on procedural issues. However, these rules are non-mandatory: the parties are permitted to choose alternative rules should they prefer a different approach.

Nonetheless, it is also possible for arbitration laws to include what are known as "mandatory rules", specifying how a particular element of the arbitral procedure must be conducted. These rules are normally aimed at ensuring that all arbitrations seated in the jurisdiction adhere to that jurisdiction's core values of due process and fairness, and as a result parties are not allowed to deviate from them. That is, an arbitral award may be annulled by the courts of the seat if the arbitration did not adhere to the jurisdiction's mandatory rules, even though both parties agreed to the deviation from those rules.

In practice, however, successful challenge of an award on the ground that the arbitral procedure violated a mandatory rule of the seat is very rare, simply because mandatory procedural rules are now rare.[33] Instead, contemporary arbitration laws overwhelmingly confer a large amount of discretion upon the arbitral tribunal in its conduct of the proceedings, recognising that a tribunal is best placed to judge the impact of a procedure in the specific context of a case. As a result, in the absence of any party agreement on procedures to be used, arbitrators are generally free to conduct an arbitration in the way they deem most appropriate, as long as due process and the right to be heard are respected.

15. Challenges can be based on procedural aspects of the arbitration: "That wasn't fair"

The next ground for challenging an arbitration award focuses on the need to ensure that arbitrations operate fairly. If arbitration was truly a completely private dispute resolution procedure, with no public consequences, then it would matter significantly less whether an arbitration was fair. After all, an arbitral award would just be a tribunal's view on how the dispute should be resolved, and could be ignored if the process from which it came was unfair. As has been discussed already, however, a major consequence of the embrace of arbitration by governments is that arbitration awards are not only enforceable, but can be enforced with very little review as to their correctness. Yet, if people are to be legally bound by arbitral awards, and particularly if the mechanisms of public justice can be invoked to enforce arbitral awards, then it is essential that courts play some monitoring role over arbitration. Otherwise legal institutions designed to deliver justice would be co-opted to commit injustice.

This concern is reflected in Article 34(2)(a)(ii) of the Model Law and Article V(1)(b) of the New York Convention, both of which state, with respect to annulment and recognition/enforcement respectively, that a challenge to an arbitral award can be successful if a party "was not given proper notice of the appointment of an arbitrator or of the arbitral proceedings or was otherwise unable to present his case".[34]

The most important thing to note about this ground for challenge is that it is purely procedural. That is, it does not give a party the right to have an award annulled or refused recognition because the award is wrong on the facts or the law. Rather, it merely requires that all parties receive proper notice of the arbitration, so that they can prepare for it adequately, including with respect to the appointment of arbitrators, and that they then be given an opportunity to actually present their case. If both of these requirements are met, then this ground for challenge cannot be relied upon, no matter how wrong the arbitral award may clearly be.

There are two distinct elements to this ground for challenge that can basically be described as "knowledge" and "opportunity", but ultimately both elements reduce to the idea that if an arbitration award is to be enforceable through the courts, then all parties must have had an "opportunity" to present their case. They may have decided not to present their case, or they may have done so badly, but they need to at least have had the "opportunity" to present their case to the tribunal.

Challenging and enforcing arbitral awards 225

The first element, "knowledge", is fairly intuitive: if you're going to arbitrate against someone, you have let them know about it. If Rosina and Laith are in a dispute, Rosina can't simply announce to Laith "Actually, we had an arbitration last week. Sorry you didn't hear about it. But you lost, so now you have to pay me." Laith has clearly been deprived of the opportunity to present his case to the tribunal, because he didn't even know there was a tribunal.

This, however, is an easy case. Rosina made no effort to notify Laith that she was commencing arbitration against him. Things can get more complex when there is disagreement about whether a party was notified of the arbitration, or whether it was even possible to notify them. For example, what if Rosina sent Laith a notice of arbitration in Chinese, even though she knows Laith doesn't understand Chinese? What if the notice was in Chinese, but at the top it said, in English, "This is a notice of arbitration"? What if Rosina is unsure how to contact Laith because he has recently moved and didn't tell her where? Can she just send the notice of arbitration to his old address, even though she isn't sure he will receive it? Things can get even more complex in the corporate context. If Simply Sweet, a candy maker, wants to commence an arbitration against Offgrid Candy, a multinational candy store chain with stores in 52 States, can it have the notice of arbitration delivered to the manager of any one of those stores, or does it have to go to someone at corporate headquarters? The manager of each store is, after all, an employee of Offgrid Candy, and in a position of managerial responsibility – although it is also likely someone who has no idea what a "notice of arbitration" is, and may simply ignore the notice when it is received.

Understanding arbitration through case-law

Arbitration notice in a foreign language

Case details: *Ekran OAO v Magneco Metrel* [2017] EWHC 2208 (Comm)

Authority deciding the case: High Court (England and Wales)

Facts of the case: An arbitral award was rendered in Russia against an English defendant. The Russian claimant sought recognition and enforcement of the award in England. The defendant, however, attempted to resist, arguing that it was not given proper notice of the arbitration. More specifically, the defendant received the arbitration claim form and a number of documents annexed to it, all written in Russian. The documents came with a letter from the tribunal; the letter was itself written in Russian, but it did contain an English heading ("The International Commercial Arbitration Court at the Chamber of Commerce and Industry of the Russian Federation") and an e-mail address at the bottom, which included the word "arbitration" in English.

Decision: The Court decided to recognise and enforce the award. It held that the fact that the notice was not in English did not, in and of itself, affect its validity. Furthermore, the court noted that the tribunal's letter containing the word "arbitration" in English was just one page long, and the defendant could have easily arranged for its translation. Because of these factors, the Court concluded that, while more efforts could

> have been made to inform the defendant, sufficient notice had been given. The problem at hand, however, necessarily requires a case-by-case analysis, taking into account the specific modes and contents of the communication received by the defendant.

In some cases, how a notice of arbitration must be served will be specified in the contract in which the arbitration clause is contained. As a result, these questions will have relatively clear answers. However, if the contract does not specify how a notice of arbitration is to be served, and what information it must contain, then whether the other party was properly notified of the commencement of the arbitration, or of the appointment of an arbitrator, will need to be decided by the reviewing court. The specific approach taken by that court will depend on the law being applied, but fundamentally the court must decide whether the notice was provided in a way reasonably calculated to let the other party know that an arbitration was being commenced or that an arbitrator had been appointed.

Ultimately, as was said originally, the requirement that a party have "knowledge" of the commencement of an arbitration or of the appointment of an arbitrator is just a consequence of the fundamental requirement that each party must have an "opportunity" to present their case to the tribunal. The second element of this ground for challenge, then, focuses directly on this requirement for an "opportunity". In other words, it addresses those situations in which the complaining party knew about the arbitration, but the arbitration was conducted in a way that made it fundamentally unfair.

While fundamental fairness is, of course, a requirement of any legal process, and of any dispute resolution procedure, the need for procedural fairness has a particular importance in arbitration. Parties litigating in court, after all, will do so in accordance with rules of civil procedure developed over many years to produce a process that it is believed will be fair to everyone who appears in court. There may be individual cases in which unfairness does occur, and those cases can be appealed to a higher court, but in any properly functioning court system the civil procedure rules will provide at least a bare minimum fair process.

Arbitration, however, as has been emphasised many times in this book, is characterised by its procedural flexibility. One of arbitration's greatest appeals is precisely that it is not bound by a strict set of procedural rules, and so the specific procedures used in any arbitration can be designed to match the parties in dispute and the subject matter of the arbitration.

Yet that procedural flexibility, while providing enormous benefits, also creates substantial risks, as procedures might be adopted that deprive one of the parties of a fair opportunity to present its case. This might be a result of specific procedural decisions made by the tribunal, of poorly designed institutional rules, or even of rules agreed to by the parties in their arbitration agreement.

If, therefore, courts asked to review arbitration awards are to be able to assure themselves that all the parties involved have received a fair process, then they must be able to review the procedures used in the arbitration, and grant a challenge where those procedures were so fundamentally unfair that one of the parties was deprived of a fair opportunity to present its case. It would, for example, be clearly unfair to give one of the parties a deadline of three weeks to make its written submission, while providing no deadline at all to the other party. More subtly, it may be unfair to conduct the arbitral proceedings in English when one of the parties does not understand English, even if their lawyers do, unless they are permitted access to a translator throughout the proceedings.

Ultimately, the guarantors of the fairness of the arbitral process are the tribunal. The parties, after all, are trying to win, and while most parties will act honestly, they can nonetheless reasonably be expected to take any procedural advantage available to them to maximise their chances of doing so. Similarly, the parties' lawyers may be professionals, bound by ethical obligations, but their role is to win the case for their party, and to use the procedural flexibility of arbitration to help them do so. If the arbitration is being administered by an institution, then the institution will have an interest in ensuring the fairness of the arbitral process, but institutions rarely have detailed knowledge of the day-to-day developments in arbitrations they administer, and so they are poorly placed to ensure the fairness of an arbitration unless clear wrongs are occurring. The tribunal, then, is the only participant in the arbitral process that can reliably ensure the fairness of the proceedings.

One complication this creates is that the tribunal is ultimately employed by the parties. Yet, as touched on in the preceding Section, there may be cases in which the tribunal's obligation to ensure that the arbitral process is fair conflicts with the procedures the parties wish to adopt. The parties may, for example, have included in their arbitration agreement that a certain procedure would be used, which the tribunal believes will undermine the fairness of the arbitration. If the procedures agreed by the parties are manifestly unfair, then the arbitrators were ethically obligated not to accept appointment to the tribunal in the first place. However, sometimes procedures that initially seem reasonable become unfair because of the specific context in which they will operate. If this happens, a tribunal's overriding obligation must be to the fairness of the arbitral process, even if this means overriding an element of the autonomy of the parties.

In other words, the tribunal must say to the parties "I know you both agreed to this process, but our judgement is that it would be unfair in the context of this arbitration as it has developed, and so we will not use it." Ideally, the tribunal and the parties will come to an agreement as to a different procedure that would not raise the same concerns. However, if the parties are insistent that their agreed procedure be used, then they have the collective power to remove the tribunal and appoint arbitrators who will apply that procedure. Arbitrators, though, can never allow themselves to knowingly participate in an arbitration that does not meet minimum requirements of fairness simply because this is what the parties want. Party autonomy is central to arbitration, but the fundamental fairness of the arbitral process matters even more.

A further complication in this context is what standards a reviewing court should apply when deciding if an arbitration has been conducted fairly. "Fair", after all, is a very vague standard, and judgements of fairness can vary greatly from one culture to another. By way of example, in an arbitration between a Panamanian party and a Pakistani party seated in Canada, should a Canadian court asked to annul the award apply Canadian standards of procedural fairness, or those of one or both of the parties? What if the enforcement of the award is being resisted in Spain? Should the Spanish court apply Spanish standards of procedural fairness, Canadian standards, the standards of one or both of the parties, something else?

Neither the Model Law nor the New York Convention specifically addresses this question. This silence has led some commentators to argue that an "international" standard of procedural fairness should be applied, rather than the fairness standards of any particular jurisdiction.[35] There is certainly a clear rationale for this view, as it reflects the cross-border nature of international arbitration and avoids the risk that one party will have its conceptions of fairness applied at the expense of the other party. However, such an approach has a fundamental problem in that it assumes that there is such a thing as an "international" standard of procedural fairness.

Yet there is certainly no universally shared conception of legal procedural fairness that can be found in every legal system around the world. Indeed, this is reflected in two of the greatest motivations that parties have for the use of international commercial arbitration: the fact that foreign court procedures may be perceived as unfair or inadequate, and the difficulties that can be involved in enforcing court judgements in other States.

It might be argued that there are nonetheless certain things that are so fundamental to a fair legal process that they can be found to some degree in every legal system, even if the specific details of how they are implemented vary from one State to another (e.g. the right to contradict the other party's evidence; the right to make submissions to the tribunal). However, the details of implementation are, of course, precisely what arbitrators must decide upon and what parties feel are unfair. Insisting that awards should only be successfully challenged if they come from a procedure that does not even plausibly reflect one of these fundamental procedural values would produce a "lowest common denominator" form of review that is inconsistent with the goal of ensuring the fundamental fairness of arbitration.

It might also be argued that international commercial arbitration should be seen in the broader context of international adjudication, such as State – State arbitration and the International Court of Justice. There are, after all, procedures agreed in these contexts that could be argued to reflect an international consensus on fair dispute resolution procedures. Such an argument, however, ignores the fact that these procedures were developed in a context in which a small minority of States held an overwhelming power to dictate what constituted acceptable procedures, and that they were developed for a particular kind of dispute between particular kinds of parties. That the government of Cambodia, for example, is willing to resolve its disputes with other governments using certain procedures is no argument for imposing those procedures on parties from Cambodia who may have very different conceptions of what constitutes a fair dispute resolution process. There is, in short, no reason why international commercial arbitration should operate on the basis of the same standards as interstate dispute settlement.

Ultimately, arguments supporting the application of an "international" standard of procedural fairness are inconsistent with the fundamental principle that arbitration is a process for resolving specific disputes between particular parties. It approaches arbitration instead as an independent process with procedural values of its own, that parties must accept if they are to take advantage of its benefits. In essence, it attempts to impose a *procedural lex mercatoria* on parties that never agreed to adopt it.

This leaves, then, the question of what standard reviewing courts should apply when considering a challenge against an arbitration award on the ground of fundamental unfairness, whether as a request for annulment or opposition to recognition/enforcement. The best answer to this question acknowledges both that arbitration is a private dispute resolution process controlled by the parties, and that the legal structures underlying the review of arbitral awards by courts, whether international treaties or local arbitration laws, are based on this principle. The parties should, that is, be held to the standards of procedural fairness in the one jurisdiction that has a direct connection with their arbitration: the arbitral seat. As long as the arbitration procedure does not violate fundamental principles of procedural fairness accepted at the seat of the arbitration, then a reviewing court should not grant a challenge to the award on the ground of the procedures used. For the courts at the seat of arbitration, this means that an award should only be annulled on this basis if the arbitral procedure substantially departed from the core procedural values of that jurisdiction. For jurisdictions other than the seat of arbitration, where recognition/enforcement may be sought, this entails that courts should not impose their own conceptions of fairness, or those of any other jurisdiction or context (e.g. "international" standards) when deciding whether the award should be denied recognition/enforcement. To do so would be to contradict the notion of party autonomy enshrined in the very laws that grant the court the power to review arbitral awards.

This does not, of course, mean that parties should be required to adhere to the same procedures as used in the courts of the seat. This would again be inconsistent with party autonomy, as manifested in arbitration's procedural flexibility. Rather, when assessing whether a party received an "opportunity" to present its case, an extremely deferential approach should be adopted, a challenge only being granted when there is clear evidence of procedural flaws that had a significant impact on the fundamental fairness of the arbitration, as judged by the standards of the seat. Any lesser unfairness was a risk the parties chose to accept as a trade-off for the other benefits that arbitration offers.

16. An award can be challenged if the dispute is not arbitrable: "Yes, I agreed to arbitration, but the law doesn't let us arbitrate this sort of thing"

As was discussed in detail in Chapter 3, in every jurisdiction there are certain types of disputes that cannot be taken to arbitration. This is recognised in Article 34(2)(b)(i) of the Model Law, which allows an award to be annulled if "the subject-matter of the dispute is not capable of settlement by arbitration" in the seat, and in Article V(2)(a) of the New York Convention, which allows recognition/enforcement to be refused if "the subject-matter of the dispute is not capable of settlement by arbitration" in the jurisdiction in which recognition/enforcement is being sought.

The important point to remember in this respect is that it is in the nature of the doctrine of arbitrability that it cannot be displaced by agreement of the parties involved in the arbitration. That is, a limitation on the arbitrability of a particular type of dispute is an instance of the State saying "You cannot arbitrate this kind of thing, even if you both want to." This is reflected in the difference in text between the Model Law provision on annulment and the New York Convention provision on recognition and enforcement. In each case, the court being asked to review the award does so with respect to its own arbitration law: the law of the seat in the case of annulment, the law of the State in which recognition/enforcement is being sought in the case of recognition/enforcement.

To give an example, presume there was an arbitration seated in the Philippines. An award was delivered by the tribunal and Martine wants to enforce that award in Trinidad and Tobago. Amarah has discovered that the dispute may not have been arbitrable under the law of the Philippines, so she goes to a court in the Philippines to seek annulment of the award. That court will decide whether to annul the award by examining the law on arbitrability of the Philippines. Unfortunately for Amarah, the court decides that the dispute was arbitrable under Philippine law, and so rejects the application for annulment. However, when Martine attempts to enforce the award in Trinidad and Tobago, where Amarah has a very nice holiday home, Amarah decides to try again, and asks the court to refuse enforcement because the subject matter of the dispute was not arbitrable. In deciding whether to enforce the award, the court in Trinidad and Tobago will not look at the rules on arbitrability of the Philippines, but will instead decide if the dispute was arbitrable under the law of Trinidad and Tobago – even though the arbitration did not take place there.

Essentially, then, this ground for challenge of an award is a way of giving appropriate recognition to the views of local jurisdictions regarding the types of disputes that should be allowed to be arbitrated. Courts at the seat of the arbitration apply their own law, because the arbitration is happening in their jurisdiction, and States have a legitimate right to control acts performed within their borders (even, in the case of the seat of the arbitration, if it happens "virtually", rather than physically). On the other hand, a court asked to recognise or enforce an award is permitted to apply its own law to the question of arbitrability in acknowledgement that courts should not be obligated to use the powers of the State to enforce an award that could not legally have been delivered in that jurisdiction.

Ultimately, however, while this ground for challenging an award remains available, it is of decreasing importance simply because, as discussed in Chapter 3, limitations on arbitrability are becoming less common throughout the world.

17. In a small number of jurisdictions challenges can be based on errors of law by the arbitrators: "The arbitrators were wrong"

As a rule, it is not possible to challenge an arbitral award because it was wrong on either the law or the facts. This is an essential restriction on the reviewing power of courts, as the parties have agreed to resolve their dispute through arbitration, but if the decision of the arbitrators can be overturned simply because a court disagrees, the parties may as well have just gone to court in the first place. The viability of arbitration as a dispute resolution mechanism, then, depends on limited substantive review of awards by courts. For this reason, the Model Law does not allow for challenges on points of law. For the same reason, the New York Convention does not allow State courts to decline recognition or enforcement simply because they think that the arbitral award may be wrong on the merits. Nonetheless, there are jurisdictions in which it is possible to challenge an arbitral award on the ground that it includes an error in the application of the law.

In a small number of jurisdictions, courts will perform a *de novo* review of arbitral awards, essentially "correcting" what they see as mistaken decisions by arbitrators. Such a practice, however, seriously undermines the autonomy of arbitration and deprives the parties of their procedural right to have their dispute resolved by their chosen tribunal: the arbitrators.

A second approach is available in the United States of America, where the Federal Arbitration Act does not allow awards to be challenged on the basis of an error of law by the tribunal, no matter how clear the error may be. However, courts in some parts of the country allow awards to be challenged on the basis of the tribunal's "manifest disregard" of the applicable law. That is, an award can be annulled if the tribunal has looked at the law and said "I don't really like the conclusion the law makes me reach, so I'm just not going to apply the law". If the tribunal was simply wrong, not matter how clearly wrong, then no review is possible.[36]

Considerably more rarely, the applicable arbitration law may expressly grant courts the power to review the correctness of an arbitral award. This sort of review is most famously available under Section 69 of the Arbitration Act 1996 of England and Wales, which grants the right to appeal on a "point of law". However, it is worth emphasising the limitations placed on this possibility of review under English law, as the existence of these limitations is often not well understood. Firstly, parties can waive their right to appeal on the basis of mistake of law in their arbitration agreement, including by agreeing to arbitrate under an institution whose rules include a waiver of any right to appeal awards.[37] Secondly, even if they have not waived this right, an appeal can only be made with the consent of all the parties to the arbitration or with leave of the court. In turn, leave of the court is granted only in very restricted situations. The mistake of law must be a mistake regarding the law of England and Wales for a court in England and Wales, or the law of Northern Ireland for a court in Northern Ireland. In addition, under Section 69(2) of the Act, the court must find that "the determination of the question will substantially affect the rights of one or more of the parties (. . .), that the question is one which the tribunal was asked to determine", that either "the decision of the tribunal on the question is obviously wrong, or (. . .) the question is one of general public importance and the decision of the tribunal is at least open to serious doubt", and finally, that "despite the agreement of the parties to resolve the matter by arbitration, it is just and proper in all the circumstances for the court to determine the question." Consequently, while it is formally possible to appeal questions of law under the English Arbitration Act 1996, successful appeals are rare.

Nonetheless, many English arbitration practitioners regard Section 69 as a favourable feature of English arbitration law considering the restrictions it includes,[38] and given the very supportive approach of English courts towards arbitration there are good arguments that it has indeed been applied in a way that is beneficial to English arbitration. It is, though, less clear that such an express legislative permission to review arbitral awards would be desirable in less developed arbitral jurisdictions, particularly in the hands of courts that are already more willing than they should be to substantively review the correctness of awards.

18. *Awards can be challenged on the ground of public policy: "This award is fundamentally unacceptable"*

Finally, there is what might be called the "nuclear option" of challenges to an arbitral award, in that it involves courts simply saying "No, this is not okay". Under Article 34(2)(b)(ii) of the Model Law, an award can be annulled if it is "in conflict with the public policy" of the seat of the arbitration. In turn, under Article V(2)(b) of the New York Convention, an award can be denied recognition/enforcement if "recognition or enforcement of the award would

232   *Challenging and enforcing arbitral awards*

be contrary to the public policy" of the jurisdiction where it is being sought. In essence, these provisions permit a court to grant a challenge to an award even when the award has not breached any of the grounds for challenge already discussed, but it is in some way irreconcilable with core values of that jurisdiction. While neither the Model Law nor the New York Convention provides any indication of what the term "public policy" means, there are two broad categories that can be identified: "procedural" and "substantive" public policy.

Procedural public policy refers to cases in which the arbitral procedure that resulted in the award somehow violates fundamental norms of procedure of the legal system of the State in which the challenge is being brought. Importantly, it is not enough that the procedure used in the arbitration differs from the procedure used in that jurisdiction's courts; flexibility of procedure is, after all, essential to arbitration. What is required is that the deviation relates to something that is viewed in that jurisdiction as an essential feature of legal procedural fairness. In France, for example, courts have held that an arbitral award can be denied recognition and enforcement if it addresses the same subject matter as another binding decision, on the ground that the matter addressed in the award is *res judicata*.[39]

What qualifies as procedural public policy will, of course, vary from one jurisdiction to the next. Indeed, the entire point of allowing courts to base the successful challenge of an award on public policy is that the court is able to protect its own jurisdiction's fundamental values. The important thing to note, then, is simply that when considering a challenge on the basis of procedural public policy, the reviewing court does not consider the merits of the tribunal's decision. It only examines the way that the arbitral proceedings were conducted.[40]

Substantive public policy, on the other hand, is focused directly on the subject matter of the dispute or on the contents of the award. It refers to cases in which either the arbitration involved an issue that the jurisdiction of the reviewing court believes should not be decided by arbitration, or the award itself is somehow fundamentally incompatible with core values of the jurisdiction.

Take the example of a contract requiring one of the parties to commit a crime. Say Serena and Stacey enter into an agreement for Serena to manufacture illegal drugs and Stacey to smuggle them into the neighbouring State. If they get into a dispute they obviously cannot take one another to court, since what they are doing is illegal. So they agree to take any disputes to arbitration. Assuming they can convince an arbitral tribunal to ignore the illegal nature of the contract and issue an award, that award will almost certainly be held by any reviewing court to be invalid on the grounds of public policy. Any other conclusion would allow criminals to avoid the restrictions of the law simply by resorting to arbitration.

Alternatively, there might be a standard commercial dispute involving the manufacture of medicines, which in itself raises no questions of public policy. However, the award delivered by the tribunal requires one party to take actions that would create a substantial risk to public health. In this case, a court may find that while the subject matter of the arbitration was arbitrable, the award as written violates public policy.

Public policy, whether substantive or procedural, is unavoidably a vague concept. For this reason it was always a concern that the inclusion of public policy as a ground for challenge in the New York Convention and then the Model Law would undermine the goals of both documents. That is, that courts would simply invoke public policy any time they didn't like an award but couldn't find a clear reason to grant a challenge against it, thereby undermining the restrictions that both documents put on the possibility of court review of arbitral awards.

In practice, however, public policy has been relatively unproblematic in most jurisdictions, and courts have embraced the idea that the term "public policy" is being used in legal instruments whose goal is to allow only a very limited review of arbitral awards, and that therefore the term "public policy" in those documents should be interpreted narrowly. Indeed, some commentators and courts have argued in the context of the New York Convention that since the Convention aims at facilitating the cross-border enforcement of arbitral awards, the public policy ground of challenge in Article V(2)(b) should be seen as referring to some form of "international public policy", rather than to the domestic public policy of the jurisdiction in which enforcement is being sought.[41] The French Code of Civil Procedure, for example, specifies that an arbitral award can be annulled or refused recognition/enforcement on the grounds of public policy only if it is contrary to "international" public policy.[42]

The difficulty of attempting to identify an international procedural public policy has already been discussed in Section 15 of this chapter, and there is little question that the same considerations apply to any argument that there exists anything solid that can be reliably said to constitute international substantive public policy. Nonetheless, jurisdictions are certainly entitled to adopt such a position as a reflection of their own domestic public policy (i.e. it is their domestic public policy that only international public policy should be applied).

Both the New York Convention and the Model Law, however, clearly refer to the domestic public policy of the jurisdiction in which annulment or recognition/enforcement are being sought. There is, therefore, no justification for interpreting either document as requiring that an "international" approach to public policy be adopted, and domestic public policy ignored.

19. Annulment and recognition/enforcement can interact in important ways

One of the themes of this chapter is that annulment and recognition/enforcement are ultimately best understood as different facets of the same fundamental process: challenge to an arbitral award. Nonetheless, despite this connection, they nonetheless remain different procedures, and not only because one (annulment) involves the courts of the seat while the other (recognition/enforcement) often involves courts elsewhere in the world. They are, in fact, qualitatively different in their intended legal effects. That is, a decision by a court of the seat to annul an award is a statement that the award should be regarded as having no legal existence, and consequently that as far as the law of the seat is concerned, no valid and binding arbitral award has been delivered. A refusal of recognition/enforcement, on the other hand, does not purport to affect the legal existence of the award, but merely constitutes a statement by the jurisdiction in question that although the award might be valid somewhere else, it is not going to be allowed to produce effects in their legal system.

A useful analogy for this contrast would be the difference between Iqra, a citizen of New Zealand, being told by the New Zealand government that as far as it is concerned she does not exist, and Iqra being told by the Italian government that she is not allowed to emigrate to Italy. The latter might be disappointing and inconvenient, but it does not have the fundamental consequences of the former.

Because, then, of the difference between these two types of challenge to arbitration awards, questions unavoidably arise regarding how they interact. It might be expected that annulment would be dispositive. That is, that if an arbitral award has been annulled at the seat of the arbitration, then it cannot exist to be enforced anywhere else, since it does not exist at the seat. After all, if you have £5,000.00 you plan to deposit in the bank, but it gets stolen the night before you are going to the bank, you can't just turn up at the bank and ask them to accept your deposit of £5,000.00 anyway: you don't have the money, so you can't deposit it. Similarly, it might reasonably be expected that if you don't have an arbitration award that is valid at the seat of the arbitration, you can't have one recognised or enforced anywhere else. The reality of arbitration, however, is more complex than that.

As has already been discussed, the purpose of the New York Convention is to facilitate the recognition and enforcement of arbitral awards. It has a "pro-enforcement bias". As a result, while Article (V)(1)(e) of the Convention allows that recognition/enforcement of an award "may" be denied if "The award has not yet become binding on the parties, or has been set aside or suspended by a competent authority of the country in which, or under the law of which, that award was made", this is, as always, permissive. That is, courts are permitted by the Convention to refuse recognition/enforcement of an award that has been annulled at the seat of arbitration, but they don't have to. They can decide to recognise or enforce the award anyway.

This is an important way in which it is true that arbitral awards are detached from the seat of the arbitration. The fact that the legal system of the seat says that an arbitral award does not exist, does not mean that it cannot be enforced elsewhere in the world.

Importantly, however, the contrary is also true. If arbitral awards should be understood as completely detached from the seat of the arbitration, then Article V(1)(e) would not be in the Convention at all. There is, after all, no provision in the Convention that allows a court to refuse recognition/enforcement of an award on the ground that it has already been refused recognition/enforcement in another State. Only the seat gets this priority. Only the seat's view of the validity of an arbitral award can serve as a justification for refusing recognition/enforcement.

The difficulty, then, is not in determining whether the annulment of an award is relevant to a decision by the courts of another jurisdiction whether or not that award should be recognised/enforced. The New York Convention makes clear that it is relevant. However, the Convention also makes clear that it is not dispositive. The difficult question, then, is how the annulment of an award should be understood as relevant to its recognition/enforcement. Article V(1)(e) lays out three different scenarios in which recognition and enforcement may be denied, and it is worth looking at each of them closely.

In the first scenario, an award has been delivered by the tribunal but "has not yet become binding on the parties". The word "binding" is key here, as it was adopted as a deliberate alteration from the use of "final" in the 1927 Geneva Convention on the Execution of Foreign Arbitral Awards ("Geneva Convention"). Under Article 1(d) of the Geneva Convention, a court was not obligated to enforce an award unless the party requesting enforcement could show, among other things, that "the award has become final in the country in which it has been made". As explained above, this led to the problem of *double exequatur*, which posed a significant obstacle to the cross-border enforcement of arbitral awards.

One of the primary goals of the New York Convention was to eliminate *double exequatur*, and as a result the Convention deliberately only requires that an award be "binding" to give rise to an obligation of enforcement, not that it be "final". The Convention itself does not clarify what the term "binding" means, and there was no agreement on this point amongst the Convention's drafters. As a result, it has been left up to enforcing courts to decide for themselves what "binding" means.

Some courts have argued that whether an award is "binding" is determined by the law of the seat, while others have argued that an "autonomous" approach should be applied, generally focusing on whether it remains possible for the substance of the award to be reviewed.[43] Ultimately, however, there is no reason to see these two approaches as inconsistent with one another, as whether or not the substance of an award can be reviewed is in part determined by the law of the seat and in part by the arbitration agreement between the parties.

The parties may, for example, have agreed to an arbitration appellate mechanism, under which either party is entitled to appeal the award to a second arbitration tribunal. Such mechanisms are rare, but are sometimes used, and when such an appeal remains available the first tribunal's award is clearly not yet "binding" on the parties, as the agreed arbitral process (i.e. including the appellate procedure) has not yet been completed.

Alternatively, the law of the seat may provide limited grounds for appeal of the substance of an award. For example, as already discussed, under Section 69 of the English Arbitration Act 1996, it is possible, under limited circumstances and for a limited period of time, for an award to be appealed to a court for review of a question of law. Importantly, however, a court evaluating an appeal under Section 69 is expected to either "confirm the award", "vary the award", or "remit the award to the tribunal, in whole or in part, for reconsideration in the light of the court's determination". It may also "set aside the award in whole or in part", but only where the court "is satisfied that it would be inappropriate to remit the matters in question to the tribunal for reconsideration". The Section 69 process, that is, is best understood not as a standard process for requesting annulment of an award, as annulment is actively discouraged by the terms of Section 69, but rather as an integral part of the arbitral process itself under English law, broadly equivalent to the ability of courts in some jurisdictions to refer specific questions of law to a higher court.[44] When court involvement in review of arbitral awards is structured in this fashion, arbitral awards are best understood as not yet being "binding" on the parties until this possibility of review has ended, on the same rationale as applies with respect to use of an appellate arbitral tribunal: the parties have agreed to arbitrate under a *lex arbitri* that incorporates a level of appellate review, and so until that possibility of review has ended, the parties' agreed arbitral procedure has not yet completed.

Importantly, however, what is also clear is that the mere possibility of future annulment does not itself prevent an award being "binding" on the parties. That is, that recognition and enforcement is possible even though annulment remains possible at the seat of the arbitration.[45] What matters, then, is how court review is approached under the law of the seat. If it is integrated into the arbitral process, as under the English Arbitration Act 1996, then no "binding" award should be seen to exist to be enforced under the New York Convention until this element of the arbitral process has concluded. On the other hand, if review of the legal correctness of the award is undertaken as part of a post-arbitration annulment procedure, then the arbitral process agreed by the parties concluded with the delivery of the award. As a result, a "binding" award exists, and can be enforced under the New York Convention, despite the possibility of substantive review of the correctness of the award during an annulment process.

In the second scenario contemplated by Article V(1)(e), the award has been delivered by the tribunal and was binding, but its binding nature has been temporarily suspended at the seat of arbitration. For instance, suspension may be possible under the *lex arbitri* once annulment proceedings have been commenced, until the court issues its decision.[46] In terms of the present discussion, this scenario is ultimately the same as the first scenario, as the award is not currently binding on the parties.

In the third scenario, the award has actually been annulled at the seat of the arbitration. It is not just that annulment proceedings are possible or currently in process. An application to annul the award was made to the courts of the seat, and that application was granted. As a result, the award no longer has legal existence under the law of the seat.

As already stated, it may initially seem that once an award no longer exists, it cannot be enforced. However, such an absolute position is just not consistent with the fact that the New York Convention expressly allows annulled awards to be enforced, should the courts of any jurisdiction choose to enforce them. Some courts, most notably in France, have adopted the opposite absolute position, arguing that an international arbitration award is not actually controlled by the seat of the arbitration, and so its annulment at the seat is not an important consideration when deciding whether or not an award should be enforced. However, as argued above, this position is not consistent with the privileged status given to the annulment of an award by the courts of the seat, as compared to a decision by another jurisdiction to deny recognition/enforcement. Finally, some courts have adopted an approach that attempts to moderate these two positions, acknowledging that there are times that an annulled arbitral award should properly be recognised and enforced, but balancing that with a desire to give recognition to the decision by the courts of the State to annul the award.

Understanding arbitration through case-law

Recognition and enforcement of awards that have been annulled at the seat of arbitration: different national approaches

Case details: *Société Hilmarton Ltd v Société Omnium de traitement et de valorisation (OTV)*, 23 March 1994

Authority deciding the case: French Court of Cassation

Facts of the case: A French company and an English company entered into a contract concerning an intermediation aimed to obtain a contract in Algeria. A dispute arose between the parties for the payment of the commission fee. An arbitral tribunal seated in Switzerland held that no commission fee was owed, as the main contract was governed by Algerian law, which prohibits this type of fee. The English company initiated annulment proceedings in Switzerland. The French company, at the same time, sought recognition of the award in France. On 17 November 1989, the competent Swiss first instance court annulled the award. On 27 February 1990, the competent French first instance court recognised the award. On 17 April 1990, the Swiss Supreme Court confirmed the decision of the lower court to annul the award. At that point, the French Court of Cassation was asked to decline the recognition of the award, pursuant to Article V(1)(e) of the New York Convention.

Decision: The Court of Cassation recognised the award, despite the fact that it had been finally annulled in Switzerland. The Court held that, since the arbitral award was international, it was not "integrated into the Swiss legal order". As such, it continued to exist, even if it had been annulled in Switzerland. According to the French approach, hence, international arbitral awards are "delocalised", and their existence cannot be determined by any national court, including the courts at the seat of arbitration. The same approach was later confirmed in *Société PT Putrabali Adyamulia v Société Rena Holding et Société Moguntia Est Epices*, French Court of Cassation, 29 June 2007.

Case details: *Nikolay Viktorovich Maximov v Open Joint Stock Company "Novolipetsky Metallurgichesky Kombinat"*, 24 November 2017

Authority deciding the case: Hoge Raad (Court of Cassation of the Netherlands)

Facts of the case: The parties entered into a sales and purchase agreement containing an arbitration clause. A dispute arose, and an arbitral tribunal operating under the auspices of the International Commercial Arbitration Court of the Chamber of Commerce and Industry of the Russian Federation issued an award in favour of the claimant. The Russian Courts, however, annulled the award, on the ground that, according to the reviewing Courts, two of the arbitrators had failed to disclose some relevant circumstances, the subject-matter was not arbitrable, and the award was against public policy. The Claimant, nonetheless, sought recognition and enforcement of the annulled award in the Netherlands.

Decision: The Dutch Court of Cassation held that, in principle, an award can be recognised and enforced in the Netherlands even if it has been annulled at the seat of arbitration. From this point of view, the Dutch approach may at first sight seem similar to the French one, outlined above. However, the Dutch Court specified that the enforcement of an annulled award is only possible under exceptional circumstances, and in particular if the award has been annulled on grounds that do not correspond to the ones set out in the New York Convention and are not consistent with international standards. Furthermore, according to the Court, an annulled award may be recognised and enforced if the foreign annulment proceedings did not provide due process. In the case at hand, however, the Court concluded that the requirements in question were not met, and thus refused to recognise and enforce the award. The Dutch approach, therefore, is significantly more restrictive than the French one, despite in principle admit the possibility of recognising and enforcing an annulled award.

238 Challenging and enforcing arbitral awards

Ultimately, the Convention reflects a balance between two principles: (1) that there is a special and unique connection between an arbitration and its seat, and (2) that an arbitration award is nonetheless not an award issued by the legal institutions of the seat. The proper approach to the interaction of annulment and enforcement, therefore, must reflect this same balance, rather than adopting entirely one or the other extreme position. It must, therefore, involve a deference to annulment decisions of the courts of the seat, but also a willingness to enforce annulled arbitral awards in some circumstances.

How that balance should be struck, however, is one of the most contentious topics in arbitration, and remains a subject of vigorous ongoing dispute between arbitration specialists. Indeed, even the authors of this book have widely divergent views on this issue. One of us,[47] believes that this question is best seen as requiring consideration of what is known in US law as "adjudicative comity", or the deference owed by a court to foreign tribunals.[48] The New York Convention gives priority to the courts of the seat in determining the validity of an arbitral award. In addition, international arbitration ultimately takes place in a cross-jurisdictional context, and it is inconsistent with that foundation for courts to refuse to respect annulment decisions delivered in other jurisdictions simply because they would have reached a different decision themselves. Approaching the question of enforcement of annulled awards through a comity-based analysis arguably best reflects both of these ideas.

By way of example, if the jurisdiction in which the reviewing court is located has a legitimate connection with the arbitration, whether through the identity of one of the parties or the transaction underlying the dispute, and the ground for annulment relied upon by the court is not one recognised in the enforcing court's jurisdiction, a court does not breach adjudicative comity by refusing to respect an annulment decision and enforcing an annulled award. In such a case, the reviewing court has a legitimate ground for relying upon its domestic standards in deciding whether the annulment decision should be respected. If, however, the reviewing court's jurisdiction has no substantive connection with the arbitration (but is, for example, merely the location of assets of one of the parties), or the ground for annulment is recognised in the reviewing court's jurisdiction but the reviewing court simply disagrees with the decision the annulment court reached, then a decision to enforce the annulled award fails to respect adjudicative comity, as it constitutes the reviewing court either involving itself in a dispute with which it has far less connection than the annulment court, or simply substituting its own judgment for that of the annulment court. Of course, any such comity-based approach to Article V(1)(e) is supplementary to, rather than a replacement of, a public policy-based refusal to enforce an annulled award under Article V(2)(b), even when the violation of public policy involves the annulment decision and how it was reached.

On the other hand, the other author of this book[49] rejects this analysis, arguing that it inappropriately places greater weight on nationality than it does on the location of the assets against which the arbitration award will be enforced. As a result, it fails to give adequate recognition to the legitimate interest of the State in which enforcement is being sought in property that falls under its legal jurisdiction.

As is perhaps well indicated by the fact that two people who can co-author an entire book could not agree on a mutually acceptable position on this issue, the question of how annulled awards should be treated when presented for enforcement in another jurisdiction is a long way from being resolved. Ultimately, however, the best resolution to this problem will be one that reflects the fundamental underlying principle of the Convention that international commercial arbitration is best supported by jurisdictions working together, rather than each insisting that their own conception of arbitration is the only one worth respecting.

Finally, it is necessary to acknowledge a procedural issue concerning the interaction between annulment proceedings at the seat of an arbitration and recognition and enforcement proceedings elsewhere. In principle, the New York Convention aims at ensuring that arbitral awards are enforced swiftly. There is, however, one significant exception: pursuant to Article VI, if an application for the annulment or suspension of an award has been made at the seat of arbitration, the court before which recognition/enforcement is being sought is expressly permitted by the Convention to adjourn its decision.

The rationale behind this rule is that if the status of the award is still to a certain extent unclear at the seat of arbitration, a court requested to recognise/enforce that award may want to wait and see if the award will be annulled before delivering its own decision. Importantly, however, this is not an obligation: the court may adjourn its proceedings if it "considers it proper", but it can also continue them notwithstanding the fact that annulment proceedings are still pending at the seat of arbitration, even to the point of granting enforcement of an award that may yet be annulled. Equally importantly, the New York Convention provides no direction to courts regarding the standards that must be applied when deciding if proceedings should be adjourned. A court may, for example, decide not to adjourn the proceedings if it considers that the request for annulment or suspension of the award is frivolous. Alternatively, it may decide that the award should be recognised and enforced whether it is ultimately annulled or not, and so there is no need to adjourn. In brief, the adjournment of recognition and enforcement proceedings is an option available to courts, but the New York Convention leaves the courts of each contracting State free to decide the standards to be used in making this decision.

It should be acknowledged, though, that adjourning recognition and enforcement proceedings can cause serious complications. Firstly, a court that decides to adjourn recognition and enforcement proceedings will then have to wait for a decision rendered by the courts at the seat: depending on the efficiency of the seat's judicial system, this may result in delay of several years before the arbitral award can be enforced. For this reason alone, the decision to adjourn proceedings is a serious one that must be taken after careful consideration, rather than adopted as a matter of policy.

Furthermore, it is possible that while the recognition and enforcement proceedings are suspended, the party resisting enforcement will dispose of the assets against which it was hoped that the award would be enforced. In such a case, the adjournment will have facilitated the avoidance of the effects of an arbitral award that may ultimately be held to be valid by the courts of the seat. Article VI of the New York Convention, however, does address this problem, providing that, on the application of the party requesting enforcement of the award, the court before which recognition/enforcement are being sought may order the party resisting recognition/enforcement to give suitable security as a condition of the adjournment being granted. In other words, the court may decide that the proceedings will only be adjourned if the party resisting recognition/enforcement provides an economic guarantee sufficient to ensure that the award can be satisfied if proceedings are resumed, such as by depositing a sum of money that the other party will be able to seize if the award is eventually enforced.

20. There are alternatives to challenging an award in court

While this Chapter has focused on the possibility of challenging an award in court, there are other alternatives that should be acknowledged, and that might be more suitable in certain circumstances.

Firstly, sometimes the problem is merely that the award includes a formal flaw that needs to be corrected. By way of example, the award may simply misspell the name of one of the parties. Small errors of this nature may seem insignificant and not worth worrying about, but if there is any risk that the award may subsequently be challenged, there is little reason to allow errors to remain that might subsequently be capitalised on by the challenging party.

As discussed in Chapter 6, once a tribunal delivers its final award, it usually becomes *functus officio*, meaning that its role is completed and so it no longer has any authority over the parties. Arbitration rules and laws, however, often expressly incorporate a procedure allowing a tribunal to make minor corrections to an award after it has been issued. For example, under Article 33 of the Model Law, an arbitral tribunal may make corrections to an award within 30 days of the receipt of the award by the parties (or any other time period agreed by the parties). However, the requested changes may only involve "errors in computation, any clerical or typographical errors or any errors of similar nature", and no substantive changes may be made. Similar provisions are, for example, included in the 2017 ICC Rules of Arbitration,[50] the JAMS International Arbitration Rules,[51] and the UNCITRAL Arbitration Rules,[52] among many others.

There will rarely be any legitimate ground for objecting to such a correction being made, precisely because of the trivial nature of the change. Potentially more complex is the parallel provision that is standardly included in arbitration rules and laws, concerning the ability of parties to request an "interpretation". Under these provisions, the tribunal may be asked not just to correct a minor formal error, but to issue an "interpretation" that explains more clearly a section of the award.[53]

In itself it is clearly desirable for parties to be able to ask the tribunal to clarify unclear points in the award. After all, the parties have spent a significant amount of time and money on the arbitration, and will be understandably unhappy if they receive an award that doesn't clearly resolve one or more of the issues the tribunal was asked to resolve.

The difficulty involved, however, is that the other party may view the request for an interpretation as an attempt to have the tribunal re-decide something that has already been decided. In other words, there is a risk that the "interpretation" delivered by the tribunal will not actually involve the tribunal clarifying what it originally meant in the award, but will instead reflect the tribunal rethinking the issue involved and making a substantive change to the award, masked as an interpretation of the original decision. This concern is reflected in the restriction in the Model Law that an interpretation may only be requested "if so agreed by the parties". In addition, the Model Law, as well as many arbitration rules, gives the tribunal significant discretion in deciding whether an interpretation should be issued.[54]

A second alternative to challenging an award in court addresses a more problematic situation, briefly discussed in Section 13 of this Chapter, namely when a tribunal has delivered an award that does not resolve all the issues submitted to it, i.e. it acts *infra petita*. As already mentioned, in some jurisdictions courts may find that an award issued *infra petita* should be annulled or denied recognition/enforcement.

It should be emphasised that simply because it initially appears that an award does not address all the issues submitted to the tribunal, does not mean that the tribunal has not actually addressed them. Ideally, of course, an award will deal with all the issues submitted to the tribunal clearly and systematically, but if an award includes a discussion resolving one issue that also implicitly resolves a second issue, the tribunal may simply omit discussion of the second issue from the award, as it is now unnecessary. This is not ideal award-writing, and should be avoided, but it is not the tribunal acting *infra petita*, and poor award writing is not a justification for annulling an award or denying it recognition or enforcement.

However, if the award does indeed fail to address some of the issues submitted to the tribunal, some arbitration laws and rules provide a means for the tribunal to issue a supplementary award, addressing only those issues omitted from the initial award. Article 33(3) of the Model Law, for example, expressly provides that "a party, with notice to the other party, may request, within thirty days of receipt of the award, the arbitral tribunal to make an additional award as to claims presented in the arbitral proceedings but omitted from the award", the supplementary award being made within 60 days.[55] Where a mechanism of this type is available, it ensures that the parties receive from the tribunal the service for which they have paid, and also eliminates the risk of an otherwise valid award being successfully challenged (where *infra petita* is available as a ground for challenge).

Finally, if the arbitration agreement allows, it is possible for an award to be appealed to a second arbitration tribunal, rather than to a court. This is most commonly available if the parties have agreed to arbitrate under rules that expressly incorporate an appellate tribunal, but it is also possible for an arbitration agreement itself to expressly include such a provision. While appellate procedures are available from leading US arbitration institutions,[56] they are less common in other jurisdictions.[57]

The benefits of using an appellate tribunal, rather than a court, are significant. The possibility of appeal removes one of the central concerns about arbitration, namely that the parties will receive a badly flawed award that they cannot challenge under the limited review available through courts. However, an appellate tribunal is still an arbitration tribunal, which means that, subject to any rules they have agreed to use, the parties have the ability to specify the qualifications of individuals who will appear on the tribunal, the level of review that the tribunal will exercise, the procedures the tribunal will use, the length of time that can be taken, and so on.

An appellate tribunal, then, can serve as an important backstop to the arbitral process, increasing the reliability of the process while minimising court intervention and the unpredictability and delays that can bring. It is another element of the procedural flexibility that makes arbitration, warts and all, such an ideal mechanism for resolving international commercial disputes.

Notes

1 Of course, legal practice is never completely uniform, and there have been cases in which national courts have allowed annulment applications to be made for arbitrations seated in other jurisdictions. This is, however, fundamentally inconsistent with the legal structures that have been developed to ensure the simultaneous fairness and independence of arbitration. Unsurprisingly, such

242 *Challenging and enforcing arbitral awards*

decisions have been heavily criticised by the overwhelming majority of arbitration practitioners and commentators.

2 The precise approach varies from one jurisdiction to another, and may involve the court issuing its own judgment that mirrors the terms of the award, or issuing a decision that confers enforceability on the award itself.

3 Under Article 34(3) of the Model Law, for example, annulment of an arbitral award must be made within three months of the date on which the party seeking annulment received the award. Similar timeframes are set out in a number of arbitration statutes, e.g. the French Code of Civil Procedure requires annulment applications to be made within one month of the notification of the award; in the United States of America, the FAA as well as the majority of state statutes set a time-limit of 90 days from the delivery of the award. With respect to enforcement, English law imposes a limit of six years, while the US Federal Arbitration Act imposes a limit of three years for awards covered by the New York Convention.

4 The European Court of Human Rights (ECtHR) has examined the compatibility of Article 192 PILA with the European Convention of Human Rights (ECHR), with particular reference to the right of access to a court. The ECtHR concluded that the Swiss statute is compatible with the ECHR, since the limitation of the right of access to a court operates on a voluntary basis and pursues the legitimate objectives of enhancing the attractiveness of Switzerland as a seat of arbitration and reducing the caseload of State courts. See *Tabbane v Switzerland* (application no. 41069/12).

5 Article 1520 Code of Civil Procedure. For a useful review of approaches taken to this issue see www.ibanet.org/Document/Default.aspx?DocumentUid=72111D60-6585-412C-B239-189ABF22108F, page 17.

6 In *West Tankers v Allianz SpA* [2011] EWHC 829 (Comm); [2012] EWCA 27, English Courts held that a negative declaratory award (simply stating that one of the parties was not liable vis-à-vis the other) could be converted into a judgment pursuant to Section 66 of the English Arbitration Act 1996. The use of Section 66, in this context, clearly did not serve the purpose of enabling West Tankers to commence enforcement proceedings, but rather operated as a mechanism to recognise the award and ensure that it could produce *res judicata* effects.

7 Article 35 of the UNCITRAL Model Law.

8 See Articles 1487–1488 of the French Code of Civil Procedure for domestic awards, and Articles 1514–1517 for foreign and international awards.

9 Some commentators have also relied upon this notion of "detachment" of arbitration in arguing for the "delocalisation" of international commercial arbitration. There is, however, nothing in the kind of "detachment" being discussed here that provides support for the broader claims of proponents of the delocalisation of international commercial arbitration. For a discussion of delocalisation theories see Emmanuel Gaillard, *Legal Theory of International Arbitration* (Martinus Nijhoff 2010).

10 Article III of the New York Convention.

11 Ibid.

12 Jan Paulsson, "May or Must Under the New York Convention: An Exercise in Syntax and Linguistics" (1998) 14(2) *Arbitration International* 227.

13 See the discussion in Chapter 3.

14 See Article 1507 of the French Code of Civil Procedure, with reference to international arbitration agreements.

15 There are exceptions to this general rule: section 69 of the English Arbitration Act, for instance, allows English courts to annul an award that is wrong on a point of law. However, this power is only exceptionally used and, as will be discussed below, the parties are free to exclude the applicability of this section in their agreement.

16 Article 36 of the UNCITRAL Model Law, governing the recognition and enforcement of both domestic and foreign arbitral awards, is a largely verbatim adoption of Article V of the New York

Convention. Therefore, in the context of this Chapter, the observations concerning Article V of the New York Convention largely apply to Article 36 of the Model Law as well.

17 This is the case under US law if the parties have given the tribunal the power to decide its own jurisdiction. See Jack M. Graves and Yelena Davydan, "Competence-Competence and Separability American Style" in Stefan Kröll, Louks Mistelis, Viscasillas Perales and V Rogers, *International Arbitration and International Commercial Law: Synergy, Convergence and Evolution – Liber Amicorum Eric Bergstein* (Kluwer 2011) 157.

18 This is the case in France and arguably most prominent arbitration jurisdictions. A useful discussion of this issue can be found in John J. Barceló III, "Kompetenz-Kompetenz and Its Negative Effect – A Comparative View", available at https://papers.ssrn.com/sol3/papers.cfm?abstract_id=3035485.

19 Article V(1)(a) of the New York Convention; Articles 34(2)(a)(i) and 36 36(1)(a)(i) of the UNCITRAL Model Law.

20 Ibid.

21 See Article V(1)(c) of the New York Convention and Articles 34(2)(a)(iii) and 36(1)(a)(iii) of the Model Law. The New York Convention says "difference", not "dispute", but this makes no substantive difference to the meaning of the text.

22 Both the Model Law and the New York Convention expressly state that "if the decisions on matters submitted to arbitration can be separated from those not so submitted, only that part of the award which contains decisions on matters not submitted to arbitration" may be successfully appealed. The Model Law adds the word "only", which was not present in the New York Convention, and makes no substantive difference – another indication that at least one person involved in the drafting of the Model Law was very passionate about proper word usage.

23 The highest court in the English legal system, now called the Supreme Court.

24 But see *Michael Wilson & Partners Limited v John Forster Emmott* [2018] EWCA Civ 51, apparently limiting the strength of the Fiona Trust presumption. For an excellent discussion of this case, see Harry Smith, "An Erosion of the Fiona Trust "One-stop Shop" Presumption?", available at http://arbitrationblog.practicallaw.com/an-erosion-of-the-fiona-trust-one-stop-shop-presumption/.

25 See, e.g. *VK Holdings (HK) Ltd v Panasonic Eco Solutions (Hong Kong) Company Ltd* [2014] HKCFI 2358 [Hong Kong]; Judgment of the Oberster Gerichtshof [Supreme Court], dated August 26, 2008 [Austria]; Judgment of the Swiss Bundesgericht [Supreme Court], dated August 6, 2012 [Switzerland]; Swedish Supreme Court, 7 April 2017, Case No. Ö 1096–16 [Sweden].

26 See e.g. Article 7(5) of the UNCITRAL Model Law.

27 See Section 20 of this Chapter.

28 Gary B Born, *International Commercial Arbitration* (2nd edn, Kluwer 2014) 3294. It is worth noting that *infra petita* was a ground for refusal of recognition and enforcement under the 1927 Geneva Convention.

29 The parties may also be able to pursue a claim against the tribunal for recovery of a portion of the tribunal's fees reflecting the work not done, if such a claim is not precluded by the applicable laws or rules on arbitrator immunity.

30 The parties may, of course, agree to a particular arbitral procedure by agreeing to arbitrate under a particular set of arbitral rules that contains that procedure. However, the reality is that all the major arbitration rules grant the tribunal substantial discretion to alter or ignore rules as they see it. As a result, agreeing on a set of institutional rules places relatively few limits on the procedures a tribunal can choose to use.

31 See e.g. *Tusculum BV v Louis Dreyfus Holding SAS* [2008] QCCS 5904; *Wuzhou Port Foreign Trade Dev. Corp. v New Chemic Ltd* [2001] 3 HKC 395; *Karaha Bodas Co., LLC v Perusahaan Pertambangan Minyak Dan Gas Bumi Negara*, 190 F.Supp.2d 936, 945 (S.D. Tex. 2001).

32 See e.g. Article 829(1)(6) of the Italian Code of Civil Procedure, stating that the failure to comply with the time-limits for the issuance of the arbitral award is a ground for annulment, as long as one of the parties has raised a complaint in this respect during the arbitration, and after the expiry of the time-limit.

33 In some jurisdictions, however, such rules still exist: consider, for instance, the aforementioned possibility of annulment for expiry of the time-limit for the making of the award under Article 829(1)(6) of the Italian Code of Civil Procedure.

34 The Model Law refers to "an arbitrator" while the New York Convention refers to "the arbitrator", but this makes no substantive difference as to the meaning of the two texts.

35 Born (n. 28) 3504–3507.

36 An excellent overview of the current rather complex status of "manifest disregard" in the United States of America is available in Jonathan J. Tompkins, "Manifest Disregard of the Law": The Continuing Evolution of an Historically Ambiguous Vacatur Standard' (2018) 12 *Dispute Resolution International* 145.

37 As do, for instance, the 2014 Arbitration Rules of the London Court of International Arbitration: see Article 26(8).

38 See, e.g. the excellent short discussion in Kate Davies, "In Defence of Section 69 of the English Arbitration Act" (2010), available at http://arbitrationblog.kluwerarbitration.com/2010/11/01/in-defence-of-section-69-of-the-english-arbitration-act/.

39 *Planor Afrique SA v Société Emirates Télécommunications corporation "Etisalat"*, 17 January 2012, Paris Court of Appeal (2012) 3 *Revue de l'Arbitrage* 569.

40 There is obviously a substantial degree of overlap between procedural public policy and the principle that parties must receive a fair opportunity to present their case (see e.g. Article V(1)(b) of the New York Convention).

41 Born (n. 28) 3655.

42 See Articles 1520 and 1525 of the French Code of Civil Procedure.

43 UNICTRAL Secretariat, "Guide on the Convention on the Recognition and Enforcement of Foreign Arbitral Awards (New York, 1958)", 2016 edition, 209–217.

44 This is sometimes referred to as "ordinary recourse", as opposed to the "extraordinary recourse" involved in an annulment procedure. See *Diag Human Se v Czech Republic* [2014] EWHC 1639 (Comm) (22 May 2014).

45 See e.g. *SPP (Middle East) Ltd. v The Arab Republic of Egypt*, District Court of Amsterdam, the Netherlands, 12 July 1984 in Pieter Sanders (ed.), *Yearbook Commercial Arbitration X* (ICCA 1985) 487–489; Oberlandesgericht München, Germany, 23 February 2007, 34 Sch 31/06; *Fertilizer Corp. of India v IDI Management*, Inc., 517 F. Supp. 948 (S.D. Ohio 1981); *Continental Transfert Technique Ltd v Federal Government of Nigeria* [2010] EWHC 780 (Comm).

46 See e.g. *Paranapanema*, São Paulo State Court, Brazil, 2 May 2013; Article 830(4) of the Italian Code of Civil Procedure.

47 Tony Cole.

48 See generally Wiliam S. Dodge, "International Comity in American Law", 115 *Columbia Law Review* 2071 (2015); see also the decision of the Second Circuit Court of Appeals in *Thai-Lao Lignite (Thailand) Co., Ltd v Government of the Lao People's Democratic Republic*, No. 14–597 (2d Cir. 2017) for one approach to the application of comity in the context of the recognition and enforcement of annulled arbitral awards.

49 Pietro Ortolani.

50 Article 36.

51 Article 38.

52 Article 38.

53 See e.g. Article 33 of the UNCITRAL Model Law.
54 See e.g. Article 33(1) of the UNCITRAL Model Law; Article 47(1) of the 2071 SCC Arbitration Rules; Article 33.4 of the 2016 SIAC Arbitration Rules.
55 See e.g. Article 27(3) of the LCIA Rules and Article 37 of the Swiss Rules.
56 See e.g. the JAMS Optional Arbitration Appeal Procedures; the AAA Optional Appellate Arbitration Rules; the CPR Appellate Arbitration Procedure.
57 Although they are certainly not unknown. See e.g. the decision of the Supreme Court of India in *M/s Centrotrade Minerals & Metal Inc. v Hindustan Copper Ltd.*, Civil Appeal No. 2562 of 2006. See also the rules of the Raad van Arbitrage voor de Bouw, an arbitral institution in the Netherlands specialising in construction arbitration.

Index

Ad hoc arbitration 2, 15–16
Administered arbitration *see* Institutional arbitration
Advantages of arbitration 2, 16–21
Agreement to arbitrate *see* Arbitration agreement
Annulment of arbitral awards: in general 205–208; grounds for annulment (in general) 216; time-limits 208; waiver of the right to seek annulment 208–209
Answer (to a request for arbitration) 137–138
Anti-suit injunction 86–87
Appointment of arbitrators 7, 97–98, 100–116
Arbitrability 1, 10–11, 51, 54–58, 229–230
Arbitral award: in general 4, 173–174; award by consent 178–180; default award 177–178; delivery 185–186; final and partial awards 174–176; requirements of validity 181–185
Arbitral institutions *see* Institutional arbitration
Arbitral order 173–174
Arbitration agreement: in general 51–96; consent 53–54; incorporation by reference 8–9; law applicable to the arbitration agreement 46–48; nature 85–86; pre-dispute agreement 51, 58–62; post-dispute agreement 51, 62; scope 82–85, 142, 218–221; separability 46–48, 62–65; validity 65–82, 142
Arbitration clause *see* Arbitration agreement
Arbitrators' contract 122–123

Bifurcation 146
Binary clause 103–104

Case management conference 142–144
Cause of action estoppel *see* Res judicata
Challenge of arbitral awards *see* Annulment of arbitral awards
Challenge of arbitrators 99, 116–120
Closing of the proceedings 153
Competence-competence 67–71
Composition of the tribunal 221–224
Compromis see Arbitration agreement
Concurring opinion 196–197

Confidentiality 3, 21, 134–136
Consumer arbitration 14
Cost: in general 21–22; advance on costs 147–149; allocation of costs 191–192

Decision on Jurisdiction *see* Award
Declaratory relief 188–189
Deliberations 154, 194–195
Dissenting opinion 196
Document production 156–158
Domestic character of arbitration 2, 11–12
Double *exequatur* 211–212, 234–235
Drawbacks of arbitration 2
Due process violations 221–229. 231–233

Emergency arbitrator 138–139
Enforceability 19–20
Error on point of law 230–231
European Convention on International Commercial Arbitration 212
Exequatur see Recognition and enforcement
Expedited arbitration 165–167
Expertise 20, 24

Finality 1, 9–10, 19
Functus officio 174–176

General terms and conditions 77–78
Geneva Convention on the Execution of Foreign Arbitral Awards 211–212, 234
Geneva Protocol on Arbitration Clauses 211

IBA Guidelines on Conflicts of Interest in International Arbitration 114–116
IBA Rules of Ethics for International Arbitrators 114–116
IBA Rules on the Taking of Evidence in International Arbitration 129, 156
Independence and impartiality 98, 111–120
Institutional arbitration 2, 15–16, 33–36, 110–111, 119

Inter-American Convention on International Commercial Arbitration 212
Interest 187–188
Interim relief *see* Provisional (interim) relief
International character of arbitration 2, 11–12
Interviews of prospective arbitrators 116
Issue estoppel *see Res judicata*

Jurisdiction 22–23, 65–82, 217–218

Lex arbitri 26, 30–33
Liability of arbitrators 99, 123–124
Litigation: comparison with arbitration 3; preclusive effect of arbitration clause 7–9

Mandatory rules 43–44
Mediation 3
Merits: choice of law agreement 36–44; *ex aequo et bono* and *amiable compositeur* 42–43; floating choice of law clauses 40; law applicable to the merits 36–46; multiple applicable laws 38–39; split clause 39–40; a-national rules 40–41
Monetary compensation 186–187
Multiparty proceedings 161–165

Neutrality 17–18
New York Convention *see* Recognition and enforcement
Number of arbitrators 105–107

Oral hearings 150–153
Order *see* Arbitral order

Party autonomy 1, 4–7, 36–44, 128–129
Post-hearing submissions 153
Power 23–24
Provisional (interim) relief 139–142
Public policy 43–44, 231–233
Punitive damages 187

Qualifications to serve as an arbitrator 109–110

Recognition and enforcement: in general 205–206; difference between recognition and enforcement 209–210; law applicable to recognition and enforcement 211; obligations arising from the New York Convention 211–213; requirements under the New York Convention 213–216; suspension of recognition and enforcement proceedings pending annulment proceedings 239
Redfern schedule 158
Remedies 186–191
Removal of arbitrators 120
Replacement of arbitrators 99
Request for arbitration 137–138
Res judicata 192–194

Seat of arbitration 29–33, 132–134
Selection of arbitrators *see* Appointment of arbitrators
Separability *see* Arbitration agreement
Separate opinion 196–197
Setting aside *see* Annulment of arbitral awards
Specific performance 189–190
Speed 18–19
State entities 2, 11–12
Statement of claim 148–150
Statement of defense 148–150
State-State arbitration 14–15

Terms of reference 144–146
Third parties: in general 88–93, 129; agency 88–89; assignment 89; group of companies 91–93; piercing the corporate veil 90
Truncated tribunal 121–122

Witnesses 158–161

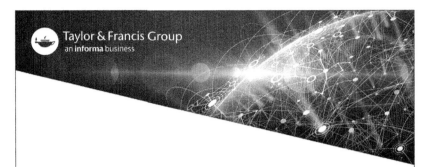